HSK核心词汇天天学

ONE HOUR PER DAY
TO A POWERFUL HSK VOCABULARY

下册
VOLUME 3

刘东青 申 培 王春颖

编著

华语教学出版社
SINOLINGUA

First Edition   2009

ISBN 978-7-80200-596-9

Copyright 2009 by Sinolingua

Published by Sinolingua

24 Baiwanzhuang Road, Beijing 100037, China

Tel: (86) 10-68320585

Fax: (86) 10-68326333

E-mail: hyjx@sinolingua.com.cn

Printed by Beijing Foreign Languages Printing House

Printed in the People's Republic of China

致学习者

　　本套书是为海外 HSK 考生及同等水平的学生编写的词汇学习用书。

　　通过使用本书，学生可以在一年内系统掌握 3000 个核心词汇。通过书中的用法示例和丰富习题，可以全面提高汉语词汇的运用能力和 HSK 考试的应试能力。本书有如下特点：

　　系统的学习计划——本书安排了为期一年的学习内容：每天学习 12 个词汇、5天的词汇学习加"周练习"构成 1 周的学习内容；每个月包括 4 周，每册书包括 4个月，3 册书共一年的学习内容，希望能帮助学习者在一年之内掌握这 3000 个词汇及示例、习题等拓展内容，达到 HSK 中级以上的要求。

　　合理的内容编排——每天学习的词汇由易到难、有难有易。每天的学习内容都包括一定比例的甲级词、乙级词、丙级词和丁级词，随着学习的深入，甲级词和乙级词会越来越少，丙级词和丁级词会越来越多。除词汇的常规项目外，本书还归纳了一些词汇的专项内容，如量词、关联词、尾词等，并配有相应的练习。

　　多样的学习板块——每天的学习项目包括词语、读音、词义、该词的同义词或反义词、常用搭配、用法示例、词义辨析以及多种形式的练习。尽管每个词的内容都十分全面，但经过作者的巧妙编排和多样的学习板块，学生能在 1 小时内轻松掌握 1 天的全部学习内容。

　　经典的语言材料——掌握词汇重在掌握其用法。本书提供了丰富、经典的例句和固定搭配，注重体现词汇的用法和 HSK 考试的重点和难点。

　　详细的英文注释——在词义、常用搭配、用法示例、词义辨析等板块均有详细的英语注释，以确保大家能够准确理解。

To the Reader

This series of textbooks contains a list of HSK words for foreign students to study and learn in preparation for the HSK.

Through the use of these textbooks, students should be able to master 3,000 words within one year. These textbooks contain many examples and exercises, which will improve students' Chinese, and ability to complete the HSK successfully.

These books have the following features:

Systematic learning program — The one-year study plan consists of three textbooks, with each book containing four months worth of study. A month of study is made up of four weeks, and each week is composed of five days of studying 12 words a day, with added 'weekly practice' sessions. This schedule will help students master the 3,000 words within one year, and will also allow them to fulfill the requirements for the intermediate level of HSK and above.

Methodical arrangement of content — The words to be studied daily range from the simple to the complex, and become more difficult as study progresses. Different levels of HSK words (e.g. A-level words, B-level, C-level, D-level) are included in the study. As students move forward, A-level and B-level words will appear less as they are replaced with more C-level and D-level ones. As well as this efficient method of studying vocabulary, these books also have added classifications and exercises for measure words, conjunctions and suffixes.

Diversity of study materials — Each daily study plan includes words and expressions, pronunciation, word definitions, synonyms and antonyms, commonly used collocations, examples of usage, as well as exercises. Despite the comprehensive coverage of each word, students can easily complete a whole day's content within one hour, due to the author's ingenious arrangement of the diverse study materials.

Typical language materials — This textbook series includes rich and illustrative sentences and allocations, and pays great attention to the usage of words, in order to help the students to learn the words and their practical applications. It also details the key or difficult points of the HSK test.

Detailed English annotations — Detailed annotations in English are given to multiple word definitions, collocations, and examples of usage, to ensure that students will understand the concise and correct meanings and usages.

9月 第1周的学习内容

星期一

zérèn
责任 （乙）名

duty; responsibility

常用搭配
对……负有责任 bear the responsibility for…
承担责任 assume responsibility
不负责任的行为 irresponsible behavior

用法示例
不要忘记你对孩子的责任。
Do not forget your duty to your child.
保护树苗是他们的责任。
It's their duty to protect the saplings.
是我错了，我愿为此承担责任。
It is my fault, and I will assume responsibility for it.

rènwu
任务 （乙）名

task; assignment

常用搭配
接受任务 accept an assignment
执行任务 carry out a task
一项艰巨的任务 an arduous task

用法示例
我很快就要完成这项任务了。
I will complete this task soon.
新政府的主要任务是降低通货膨胀的水平。
The new government's main task is to reduce the level of inflation.
我们保证完成任务。
We guarantee to fulfill our mission.

fùzé
负责 （甲）动

be in charge of; be responsible for

常用搭配
对……负责 be responsible for…
负责照看孩子 be in charge of looking after a child
负责人 person in charge

用法示例
这里谁负责？
Who is in charge here?

警察负责执法。
The police are responsible for the enforcement of the law.
公共汽车司机应对乘客的安全负责。
The bus driver is responsible for the passengers' safety.

nánkàn
难看 反好看 （乙）形

ugly; disgraceful

常用搭配
难看的家具 ugly furniture
难看的疤 a hideous scar

用法示例
这双鞋多难看呀！
What an ugly pair of shoes!
我觉得那座建筑物很难看。
I think the building is very ugly.
她的新衣服太贵了，而且很难看。
Her new coat is too expensive and very ugly.

bù'ān
不安 （丙）形

uneasy; restless; worried

常用搭配
坐立不安 on pins and needles
不安的情绪 an uneasy mood
感到不安 to feel uneasy

用法示例
男孩因离开妈妈而变得不安。
The boy was restless after leaving his mother.
这条消息使我感到十分不安。
The news had me worried.
世界局势动荡不安。
The world's situation is characterized by turbulence and intranquility.

cánkuì
惭愧 同羞愧 （丙）形

ashamed

常用搭配
为……而惭愧 be ashamed of…

用法示例
他很惭愧，他说了谎。
He was ashamed that he had lied.
他为他的行为感到惭愧。
He is ashamed of his behavior.
我昨天表现不好，现在感到很惭愧。
I behaved badly yesterday and I am ashamed now.

zébèi
责备
回 责怪 zéguài （丙）动

blame

常用搭配

他责备我。He blamed me.
他应该受到责备。He is to blame.

用法示例

孩子们不应受到责备。
The children were not to blame.
我并不是在责备他。
I am far from blaming him.
你不能责备任何人。
You can't blame anyone.

jīzhì
机智 （丁）形

tactful; witty

常用搭配

机智的警察 resourceful police

用法示例

他机智地回答了记者的问题。
He answered the reporter's question tactfully.
这位外交官十分机智。
The diplomat is very tactful.
他机智地给警察打了电话。
He had the wit to telephone the police.

jīling
机灵
回 迟钝 chídùn （丁）形

clever; smart

常用搭配

他很机灵。He is quite smart.   机灵鬼 cunning person
机灵的孩子 a clever child

用法示例

你骗不了他，他特别机灵。
You won't catch him. He's very sharp.
他真是个小机灵鬼儿。
He really is a smart child.
她关掉了煤气，够机灵的。
She was intelligent enough to turn off the gas.

bùkān
不堪 （丁）动／副

① cannot bear ② utterly

常用搭配

狼狈不堪 be in a very sorry plight
穿得破烂不堪 be dressed in rags
不堪回首 can't bear to look back on

用法示例

他的房间总是凌乱不堪。
His room is always in clutter.
厨房肮脏不堪。
The kitchen is absolutely filthy.

后果将不堪设想。
The consequences would be too ghastly to contemplate.

nánkān
难堪 （丁）形

embarrassing

常用搭配

感到难堪 feel embarrassed
处于难堪的境地 be in an extremely awkward situation
难堪的事 a bitter pill to swallow

用法示例

他在餐桌上举止粗鲁，在座的人感到很难堪。
His rude behavior at the dinner table caused much embarrassment.
他叫家里人难堪。
He's an embarrassment to his family.
你是想让我难堪吗？
Are you trying to embarrass me?

kāndēng
刊登 （丁）动

publish (in a newspaper or a magazine)

常用搭配

刊登广告 publish advertisements

用法示例

这家杂志刊登了一名高中生写的小说。
The magazine published a novel written by a high school student.
该报每周刊登一篇优秀运动员的简介。
The newspaper publishes a profile of a leading sportsman every week.
杂志刊登了这个电影明星的巨幅照片。
The magazine published a big picture of the movie star.

 词义辨析

机智、机灵

"机智"和"机灵"都是形容词，都有聪明、灵活的意思，都可以用作定语、谓语和补语。"机智"强调洞察敏锐，反应迅速，应变能力强，常常用来形容警察、士兵等成年人，还常用作状语；"机灵"强调聪明伶俐，惹人喜爱，常常用来形容小孩或小动物，不能用作状语。例如：①机智的士兵，②机灵的猴子，③他机智地回答了律师的问题。

Both 机智 and 机灵 are adjectives, meaning "clever, smart"; both of them can function as an attributive, a predicate or a complement. 机智 stresses "keenness and quickness of perception or reaction", and is often used to describe a policeman or a soldier. It can also function as an adverbial; while 机灵 stresses "clever and lovely", and is often used to describe a child or a small animal. It can not function as an adverbial. For example: ① a tactful soldier; ② a clever monkey; ③ He answered the lawyer's questions tactfully.

 练习

练习一、根据拼音写汉字，根据汉字写拼音

kān (   ) (   )kān　zé (   ) (   )kuì　rèn (   )
(   )登　难(   ) (   )备　惭(   ) (   )务

练习二、搭配连线

(1) 承担　　　　　　　　A. 不堪
(2) 狼狈　　　　　　　　B. 不安
(3) 受到　　　　　　　　C. 任务
(4) 执行　　　　　　　　D. 责任
(5) 感到　　　　　　　　E. 责备

练习三、从今天学习的生词中选择合适的词填空

1. 发生这样的事，学校有不可推卸的 _____。
2. 这个星期天天加班，每天回家时都感到疲惫 _____。
3. 我不知道这个聚会如此正式，大家都穿着正装，只有我穿着运动服，我感到很 _____。
4. 别 _____ 她了，她太善良了，所以才相信了那个骗子的话。
5. 妻子在动手术，丈夫 _____ 地在手术室外边走来走去。
6. 三个孩子中，老二最 _____，所以最得大家的宠爱。
7. 他工作太忙，一直没有找到合适的对象，于是在报纸上 _____ 了一则征婚启事。
8. 副总经理 _____ 公司的财务，财务方面的事可以直接请示他。
9. 他 _____ 地把三个歹徒困在了电梯里，并马上给警察局打了电话。
10. 这么简单的问题都没回答上来，我感到万分 _____。

🔑 答案

练习一：
略

练习二：

(1) D	(2)A	(3)E	(4)C	(5)B

练习三：

1. 责任	2. 不堪	3. 难堪	4. 责备	5. 不安
6. 机灵	7. 刊登	8. 负责	9. 机智	10. 惭愧

 星期二

dàodá
到达　　　　　　　　　（乙）动

reach; arrive

常用搭配

准时到达 arrive on time
到达上海 arrive in Shanghai
到达顶点 come to a head

用法示例

那辆火车三点钟准时到达。
The train arrived at three o'clock on the dot.
我们终于到达了目的地。
We eventually arrived at our destination.
你必须提前两小时到达机场。
You must arrive at the airport two hours early.

dádào
达到　　　　　　　　　（乙）动

reach; achieve

常用搭配

达到目的 achieve one's purpose
达到世界先进水平 meet advanced world standards
达到标准 meet the standard

用法示例

他已经达到了事业的顶峰。
He has reached the zenith of his career.
水源污染已经达到危及居民健康的程度。
Pollution of the water supply reached a level pernicious to the health of the citizen.
这架飞机可以达到每小时一千公里的速度。
This plane can reach a speed of 1,000 kilometers an hour.

kāimíng
开明　　　🔘明智　　　（乙）形
　　　　　míngzhì

enlightened; open-minded

常用搭配

开明的国王 open-minded king
开明的思想 liberal ideas

用法示例

他是一位开明的领导，愿意接受别人的意见。
He is an open-minded leader who likes to accept advice from others.
一个开明的政府应当允许自由发表政见。
An enlightened government should permit the free expression of political opinion.
开明的人知道教育的价值。
An enlightened person knows the value of education.

hūnmí
昏迷　　　反 苏醒 **sūxǐng**　　　（乙）动

to lose consciousness; be comatose

常用搭配

从昏迷中醒来 rouse from a coma

陷入昏迷 lapse into coma

用法示例

他昏迷了几天，但现在清醒了。

He was in a coma for days, but now he's conscious again.

他受了伤，而且昏迷了。

He is hurt and still remains unconscious.

三个月前，这个姑娘就昏迷了，至今还没有苏醒过来。

The girl went into a coma three months ago, and has not woken up yet.

huíxiǎng
回想　　　（丙）动

recall; recollect

常用搭配

回想我的学生时代 recall my schooldays

回想童年生活 recollect the days of one's childhood

用法示例

我开始回想我的童年。

I began to think back to my childhood.

我躺在床上回想王伯伯给我讲的那些事。

I lay in bed and recalled the things Uncle Wang had told me.

她在努力回想上周四发生的事。

She is trying to recollect what happened last Thursday.

dáchéng
达成　　　（丙）动

reach (an agreement)

常用搭配

达成协议 reach an agreement

达成一致意见 reach a consensus

达成谅解 reach an understanding

用法示例

由于他们态度强硬，我们无法达成协议。

Owing to their intransigent attitude, we were unable to reach an agreement.

他们最后达成了谅解。

They finally reached an understanding.

双方没有达成妥协。

Neither party struck a compromise.

fāyù
发育　　　（丙）动

grow; develop

常用搭配

正常发育 the proper growth

发育不良 runtishness

发育健全 physically well-developed

用法示例

胎儿发育良好。

The fetus is developing well.

有的儿童比其他儿童发育得慢。

Some children develop more slowly than others.

运动和食物对孩子的发育十分重要。

Exercise and food are important to the proper growth of a child.

gōngnéng
功能　　　（丙）名

function

常用搭配

心脏的功能 the function of the heart

教育的功能 the function of education

用法示例

你知道大脑的功能吗？

Do you know the function of the brain？

这台机器有什么功能？

What functions does this machine have?

耳朵的功能是听。

The function of the ear is to listen.

gōngxiào
功效　　　同 效果 **xiàoguǒ**　　　（丁）名

efficacy; efficiency

常用搭配

提高功效 improve efficiency

机器的功效 efficacy of a machine

用法示例

我们正在测试新药的功效。

We are testing the efficacy of a new drug.

这种药草有退热的功效。

This kind of herb is efficacious against fever.

这台新复印机比那台旧的功效高。

This new copy machine is more efficient than the old one.

kāilǎng
开朗　　　反 内向 **nèixiàng**　　　（丁）形

① open and clear ② optimistic

常用搭配

性格开朗 a cheerful disposition

用法示例

我们在密林中穿行，约数百米，便豁然开朗。

We pushed ourselves through the thick forest for a few hundred meters and then reached an open space.

这个女孩的性格十分开朗，在各项活动中都很活跃。

The girl's character is very open and clear, and she is a very eager participant in all kinds of activities.

fācái
发财　　　（丁）动

get rich

常用搭配

发大财 get very rich

恭喜发财！May you prosper!

用法示例

现在很多人都想要发财致富。
Many people are trying to get rich nowadays.
她生活的唯一目的似乎就是发财。
Getting rich seems to be her only purpose in life.
他靠经营旅馆发了财。
He got rich by running hotels.

fāpiào
发票　　　　　　　　　　　　　（丁）名

① receipt ② invoice

常用搭配

给（某人）开（某物的）发票 to invoice sb. for sth.

用法示例

你付了款，就给你发票。
After you have paid, a receipt is given to you.
制造厂家给我公司开了一张两部打字机的发票。
The manufacturer invoiced our company for two typewriters.
经过签字的发票表示货物已经收到。
A signed invoice presumes receipt of the shipment.

 **词义辨析**

到达、达到

"到达"和"达到"都有到的意思。"到达"强调到了某一地点，宾语一般是处所名词；"达到"强调取得了预期的结果，多与"理想"、"目的"、"标准"、"水平"等抽象名词搭配使用。例如：①到达北京，②到达机场，③达到目的，④达到标准。

Both 到达 and 达到 mean "to reach or to arrive in". 到达 stresses "to reach a place"; its object is usually the name of a place; while 达到 stresses "to accomplish something successfully"; it is usually collocated with abstract nouns such as "理想" (ideal), "目的" (purpose), "标准" (standard), "水平" (level). For example: ① to arrive in Beijing, ② to arrive at the airport, ③ to accomplish one's purpose, ④ to meet the standard.

 **练习**

练习一、根据拼音写汉字，根据汉字写拼音

（　）xiǎng （　）dào　hūn（　）（　）xiào（　）piào
回（　）　达（　）　（　）迷　功（　）　发（　）

练习二、搭配连线

(1) 准时　　　　　　A. 标准
(2) 性格　　　　　　B. 健全
(3) 达到　　　　　　C. 到达
(4) 达成　　　　　　D. 开朗
(5) 发育　　　　　　E. 谅解

练习三、从今天学习的生词中选择合适的词填空

1. 她的父母很 _____，从不强迫她做任何事情。
2. 他最初是靠做钢材生意 _____ 的，之后开办了自己的公司。
3. 晕倒后，她在医院 _____ 了三天三夜。
4. 这项专利技术已经 _____ 了世界先进水平。
5. 我想买个便宜的手机，我只是打打电话、发发短信，不需要那么多 _____。
6. 经过历时两周的自驾车旅行，昨天他已安全 _____ 目的地。
7. 她是个性格 _____ 的女孩，喜欢运动和交际。
8. 谈判双方最终 _____ 了协议，会后举行了签字仪式。
9. _____ 当年的那些事，他有些伤感。
10. 怀孕期间应该定期去医院检查，以便掌握胎儿生长 _____ 的情况。

 **答案**

练习一：
略
练习二：
(1) C　　　(2)D　　　(3)A　　　(4)E　　　(5)B
练习三：
1. 开明　　2. 发财　　3. 昏迷　　4. 达到　　5. 功能
6. 到达　　7. 开朗　　8. 达成　　9. 回想　　10. 发育

星期三

dāying
答应 （乙）动

promise; reply; answer; agree; consent

常用搭配
他答应帮助我们。He promised to help us.
答应她的请求 consent to her request

用法示例
她答应弟弟给他买辆自行车。
She promised her brother that she would buy him a bike.
他勉强答应了。
He gave a reluctant promise.
我答应决不泄漏他的秘密。
I promise never to reveal his secret.
我敲了下门,但没人答应。
I knocked at the door several times, but there was no answer.

chuánbō
传播 （乙）动

disseminate; spread

常用搭配
传播佛教 disseminate Buddhism
传播消息 spread news
传播中国文化 diffuse Chinese culture

用法示例
他们利用报刊来传播政治观点。
They use the press to disseminate political views.
传教士到远方去传播他们的信仰。
Missionaries went far afield to propagate their faith.
印刷术的发明有助于知识的传播。
The invention of printing helped the diffusion of learning.

bāokuò
包括 同 包含（bāohán） （乙）动

comprise; include

常用搭配
名单上包括你。You are included on the list.

用法示例
一套餐具包括刀、叉、匙等。
A cutlery set includes knives, forks, spoons, etc.
账单中包括服务费吗?
Is service included in the bill?
纽约市包括五个行政区。
New York City consists of five boroughs.

bōxuē
剥削 （丙）动／名

① exploit ② exploitation

常用搭配
剥削工人 exploit workers
剥削阶级 the exploiting class

用法示例
老板剥削员工。
The boss exploited his men.
在旧社会工人农民是被剥削的阶级。
In the old society workers and farmers were the exploited classes.

bāohán
包含 （丙）动

contain; include

常用搭配
这句话包含几层意思。
This statement has several implications.

用法示例
"美"这个词包括许多意思。
The word "beauty" comprehends various meanings.
书中包含了许多科学领域。
This book embraces many fields of science.

bāowéi
包围 （丙）动

surround; encircle

常用搭配
被警察包围了 be surrounded by police
包围圈 ring of encirclement

用法示例
敌军包围了这座城市。
Enemy troops had encircled the city.
我们被敌人包围了。
We have been surrounded by the enemy.

chuándá
传达 （丙）动

convey

常用搭配
传达文件 relay a document
传达命令 convey orders
传达室 reception office

用法示例
将军亲自向他们传达了总统的命令。
The general personally conveyed the president's order to them.
我把消息传达给他了。
I conveyed the information to him.
我们用电子邮件传达指示。
We transmitted the instructions by electronic mail.

cāngcù
仓促 反 慎重（shènzhòng） （丁）形

hasty

常用搭配
仓促的决定 a hasty decision

走得仓促 leave in a hurry
用法示例
他们仓促地结婚,不久就离婚了。
They married in haste and divorced soon.
他们仓促地采取了行动。
They acted in haste.
我们不应仓促地下结论。
We should not draw a conclusion hastily.

cōngmáng
匆忙   ⊜ 急忙 jímáng   (丙)形
hurried
常用搭配
匆忙做出决定 make a hasty decision
他总是匆匆忙忙的。He is always in a hurry.
用法示例
匆忙之中,他忘了带眼镜。
In his hurry, he forgot to bring his glasses with him.
她匆匆忙忙地去了银行。
She went to the bank in a hurry.
我匆忙离开学校,甚至没有时间跟你道别。
I left the school in a hurry and had no time to even say good-bye to you.

chuánshòu
传授   (丁)动
impart
常用搭配
传授技术 pass on one's skills
口头传授秘诀 transmit a secret process orally
用法示例
教师的职责是传授知识。
A teacher's function is to impart knowledge.
他把技术知识毫无保留地传授给了我们。
He unreservedly passed on to us his technical know-how.

bāozhuāng
包装   (丁)动 / 名
pack; package
常用搭配
包装箱 packing chest
包装纸 wrapping paper
用法示例
铝箔用于包装食物。
Aluminum foil can be used for wrapping food.
他们的产品总是包装得非常精美。
Their products are always attractively packaged.
在外包装上请标明"小心轻放"字样。
On the outer packing please mark the words, 'Handle with care'.

fánmáng
繁忙   ⊗ 悠闲 yōuxián   (丁)形
busy; bustling

常用搭配
繁忙的季节 busy season
工作繁忙 busy with one's work
繁忙的一天 a busy day
用法示例
这个港口总是很繁忙。
The port is always busy.
上午护士们十分繁忙。
The nurses are very busy in the morning.
春节前商店里十分繁忙。
The shops are very busy before the Spring Festival.

 词义辨析

包括、包含

"包括"和"包含"都是动词,都有以……为组成部分的意思。"包括"的对象比较具体,往往指相对独立的各个部分、因素或成员。"包含"的对象一般是抽象的,像"道理"、"意义"、"内容"等。例如:①这套房子包括卧室、厨房和卫生间。②这段话包含三层意思。

Both 包括 and 包含 are verbs, meaning "to have as component parts; include or comprise". The objects of 包括 are something concrete, which are independent parts, elements, or members; while the objects of 包含 are something abstract, such as "道理" (principles), "意义" (significance), "内容" (contents), etc. For example: ① The apartment includes bedrooms, a kitchen and a bathroom. ② This paragraph contains three dimensions of meaning.

 **练习**

练习一、根据拼音写汉字，根据汉字写拼音

dā（　　） bō（　　） （　　）wéi cōng（　　） cāng（　　）
（　　）应 （　　）削 包（　　） （　　）忙 （　　）促

练习二、搭配连线

(1) 工作　　　　　　　　A. 佛教
(2) 传授　　　　　　　　B. 繁忙
(3) 传播　　　　　　　　C. 工人
(4) 传达　　　　　　　　D. 技术
(5) 剥削　　　　　　　　E. 命令

练习三、从今天学习的生词中选择合适的词填空

1. 他把自己经验和技术毫无保留地 _____ 给了大家。
2. 调查发现，人们在买东西时除了看商品本身外，还很重视商品的 _____。
3. 今天开会的目的是为了 _____ 上级单位的指示。
4. 我们把敌人 _____ 了起来，他们被迫投降了。
5. 奴隶主靠 _____ 奴隶的劳动过着安逸的生活。
6. 互联网可以使信息在很短的时间内 _____ 到世界各地。
7. 这句话 _____ 两层意思。
8. 我走得太 _____，没带手机，也没带手表。
9. 这间房子的租金是 1500 块，水电费不 _____ 在内。
10. 由于时间 _____，我们在这个城市只游览了一天。

答案

练习一：
略

练习二：
(1) B　　(2) D　　(3) A　　(4) E　　(5) C

练习三：
1. 传授　　2. 包装　　3. 传达　　4. 包围　　5. 剥削
6. 传播　　7. 包含　　8. 匆忙　　9. 包括　　10. 仓促

 星期四 Thursday

fǎnyìng
反映　　　　　　　　（乙）动／名

① reflect; report　② reflection

常用搭配
反映民意 reflect public opinion
向上级反映情况 report the situation to a superior

用法示例
衣着可以反映一个人的个性。
Your clothes are a reflection of your personality.
某一时期的文学可反映出该时期的价值观和审美观。
The literature of a period reflects its values and tastes.
选举结果充分反映了民意。
The election results mirror public opinion well.

fǎnyìng
反应　　　　　　　　（乙）动／名

① response　② react　③ reaction

常用搭配
化学反应 chemical reaction
生理反应 physiological response
过敏反应 allergic reaction

用法示例
他对你的建议有什么反应？
What was his reaction to your proposal?
你妈妈对这个消息的反应怎样？
How did your mother react to the news?
她的反应是非常生气。
She reacted by getting very angry.

bàozhǐ
报纸　　　　　　　　（乙）名

newspaper

常用搭配
送报纸 deliver newspapers
买一份报纸 buy a copy of a newspaper

用法示例
我是从报纸上得知这个消息的。
I learned this from the newspaper.
这位校长受到了当地报纸的批评。
The headmaster was criticized by the local paper.

guānjiàn
关键　　　　　　　　（乙）名／形

① key　② crucial

常用搭配
在关键时刻 at the crucial moment　　关键人物 keyman
关键因素 key factor

【用法示例】

谈判正处于一个关键的阶段。

Negotiations were at a crucial stage.

这就是问题的关键所在。

This is the crux of the matter.

他在上一场比赛中起到了关键作用。

He played a key role in last match.

guāntóu
关头 （丙）名

juncture; moment

【常用搭配】

紧要关头 the critical moment

在最后关头 at the last moment

【用法示例】

她在危急关头总是挺身而出。

She's always comes forward during moments of crisis.

现在企业的改革正处在紧要关头。

The reforms of enterprise are now at the critical moment.

那是我人生历程中的重要关头。

It was an important juncture in my career.

dàibǔ   shìfàng
逮捕   ⊠ 释放   （丙）动

arrest

【常用搭配】

逮捕证 arrest warrant

警察逮捕了小偷。

The police arrested the thief.

【用法示例】

那个破坏者已经被警察逮捕了。

The destroyer has been arrested by the police.

几天前,这些歹徒被逮捕了。

These bandits were arrested several days ago.

警察逮捕了他和他的两个同谋。

The police arrested him and his two accomplices.

ángguì
昂贵 （丁）形

expensive; costly

【常用搭配】

昂贵的钻石戒指 an expensive diamond ring

昂贵的跑车 an expensive sports car

【用法示例】

这套水晶玻璃酒杯非常昂贵。

This set of crystal wine cups is very expensive.

这套红木家具一定特别昂贵。

This set of mahogany furniture must be very expensive.

他的黑色皮沙发看上去很昂贵。

His black leather couch looks expensive.

zèngsòng   zèngyǔ
赠送   ⊜ 赠与   （丙）动

give as a present; to present

【常用搭配】

向图书馆赠送书籍 present a library with books

互相赠送礼品 exchange gifts

【用法示例】

我们将赠送给他一块金表。

We'll present a gold watch to him.

样品是免费赠送的。

The sample is free of charge.

超级市场向今天来的每位顾客赠送一盒糖。

The supermarket is giving away a box of sugar to everyone who comes today.

bàokān
报刊 （丙）名

newspapers and periodicals

【常用搭配】

订阅报刊

subscribe to newspapers and periodicals

报刊杂志 newspapers and magazines

【用法示例】

他们利用报刊发布消息。

They use the press to disseminate information.

报刊杂志刊登了许多关于她的文章。

The newspapers and magazines carry a lot of articles about her.

bàodá
报答 （丁）动

repay; requite

【常用搭配】

不图报答 expect no return

报答某人的好意 repay sb. for his kindness

【用法示例】

我怎样才能报答你的好意呢?

How can I ever repay you for your kindness?

他给了我那么大的帮助,我一定会报答他的。

He helped me so much. I will surely repay him.

zēngtiān   xuējiǎn
增添   ⊠ 削减   （丁）动

add to

【常用搭配】

增添设备 get additional equipment

【用法示例】

旗帜给街道增添了色彩。

The banners lent color to the streets.

制度创新为企业增添了活力。

System innovations enliven enterprises.

友谊可以增添欢乐,减轻悲伤。

Friendship multiplies joys and divides grieves.

fǎncháng   yìcháng
反常   ⊜ 异常   （丁）形

unusual; abnormal

常用搭配

反常现象 abnormal phenomena
反常的天气 abnormal weather

用法示例

这孩子是不是有点反常？
Is the child abnormal in any way?
我们认为这样的反常现象不会持续很久。
We do not think such an abnormal phenomenon will last long.

 **词义辨析**

反映、反应

1. "反应"和"反映"都可以用作名词和动词,但它们的意思不同,"反应"指受到刺激而发生的变化,如"过敏反应"、"化学反应",还指在某种刺激或提示的影响下而采取的行动;"反映"指通过一种形式表现事物内在的、真实的性质,还指向上级汇报情况或意见。例如:①他们对我们的求援没有反应。②吃了药以后,她反应得很厉害。③这封信是否反映了你真实的想法?

Both 反应 and 反映 are verbs and nouns, but they are different in meaning. 反应 means "a response to a stimulus", such as "过敏反应" (allergic reaction), "化学反应" (chemical reaction), and it also means "to act in response to, or under the influence of a stimulus"; while 反映 means "to show something internal or real through certain a form". It also means "to report situations or opinions of others to a higher level". For example: ① They gave no response to our call for help. ② After taking the medicine she reacted strongly. ③ Does this letter reflect how you really think?

2. 作为动词,"反应"和"反映"的用法也不同,"反应"一般不带宾语,不能重叠使用;"反映"可以带宾语,可以重叠使用。例如:我一定把你的意见向上级反映反映。

As verbs, 反应 and 反映 are different in usage. 反应 does not go with objects. And it can not be used in a repeated form; while 反映 can be followed by objects, and it can be used in repeated form. For example: I will surely report your opinion to a higher level.

 **练习**

练习一、根据拼音写汉字，根据汉字写拼音

( )dá ( )tiān ( )jiàn ( )bǔ áng ( )
报( ) 增( ) 关( ) 逮( ) ( )贵

练习二、搭配连线

(1) 反映   A. 反应
(2) 化学   B. 报刊
(3) 赠送   C. 设备
(4) 订阅   D. 礼品
(5) 增添   E. 情况

练习三、从今天学习的生词中选择合适的词填空

1. 北京的夏天通常比较热,不过今年的天气有些 _____。
2. 警察 _____ 这个嫌疑人时他正想化妆潜逃。
3. 他给了我那么大的帮助,我该如何 _____ 人家呢?
4. 群众对这起贪污案件的 _____ 很强烈,今后我们还要加强廉政建设。
5. 这条新闻成了当天各 _____ 的头条。
6. 演出结束后,小朋友们给演员 _____ 了花篮。
7. 一次的考试成绩不一定能 _____ 出学生真实的水平。
8. 能否办成这件事, _____ 要看领导是不是支持。
9. 出席晚会时,这个明星戴了一条 _____ 的钻石项链。
10. 在这紧要 _____ 你可千万不能泄气啊。

答案

练习一:
略

练习二:
(1) E   (2)A   (3)D   (4)B   (5)C

练习三:
1. 反常   2. 逮捕   3. 报答   4. 反应   5. 报刊
6. 赠送   7. 反映   8. 关键   9. 昂贵   10. 关头

星期五

cóngshì
从事 （乙）动
① undertake ② deal with ③ handle

常用搭配
从事商业活动 undertake commercial activity
从事科学研究 be engaged in scientific research.

用法示例
你毕业之后想要从事什么工作？
What will you do after graduating from school?
要想从事这个工作，你必须有硕士文凭。
To do this job, you must have a Master degree.
做这样的事情要慎重从事。
Be cautious in doing such a thing!

ānquán píngān
安全 ⑩ 平安 （丙）形／名
① safe ② safety ③ security

常用搭配
安全的地方 a safe place　　安全感 a sense of security
安全第一 safety first

用法示例
我将保证你的安全。
I'll undertake your security.
他们安全地越过了公路。
They crossed the road in safety.
这些玩具对小孩安全吗？
Are these toys safe for small children?

wèidào zīwèi
味道 ⑩ 滋味 （乙）名
flavor; taste

常用搭配
柠檬的味道 taste of lemon
味道好极了。It's so delicious.

用法示例
我不喜欢洋葱的味道。
I don't like the flavor of onions.
这种酒的味道美极了。
This wine is pleasing to the palate.
汤的味道很好。
The soup is delicious.

késou
咳嗽 （甲）动
cough

常用搭配
咳嗽得嗓子嘶哑 cough oneself hoarse

咳嗽的声音 sound of cough

用法示例
请医生开点咳嗽药。
Ask the doctor to prescribe something for that cough.
这孩子咳嗽了一整夜。
The child was coughing all night.
孩子咳嗽得很厉害，所以他妈妈带他去看医生。
The child had a bad cough, so his mother took him to the doctor.

āndìng
安定 （乙）形／动
① stable ② calm and orderly ③ pacify

常用搭配
维护社会安定 maintain social stability
安定团结 stability and unity

用法示例
他放弃了安定的生活，决心自己创业。
He gave up a stable life and decided to set up his own business.
我们都应该维护社会安定。
We should all keep the peace.
局势安定下来了。
The situation has settled down.

tíwèn
提问 （丙）动
raise questions; ask a question

常用搭配
向他提问 ask him a question

用法示例
会后请听众提问。
Questions are invited after the meeting.
当老师提问时学生们都举起了手。
The pupils all put up their hands when the teacher asks them questions.

cáigàn běnlǐng
才干 ⑩ 本领 （丁）名
ability; competence

常用搭配
天生的才干 raw talent　　杰出的才干 outstanding abilities

用法示例
我们相信他的才干。
We believe in his ability.
人人都知道她很有才干。
Her talents are well known.
他有能在本行业中领先的才干。
His ability carried him to the top of his profession.

cáinéng
才能 （丙）名
talent; ability

常用搭配
管理才能 administrative talent

有多种才能的人 a man of many abilities

用法示例

经理没有发现她潜在的才能。
The manager did not see her hidder abilities.
他显示出领导才能。
He shows the quality of leadership.
我们为他找到了更容易发挥才能的工作。
We found him a job that will better utilise his abilities.

wèiwèn
慰问 （丙）动

① condole ② express sympathy, greetings, consolation, etc.

常用搭配

慰问灾民 extend one's regards to sufferers
表示亲切慰问 express one's sincere solicitude

用法示例

她的丈夫在这次事故中受伤了,她的朋友们都向她表示慰问。
Her friends consoled her when her husband was hurt in the accident.
市长向在除夕之夜还坚持工作的人们表示慰问。
The mayor expressed his sympathy to those who were working on New Year's Eve.
听到这些我很遗憾。请接受我最诚挚的慰问。
Oh, I'm sorry to hear that. Please accept my deepest sympathies.

cóngzhōng
从中 （丁）副

① therefrom ② from

常用搭配

从中作祟 play tricks in secret

用法示例

我想我们能从中学到许多。
I think we may learn much from it.
这些都是事实,你能从中得出什么结论?
Those are the facts; what do you conclude from them?
多少公司要从中获利呢?
How many companies are to make profits for themselves?

cóngtóu
从头 （丁）副

① from the beginning ② anew

常用搭配

从头做起 start from the very beginning
从头到脚 from head to foot   从头至尾 from first to last

用法示例

他从头到脚都湿透了。
He was wet from top to toe.
我把这本书从头到尾看完了。
I've read the book from beginning to end.
他损失了所有的钱,只好再从头做起。

He lost all his money and had to start again, completely from scratch.

wèijù   kǒngjù
畏惧 ⑤ 恐惧 （丁）动

fear; dread

常用搭配

无所畏惧 be fearless
使某人畏惧 inspire a man with awe

用法示例

法官坚决维护法律,既不畏惧也不偏袒。
The judge administers to the law, without fear or favor.
他和这位强手比赛并不感到畏惧。
He played fearlessly against his strong opponent.
这些年轻人不畏惧任何困难。
No difficulty could awe these young men.

 词义辨析

才能、才干

"才能"和"才干"都是名词,都有能力的意思,常常可以互换使用。但是"才能"主要指知识和能力,强调内在的能力或才华,如科学研究的才能,文学创作的才能;"才干"主要指在实践中表现出来的处理问题的具体能力,包括组织、管理等方面的能力。

Both 才能 and 才干 are nouns, meaning "ability". Sometimes they are exchangeable. 才能 mainly indicates knowledge and ability, and stresses innate ability or talent, such as "科学研究的才能" (ability of scientific research), "文学创作的才能" (talent to write literature works); while 才干 mainly indicates practical capability or skill to deal with something, including the ability to organize or administrate, etc.

 练习

练习一、根据拼音写汉字,根据汉字写拼音
ké（　） wèi（　） wèi（　） wèi（　）（　）gàn
（　）嗽 （　）问 （　）道 （　）惧　才（　）

练习二、搭配连线
(1) 杰出的　　　　　　　A. 局面
(2) 亲切的　　　　　　　B. 才干
(3) 安定的　　　　　　　C. 味道
(4) 安全的　　　　　　　D. 慰问
(5) 难闻的　　　　　　　E. 地方

练习三、从今天学习的生词中选择合适的词填空
1. 我猜他有吸烟的习惯,他身上有股淡淡的烟草的_____。
2. 讲座的最后一个环节是与学生现场交流,请学生_____。

3. 战争过后,人们都渴望过 _____ 的生活。

4. 他把房子重新装修了一下,然后又卖了,_____ 赚了十五万。

5. 这个孩子从小就表现出了非凡的领导 _____。

6. 他 _____ 科研工作十五年了。

7. 晚上出门的时候,凯特的妈妈一再嘱咐女儿要注意 _____,早点儿回家。

8. 他做生意失败了,但他并不气馁,想 _____ 再来。

9. 他把活动搞得有声有色,得到了各方面的好评,领导也十分欣赏这个年轻人的 _____。

10. 政府每年春节时都对孤寡老人进行 _____。

 **答案**

练习一:
略

练习二:
(1) B   (2)D   (3A   (4)E   (5)C

练习三:
1. 味道   2. 提问   3. 安定   4. 从中   5. 才能
6. 从事   7. 安全   8. 从头   9. 才干   10. 慰问

第9月,第1周的练习

练习一. 根据词语给加点的字注音
1.( )   2.( )   3.( )   4.( )   5.( )
惭愧   剥削   逮捕   赠送   增添

练习二. 根据拼音填写词语
wèi   wèi   wèi   kān   kān
1.( )问 2.( )惧 3.( )道 4.( )登 5.难( )

练习三. 辨析并选择合适的词填空
1. 这个小男孩长着一双漂亮的大眼睛,看上去很( )。(机智、机灵)

2. 当记者问到一些隐私问题时,他回答得都很( )。(机智、机灵)

3. 这项技术已经( )世界先进水平。(到达、达到)

4. 飞机下午三点( )了首都机场。(到达、达到)

5. 他每个月的工资收入有两万多,其中不( )额外的收入。(包括、包含)

6. 这首小诗( )着作者真挚的情感和殷切的希望。(包括、包含)

7. 对于这种尖锐的提问,他的( )很平淡。(反映、反应)

8. 学生没有得到满意的答复,于是就把问题( )到了校长那里。(反映、反应)

9. 父母希望他把自己的聪明( )用在做生意上,而不是整天打电脑游戏。(才干、才能)

10. 他上大学时就表现出了非凡的领导( )。(才干、才能)

练习四.选词填空
仓促   开朗   惭愧   传达   传授
繁忙   开明   难堪   难看   传播

1. 孩子在众人面前的粗野行为让他的父母十分( )。

2. 他是一位十分( )的领导,能够听取各方面的意见,也乐于接受新鲜事物。

3. 年底,业务量骤增,他工作非常( )。

4. 这种流感病毒( )的速度非常快,学校里大部分学生都患上了感冒。

5. 因为没考上大学,她觉得非常( ),很对不起父母。

6. 他的决定太( )了,当时真应该仔细考虑考虑。

7. 中国人觉得这个模特长得很( ),可是外国人觉得她很漂亮。

8. 母亲把做这些菜的秘诀都( )给了女儿。

9. 她妹妹是个内向的女孩,而她的性格却非常( )。

10. 各单位向职工及时( )了政府的会议精神。

练习五.写出下列词语的同义词
1. 味道( )   2. 责备( )
3. 功效( )   4. 匆忙( )
5. 赠送( )

练习六.写出下列词语的反义词
1. 仓促( )   2. 开朗( )
3. 增添( )   4. 逮捕( )
5. 机灵( )

 **答案**

练习一.
1.kuì   2.xuē   3.bǔ   4.zèng   5.zēng

练习二.
1. 慰   2. 畏   3. 味   4. 刊   5. 堪

练习三.
1. 机灵   2. 机智   3. 达到   4. 到达   5. 包括
6. 包含   7. 反应   8. 反映   9. 才干   10. 才能

练习四.
1. 难堪   2. 开明   3. 繁忙   4. 传播   5. 惭愧
6. 仓促   7. 难看   8. 传授   9. 开朗   10. 传达

练习五.
1. 滋味   2. 责怪   3. 效果   4. 急忙   5. 赠与

练习六.
1. 慎重   2. 内向   3. 削减   4. 释放   5. 迟钝

9月 第 2 周的学习内容

星期一 Monday

bàoqiàn
抱歉 （乙）形
① be sorry ② feel apologetic

常用搭配
真抱歉。I am really sorry.

用法示例
我为此感到非常抱歉。
I'm extremely sorry for that.
真抱歉给你添了这么多麻烦。
I am so sorry to give you so much trouble.
很抱歉，我不能参加你们的晚会了。
I'm sorry, I can't come to your party.

jùtǐ
具体 反 抽象 chōuxiàng （乙）形
specific; concrete

常用搭配
具体日期 specific date　具体情况 set conditions
具体细节 concrete details

用法示例
我们应该对具体问题作具体分析。
We should make a concrete analysis of a specific problem.
对于解决这个问题，你有什么具体的想法？
Do you have any concrete thoughts on how to solve the problem?
我们确定了下次开会的具体时间。
We fixed a definite time for the next meeting.

guīlù
规律 （乙）名
regular pattern

常用搭配
历史规律 law of history　发展规律 law of development
客观规律 objective law

用法示例
我们有必要了解市场经济的规律。
It's necessary for us to understand the rules of a market-oriented economy.
供求规律决定商品的价格。
The law of supply and demand governs the prices of goods.

我研究历史是为了了解历史规律。
I research history in order to understand historys laws.

chōuxiàng
抽象 （乙）形
abstract

常用搭配
抽象概念 an abstract concept
抽象派艺术 abstract art

用法示例
这些是抽象名词，如真理和正义。
These are abstract words, like truth and justice.
我们可以欣赏美的事物，然而美本身却是抽象的。
We may enjoy beautiful things, but beauty itself is abstract.
不要这样抽象地谈问题。
Don't speak in such abstract terms.

shěde
舍得 （丙）动
be willing to part with (sth)

常用搭配
舍不得 hate to part with
舍得下功夫 not begrudge time spent on practice

用法示例
在这种时候，我什么都舍得。
At a time like this, I begrudge nothing.
我舍不得花这么多钱买衣服。
I hesitate to spend so much money on clothes.
我与他们一起度过那么多难忘的日子，真舍不得离开他们。
I spent so many unforgettable days with them that I was loath to part with them.

chǔcún
储存 反 清除 qīngchú （丁）动
store

常用搭配
储存食物 store food　储存余粮 store up surplus grain
储存战略物资 stockpile strategic materials

用法示例
他们把货物储存在一个仓库里。
They stored their goods in a warehouse.
易坏的食物应储存在冰箱里。
Perishable food should be stored in a refrigerator.
这个棚子能储存 30 箱苹果。
The shed will store 30 boxes of apples.

gēngxīn
更新 （丁）动
update; renew

常用搭配
更新信息 update information
更新设备 renew equipments

用法示例
我们每星期更新一次数据。
We update the data once a week.
这些旧桌椅该更新了。
These old chairs and tables should be replaced.
产品该更新换代了。
The older generation of products should be replaced by newer ones.

gēngzhèng
更正 gǎizhèng ◎ 改正 （丁）动
correct (of errors in published statements)

常用搭配
更正报价单 make a correction to the price list
加以更正 make corrections

用法示例
你把我的名字写错了，请予以更正。
You spelled my name wrong. Please correct it.
他要求出版社更正广告的内容。
He demanded the press make corrections to the content of the ads.
那个错误可以更正。
That mistake can be rectified.

zhòuwén
皱纹 （丙）名
wrinkle

常用搭配
脸上有皱纹。 There are some wrinkles on one's face.

用法示例
她的眼角开始有皱纹了。
She's beginning to get wrinkles round her eyes.
老人的脸上布满了皱纹。
The old man's face was covered in wrinkles.
祖父脸上有许多皱纹。
Grandfather has many wrinkles on his face.

chóubèi
筹备 zhǔnbèi ◎ 准备 （丁）动
make preparations

常用搭配
筹备委员会 preparatory committee
筹备国庆庆祝活动
make preparations for the National Day celebrations

用法示例
女王访问的筹备工作已基本就绪。
Preparations for the Queen's visit are almost complete.

你能帮我筹备此次会议吗？
Can you help me prepare for the conference?

chǔbèi
储备 （丁）动
① store up ② reserve

常用搭配
储备粮食 store up grain
物资储备 material reserve
石油储备 petroleum reserves

用法示例
他们已经储备了过冬用的煤。
They have laid in a stock of coal for winter.
我们应该为明年储备更多的粮食。
We should reserve more grain for the next year.
黄金储备已经耗尽。
The gold reserve had been exhausted.

hégé
合格 （丙）形
① qualified ② eligible

常用搭配
合格的教师 qualified teacher
合格的医生 qualified doctor
不合格 not up to standard

用法示例
我认为他是一个不合格的领导。
I don't consider him a qualified leader.
在 36 个儿童中，有半数合格。
Out of 36 children, half passed.
这种产品不合格。
This product does not measure up.

 词义辨析

更新、更正

"更新"和"更正"都是动词，"更新"指用新的代替旧的，宾语可以是设备、数据、资料等。"更正"的意思是改正，指用正确的代替错误的，宾语往往是错误的文字信息及内容。例如：①我们的主页每天更新一次。②广告中的地址是错的，所以他要求出版社予以更正。

Both 更新 and 更正 are verbs. 更新 means "to replace the old one with a new one"; its objects are equipment, figures, data, etc. While 更正 indicates "to make a correction", "to replace the wrong one with a correct one"; its objects are mainly wrong factual information or content. For example: ① Our homepage is updated once every day. ② The address was wrong in the ads, so he demanded the press make a correction.

 **练习**

练习一、根据拼音写汉字,根据汉字写拼音

( )qiàn　chōu( )　( )xīn　chǔ( )　guī( )
抱( )　( )象　更( )　( )存　( )律

练习二、搭配连线

(1) 更新　　　　　　A. 概念
(2) 储存　　　　　　B. 细节
(3) 抽象　　　　　　C. 设备
(4) 客观　　　　　　D. 食物
(5) 具体　　　　　　E. 规律

练习三、从今天学习的生词中选择合适的词填空

1. 现在的电子产品 _____ 换代很快,过半年这种数码相机可能就会降价。

2. 为自己的家人,他一向都很 _____ 花钱。

3. 杂志社将在后一期上对错别字作 _____。

4. 这件事情我只知道个大概,_____ 细节不太清楚。

5. 这里的冬天很冷,而我们燃料 _____ 得又不太充足,所以我们得节约用煤。

6. 我们的地下室是用来 _____ 原料的。

7. 会议下周就要召开了,会议的 _____ 工作已经进行得差不多了。

8. 这个概念很 _____,理解起来有点困难。

9. 这种产品因质量不 _____ 而被退回了工厂。

10. 他的生活很有 _____,每天早上六点起床,晚上十点睡觉。

答案

练习一:
略

练习二:

(1) C	(2)D	(3)A	(4)E	(5)B

练习三:

1. 更新	2. 舍得	3. 更正	4. 具体	5. 储备
6. 储存	7. 筹备	8. 抽象	9. 合格	10. 规律

 星期二

chūbǎn
出版　　　　　　　　　　（乙）动

publish

常用搭配

出版商 publisher
出版新书 publish a new book
新出版的小说 newly published novel

用法示例

这本词典是什么时候出版的?
When was the dictionary published?
这本书是 1988 年出版的。
The book was published in 1988.
出版社侵犯了他的版权。
The publisher infringed on his copyright.

shìyòng　　　　　　　　　　*shìhé*
适用　　　　　同 适合　　　　（乙）形

applicable

常用搭配

适用于…… apply to…
对……不再适用 be no more applicable to…

用法示例

法律适用于所有的人,不分种族或信仰。
The laws apply to everyone irrespective of race, or creed.
这项规定不适用于外国人。
This rule is not applicable to foreigners.
这项规则并不适用于所有的情况。
The rule cannot be applied in every case.

shìyìng
适应　　　　　　　　　　（乙）动

adapt; accommodate

常用搭配

适应新环境 adapts to new circumstances
适应社会需要 fit in with the needs of society

用法示例

她很快就适应了这种寒冷的气候。
She adapted quickly to the cold climate.
他们的眼睛慢慢适应了黑暗的环境。
Their eyes slowly adapted to the dark.
他不适应这种乡村小镇的单调生活。
He was not used to the tedious life in this small country town.

shèfǎ
设法　　　　　　　　　　（丙）动

try to; manage to

常用搭配

设法离开 try to leave

设法逃脱 manage to escape

用法示例

他设法自己克服困难。

He managed to overcome the difficulty by himself.

只要有可能,他总是设法帮助我。

Wherever possible, he tries to help me.

母亲设法培养儿子对音乐的兴趣。

The mother tried to foster her son's interest in music.

zhuózhòng
着重 （丙）动

stress; emphasize

常用搭配

着重指出 point out emphatically

着重讨论 discuss emphatically

用法示例

部长着重指出了基础教育的重要性。

The minister emphasized the importance of basic education.

政府今年将着重解决供需矛盾的问题。

The government will make a special effort to solve the conflict of demand and supply this year.

李教授今天只着重谈了一个问题。

Professor Li focused on one question in particular today.

zhuóshǒu
着手 〓 dòngshǒu 动手 （丙）动

① commence ② set about

常用搭配

着手收集资料 set about collecting data

着手进行实验 commence experimentation

用法示例

他着手创办新企业。

He embarked on a new enterprise.

他已经着手写学位论文了。

He has commenced writing his thesis.

中国着手进行大规模的改革。

China embarked on a massive program of reform.

bàochóu
报仇 〓 fùchóu 复仇 （丙）动

revenge

常用搭配

为他哥哥报仇 revenge for his brother

用法示例

哈姆雷特为他死去的父亲报仇。

Hamlet avenged his dead father.

他们决定向敌人报仇。

They decided to take revenge on their enemies.

骑士发誓要为他妻子报仇。

The knight swore he would avenge his wife's death.

bàofù
报复 （丙）动/名

① retaliate ② reprisals

常用搭配

进行报复 make reprisals

报复老板 take revenge on one's boss

图谋报复 nurse thoughts of revenge

用法示例

王寒上了哥哥的当,发誓要报复。

Wang Han swore to take revenge on his brother, who'd played a trick on him.

我做那件事并不是出于报复。

I did not do it out of revenge.

我们若征收进口税,别的国家就可能报复我们。

If we impose import duties, other countries may retaliate against us.

zháoliáng
着凉 〓 gǎnmào 感冒 （丙）动

catch a cold; take a chill

常用搭配

他着凉了。He has caught a chill.

用法示例

别着凉。快去把湿衣服换掉。

I can't have you catching cold. Run and change your wet things.

他浑身湿透了,说不定会着凉的。

He is soaked to the bone and might catch a cold!

恐怕我是着凉了。

I'm afraid I've caught a chill.

zhuóxiǎng
着想 （丁）动

give consideration to (others)

常用搭配

为集体利益着想 think about the interests of the collective

用法示例

人人都会为自己的利益着想。

Every miller draws water to his own mill.

他从不为别人着想。

He never considers others.

她是为你着想才那样做的。

She did that for your own good.

chūchǎn
出产 （丁）动

output

常用搭配

出产优质水稻 produce good rice

出产率 rate of output

用法示例

加拿大出产优质小麦。

Canada produces good wheat.

江西景德镇出产精美的瓷器。

Jingdezhen in Jiangxi Province produces fine porcelain.

用法 *yòngfǎ* （丁）名

usage

常用搭配

用法说明 direction(for use)

习惯用法 idiomatic usage

用法示例

请注意这个词的用法。

Please pay attention to the use of this word.

你得学习工具的用法。

You need to learn the use of tools.

 词义辨析

报仇、报复

"报仇"和"报复"都表示对损害过自己的人进行的回击,都可以用作动词和名词。"报仇"语气重,是不及物动词,不能带宾语;"报复"的语气轻,是及物动词,能够带宾语。例如:①我不小心弄坏了玛丽的钢笔,出于报复,她撕掉了我的作业。②我担心有人会报复法官。③他叔叔杀了他爸爸,长大后他(为父亲)向叔叔报仇。

Both 报仇 and 报复 mean "to inflict punishment in return for injury". They can be used as verbs and nouns. 报仇 is more serious than 报复. 报仇 is also an intransitive verb, and it does not go with objects; while 报复 is a transitive verb, and it can be followed by objects. For example: ① I broke Mary's pen by accident, and in revenge she tore up my school work. ② I am afraid someone will retaliate on the judge. ③ His uncle killed his father, he took revenge on his uncle (for his father) when he was grown-up.

 练习

练习一、根据拼音写汉字,根据汉字写拼音

( )liáng zhuó( ) shì ( ) ( )bǎn ( )fǎ

着( ) ( )重 ( )应 出( ) 用( )

练习二、搭配连线

(1) 出版　　　　　　A. 逃脱

(2) 适应　　　　　　B. 强调

(3) 着重　　　　　　C. 仇人

(4) 报复　　　　　　D. 环境

(5) 设法　　　　　　E. 新书

练习三、从今天学习的生词中选择合适的词填空

1. 南非因 _____ 钻石而闻名。

2. 新领导上任以后,先了解公司的情况,然后就 _____ 进行管理体制改革。

3. 别生父母的气了,父母这样做可都是为你的前途 _____。

4. 这项任务很艰巨,但我们一定会 _____ 按时完成。

5. 侵略者杀害了这个孩子的父母,孩子发誓要为父母 _____。

6. 这次会议 _____ 讨论了两个问题。

7. 睡觉时不要把空调的温度调得太低,小心 _____。

8. 他给领导提意见,后来遭到 _____,被调到别的部门了。

9. 热带国家来的留学生很难 _____ 北京冬天的气候。

10. 形势发生了很大的变化,以前的法规已经不 _____ 了。

答案

练习一:

略

练习二:

(1) E　　(2)D　　(3)B　　(4)C　　(5)A

练习三:

1. 出产　2. 着手　3. 着想　4. 设法　5. 报仇

6. 着重　7. 着凉　8. 报复　9. 适应　10. 适用

星期三 Wednesday

bǎngyàng
榜样 　　　　　　　　　　　（乙）名

model; example

常用搭配

树立榜样 set an example
好榜样 good example

用法示例

她很勤奋,为其他人树立了榜样。
Her diligence has set an example to the others.
玛丽很勇敢,是我们大家的榜样。
Mary is so brave that she is an example to us all.
榜样的力量是无穷的。
A fine example has boundless power.

jīguān
机关 　　　　　　　　　　　（乙）名

organ

常用搭配

国家机关 state organs　　机关报 official newspaper
机关干部 office staff

用法示例

联邦调查局是司法部的一个机关。
The FBI is an organ of the Justice Department.
议会是政府的主要机关。
Parliament is the chief organ of government.

jīchuáng
机床 　　　　　　　　　　　（乙）名

machine tool

常用搭配

修理机床 repair a machine tool
一台机床 a machine tool

用法示例

我们可以供应各种型号的机床。
We can supply machine tools of all types and sizes.
由于使用不当,机床出故障了。
The machine tool didn't work because it was improperly used.

bàochou
报酬 　　圈 酬劳 chóuláo 　　　（丙）名

reward; pay

常用搭配

付给他报酬 give him a reward　　得到报酬 get paid
不计报酬 not concerned about pay

用法示例

尽管他努力工作,却没有得到报酬。
He hasn't received his reward even though he works hard.

女工们要求得到合理的报酬。
Women workers request equal pay.
他那份工作报酬很少。.
He gets paid peanuts for doing that job.

zīgé
资格 　　圈 资历 zīlì 　　　（丙）名

qualifications

常用搭配

入学资格 admission qualification
具备……资格 have qualifications for…

用法示例

目前他还不具备行医资格。
He hasn't achieved medical qualifications yet.
她没有资格申请助学金。
She is not qualified for an award.
他承认自己没有资格担任那个职务。
He recognized that he was not qualified for the post.

zījīn
资金 　　　　　　　　　　　（丙）名

fund; capital

常用搭配

建设资金 funds for construction
流动资金 current funds

用法示例

这个项目因缺少资金而放弃了。
The project was abandoned due to a lack of funds.
我们的公司需要资金。
Our company is in want of financing.
他们把资金投资于股票和债券了。
They invested their capital in stocks and bonds.

bìngliè
并列 　　　　　　　　　　　（丁）动

be juxtaposed

常用搭配

并列第三 tie for the third place
并列句 a coordinate sentence

用法示例

英国队和意大利队并列第二。
Britain are tied with Italy for the second place.
他们在跳高比赛中并列第一名。
They tied for the first place in the high jump.

bìngpái
并排 　　　　　　　　　　　（丁）动

① side by side ② abreast

常用搭配

并排走 walk side by side　　并排前进 to march abreast

用法示例

总经理和董事长并排坐在桌子后面。
The general manager and the chairman are sitting behind the desk side by side.

两辆车并排行驶。

Two cars drove side by side.

不要并排骑车。

Don't all cycle abreast.

摆脱 bǎituō （丙）动

① break away ② get rid of

常用搭配

尽快摆脱他 get rid of him as soon as possible

用法示例

如今,人们已经摆脱了一些习俗的束缚。

Nowadays, people have shaken off the shackles of some conventions.

我们趁黑摆脱了跟踪的人。

We managed to lose our pursuers in the darkness.

他这人真讨厌!我很庆幸能摆脱他。

He was a boring nuisance! I'm glad to be rid of him.

抱负 bàofù 回理想 lǐxiǎng （丁）名

ambition

常用搭配

实现他的抱负 fulfill his ambition

很有抱负 have high aspirations

用法示例

她的抱负是成为一名总统。

Her ambition is to attain the presidency.

她声称她的抱负是要当政治家。

Her declared ambition is to become a politician.

你有什么抱负?

Do you have any ambitions?

式样 shìyàng （丁）名

style

常用搭配

新颖的式样 novel style

春季流行式样 the spring fashion

用法示例

这件衣服的式样真高雅,它一定会流行好几年。

This dress is such a good style; it will be fashionable for many years.

请你照这个式样给我裁剪大衣。

Please cut out my overcoat according to this pattern.

这种式样过时了。

This fashion is out of date.

示范 shìfàn 回演示 yǎnshì （丁）动

① demonstrate ② show how something is done

常用搭配

做示范 to give a demonstration

起示范作用 play an exemplary role

示范效应 demonstration effect

用法示例

请示范机器的使用方法。

Please demonstrate how the machine works.

她给我们作示范,演示怎样操作这台机器。

She gave us a demonstration of the machine to show how it worked.

她示范了最有效的自卫方法。

She demonstrated how best to defend oneself.

 词义辨析

并排、并列

"并排"和"并列"都是动词,都指置于相同位置的意思。"并排"指位置与人或物平行不分前后,也可以修饰动作,如"并排骑车"、"并排走"、"并排站"等;"并列"强调名次与人相等,不分主次、优劣,很少修饰动词,如:并列第三名。

Both 并排 and 并列 are verbs, meaning "to place alongside of". 并排 indicates side by side with somebody or something; it can modify a verb, such as 并排前进 (to march abreast), 并排走 (to walk side by side), 并排站 (to stand side by side), etc, while 并列 stresses one's place in a competition is the same as another's, and it hardly modifies a verb; e.g. tie for the third place.

 **练习**

练习一、根据拼音写汉字，根据汉字写拼音

zī（　　）　（　　）tuō　shì（　　）　（　　）chou bǎng（　　）
（　　）格　摆（　　）　（　　）范　报（　　）　（　　）样

练习二、搭配连线

(1) 树立　　　　　　　A. 干部
(2) 付给　　　　　　　B. 第一
(3) 摆脱　　　　　　　C. 榜样
(4) 并列　　　　　　　D. 报酬
(5) 机关　　　　　　　E. 束缚

练习三、从今天学习的生词中选择合适的词填空

1. 世界上的伟人们一般在青少年时代就树立了远大的 _____。

2. 这次期中考试，他们两个人都是 100 分，在我们班 _____ 第一名。

3. 这件衣服看上去还很新，不过衣服的 _____ 已经过时了。

4. 这家企业引进了几台先进的 _____，这种设备在国内是一流的。

5. 启动这个项目需要大量 _____，但目前我们公司还不具备这个经济实力。

6. 他为了 _____ 前女友的纠缠，去另一个城市工作了。

7. 他通过了考试，取得了律师 _____ 证书。

8. 照片中和我父亲 _____ 坐着的是我母亲。

9. 这个工作的压力很大，但是 _____ 也很丰厚，我还不想马上换工作。

10. 辞职前，他是一名政府 _____ 的公务员。

答案

练习一：
略

练习二：
(1) C　　　(2)D　　　(3)E　　　(4)B　　　(5)A

练习三：
1. 抱负　　2. 并列　　3. 式样　　4. 机床　　5. 资金
6. 摆脱　　7. 资格　　8. 并排　　9. 报酬　　10. 机关

星期四 Thursday

fāhuī
发挥 （乙）动

perform; bring into play

常用搭配

发挥作用 perform a function
发挥艺术天赋 turned one's artistic gifts to good account

用法示例

互联网在现代生活中发挥着重要作用。
The internet plays an important role in modern life.
在新的岗位上，他充分发挥了自己的才能。
He makes full use of his talent in this new position.

fādǒu
发抖 （乙）动

tremble; shiver

常用搭配

吓得发抖 tremble with fear　　冷得发抖 shiver with cold

用法示例

这孩子冷得直发抖。
The child shivered with cold.
他害怕得声音发抖。
His voice shook with fear.
他气得发抖。
He was trembling with rage.

qìngzhù
庆祝 圓 庆贺 qìngzhù （乙）动

celebrate

常用搭配

举行庆祝会 hold a celebration
庆祝新年 celebrate the New Year
庆祝国庆 celebrate the National Day

用法示例

他们兴高采烈地庆祝胜利。
They celebrated their victory cheerily.
你是怎样庆祝结婚周年纪念日的？
How did you celebrate your wedding anniversary?
我们开瓶香槟酒庆祝一下吧。
Why don't we crack open a bottle of champagne to celebrate?

huìbào
汇报 圓 报告 bàogào （丙）动/名

① give an account of ② report

常用搭配

向总部汇报 report to headquarters
汇报情况 report the condition

汇报工作 report to sb. on one's work

【用法示例】

他每周得向总经理汇报一次工作。

He has to the report his work to the general manager once a week.

他因没有对事故进行汇报而受到批评。

He was criticized for failing to report the accident.

chuánshuō
传说 （丙）动／名

① it is said ② legend

【常用搭配】

古老的传说 an ancient legend

美丽的传说 a beautiful legend

【用法示例】

传说这个湖是仙女的镜子。

It was said that the lake was a fairy's mirror.

有一个关于这个湖的传说。

There is a legend about the lake.

外界传说外交部长打算辞职。

It is common knowledge that the foreign minister intended to resign.

gōngdào
公道　🔄偏袒　（丁）形

piāntǎn

fair; equitable

【常用搭配】

价格公道 reasonable prices

主持公道 do justice

【用法示例】

说句公道话,她确实应该获胜。

To do her justice, she did deserve to win.

我认为价格很公道。

I think the price is very reasonable.

gōngzhèng
公正 （丙）形

just

【常用搭配】

公正的裁决 a just verdict

公正的领导 an impartial leader

【用法示例】

他是一位公正的法官。

He is an impartial judge.

应该公正地对待每一个人。

Everyone should be treated with justice.

你必须做事公正。

You must play fair.

gōngpíng
公平 （丁）形

fair; impartial

【常用搭配】

公平交易 a fair deal　公平竞争 a fair competition

这不公平! It's not fair.

【用法示例】

用五个苹果换五个鸡蛋公平吗?

Is five apples for five eggs a fair exchange?

他们很公平地分担家务。

They shared the housework fairly.

对学生而言,这并不公平。

It is not fair on the students' part.

zōngjiào
宗教 （丙）名

religion

【常用搭配】

宗教问题 a religious question

宗教活动 religious activities

【用法示例】

我对宗教问题和道德问题不感兴趣。

I am unconcerned with questions of religion or morality.

宗教是一个必须慎重处理的问题。

Religion is a subject that must be approached with great delicacy.

几乎每个国家都有某种形式的宗教。

Almost every country has some form of religion.

chuánzhēn
传真 （丁）名

fax; facsimile

【常用搭配】

接收传真 receive a fax

发传真 send a fax

【用法示例】

上星期我正在度假,没收到你的传真。

I was on vacation last week and didn't receive your fax.

你仔细考虑过之后,请发个传真告诉我。

After you think it over, please let me know by fax.

请把名单传真给我。

Please fax me the name list.

qìnghè
庆贺 （丁）动

congratulate and celebrate

【常用搭配】

值得庆贺的事情 a matter for congratulations

【用法示例】

我们今晚出去好好玩玩,以示庆贺。

We are celebrating by stepping out tonight.

他举行宴会庆贺女儿的生日。

He celebrated his daughter's birthday with a banquet.

zhùfú
祝福　🔄诅咒　（丁）动

zǔzhòu

bless; give a benediction

【常用搭配】

神的祝福 the blessing of the lord

美好的祝福 good wishes

用法示例

当我离开的时候,她向我祝福。
She conferred her benediction on me when I left.
请接受我的祝福。
Please accept my benediction.

 词义辨析

公平、公正、公道

　　"公平"、"公正"和"公道"都是形容词,都有对各方都平等对待的意思,有时这些词可以互换使用。"公平"和"公道"都强调合理,"公正"强调不偏袒。"公正"和"公道"都可以作定语,形容人的品德,"公平"不可以。"公道"可以用作名词,"公正"和"公平"不可以。在下列的固定搭配中三个词不能互相替换:公平交易、公平竞争、公正的裁判、公正的裁决、价格公道、主持公道、讨个公道等。

　　公平, 公正, 公道 are adjectives, meaning "impartial, just to all parties"; sometimes they are exchangeable. 公正 and 公道 stress "being reasonable", 公正 stressed "being free of favoritism"; 公正 and 公道 can function as attributives, and they are used to describe the good virtue of somebody; 公平 can not be used like that. 公道 is also a noun; 公正 and 公平 can only be adjectives. The three words are not exchangeable in the following collocations: 公平交易 (a fair deal), 公平竞争 (a fair competition), 公正的裁判 (an impartial judge), 公正的裁决 (a just verdict), 价格公道 (reasonable prices), 主持公道 (do justice), 讨个公道 (ask for justice), and so on.

 练习

练习一、根据拼音写汉字,根据汉字写拼音

zōng (　　) qìng (　　) chuán (　　) (　　) dǒu zhù (　　)
(　　) 教　(　　) 贺　(　　) 说　　发 (　　)(　　) 福

练习二、搭配连线

(1) 价格　　　　　　　　A. 传真
(2) 公平　　　　　　　　B. 公道
(3) 美好　　　　　　　　C. 竞争
(4) 接收　　　　　　　　D. 情况
(5) 汇报　　　　　　　　E. 祝福

练习三、从今天学习的生词中选择合适的词填空

1. 导游带领我们游览美景的同时,还给我们讲了一些关于这里的古老 _____。
2. 这个市场卖的水果价钱 _____,我常去那儿买。
3. 出门的时候衣服穿少了,她冷得直 _____。
4. 我相信法庭会对此事做出 _____ 的判决。
5. 中国公民有自由信仰 _____ 的权利。
6. 命运有时对人很不 _____,可是我们不能屈服于命运。
7. 老师让孩子们在画画时充分 _____ 自己的想象力。
8. 你能不能把那份资料 _____ 给我?我有急用。
9. 今晚在学校礼堂有场毕业班的 _____ 演出。
10. 我们队获得了冠军,赛后,我们决定邀请教练一起去酒吧 _____ 一下。

答案

练习一:
略
练习二:
(1) B　　　(2) C　　　(3) E　　　(4) A　　　(5) D
练习三:
1. 传说　　2. 公道　　3. 发抖　　4. 公正　　5. 宗教
6. 公平　　7. 发挥　　8. 传真　　9. 汇报　　10. 庆贺

星期五

mìmì
秘密　⊠公开　（乙）形／名

secret

常用搭配

泄漏秘密 reveal a secret　保守秘密 keep a secret
秘密行动 secret action

用法示例

不要对任何人讲我们的计划,要保守秘密,这是一个秘密计划。

Don't tell anyone about our plan; keep it a secret — it's a secret plan.

她很谨慎,不会泄露秘密。

She is cautious of telling secrets.

他们在秘密地进行谈判。

They are negotiating in secret.

shàngdàng
上当　⊜受骗　（乙）动

be deceived; be fooled

常用搭配

他上当了。He was taken in.

用法示例

别想骗我,我不会轻易上当的。

Don't try to cheat me; I can't be fooled easily.

不要上坏人的当。

Don't let yourself be fooled by evil people.

别上当——他是骗子。

Don't be taken in — he's just a quack.

你上当了,他不过是开个玩笑。

You were deceived. He was only joking.

zìyóu
自由　（乙）名／形

① freedom ② free

常用搭配

言论自由 freedom of speech
信仰自由 freedom of beliefs
自由讨论 have a free exchange of views

用法示例

奴隶们希望获得自由。

The slaves wish to be free.

老太太过着一种自由、安逸的生活,从不为任何事情操心。

The old lady leads a free and easy life, and is never troubled much about anything.

我将自由自在地过这个暑假。

I will be as free as the wind in the summer vacation.

shāngrén
商人　（丙）名

businessman; merchant

常用搭配

丝绸商人 a silk merchant　精明的商人 a shrewd trader
奸诈的商人 a fraudulent businessman

用法示例

这个商人贿赂他。

The businessman offered bribes to him.

他是一个精明的商人,深知自己的利益所在。

He was a shrewd businessman. He knew which side his bread was buttered on.

yuánshǐ
原始　（丙）形

primitive; primeval

常用搭配

原始社会 primitive society　原始森林 primeval forest
原始资料 original data

用法示例

原始人住在山洞里。

Primitive men lived in caves.

他找到了那次会议的原始记录。

He found the original record of that meeting.

原始社会的结构并不一定就是简单的。

The constitution of a primitive society is not necessarily simple.

yuánxiān
原先　（丙）名

① original ② originally

常用搭配

原先的计划 the original plan

用法示例

房子原先的主人搬出去了。

The original owner of the house moved out.

他原先在大学工作,但现在是律师。

He formerly worked in a university, but now he's a lawyer.

她说她原先看过这部电影。

She said she had seen the film before.

jīmì
机密　（丁）形／名

① secret ② classified (information)

常用搭配

机密文件 classified documents　国家机密 state secrets

用法示例

这份情报是机密,只有少数几个高级官员能看。

This information is classified; only a few top officials can see it.

政府雇员宣誓不泄露官方机密。

Government employees swear an oath not to reveal official secrets.

我当时正在销毁机密文件。

I was shredding top-secret documents at that time.

yuánzǐ
原子 （丙）名
atom
常用搭配
原子弹 atom bomb　原子能 atomic energy
氮原子 atom of nitrogen
用法示例
一个水分子是由两个氢原子和一个氧原子构成的。
A molecule of water is made up of two atoms of hydrogen and one atom of oxygen.
一颗原子弹能摧毁一座城市。
An atom bomb would destroy a city.
自从原子动力问世以后，工业发生了巨大的变化。
Since the advent of atomic power, there have been great changes in industry.

shūjí
书籍 （丙）名
book
常用搭配
各种书籍 all kinds of books
用法示例
我在图书馆里查阅了大量法律书籍。
I have consulted a large number of law books in the library.
一个学生如果没有了书籍，将怎么办？
What would a student do if he were deprived of his books?
他搜集了许多珍贵书籍。
He has collected a lot of rare books.

shāngbiāo
商标 （丁）名
trademark
常用搭配
注册商标 register trademarks
名牌商标 a well-known brand
用法示例
你注意到瓶子上的商标了吗？
Have you noticed the trademark on the bottle?
我想知道这种啤酒的商标。
I want to know the trade name of the beer.
你知道这种商品的商标吗？
Do you know the trade name of this kind of merchandise?

shàngrèn
上任　⊗卸任 （丁）动
take office
常用搭配
新官上任三把火。A new broom will sweep clean the old cobwebs.
用法示例
新领导已上任。
The new leader has come into office.
上任后，我仍旧坚守三个信念。
Since assuming office, I have held firmly to three values.

róngyù
荣誉　⊜荣耀 （丁）名
honor
常用搭配
荣誉学位 an honorary degree
用法示例
他玷污了家族的荣誉。
He stained the family honor.
我不配获得这样的荣誉。
I am unworthy of such an honor.

 词义辨析

秘密、机密
　　"秘密"和"机密"都是形容词和名词，都有保持不被人知道或发现的意思。"秘密"使用范围比较广，可以用于正式场合、非正式场合、组织及任何个人，还可以作状语。"机密"有重要而隐秘的含义，用于正式场合或国家、团体，不能用于私人之间的隐秘的事情，不能作状语。例如：①这是一份机密情报，只有部长本人能看。②她告诉我一个小秘密，她在和李强秘密地约会。

　　Both 秘密 and 机密 are adjectives and nouns, meaning "being kept concealed". 秘密 can be applied in most circumstances, either formal occasions or informal occasions; it can be used to describe any organization or any individual, and it can function as an adverbial. 机密 indicates "secret and important"; it is just applied to formal occasions, and it can not function as an adverbial. For example: ① This is a classified document that only the Minister himself can read. ② She told me her secret which is that she is secretly dating Li Qiang.

 练习

练习一、根据拼音写汉字，根据汉字写拼音
mì（　）（　）jí　shāng（　）（　）yù（　）shǐ
（　）密　书（　）　（　）标　荣（　）原（　）
练习二、搭配连线
(1) 保守　　　　　A. 森林
(2) 注册　　　　　B. 秘密
(3) 原始　　　　　C. 商标
(4) 机密　　　　　D. 讨论
(5) 自由　　　　　E. 文件
练习三、从今天学习的生词中选择合适的词填空
1. 总经理在 _____ 之前已经摸清了公司的基本情况。
2. 这个 _____ 已经被别人注册了，你要是使用就是侵权。
3. 由于军事 _____ 被泄露，战略计划不得不临时更改。
4. 一个人生活确实很 _____，但有时也会觉得孤单。

5. 一个中国朋友说我 _____ 了,这个东西其实没那么贵。

6. 他爸爸原先是个机关干部,后来和朋友一起经商,成了一名非常成功的 _____。

7. 运动员们在赛场上为祖国的 _____ 而战。

8. 虽然遇到一些困难,但是我们决定继续按照 _____ 的计划进行改革。

9. 他的书房里摆了很多 _____,看来他是个很喜欢看书的人。

10. 在这一带发现了许多 _____ 动物的化石。

答案

练习一:
略
练习二:
(1) B   (2)C   (3)A   (4)E   (5)D
练习三:
1. 上任   2. 商标   3. 机密   4. 自由   5. 上当
6. 商人   7. 荣誉   8. 原先   9. 书籍   10. 原始

第9月,第2周的练习

练习一.根据词语给加点的字注音

1.( )   2.( )   3.( )   4.( )   5.( )
　着凉　　　着重　　　更正　　　上当　　　书籍

练习二.根据拼音填写词语

bào　　　bào　　　shì　　　shì　　　shì
1.( )歉 2.( )酬 3.( )样 4.( )范 5.( )应

练习三.辨析并选择合适的词填空

1. 你们把我们学校的名字写错了,我要求你们立即( )。(更新、更正)

2. 他这几天出差,所以他的网络日记没有及时( )。(更新、更正)

3. 孩子下决心将来一定给死去的父母( )。(报仇、报复)

4. 他对领导不满意但又不敢提意见,他怕领导( )他。(报仇、报复)

5. 他们俩考试的总成绩相等,是( )第二名。(并列、并排)

6. 照片中的姐妹俩( )站在花坛的前边。(并列、并排)

7. 他是个( )无私的人,大家很信任他。(公道、公正、公平)

8. 这个市场卖的蔬菜水果比别的市场价钱( )。(公道、公正、公平)

9. 大家都要遵守市场经济规则,( )竞争,不能相互欺骗。(公道、公正、公平)

10. 他拒绝接受赔款,坚决要把坏人告上法庭,为死去的妻

子讨回( )。(公道、公正、公平)

11. 这是一份( )文件,只有董事会的成员才能看。(机密、秘密)

12. 这是我们俩之间的( ),你可不能告诉别人。(机密、秘密)

练习四.选词填空

储备　　适用　　资格　　庆祝　　摆脱
筹备　　适应　　资金　　祝福　　荣誉

1. 刚开始工作时,工作压力特别大,我感到有点不( )。

2. 运动员们努力拼搏,为祖国赢得了( )。

3. 学校组织了一次晚会来( )新年的到来。

4. 他做生意的( )不足,所以他向银行申请了贷款。

5. 为了抵御可能出现的燃料短缺,我们提前( )了一些石油和煤。

6. 勤俭节约的原则无论对富人还是穷人都( )。

7. 朋友们( )这对新人婚姻美满,白头偕老。

8. 我自己在这方面做得并不好,所以我觉得自己没有( )批评别人。

9. 孩子为了( )父母的管束竟然离家出走了!

10. 这个有名的导演最近正在( )拍摄一部新电影。

练习五.写出下列词语的同义词

1. 报仇( )　　　　2. 汇报( )
3. 荣誉( )　　　　4. 筹备( )
5. 资格( )

练习六.写出下列词语的反义词

1. 上任( )　　　　2. 祝福( )
3. 秘密( )　　　　4. 具体( )
5. 储存( )

答案

练习一.
1.zháo   2.zhuó   3.gēng   4.dàng   5.jí
练习二.
1. 抱   2. 报   3. 式   4. 示   5. 适
练习三.
1. 更正   2. 更新   3. 报仇   4. 报复   5. 并列
6. 并排   7. 公正   8. 公道   9. 公平   10. 公道
11. 机密   12. 秘密
练习四.
1. 适应   2. 荣誉   3. 庆祝   4. 资金   5. 储备
6. 适用   7. 祝福   8. 资格   9. 摆脱   10. 筹备
练习五.
1. 复仇   2. 报告   3. 荣耀   4. 准备   5. 资历
练习六.
1. 卸任   2. 诅咒   3. 公开   4. 抽象   5. 清除

9月 第3周的学习内容

星期一 Monday

yǒngqì
勇气 （乙）名

courage

常用搭配

丧失勇气 lose courage
鼓起勇气 muster up courage

用法示例

他在面临危险的时候表现出了非凡的勇气。
He showed remarkable courage when faced with danger.
我觉得我没有勇气告诉他这个坏消息。
I don't think I have the courage to tell him the bad news.
他鼓起勇气参加了比赛。
He mustered his courage to take part in the game.

yǒnggǎn
勇敢　　　反 怯懦 qiènuò　　（乙）形

brave; courageous

常用搭配

勇敢的行为 a courageous deed
机智勇敢 brave and resourceful

用法示例

你真勇敢。
You are so brave.
他是一位勇敢的士兵。
He is a dauntless soldier.
他勇敢地从失火的房子里救出了孩子。
He bravely saved the child from the burning house.

xīshēng
牺牲 （乙）动

sacrifice

常用搭配

做出牺牲 make a sacrifice
牺牲生命 sacrificed one's life
不怕牺牲 fear no sacrifice

用法示例

以牺牲健康来求得工作上的成功是不值得的。
Success in your job is not worth the sacrifice of your health.
他为救落水的孩子而牺牲了。
He sacrificed his life to save the drowning child.

为供他上学,他的父母做出了很大牺牲。
His parents made many sacrifices to pay for his education.

zhìyuàn
志愿 （丙）名

① aspiration ② ideal

常用搭配

学生的志愿 students' aspiration
志愿者 volunteer
志愿献血者 volunteer blood donor

用法示例

他的志愿是作一名优秀的科学家。
His aspiration is to be an eminent scientist.
他志愿参军,保卫祖国。
He volunteered to join the army and defend his country.
医院的志愿人员分成了三组。
The hospital volunteers formed themselves into three groups.

biānjí
编辑 （丙）动/名

① edit; compile ② editor

常用搭配

编辑报纸 edit a newspaper
责任编辑 managing editor
编辑部 editorial department

用法示例

她的工作是编辑杂志。
Her work is to edit the magazine.
这份报纸的编辑是一个负责任的年轻人。
The editor of the newspaper is a responsible young man.
编辑删掉了文章的最后一段。
The editor deleted the last paragraph from the article.

gòusī
构思 （丙）动/名

① conceive ② conception

常用搭配

构思一部小说 to conceive a novel
构思巧妙 be ingenious in conception
大胆的构思 be bold in conception

用法示例

构思这本书只用了五分钟,但写这本书却花了一年。
The conception of the book took five minutes, but writing it took a year.
这个计划在构思上很有想象力。
The plan is very imaginative in conception.
影片的构思相当巧妙。
The plot of the film is ingeniously conceived.

gòuxiǎng
构想　⊜ 设想 shèxiǎng　（丁）动

conceive

常用搭配

大胆的构想 conceive bravely

去月球旅行的构想 propose traveling to the moon

用法示例

他构想了一个增加利润的计划。
He conceived a plan to increase profits.

一百多年前就有人提出了建设海底隧道的构想。
The notion of building a Channel Tunnel was put forward more than a century ago.

biānyuán
边缘　（丙）名

brink; edge

常用搭配

悬崖的边缘 the brink of a cliff

在死亡的边缘 on the brink of the grave

用法示例

这盘子的边缘是蓝色的。
The edge of the plate was blue.

这家公司就处在破产的边缘。
The company is on the edge of bankruptcy.

这边缘必须切割到 0.02 毫米的精密度。
The edge must be machined to 0.02 millimeters.

sǐwáng
死亡　⊗ 出生 chūshēng　（丙）动

① die ② death

常用搭配

因病死亡 to die of an illness

死亡率 death rate

用法示例

病人因出现并发症而死亡。
Complications set in, and the patient died.

车祸造成多人死亡。
Car accidents cause many deaths.

去年的出生人数大于死亡人数。
Last year there were more births than deaths.

biānjìng
边境　（丁）名

border; boundary

常用搭配

封锁边境 close the frontiers　开放边境 open the borders

边境冲突 border clash

用法示例

恐怖分子越过边境逃走了。
The terrorists escaped over the border.

边境上的紧张局势加重了我们对战争的忧虑。
The serious incident along the border increased our fears of war.

双方军队在边境的冲突引发了战争。
A border clash between the two armies started the war.

zhìqì
志气　（丁）名

ambition

常用搭配

有志气
have high aspirations

有志气的人
a man of iron will

用法示例

别看他年纪小，可志气并不小。
Although he is young in age, he is strong in will.

他们虽穷却很有志气。
They are ambitious although they are poor.

liángxīn
良心　⊜ 良知 liángzhī　（丁）名

conscience

常用搭配

没良心 be heartless

违背良心 go against one's conscience

良心不安 have an uneasy conscience

用法示例

为了不受良心的谴责，她把偷他的钱还给他了。
For the sake of her conscience, she gave him back the money she'd stolen.

现在想凭借道歉获得良心上的安慰已经太晚了。
It's too late to salve your conscience by apologizing.

 词义辨析

牺牲、死亡、死

1. "牺牲"、"死亡"和"死"都是动词，都表示丧失生命。"牺牲"的语气很庄重，指为坚持信仰或为了国家、集体或他人的利益而失去生命。"死亡"的语气很正式，指因病、意外、灾难等情况而失去生命。"死"的语气很随意，指失去生命，无论什么情况。例如：①二十名战士在战争中牺牲了。②车祸造成两人死亡。③我听说那个老人已经死了。

牺牲，死亡 and 死 are verbs, meaning "to die". The tone of 牺牲 is quite serious, indicating to die as a martyr or to sacrifice one's life for the country's interest or collective interests. The tone of 死亡 is formal, indicating to die of an illness, accident or disaster. The tone of 死 is colloquial, meaning to die under any circumstances. For example: ① Twenty soldiers died in battle. ② The traffic accident caused two deaths. ③ I heard that the old man had died.

2. "牺牲"还表示放弃或损害一方的利益，还可以带宾语，"死"和"死亡"都没有这种用法。"死"可以用于描述其他事物失去生命，"死亡"和"牺牲"只用于人。例如：①

他的父母为供他上学而做出了很大牺牲。②为了帮助我们,老师牺牲了自己的假期。③上个星期,我的狗死了,姐姐的花也死了。

牺牲 also means "to give up or do something at the expense of something; it can be followed by objects. 死 and 死亡 can not be used like this. While 死 can be used to describe something dead; 死亡 and 牺牲 are just applied to modify people. For example: ① His parents made great sacrifices to pay for his education. ② Our teacher sacrificed his holiday to help us. ③ Last week my dog died and my sister's flower perished, too.

 练习

练习一、根据拼音写汉字,根据汉字写拼音
( )gǎn ( )shēng biān( ) biān( ) ( )wáng
勇( ) 牺( ) ( )辑 ( )缘 死( )

练习二、搭配连线
(1) 鼓起　　　　　　A. 报纸
(2) 违背　　　　　　B. 勇气
(3) 牺牲　　　　　　C. 冲突
(4) 边境　　　　　　D. 生命
(5) 编辑　　　　　　E. 良心

练习三、从今天学习的生词中选择合适的词填空
1. 教授呼吁立即停止捕杀那些处于灭绝 _____ 的珍稀野生动物。
2. 这个小孩虽然年龄很小,但很有 _____,从小就有远大的理想。
3. 那个战士为救落水儿童 _____ 了自己年轻的生命。
4. 高考时,小王报的第一 _____ 是北京大学。
5. _____ 一点,不要怕,大家都会帮助你的。
6. 她在出版社工作,是一名 _____。
7. 这支军队是边防军,他们的任务是守卫 _____。
8. 当警方发现受害者时,受害者已经 _____。
9. 小伙子爱上了一位姑娘,可他只是把爱藏在心里,没有 _____ 对她表白。
10. 这部影片的 _____ 非常巧妙,是部难得的好影片。

 答案

练习一:
略
练习二:
(1) B　　(2)E　　(3)D　　(4)C　　(5)A
练习三:
1. 边缘　　2. 志气　　3. 牺牲　　4. 志愿　　5. 勇敢
6. 编辑　　7. 边境　　8. 死亡　　9. 勇气　　10. 构思

 星期二

shāowēi
稍微 （乙）副
① slightly ② little
常用搭配
稍微多一些 a little more
稍微搁点盐 add a little salt
觉得稍微有点冷 feel a bit cold
用法示例
他今天早晨稍微好了一些。
He's a little better this morning.
稍微当心一点,这种事情就不会发生。
A little care would have prevented it.
他比他的弟弟稍微高一些。
He is a little taller than his younger brother.

chóngfù
重复 （乙）动
repeat; duplicate
常用搭配
请再重复一遍。Please repeat it one more time.
重复劳动 repeated effort
用法示例
他一字不差地重复了她的话。
He repeated her statement word for word.
这项研究仅仅是重复了别人已经做过的工作。
This research merely duplicates work already done elsewhere.
他重复了几遍直到记住为止。
He repeated it several times over until he could remember it.

zhuàngtài
状态 （乙）名
① state ② state of affairs
常用搭配
紧急状态 state of emergency
战争状态 state of war
状态良好 in good condition
用法示例
我更爱看处于野生状态的动物。
I prefer to see animals living in their natural state.
冰是水的固体状态。
Ice is water in its solid state.
他处于十分焦虑的状态。
He was in a state of great agitation.

zhuàngdà 　　　　**wěisuō**
壮大 反 萎缩 （丙）动
strengthen; enhance

常用搭配

壮大军事实力 strengthen military force

壮大革命力量 expand the revolutionary forces

用法示例

他们在政府中的势力正在壮大。

Their influence in government is strengthening.

这有利于军队的发展和壮大。

It is good for the development and enhancement of the army.

他们的组织日益壮大。

Their organization is getting more and more powerful.

bèijǐng
背景 （丙）名

background; backdrop

常用搭配

家庭背景 family background　背景音乐 background music

教育背景 academic background

用法示例

这是我的照片,背景是我家的房子。

This is a photo of mine with our house in the background.

这部小说以战前的伦敦为背景。

The novel is set in pre-war London.

fǔyǎng
抚养 （丙）动

bring up; raise

常用搭配

抚养孩子 raise children

用法示例

他说他妻子的职责就是生育和抚养后代。

He said it was his wife's duty to bear and raise children.

她不得不独力抚养她的孩子。

She had to bring up her baby alone.

这个被遗弃的孩子是由政府抚养大的。

The abandoned boy was brought up by the government.

fǔyù
抚育 （丙）动

① nurture ② to provide loving care and attention

常用搭配

抚育子女 nurture children

抚育之恩 benevolence of nurturing

抚育烈士子女

bring up the children of revolutionary martyrs

用法示例

她把那孩子当作自己的儿子来抚育。

She nurtured the child as if he were her own son.

在父母的抚育下,我度过了幸福的童年。

I spent a happy childhood in the care of my parents.

hūshì
忽视　　　　　zhòngshì
⊗重视 （丙）动

neglect; ignore

常用搭配

忽视了这个问题 neglect the problem

忽视了她的感受 neglect her feelings

不可忽视的力量 a force not to be ignored

用法示例

你可不能忽视安全问题!

You can't just disregard the security problem!

教师在学习中的关键作用是不容忽视的。

The key role of the teacher in the learning process should not be neglected.

秘书是个很细心的人,她从不忽视任何细节。

The secretary is very careful and never overlooks any detail.

cáipàn
裁判 （丙）名/动

① referee ② judge

常用搭配

总裁判 chief referee

用法示例

裁判员判定罚一个任意球。

The referee awarded a free kick.

裁判哨子一响,比赛开始了。

The referee whistled and the game began.

他在网球比赛中担任裁判。

He umpired the tennis match.

bèipàn　　　pànbiàn
背叛　◎叛变 （丁）动

betray

常用搭配

背叛祖国 betray one's country

背叛妻子 betray one's wife

用法示例

他背叛了他的国家。

He betrayed his country.

我担心他会背叛我们。

I have a fear that he will betray us.

zhuàngguān
壮观 （丁）形

grand; spectacular

常用搭配

宏伟壮观的宫殿 the splendour of a palace

壮观的景象 grand view

用法示例

当我们爬上山顶时,我们看到了云海的壮观景象。

We had a grand view of a sea of clouds when we climbed to the top of the mountain.

他生平从未见过如此壮观的场面。

He had never before gazed up on such splendor.

瀑布的壮观景象真是好看极了。

The magnificence of the waterfall is a joy to behold.

yōumò
幽默 fēngqù ⑩ 风趣 （丁）形

① humor ② humorous

常用搭配

幽默感 sense of humor
黑色幽默 black humor
幽默故事 a humorous story

用法示例

他是一个幽默的人。
He is a humorous man.
她缺乏幽默感。
She had no sense of humor.
你真幽默！
You are so humorous!

 **词义辨析**

抚养、抚育

　　"抚养"和"抚育"都是动词,都有照料孩子成长的意思。"抚养"指供给衣、食、住或其他生活必需品,它的对象只能是人;"抚育"指抚养和教育两层意思,它的对象可以是人,也可以是动物或植物。例如:①孩子的父母去世后,孩子的叔叔负责抚养他们。②她把那孩子当作自己的孩子来抚育。③熊猫妈妈负责抚育熊猫宝宝。

　　Both 抚养 and 抚育 are verbs, meaning "to bring up". 抚养 indicates to provide a child with clothing, food, accommodation, and other necessities. Its objects are just people. 抚育 includes to bring up and to educate; its objects can be people, animals or plants. For example: ① The children's uncle is responsible for bringing up them after their parents died. ② She nurtured the child as if he were her own son. ③ The mother of the panda is responsible for raising her.

 **练习**

练习一、根据拼音写汉字,根据汉字写拼音

(　)pàn　(　)pàn fǔ(　)　(　)fù　(　)wēi
背(　)　裁(　)　(　)育　重(　)　稍(　)

练习二、搭配连线

(1) 幽默　　　　　A. 景象
(2) 紧急　　　　　B. 状态
(3) 壮观　　　　　C. 背景
(4) 政治　　　　　D. 孩子
(5) 抚养　　　　　E. 故事

练习三、从今天学习的生词中选择合适的词填空

1. 他说话很 _____ ,这使会议的气氛变得轻松多了。
2. 最近,队员的竞技 _____ 都不错,我们对打赢比赛充满信心。
3. 有的父母给孩子提供了优越的生活条件,却 _____ 了与孩子进行沟通和交流的重要性。
4. 良好的教育 _____ 会使求职者更具竞争力。
5. 这是世界上最大的瀑布,水从高处倾泻下来,相当 _____ 。
6. 这个间谍 _____ 了自己的祖国,逃到了另外一个国家。
7. 我们能不能 _____ 休息一会儿再工作,我有点累了。
8. 有的学生说没有听清楚,于是老师又 _____ 了一遍。
9. 这是个单亲家庭,妈妈自己 _____ 两个孩子长大成人。
10. 球迷们很生气,因为他们觉得 _____ 的裁决不公正。

答案

练习一:
略

练习二:
(1) E　　(2) B　　(3)A　　(4)C　　(5)D

练习三:
1. 幽默　2. 状态　3. 忽视　4. 背景　5. 壮观
6. 背叛　7. 稍微　8. 重复　9. 抚养　10. 裁判

星期三

cùjìn
促进　　　反 妨碍　　　（乙）动

promote

常用搭配
促进合作 promote cooperation
促进发展 promote development
促进相互了解 further mutual understanding

用法示例
该组织旨在促进各国之间的交流。
The organization works to promote communication between nations.
人工供暖能促进植物生长。
Artificial heating hastens the growth of plants.
锻炼能促进血液流动。
Exercise stimulates the flow of blood.

shànyú
善于　　　（乙）动

be good at

常用搭配
善于应变 be good at dealing with an emergency
善于观察 be good at observation

用法示例
她善于妥善解决这类小问题。
She is good at smoothing over these little problems.
他善于学习语言。
He is good at learning languages.
我们经理善于和各种顾客打交道。
Our manager is good at dealing with all kinds of customers.

yízhì
一致　　　反 分歧　　　（乙）形

unanimous; identical (views or opinions)

常用搭配
一致同意 agree unanimously
观点一致 hold identical views

用法示例
他的想法和我的不一致。
His ideas do not conform to mine.
他们一致反对建设新的停车场。
They are unanimous in their opposition to the building of new parking lot.
他言行一致。
His behavior conforms to his words.

jiàshǐ
驾驶　　　（丙）动

drive

常用搭配
驾驶执照 driving license
小心驾驶。Drive with caution!
驾驶飞机 pilot an airplane

用法示例
他熟练地驾驶着汽车穿过街道。
He steered the car skillfully through the streets.
他的驾驶执照上有危险驾驶记录。
He's had his license put on file for dangerous driving.

jiǎshǐ
假使　　　同 倘若　　　（丙）连

① suppose ② given ...

常用搭配
假使有机会……Given a chance…
假使我们中了彩票……Supposing we win the lottery…

用法示例
假使他来不了,谁干这工作?
Supposing he can't come, who will do the work?
假使你不能去旅行,你会有什么感受?
Suppose you couldn't go on the trip. How would you feel?
假设你父亲现在看到了你,你会怎么说?
Suppose your father sees you now, what would you say?

cùshǐ
促使　　　（丙）动

induce; prompt

常用搭配
促使他离开 prompt him to leave
促使他做出决定 prompt him to make the decision

用法示例
他说是贫穷促使他犯罪的。
He said he had been forced into crime by poverty.
是什么促使你做出这样的事来?
What prompted you to do such a thing?
他含糊其词的答复促使我又提出了一个问题。
His evasive reply prompted me to ask him another question.

cǐkè
此刻　　　（丙）名

now; this moment

常用搭配
此时此刻 at this very moment

用法示例
他此刻正在主持会议。
He's chairing a meeting at the moment.
他此刻正在去机场的路上。
He is on his way to the airport now.
此刻我正在工作,过一会儿再给我打电话吧。
At the moment I am working. Can you call me later ?

cìjī
刺激　　　（丙）动／名

① stimulate; irritate ② stimulation; excitement

常用搭配

刺激神经 stimulate nerves

刺激经济增长 stimulate the economic growth

别刺激他了！ Don't annoy him!

用法示例

羊毛刺激我的皮肤。

Wool irritates my skin.

他们利用电视广告来刺激需求。

They use television advertising to stimulate demand.

我们有些人崇尚安宁与舒适，有些人重视快乐与刺激。

Some of us value peace and comfort very highly whilst, others value pleasure and excitement.

tóuzī
投资　　　　　　　　（丁）名/动

① investment ② invest

常用搭配

投资于房地产 invest in real estate

短期投资 short-term investment

用法示例

国家计划投资 200 万元修建铁路。

The state has planned to invest two million in the railway.

由于投资不足，我们的工业生产一直停滞不前。

Due to low investment, our industrial output has remained stagnant.

我认为，这是很可靠的投资。

In my opinion, it is a very sound investment.

cǐhòu
此后　　　　　　　　（丁）连

① after this ② hereafter

常用搭配

此后不久 soon after this

用法示例

此后不久，她便成为一名全国闻名的流行歌手。

Not long after that, she made a national name for herself as a pop singer.

她 1958 年去了农村，此后一直在那儿工作。

She went to the countryside in 1958 and has worked there ever since.

shàncháng
擅长　　　　　　　　（丁）动

be good at; be expert in

常用搭配

他擅长数学。 He is skilled at math.

她擅长于写作。 She is good at writing.

用法示例

他擅长绘画和弹钢琴。

He excels in painting, and playing the piano.

李先生擅长于做很多事情，但他从来不表现自己。

Mr. Li is an expert at a lot of things, but he always hides his light under a bushel.

这个作家不太擅长写对白。

The writer is not very good at writing dialogues.

shànzì　　　　　　　sīzì
擅自　　◉ 私自　　　（丁）副

act without authorization

常用搭配

擅自决定 make arbitrary decisions

擅自作主 act without authorization

擅自更改 make an unauthorized change

用法示例

她未请示上级擅自把这些请柬都发了出去。

She issued these invitations without any reference to her superiors.

译者不应该擅自把自己的意思加进译文中。

A translator shouldn't insert his own opinions into what he's translating.

卫兵擅自离开了他的岗位。

The guard deserted his post.

 词义辨析

擅长、善于

"擅长"和"善于"都是动词，都有在某方面具有突出才能的意思。"擅长"的宾语往往比较具体，通常是名词，如：唱歌、跳舞、书法、绘画、运动等，常常用作"擅长于……"；"善于"的宾语往往是比较抽象，多数是动词，如：①他善于寻找机会。②我不善于跟陌生人交流。

Both 擅长 and 善于 are verbs, meaning "to be good at something". The objects of 擅长 are something concrete (and most of which are nouns), such as: "唱歌" (singing), "跳舞" (dancing), "书法" (calligraphy), "绘画" (painting), "运动" (sports), etc., and it is often used as "擅长于…"; while the objects of 善于 are usually something abstract (and most of which are verbs). For example: ① He is good at seeking out chances. ② I am poor at communicating with strangers.

 **练习**

练习一、根据拼音写汉字，根据汉字写拼音

jià（　）　shàn（　）（　）jī　（　）kè（　）zī
（　）驶　（　）长　刺（　）　此（　）　投（　）

练习二、搭配连线

(1) 擅自　　　　　　　　A. 绘画
(2) 擅长　　　　　　　　B. 一致
(3) 驾驶　　　　　　　　C. 观察
(4) 言行　　　　　　　　D. 决定
(5) 善于　　　　　　　　E. 执照

练习三、从今天学习的生词中选择合适的词填空

1. 我们都认为他对人很热情,也很有能力,所以 _____ 推选他当班长。
2. _____ 把你一个人留在一座孤岛上,你会怎么办?
3. 他来中国留学的时候已经四十岁了,是什么 _____ 他做出这样的决定呢?
4. 他最 _____ 打篮球,是我们学校篮球队的队长。
5. 中国对来华 _____ 的外国企业实行很多优惠政策。
6. 两国贸易的发展 _____ 了双方经济的交流、加强了两国人民的了解。
7. 这个人科研能力一般,但他很 _____ 交际。
8. 没有父母的同意,你不能 _____ 使用这笔钱。
9. 那一次是他们最后一次见面, _____ 他再也没见过她。
10. 这种行动很 _____ ,但也很危险。

答案

练习一：
略

练习二：

(1) D	(2)A	(3)E	(4)B	(5)C

练习三：

1. 一致	2. 假使	3. 促使	4. 擅长	5. 投资
6. 促进	7. 善于	8. 擅自	9. 此后	10. 刺激

星期四

bùzhì
布置　　　　　　　　　　　　　（乙）动
arrange; decorate

〔常用搭配〕
布置房间 decorate a room
布置作业 assign homework

〔用法示例〕
房间布置得很好。
The room is well decorated.
他们在布置房子准备过新年。
They are decorating the house for the New Year.

shīgōng
施工　　　　　　　　　　　　（乙）名/动
① construction ② build

〔常用搭配〕
施工队 construction team　　施工图 construction drawing

〔用法示例〕
该房子正在施工中。
The house is under construction.
工人们已经开始施工了。
Workers have already started construction work.

xióngwěi　　　　　　　hóngwěi
雄伟　　　　同 宏伟　　　　　（乙）形
grand; majestic

〔常用搭配〕
一座雄伟的大教堂 a magnificent cathedral
雄伟的泰山 the majestic Mount Tai

〔用法示例〕
长城以其雄伟壮丽而著名。
The Great Wall is known for its magnificence.
那是一座雄伟的宫殿。
It is a very stately palace.
雄伟的人民大会堂给他们留下了深刻的印象。
The magnificent Great Hall of the People impressed them tremendously.

shīféi
施肥　　　　　　　　　　　　　（丙）动
fertilize

〔常用搭配〕
给花施肥 manure flowers
合理施肥 adequate fertilization

〔用法示例〕
农民们正在为田地施肥。
The peasants are fertilizing the field.

为花园施肥有利于植物的生长。
Fertilizing the garden is good for plants' growth.
我帮助父亲给庄稼施肥。
I help my father fertilize the crops.

xíngshǐ
行驶 （丙）动
(vehicle, ship) go, run

常用搭配
安全行驶 travel safely
超速行驶 travel at a high speed

用法示例
火车在轨道上行驶。
Trains run on rails.
汽车在高速公路上飞速行驶。
The car is whizzing along the motorway.
轮船正在以每小时 50 海里的速度行驶。
The ship is traveling at a speed of 50 sea miles an hour.

bùshǔ **ānpái**
部署 ◎安排 （丙）动/名
① deploy ② disposition

常用搭配
军队的部署 disposition of troops
战斗部署 battle disposition

用法示例
炮兵部署在西边。
Artillery was deployed in the west.
他们在猜测敌军的部署。
They are guessing at the deployment of the enemy troops.
我们想知道他们是如何部署军队的。
We want to know how they deployed their troops.

chuánrǎn
传染 （丙）动
infect; be contagious

常用搭配
通过空气传染 airborne infections
传染病 contagious diseases
传染病病房 a contagious ward

用法示例
他被传染上了流感。
He was infected with the flu.
班上的一个孩子发烧了，不久传染给了其他孩子。
One of the boys in the class had a fever and he soon infected other children.
这种传染病是由蚊子传播的。
This infection is transmitted by mosquitoes.

bàoxiāo
报销 （丁）动
① reimburse ② submit an expense account

常用搭配
报销单 expense account

报销通讯费 reimburse a communication fee
用法示例
一切费用都能给你报销。
All of your expenses will be reimbursed.
我要找经理报销差旅费。
I will ask our manager to reimburse my travel expenses.
我去财务科报销了。
I went to submit an expense account to the finance office.

péixùn **xùnliàn**
培训 ◎训练 （丁）动
train

常用搭配
职业培训 occupational training
短期培训 short-term training

用法示例
人事部门正在组织新雇员的培训。
The personnel department is organizing training for the new members of staff.
他受过工程师资格培训。
He was trained as an engineer.

chuándì
传递 （丁）动
pass on to someone else

常用搭配
传递消息 convey news
传递眼色 give a wink
传递奥运火炬 pass on the Olympic torch

用法示例
人们一桶一桶地传递水，以便把火扑灭。
The bucket of water is passed from hand to hand to put the fire out.
请把这份文件传递给其他人。
Please pass on the document to others.

shīxíng **shíshī**
施行 ◎实施 （丁）动
put into practice; take effect

常用搭配
自公布之日起施行 to come into force upon promulgation
施行细则 rules for implementation

用法示例
这一税收制度一旦施行，必定会危害国民经济。
This tax can not be introduced without causing damage to the economy.
本条例自即日起施行。
The regulations came into force as of today.

shìxíng
试行 （丁）动
try; test out

常用搭配
试行生产 trial production

在试行期 in a trial period

用法示例

这些规定已开始试行。
The regulations have been put into practice on a trial basis.
先试行,再推广。
First try it out, then implement it.

 **词义辨析**

部署、布置

1．"布置"和"部署"都是动词,都有对活动做出安排的意思。"布置"多指安排具体的工作任务;"部署"多指对重大活动进行系统的、策略性的计划和安排。例如:①上午,经理布置完今天的工作就离开公司了。②他们在为战斗部署军队。

Both 布置 and 部署 are verbs, meaning "to make an arrangement for some activities". 布置 indicates to arrange concrete tasks or work; 部署 indicates "to arrange systematically or strategically an important activity. For example: ① This morning, our manager left the company after he assigned the tasks of today. ② They are deploying troops for the battle.

2．"布置"的对象还可以是一个场所,表示在一个地方安排和摆放各种物品,使其适合于某种需要的意思,"部署"没有这种用法。"部署"还是名词,"布置"不是。例如:①明天就是圣诞节了,学生们在布置教室。②根据政府的部署,我们将开发中国西部地区。

The objects of 布置 can be places, indicating "to put things in a place according to one's need or liking." 部署 can not be used like this; 部署 can also be a noun, while 布置 is not. For example: ① Tomorrow is Christmas; students are rearranging the desks and chairs, and putting up some decorations in the classroom. ② According to the arrangement of the government, we will develop the western areas of China.

 **练习**

练习一、根据拼音写汉字,根据汉字写拼音

( )rǎn ( )xiāo xióng ( ) shī ( )( )shǔ
传( ) 报( ) ( )伟 ( )肥 布( )

练习二、搭配连线

(1) 职业　　　　　　　　A. 行驶
(2) 传递　　　　　　　　B. 房间
(3) 战斗　　　　　　　　C. 培训
(4) 超速　　　　　　　　D. 部署
(5) 布置　　　　　　　　E. 消息

练习三、从今天学习的生词中选择合适的词填空

1. 他给花 _____ 以后,果然长得比以前好多了。
2. 为了引进新技术,公司派他去国外参加为期两个月的业务 _____。
3. 公司给我 _____ 我来中国学习汉语的费用。
4. 中央召开能源大会, _____ 今后五年能源发展的重点工作。
5. 这座高大 _____ 的纪念碑是我们城市的标志性建筑。
6. 该项条例自今年十月一日起 _____。
7. 这种病很可怕,会通过呼吸道 _____,我们得立即隔离这些病人。
8. 这项研究成果先要小面积 _____,有了一定经验后再大面积推广。
9. 她把家 _____ 得非常温馨。
10. 高考期间,所有学校附近的工程暂时停止 _____。

答案

练习一:
略
练习二:
(1) C　　　(2)E　　　(3)D　　　(4)A　　　(5)B
练习三:
1. 施肥　　2. 培训　　3. 报销　　4. 部署　　5. 雄伟
6. 施行　　7. 传染　　8. 试行　　9. 布置　　10. 施工

星期五

chónggāo
崇高　　　　同 高尚　　　　（乙）形

sublime; lofty

（常用搭配）

崇高的思想 a sublime thought

崇高的事业 a lofty cause

（用法示例）

他对人生抱有崇高的理想。

He has lofty ideals about life.

追求崇高的政治目标。

Pursue lofty political goals

zhǔdòng
主动　　　　反 被动　　　　（乙）形

on one's own initiative

（常用搭配）

主动学习 study on one's own initiative

争取主动 try to take the initiative

（用法示例）

他主动帮助我。

He helped me on his own initiative.

在谈判中我们赢得了主动权。

We won control in the negotiation.

他工作很主动。

He displays great initiative in his work.

bèidòng
被动　　　　　　　　　　　（丙）形

passive

（常用搭配）

感到被动 feel being passive

被动的局面 passive situation

陷于被动地位 land oneself in a passive position

（用法示例）

他在婚姻中扮演了一个被动的角色。

He played a passive role in the marriage.

通过进攻,我们使敌人陷入被动。

By attacking, we put the enemy in a weaker position.

在比赛中我们尽量摆脱被动。

We tried to get rid of passiveness in the match.

zhuàndòng
转动　　　　　　　　　　　（丙）动

turn

（常用搭配）

转动钥匙 turn the key

飞快地转动 turn around fast

（用法示例）

他轻轻地转动手柄,打开了门。

He rotated the handle gently, and opened the door.

按逆时针方向转动钥匙。

Turn the key anticlockwise.

如果你给这把锁涂上油,转动起来就容易了。

If you grease the lock, it will turn more easily.

zhǔlì
主力　　　　　　　　　　　（丙）名

main force

（常用搭配）

主力队员 top player of a team

主力部队 principal force

主力兵团 main formations

（用法示例）

主力部队遭到了敌人的伏击。

The main force was ambushed by the enemy.

他是我们足球队的主力。

He is a top player in our football team.

gēnggǎi
更改　　　　　　　　　　　（丁）动

alter; change

（常用搭配）

更改遗嘱 alter one's will

更改进度表 make a change in a schedule

更改路线 change the route

（用法示例）

没有我的允许,你不能更改合同。

You shouldn't alter the contract without my permission.

他们得更改原先的计划。

They have to change their original plan.

gēnghuàn
更换　　　　同 更新　　　　（丁）动

replace; change

（常用搭配）

更换轮胎 replace a tire

更换设备 replace equipment

更换磨损零件 replace worn parts

（用法示例）

他更换了电池。

He replaced the battery.

请问,能给我更换座位吗?

Excuse me, but could you change seats with me?

如果你对它不满意,你可以在一周之内来本店更换。

If you are not satisfied with it, you can come to the shop and change it for another one within one week.

bàifǎng
拜访　　　　　　　　　　　（丙）动

pay a visit; call on

常用搭配

拜访某人 pay sb a visit

定期拜访…… make a regular visit to…

用法示例

明天我将要去拜访这个作家。

Tomorrow I'll pay a call on the writer.

他们动身去拜访那位教授。

They were off to visit the professor.

我将在圣诞节前后去拜访您。

I will visit you around Christmas.

fángyù
防御 　　反 jìngōng 进攻 　　（丙）动

defense

常用搭配

防御敌人 defend oneself against enemy

防御计划 plan of defense

用法示例

敌人冲破了我们的防御工事。

The enemy brushed aside our defenses.

我们必须加强防御设施以抵御进攻。

Our defensive structures must be reinforced against attack.

枪是攻击武器还是防御武器，要根据你的目的来确定。

Whether a gun is a weapon of offence, or a weapon of defense depends on which end of it you are on.

chóngbài
崇拜 　　（丁）动

worship; adore

常用搭配

对自然的崇拜 nature worship

盲目崇拜 worship blindly

个人崇拜 a cult of personality

用法示例

我并不崇拜那个影星。

I am not a fan of that film star.

这小孩崇拜他的父亲。

The boy worshipped his father.

她很崇拜他，听不进别人对他的批评。

She worshipped him and refused to listen to his critics.

zhǔbàn
主办 　　（丁）动

host (a conference or sports event)

常用搭配

主办单位 host unit 　　主办产品交易会 hold a product fair

用法示例

哪个国家是下届奥运会的主办国？

Which country will be the host of the next Olympic Games?

今年的运动会由哪国主办？

Which country is hosting the Games this year?

这次报告会是由科学院主办的。

The lecture was given under the auspices of the Academy of Science.

zhuǎnzhé
转折 　　（丁）动 / 名

① a turn in the course of events ② transition

常用搭配

转折点 turning point

历史的转折 a turning point in history

戏剧性的转折 a dramatic turn

用法示例

她的印度之行成了她一生的转折点。

Her visit to India proved to be a watershed moment in her life.

这是我国历史上的一个伟大的转折。

This is a great turning point in China's history.

 词义辨析

更改、更换

"更改"和"更换"都是动词，都有改变的意思。"更改"指某部分或某方面有所变动或修改，不用于人；"更换"指用新的或合适的代替以前的，更换的对象一般比较具体，可以用于人。例如：①会议的日期需要更改一下。②对这项安排做了一些更改。③要定期更换空调的过滤网。④这一届领导班子的任期已到，人员要适当更换。

Both 更改 and 更换 are verbs, meaning "to change". 更改 indicates to make some changes or corrections in some parts or some aspects, but it is not applied to modifying people; 更换 indicates "to replace the original one with a new one or a suitable one"; the object of it is usually something concrete, and it can be used to modify people. For example: ① The date of the meeting needs to be changed. ② Some corrections have been made to the arrangement. ③ The filter of the air conditioner should be changed regularly. ④ The leaders terms are ending and some of them will be replaced.

 练习

练习一、根据拼音写汉字，根据汉字写拼音

chóng（ 　 ） 　 zhé（ 　 ） 　 huàn（ 　 ） 　 yù bài（ 　 ）

（ 　 ）高 　 转（ 　 ） 　 更（ 　 ） 　 防（ 　 ）访

练习二、搭配连线

(1) 更换 　　　　　　A. 队员

(2) 更改 　　　　　　B. 崇拜

(3) 主力 　　　　　　C. 主动

(4) 盲目 　　　　　　D. 轮胎

(5) 积极 　　　　　　E. 计划

练习三、从今天学习的生词中选择合适的词填空
1. 他向左 _____ 一下门把手,门马上就开了。
2. 他每去一个城市旅游,都要去 _____ 名人的故居。
3. 夏天 _____ 紫外线的最好方法是涂抹防晒油。
4. 谈恋爱时,男孩子要 _____ 一点,姑娘们一般比较害羞。
5. 他是我弟弟最 _____ 的球星。
6. 冰箱的一个零件坏了,需要 _____。
7. 刚开始谈判,公司就陷于 _____ 地位。
8. 开会的日期 _____ 了,请大家相互转告一下。
9. 老师教育我们从小要有 _____ 的理想。
10. 这次知识竞赛是国家教育部 _____ 的。

 **答案**

练习一:
略
练习二:
(1) D (2)E (3)A (4)B (5)C
练习三:
1. 转动 2. 拜访 3. 防御 4. 主动 5. 崇拜
6. 更换 7. 被动 8. 更改 9. 崇高 10. 主办

第9月,第3周的练习

练习一.根据词语给加点的字注音
1.( ) 2.( ) 3.( ) 4.( ) 5.( )
  重复   防御   刺激   编辑   雄伟

练习二.根据拼音填写词语
  pàn   pàn   shǐ   shǐ   zhuàng
1. 裁( ) 2. 背( ) 3. 促( ) 4. 行( ) 5. ( )态

练习三.辨析并选择合适的词填空
1. 这个人在郊区被发现时已经( )三天了。(牺牲、死亡)
2. 我们向在战争年代为了保卫祖国而( )的烈士们致敬。(牺牲、死亡)
3. 在饲养员的精心( )下,小熊猫长得又健康又可爱。(抚育、抚养)
4. 父母去世时他才三岁,他是由哥哥和嫂子( )大的。(抚育、抚养)
5. 他( )弹钢琴,曾获得钢琴比赛的第一名。(善于、擅长)
6. 他( )学习别人的优点,所以进步很快。(善于、擅长)
7. 各部门经理都来开会,一起研究了下半年的工作( )。(布置、部署)
8. 周末老师没有( )家庭作业,她让我们去逛胡同,了解北京的胡同文化。(布置、部署)
9. 不知什么原因,总统乘坐的专机在回国时( )了航线。

(更改、更换)
10. 机器还能用,只要把磨损的零件( )了就行。(更改、更换)

练习四.选词填空
构思   促使   行驶   试行   主动
构想   假使   施行   施工   被动
1. 学生不应该( )地接受老师的指导和监督,而是要积极思考,主动学习。
2. 建筑工人正在加紧( ),争取在冬天到来之前建好那条公路。
3. 老师和警察都在思考,是什么( )这个孩子成了杀人犯呢?
4. 很久以前就有人提出应该在两座岛之间建一座大桥,现在这个( )终于变成了现实。
5. 这个法案只是( ),在实践过程中还会做相应的调整。
6. 我们到了这个城市后去看看他,( )他不在,我们就继续去下一个城市旅行。
7. 汽车在高速路上飞速( )。
8. 这个剧本的( )已经出来了,剩下的事情只是动笔写出来的问题了。
9. 有几个志愿者( )要求去农村学校工作。
10. 世界上很多国家都( )八小时工作制。

练习五.写出下列词语的同义词
1. 幽默( )   2. 良心( )
3. 雄伟( )   4. 更换( )
5. 假使( )

练习六.写出下列词语的反义词
1. 主动( )   2. 促进( )
3. 壮大( )   4. 勇敢( )
5. 忽视( )

 **答案**

练习一.
1.chóng 2.yù 3.cì 4.jí 5.xióng
练习二.
1. 判 2. 叛 3. 使 4. 驶 5. 状
练习三.
1. 死亡 2. 牺牲 3. 抚育 4. 抚养 5. 擅长
6. 善于 7. 部署 8. 布置 9. 更改 10. 更换
练习四.
1. 被动 2. 施工 3. 促使 4. 构想 5. 试行
6. 假使 7. 行驶 8. 构思 9. 主动 10. 施行
练习五.
1. 风趣 2. 良知 3. 宏伟 4. 更新 5. 倘若
练习六.
1. 被动 2. 妨碍 3. 削弱 4. 怯懦 5. 重视

9月 第 4 周的学习内容

星期一 (Monday)

gàobié
告别 ⓔ 辞别 cíbié （乙）动

bid farewell to; say good-bye to

常用搭配

挥手告别 give sb a farewell wave
告别宴会 farewell banquet

用法示例

她发表了热情的告别演说。
She gave a passionate farewell speech.
我们向他们告别后就离开了。
Bidding them adieu, we departed.
我们在机场互相告别了。
We said good-bye to each other at the airport.

línjū
邻居 ⓔ 街坊 jiēfang （乙）名

neighbor

常用搭配

他们是邻居。They are neighbors.
隔壁的邻居 a next-door neighbor

用法示例

她委托邻居照顾她的孩子。
She entrusted her child to the care of a neighbor.
我从邻居那里借了割草机。
I borrowed a mower from my neighbor.
那是邻居家的猫。
That is the cat of a neighbor.

hūnyīn
婚姻 （乙）名

marriage

常用搭配

美满的婚姻 a happy marriage
婚姻指导 marital guidance
婚姻介绍所 marriage bureau

用法示例

他的婚姻生活很幸福。
His marriage is full of happiness.
父亲决不会同意我们的婚姻。
My father will never give his consent to our marriage.

duìfāng
对方 （乙）名

① counterpart ② opposite side

常用搭配

对方的利益 interests of the opposite side
嘲笑对方 laugh at the opposite side

用法示例

他们站在那里，互相怒视着对方。
They stood there, glaring at each other.
面对我们摆出来的证据，对方只得做出让步。
After being confronted with our evidence, the other side had to back down.
我想知道对方的想法。
I want to know the opinions of the opposite side.

kāimù
开幕 （丙）动

open (a conference)

常用搭配

开幕式 opening ceremony
开幕辞 opening address

用法示例

奥运会的开幕式非常壮观。
The opening ceremony of the Olympic Games was very grand.
交易会将于 5 月 19 日开幕。
The fair is to open on May the 19th.
大会于今天上午开幕了。
The conference inauguration was this morning.

bìmù
闭幕 ⓔ 落幕 luòmù （丙）动

① close (æconference) ② the curtain falls

常用搭配

胜利闭幕 successfully bring down the curtain
闭幕式 closing ceremony

用法示例

闭幕式将在明天举行。
The closing ceremony is going to be held tomorrow.
会议定于 5 月 30 日闭幕。
The conference is scheduled to close on May the 30th.

gébì
隔壁 （乙）名

next door

常用搭配

住在隔壁 live next door
隔壁的房间 the room next door

【用法示例】

他是我的邻居,就住在我家隔壁。

He is my neighbor, he only lives next door.

我们计划买下隔壁的房子。

We plan to buy the house next to ours.

我们在上海时李先生就住在我家隔壁。

Mr. Li lived next door to us when we were in Shanghai.

dī

滴 （乙）动／量

① to drip ② drop

【常用搭配】

几滴水 a few drops of water

两滴眼泪 two drops of tears

一滴牛奶 a drop of milk

【用法示例】

水笼头正在滴水。

Water is dripping from that faucet.

雨水从树上滴落下来。

The rain was dripping from the trees.

几滴雨水落在了屋顶上。

A few drops of rain landed on the roof.

血从伤口一滴一滴地流出来。

Blood trickled from the wound.

duìmén

对门 （丙）名

the building or room opposite

【常用搭配】

住在对门 live in the opposite house

【用法示例】

他住在我家对门。

He lives the house that is opposite to mine.

住在我对门的人是一名警察。

The man who lives in the room opposite to mine is a policeman.

bìsè

闭塞 （丁）形／动

① unenlightened; out of the way ② block

【常用搭配】

消息闭塞 ill-informed

【用法示例】

我很不喜欢住在闭塞的乡村。

I hate being shut away in the country.

他思想闭塞僵化。

He has a closed mind.

以前这一带交通闭塞。

In the past this district was very hard to reach.

kāItuò

开拓 （丁）动

kāichuàng

◎ 开创

open up

【常用搭配】

开拓新的市场 open up new markets

开拓精神 pioneering spirit

开拓型人才 talent of the pioneering type

【用法示例】

他的小说开拓了想象力的新天地。

His stories opened up new worlds of imagination.

为了帮助他们开拓亚洲市场,你有什么具体计划?

Do you have any particular plan to help them open up the Asian market?

línguó

邻国 （丁）名

neighboring country

【用法示例】

这个国家同意为了各自的安全而与邻国结盟。

The country agreed to unite with the neighboring country for their mutual safety.

我们必须促进与邻国的贸易。

We must promote trade with our neighboring countries.

俄罗斯和蒙古国是邻国。

Russia and Mongolia are neighboring countries.

 词义辨析

邻居、隔壁、对门

三个词都是名词,都表示位置相近的地方。"邻居"指在附近或同一街区,也指生活在附近的人或家庭,强调人与人之间的关系,"邻居"可以有很多。"隔壁"和"对门"强调地点和地点之间的关系,"隔壁"指在旁边,隔着一堵墙或屏障,"隔壁"只能有一个或两个,"对门"指在对面,门对着门,隔着一条过道或街道,严格地讲,"对门"只能有一个。例如:①他是我的邻居。②他住在我隔壁的房间。③我们商店和马路对面的银行是对门。

The three words are nouns, mean "places located near one another". 邻居 indicates "near or in a same block" and "people or family who live nearby". It stresses the relation ship between people, and that there may be a lot of 邻居; While 隔壁 and 对门 stress the relationship between places, 隔壁 indicates "next door", "be separated only by a wall or a screen", and there may be one or two 隔壁; while 对门 indicates "the opposite, door to door, be separated by corridor or a street", literally there is just one 对门. For example: ① He is my neighbor. ② He lives in the room next to mine. ③ Our shop is opposite a bank on the other side of the road.

 **练习**

练习一、根据拼音写汉字，根据汉字写拼音
（　）mù lín（　）（　）tuò（　）bì（　）yīn
闭（　）　（　）居　开（　）　隔（　）　婚（　）

练习二、搭配连线
(1) 闭塞的　　　　　A. 房间
(2) 隔壁的　　　　　B. 利益
(3) 美满的　　　　　C. 邻国
(4) 对方的　　　　　D. 乡村
(5) 友好的　　　　　E. 婚姻

练习三、从今天学习的生词中选择合适的词填空
1. 汽车展览会明天上午在国际展览中心 _____，届时可以看到最新型的跑车。
2. 山本要回国了，昨天我们全班一起吃饭 _____。
3. 我弟弟就住在 _____，如果我有事找他，我就敲一敲墙，他听到了就会过来。
4. 小城市的信息相对 _____，但自从有了网络，天下大事都能随时掌握了。
5. 近年来，我国跟 _____ 发展边境贸易，当地人们的生活水平有了显著提高。
6. 这种产品刚刚进入亚洲市场，还有很大的 _____ 空间。
7. 全国人民代表大会刚刚 _____，参加会议的代表也陆续回到了自己的工作岗位上。
8. 我们是 _____，小时候常常在一起玩。
9. 在谈判的时候，我们要坚持自己的立场，也要研究 _____ 的意图。
10. 每天一开门我就能看见 _____ 门上贴的大大的双"喜"字。

答案

练习一：
略

练习二：
(1) D　　(2) A　　(3) E　　(4) B　　(5) C

练习三：
1. 开幕　2. 告别　3. 隔壁　4. 闭塞　5. 邻国
6. 开拓　7. 闭幕　8. 邻居　9. 对方　10. 对门

 星期二

bìyè 毕业　（乙）动
graduate
常用搭配
毕业典礼 graduation ceremony
大学毕业生 a graduate from college
用法示例
他 1989 年毕业于牛津大学。
He graduated from Oxford in 1989.
他已经大学毕业十年了。
He has been graduated from college for ten years now.
他将要在七月份毕业。
He will graduate from the school in July.

rèxīn 热心　（乙）形
zealous; warmhearted; enthusiastic
常用搭配
热心人 a warmhearted man
热心观众 a zealous audience
对……热心 be enthusiastic about sth
用法示例
他热心地帮助他人。
He is enthusiastic about helping others.
这位老工程师对工作总是很热心。
The old engineer is always enthusiastic about work.
他是一位热心的退休工人。
He is a warmhearted retired worker.

lǐngxiù 领袖　（乙）名
leader
常用搭配
伟大的领袖 great leader
党的领袖 leader of a party
用法示例
领袖的逝世对党是巨大的损失。
The death of its leader was a body-blow to the party.
人民想让他当领袖。
The people want him as their leader.
该国需要一个能使全国团结起来的领袖。
The country needs a leader who will unite the nation.

zhuàngkuàng 状况　圆 qíngxíng 情形　（乙）名
condition; state

常用搭配

经济状况 economic conditions

天气状况 weather conditions

财务状况 financial situation

用法示例

他的健康状况令人十分满意。

The condition of his health is fairly satisfactory.

他正在看一篇关于道路状况的报告。

He is reading a report on the state of the roads.

毕竟 *bìjìng* （丙）副

after all

常用搭配

个人的力量毕竟是有限的。

After all, individual strength is limited.

用法示例

不要责备他,他毕竟是个新手。

Don't blame it on him, after all he is a new comer.

你应该对他宽容些,毕竟他还是个孩子。

You should be charitable to him; he is a child after all.

你应该原谅他的健忘,毕竟他已经七十多岁了。

You should forgive him for his forgetfulness; after all, he is over seventy.

潮湿 *cháoshī* 反干燥 *gànzào* （丙）形

moist; damp

常用搭配

潮湿的空气 humid air   潮湿的衣服 damp clothes

用法示例

这里太潮湿了。

There is a lot of dampness here.

气候潮湿时,面包容易发霉。

Bread tends to go mouldy in humid weather.

这座旧房子很潮湿。

The old house is very damp.

腐败 *fǔbài* 反廉洁 *liánjié* （丁）形

corrupt

常用搭配

腐败的官员 a corrupt official

腐败的政府 a corrupt government

用法示例

这是一场反腐败的运动。

It's a crusade against corruption.

他说前政府已经腐败透顶。

He said that the previous government had been riddled with corruption.

腐败妨碍社会的发展。

Corruption stands in the way of the society's development.

腐化 *fǔhuà* 同堕落 *duòluò* （丁）形

corrupt; depraved

常用搭配

生活腐化 lead a dissolute life

腐化堕落 become corrupt and degenerate

用法示例

他浑身散发着腐化堕落的气味。

He has an air of corruption about him.

这座城市充斥着腐化现象。

The city was riddled with corruption.

丸 *wán* （丙）量／名

① measure word for pills ② pellet

常用搭配

一丸药 a pill   肉丸 meatball

用法示例

睡觉前,他吃了两丸药。

He took two pills before going to bed.

一个瓶子里有六丸药。

There are six pills per bottle.

热潮 *rècháo* （丁）名

upsurge

常用搭配

生产热潮 a vigorus fervor of production

掀起群众性体育运动的热潮

start a vigorous mass campaign for sports

用法示例

圣诞争购热潮前,超市的货架堆满了商品。

The shelves in the supermarket are full of items before the Christmas rush.

三月,华南正处在春耕的热潮中。

In March, spring farming is in full swing in Southern China.

潮流 *cháoliú* （丁）名

tide; trend

常用搭配

流行音乐的潮流 the trends of pop music

历史的潮流 the tide of history

用法示例

报纸影响思想潮流。

Newspapers influence the tide of thought.

青少年经常反潮流而动。

Teenagers often go against the tide.

趋势 *qūshì* （丁）名

trend; tendency

常用搭配

现代生活的趋势 the trend of modern living

舆论的趋势 the tide of public opinion

用法示例

物价仍有上涨趋势。
Prices are still on the upward trend.
新法律有限制新闻自由的趋势。
Recent laws have tended to restrict the freedom of the press.

 词义辨析

腐败、腐化

"腐败"和"腐化"都是形容词,都有思想行为堕落的意思,有时可以互换使用。"腐败"往往用于制度、机构、官员等,也可以表示物体腐烂。"腐化"往往用于个人行为或现象,也可以用作动词,可以带宾语,表示"使……堕落","腐败"没有这样的用法。例如:①腐败的官员将很快受到惩罚。②年轻的时候,他过着腐化的生活。③他们想通过行贿来腐化领导。

Both 腐败 and 腐化 are adjectives, meaning "to be corrupt", sometimes they are interchangable. 腐败 is usually applied to systems, institutions, and officials, and it also means "something is rotten"; while 腐化 is usually applied to somebody or some phenomena, and is also a verb which can be followed by objects, indicating "to make somebody corrupt". 腐败 can not be used like this. For example: ① The corrupt officials will be punished soon. ② He lead a dissolute life when he was young. ③ They wanted to corrupt the leader through bribery.

 练习

练习一、根据拼音写汉字,根据汉字写拼音

cháo ( ) ( )xiù fǔ ( ) qū ( ) ( )kuàng
( )湿 领( ) ( )败 ( )势 状( )

练习二、搭配连线

(1) 腐败的   A. 趋势
(2) 发展的   B. 领袖
(3) 潮湿的   C. 邻居
(4) 伟大的   D. 空气
(5) 热心的   E. 政府

练习三、从今天学习的生词中选择合适的词填空

1. 奥运会后掀起了一股体育锻炼的_____。
2. 我的家乡是沿海城市,那里的冬季寒冷而_____。
3. 这个政府官员被抓后,发现了大量生活_____堕落的证据。
4. 大学改革和发展的_____是让更多的人有接受高等教育的机会。
5. 谁也无法阻挡中国改革发展的历史_____。
6. 我刚参加工作时,单位的同事都很_____地给我介绍对象。
7. 她大学一_____就在这里教书,现在已经是校长了。
8. 政府因_____而受到民众指责。
9. 工作时一定要有团队意识,个人的力量_____有限。
10. 近几年他父亲的健康_____急剧下降。

答案

练习一:
略
练习二:
(1) E   (2)A   (3)D   (4)B   (5)C
练习三:
1. 热潮   2. 潮湿   3. 腐化   4. 趋势   5. 潮流
6. 热心   7. 毕业   8. 腐败   9. 毕竟   10. 状况

星期三

bǎozhèng
保证 （乙）动/名
① to ensure ② guarantee

常用搭配
我向你保证。I assure you.

用法示例
我可以向你保证这消息是可靠的。
I can assure you of the reliability of the news.
我们保证把工作做好。
We guarantee that the work shall be done in the right way.
预防措施保证了他们的安全。
Precautions ensured their safety.

àihù
爱护 （乙）动
cherish; take good care of

常用搭配
爱护工具 care for tools
爱护眼睛 take good care of the eyes

用法示例
这些小动物需要爱护。
These little animals need care and protection.
我们应该爱护古代建筑，不能破坏它们。
We should take good care of ancient buildings rather than damage them.

shàngjí
上级 反 下级 **xiàjí** （乙）名
higher authorities; superiors

常用搭配
上级官员 a superior officer
上级法院 a higher court
对上级负责 be responsible to a higher authority

用法示例
他总是听从于上级的指示。
He always does what his superiors tell him.
她没有请示上级就做了这个重要决定。
She made the important decision without any reference to her superiors.

línghuó
灵活 反 僵硬 **jiāngyìng** （乙）形
nimble; flexible

常用搭配
头脑灵活 an agile mind
灵活的政策 a flexible policy
灵活的动作 nimble action

用法示例
我们的计划十分灵活，因为我们有足够的时间。
Our plans are quite flexible, because we have enough time.
我们需要更加灵活的外交政策。
We need a foreign policy that is more flexible.
这名运动员像鹿一样灵活。
This athlete is as nimble as a deer.

júbù
局部 反 整体 **zhěngtǐ** （丙）名
part

常用搭配
局部战争 local war
局部麻醉 local anesthesia
局部感染 local infection

用法示例
明天北京局部地区将下雪。
It will snow in parts of Beijing tomorrow.
局部服从整体。
The part must be subject to the whole.

júmiàn
局面 （丙）名
situation

常用搭配
当前的局面 present situation
处于尴尬的局面 be in an embarrassing situation

用法示例
这样的局面对我们不利。
This situation is unfavorable for us.
必须采取措施以应付这种局面。
Measures must be taken to address the situation.
我很钦佩你如此巧妙地处理了这种局面。
I admired your delicate handling of the situation.

bǎozhàng
保障 （丙）动/名
① ensure; safeguard ② assurance

常用搭配
保障供给 ensure supplies
保障人民言论自由
guarantee freedom of speech for the people

用法示例
法律保障公民的合法权益。
The law can protect the rights and interests of citizens.
我觉得自己的生活缺乏保障。
I think my life is lacking in security.
请您放心，还款是有保障的。
Please rest assured that repayment is guaranteed.

sōu
艘 （丙）量
measure word for ships

常用搭配

一艘轮船 a ship

两艘军舰 two warships

用法示例

一周后,他们发现了那艘失事的轮船。

One week later, they found the wrecked ship.

海上有一艘巨型油轮。

There is a large oil tanker on the sea.

泰坦尼克号是一艘豪华游轮。

The Titanic was a luxury passenger liner.

lěngquè

冷却　　　　🈲加热　　　（丙）动

jiārè

be cool; to cool off

常用搭配

冷却系统 a cooling system

用法示例

蒸汽冷却时凝结成水。

Steam condenses into water when it cools down.

把它泡在水中冷却一下。

Put it in water to cool it down.

把啤酒放进冰箱里冷却一下,味道会更好。

Put the beer in the refrigerator to chill, and it will be more delicious.

àidài

爱戴　　　　　　　　　　（丁）动

love and esteem

常用搭配

深受爱戴 be very much admired

赢得……的爱戴 gain the love and esteem of…

用法示例

林肯是美国人民爱戴的总统。

Abraham Lincoln was a president loved by the American people.

校长的仁慈和耐心使他受到了所有学生的爱戴。

The headmaster's kindness and patience endeared him to all students.

总理赢得了人民的爱戴。

The Premier gained the love and esteem of the people.

àixī

爱惜　　　　　　　　　　（丁）动

treasure; cherish

常用搭配

爱惜粮食 cherish food

爱惜时间 treasure time

用法示例

她很爱惜她的新车。

She cherishes her new car very much.

年轻人往往不懂得爱惜身体的重要性。

Young men usually don't understand the importance of cherishing their health.

àishì

碍事　　　　　　　　（丁）形/动

① hindrance ② be in the way

常用搭配

我在这儿碍事吗？ Am I in your way here?

用法示例

有些小炊具非但没用反而碍事。

Some kitchen gadgets are more of a hindrance than a help.

把这些书堆起来,它们太碍事。

Put these books in a pile please. They are in the way.

 **词义辨析**

保障、保证

　　"保障"和"保证"都可以表示确保。"保障"强调维护,使不受侵害或损害,它的对象一般是已经存在的事物,如:安全、财产、权力、利益等抽象的事物;"保证"强调一定做到,确保完成,它的对象经常是没有做或没有完成的事,如:工作、计划、行动等具体的事情或活动。

　　Both 保障 and 保证 mean "to ensure". 保障 stresses to keep things from being violated or damaged, and its objects are usually something abstract, such as "安全" (security), "财产" (property), "权力" (right), "利益" (interests). 保证 stresses to certify that one can provide a guarantee, and the objects of it are usually concrete activities, such as "工作" (work), "任务" (task), "计划" (plan), "行动" (action).

 **练习**

练习一、根据拼音写汉字，根据汉字写拼音

ài（ ） （ ）dài （ ）zhàng （ ）bù líng （ ）

（ ）事 爱（ ） 保（ ） 局（ ）（ ）活

练习二、搭配连线

(1) 上级   A. 感染

(2) 头脑   B. 官员

(3) 局部   C. 供给

(4) 保障   D. 粮食

(5) 爱惜   E. 灵活

练习三、从今天学习的生词中选择合适的词填空

1. 很多中国人重视儿子是因为他们担心老了以后生活没有_____。

2. 体操运动员的身体非常柔软、_____。

3. 你借给我的钱我_____在一个星期之内还给你。

4. 这篇文章整体来说不错，_____地方再好好修改一下。

5. 他很_____这双运动鞋，因为这是他攒了三个月的零花钱才买到的。

6. 桌子放在门口太_____，把它搬走吧。

7. 会上大家都不发言，_____有点尴尬。

8. 这位总统享有很高的威望，尤其受到年轻人和平民的_____。

9. 面条煮好以后先在凉水里_____一下，我喜欢吃凉面条。

10. _____领导要到我们这里视察工作。

答案

练习一：

略

练习二：

(1) B   (2)E   (3)A   (4)C   (5)D

练习三：

1. 保障   2. 灵活   3. 保证   4. 局部   5. 爱惜

6. 碍事   7. 局面   8. 爱戴   9. 冷却   10. 上级

星期四 Thursday

suǒ
所 （乙）名／量

① place ② classifier for houses or school, etc.

常用搭配

派出所 police station   诊所 clinic

一所老房子 an old house

用法示例

他通过职业介绍所找到了工作。

He found a job through an employment agency.

牛津大学是一所综合大学。

Oxford University is a comprehensive university.

我家附近有一所新的幼儿园。

There is a new kindergarten near my home.

línjìn
临近 （丁）动

be close to; approach

常用搭配

新年临近了。New year is approaching.

临近黎明 close on daybreak

用法示例

考试临近了，学生们都在努力学习。

The exam is approaching, so the students are hard their studies.

冬天临近了，天气要冷了。

The approach of winter brings colder weather.

圣诞节临近了。

Christmas is drawing near.

dàdǎn
大胆 （乙）形

bold; daring

常用搭配

大胆的行动 a bold action

大胆的假设 a daring assumption

用法示例

有一次他大胆提出了自己的看法。

Once he made bold, and spoke out about his views.

在学习汉语时，应当大胆地用汉语和朋友交谈。

When learning Chinese, one should be bold, and talk in the language with one's friends.

línshí
临时   同 **zànshí** 暂时   （乙）形

temporary; interim

常用搭配

临时主席 a temporary chairperson

临时政府 an interim government

【用法示例】

老板雇佣了一些临时工。

The boss hired some temporary workers.

他做临时工作已一年了,想找个固定的工作。

He's been temping for a year now and wants a permanent job.

双方签订了一项临时协议。

Both sides signed an interim agreement.

qǔxiāo

取消 　　　　　　　　　　　　（乙）动

cancel

【常用搭配】

取消计划 cancel a plan　　取消考试 cancel the exam

【用法示例】

由于下雨,取消了比赛。

Owing to the rain, the match was cancelled.

因为天气不好,他们的旅行计划被取消了。

Their travel plan was cancelled because of the bad weather.

委员会决定取消对那个项目的资助。

The committee decided to withdraw financial support for the scheme.

qūzhé

曲折 　　　　　　　　　　　　（丙）形

winding; complicated

【常用搭配】

曲折的小路 a zigzag path

曲折的情节 complicated plot

【用法示例】

在前进的道路上,我们必定会遇到曲折。

As we move forward we a bound to run into complications.

小说的情节曲折而引人入胜。

The plot of the novel is very complicated and absorbing.

成功的道路是曲折的。

The road to success is winding.

cí'ài

慈爱 　　　　　　　　　　　　（丁）形

kindly (particularly show by elders to children)

【常用搭配】

对……慈爱 to have charity for

慈爱的父母 loving parents

【用法示例】

她慈爱地望着她的孩子。

She looked at her child kindly.

我永远也忘不了爷爷那慈爱的目光。

I will never forget the loving expression in my grandpa's eyes.

cíxiáng

慈祥　　　　xiōng'è　反 凶 恶　　　　（丁）形

kindly (person)

【常用搭配】

慈祥的老人 a kind old man

慈祥的面孔 a kindly face

【用法示例】

他母亲十分慈祥。

His mother is very kind.

那位慈祥的老人给了他一些钱。

That kind old man offered him some money.

lěngjìng

冷静　　　chénzhuó　同 沉着　　　　（丙）形

calm; composed

【常用搭配】

头脑冷静 a cool head

保持冷静 keep calm

遇事冷静 Keep calm when problems crop up

【用法示例】

即使在争辩时,你也要尽力保持冷静。

Even whilst arguing, you should try to keep your cool.

我告诫自己要冷静下来。

I told myself to calm down.

她冷静地回答他们的问题。

She answered their questions calmly.

qǔdài

取代 　　　　　　　　　　　　（丁）动

replace; take the place of

【常用搭配】

取代某人 take the place of sb

【用法示例】

没有什么东西能取代母爱。

Nothing can replace a mother's love.

汽车已经取代了自行车,成为了最重要的交通工具。

The bikes were superseded by cars as the most important mode of transport.

帆船已被汽船所取代。

Sailing ships were superseded by steamships.

qūfú

屈服 　　　　　　　　　　　　（丁）动

yield to; give in

【常用搭配】

向敌人屈服 yield to enemies

从不屈服 never give in

屈服于外界的压力

yield to outside pressure

【用法示例】

我们绝不会向侵略者屈服。

We will never yield to invaders.

在足够的证据面前,这个罪犯屈服了。

In the face of so many witnesses, the criminal gave in.

他宁死也不屈服。

He would rather die than yield.

chèxiāo
撤销 ⓘ 保留 （丁）动

băoliú

discharge; revoke

【常用搭配】

撤销指控 withdraw an accusation

撤销命令 recall an order

撤销合同 cancellation of a contract

【用法示例】

她的执照被撤销了。

Her license was revoked.

董事会撤销了他总经理的职务。

The board of directors dismissed him from his post of general manager.

 词义辨析

慈爱、慈祥

"慈爱"和"慈祥"都是形容词,都有温柔和善的意思。"慈爱"强调年长者对年幼者的内在情感,可以用于年老的长辈、领导等对年轻人的关爱,可以用作状语。"慈祥"强调老人外在的神色、面容和态度,不能用作状语。如:①她慈爱地看着她的孩子。②她奶奶看上去十分慈祥。

Both 慈爱 and 慈祥 are adjectives, meaning "kindly and amiable". 慈爱 stresses the inner affection shown by elders toward children, is applied to describing the tender feelings of seniors to juniors, and can function as an adverbial; while 慈祥 stresses the looks, manners, or attitudes of old men, and it can not function as an adverbial. For example: ① She looked at her child kindly. ② Her grandma looks very kindly.

 练习

练习一、根据拼音写汉字,根据汉字写拼音

( )xiāo　　qū( )　cí( )( )zhé　( )xiāo

撤( )　( )服　( )详　曲( )　　取( )

练习二、搭配连线

(1) 临时　　　　　　A. 屈服

(2) 取消　　　　　　B. 政府

(3) 保持　　　　　　C. 曲折

(4) 情节　　　　　　D. 冷静

(5) 绝不　　　　　　E. 计划

练习三、从今天学习的生词中选择合适的词填空

1. 贪污事件被揭发后,他的局长职务被 _____ 了。

2. 当你遇到麻烦时,一定要 _____,千万不能太激动。

3. 原定在今天下午召开的会议因紧急情况 _____。

4. 这个老太太非常 _____,她让我想起了我去世的奶奶。

5. 出名前,这个模特的经历非常 _____。

6. 他提出的设想非常 _____,我保证很多人连想都不敢想。

7. 在 _____ 考试的那两个星期,同学们都在紧张地复习。

8. 人们把受伤的人送进了最近的一 _____ 医院。

9. 出国期间,他的位置被别人 _____ 了。

10. 奶奶 _____ 地看着我,嘱咐我一个人出门在外要多加小心。

答案

练习一:

略

练习二:

(1) B　　　(2) E　　　(3) D　　　(4) C　　　(5) A

练习三:

1. 撤销　　2. 冷静　　3. 取消　　4. 慈祥　　5. 曲折

6. 大胆　　7. 临近　　8. 所　　　9. 取代　　10. 慈爱

dài
袋 （乙）名／量
① sack; bag ② measure word for bagged things

常用搭配
睡袋 sleeping bag
垃圾袋 garbage bag
两袋大米 two sacks of rice
一袋玩具 a sack of toys

用法示例
别把购物袋扔了，还可以再用。
Do not throw away your shopping bag, it can be reused.
给我一袋土豆。
Give me a sack of potatoes.
他买了两袋水泥。
He bought two bags of cement.

ānxīn
安心 （乙）动
feel at ease; keep one's mind on something

常用搭配
安心学习 keep one's mind on studying

用法示例
别着急，安心养病。
Just take care of yourself and don't worry about other things.
听说孩子们都很安全，她才安心。
Her mind was at ease knowing that the children were safe.
安心工作，别为我担心。
Keep your mind on work. Don't worry about me.

xuèyè
血液 （乙）名
blood

常用搭配
血液循环 the circulation of blood

用法示例
血液在体内循环。
Blood circulates through the body.
心脏把血液送至血管。
The heart pumps blood into the veins.

zhōngyú
终于 （乙）副
at last; finally

常用搭配
他们终于做完了。Finally, they finished it.
终于找到了。Found it at last.

用法示例
拖了那么久，他终于完成了论文。
He finished his paper at last after much delay.
他终于成功地解决了这个问题。
At last he successfully solved the problem.
推迟了三次之后，我们终于去希腊度假了。
After putting it off three times, we finally spent a holiday in Greece.

zìsī
自私 反 无私 **wúsī** （丙）形
selfish

常用搭配
自私的行为 selfish behavior
自私的人 selfish person

用法示例
自私的人总是想着自己。
A selfish person always thinks about himself.
这种行为说明他很自私。
This behavior illustrates his selfishness.
这两兄弟经常吵架；一个很固执，另一个很自私。
The two brothers often quarrel with each other; one is stubborn, and the other is selfish.

sīyǒu
私有 反 公有 **gōngyǒu** （丙）形
① private ② privately owned

常用搭配
私有财产 private property
私有制 private ownership

用法示例
他把妻子当成自己的私有财产。
He considers his wife to be his private property.
近年来私有企业发展得很快。
The privately owned enterprises have developed quickly in recent years.

cuīhuǐ
摧毁 同 捣毁 **dǎohuǐ** （丙）动
destroy; demolish

常用搭配
被彻底摧毁 be destroyed completely
摧毁敌人的防线 smash the enemy's defense

用法示例
炸弹摧毁了许多工厂。
The bombs demolished the factories.
机场被敌人彻底摧毁了。
The airport was totally demolished by the enemy.
突击队员在敌后来了一个突然袭击，摧毁了雷达站。
The commandos made a lightning fast attack behind enemy lines and destroyed the radar station.

cuīcán
摧残 [（]迫害 pòhài （丁）动
① ravage ② ruin

常用搭配
受到摧残 be ravaged
摧残人性 destroy humanity

用法示例
十年来,这个国家饱受战争的摧残。
The country has suffered from the ravages of war for ten years.
他的身体正遭受毒品的摧残。
His health is being destroyed by drugs.
寒风摧残了初绽的花朵。
The icy breeze nipped at the young blooms.

zhōngyú
忠于 （丁）动
be loyal to

常用搭配
忠于祖国 be loyal to one's country
忠于事业 be loyal to a cause

用法示例
士兵们忠于他们的国家。
The soldiers are loyal to their country.
他们宣誓忠于女王陛下。
They swore allegiance to the Queen.
这条狗忠于它的主人。
The dog remained faithful to his master.

ānwěn
安稳 （丁）形
smooth and steady; safe and secure

常用搭配
睡得安稳 sleep peacefully

用法示例
船航行得很安稳。
The boat sailed smoothly.
她放弃了安稳的工作,办起了自己的公司。
She gave up her stable job and set up her own company.

sīzì
私自 （丁）副
① privately ② without permission

常用搭配
私自离开 leave without permission
私自改变计划 change the plan privately
私自出售公物 sell public property without authorization

用法示例
不能私自把参考书带出阅览室。
No reference books are to be taken out of the reading room without permission.
其他同学在上课的时候,他们俩私自出去玩儿了。
When other students were having class, those two went

out to play without permission.
晚上十点以后,谁也不能私自离开宿舍。
After 10:00 pm no one is allowed to leave the dorm without permission.

zhōngzhǐ
终止 （丁）动
① stop ② come to a close

常用搭配
终止合同 terminate a contract
终止交易 close a deal
终止外交关系 suspend diplomatic relations

用法示例
这个项目已经终止了。
This project has been shut down.
我们得想个办法终止他们的活动。
We ought to find a way to put a stop to their activities.
他们要求终止一切不平等条约。
They demanded an end to all unequal treaties.

 词义辨析

摧毁、摧残

"摧毁"和"摧残"都是动词,都有用强大的力量迫害的意思。"摧毁"是中性词,指进行彻底地破坏,它的对象一般不是人,而是建筑物、国家政权、集团势力等,否定形式可以用作"摧不毁";"摧残"是贬义词,指恶的力量对有生命、有价值的人或物的故意迫害、伤害和折磨,它的对象一般是人的身体和精神、文化、艺术等,否定形式不可以用作"摧不残"。例如:①我们成功地摧毁了敌人的仓库。②女孩在狱中受到了精神和肉体的摧残。

Both 摧毁 and 摧残 are verbs, meaning "to destroy with great force". 摧毁 has a neutral sense, and indicates to ruin completely. Its objects are not people but buildings, state political power, force of an organization, etc.; its negative form can be used as "摧不毁". 摧残 has a derogatory sense, and indicates the evil force that damages, hurts or ravages something which is living or valuable, so its objects are the bodies or minds of people, culture, art, etc. its negative form can not be used as "摧不残". For example: ① We demolished the enemy's storehouse successfully. ② The young girl was physically devastated and mentally in prison.

 **练习**

练习一、根据拼音写汉字，根据汉字写拼音

( )cán ( )wěn zhōng ( )sī ( ) ( )yè

摧( ) 安( ) ( )止 ( )有 血( )

练习二、搭配连线

(1) 终止   A. 祖国

(2) 私有   B. 合作

(3) 受到   C. 防线

(4) 忠于   D. 财产

(5) 摧毁   E. 摧残

练习三、从今天学习的生词中选择合适的词填空

1. 图书馆的书籍不能 _____ 带出,要到图书管理员那里登记。

2. 他们夫妻俩虽然收入不高,但生活过得很 _____。

3. 由于对方国内发生了战争,我们与他们的合作被迫 _____ 了。

4. 她在狱中受到敌人的百般 _____,但她始终没有屈服。

5. 文艺作品要 _____ 现实,反映现实。

6. 警方 _____ 了一个贩卖毒品的犯罪团伙。

7. 他在超市买了一 _____ 大米,一些水果和蔬菜。

8. _____ 考完试了,现在可以好好放松放松了。

9. 在一些国家,土地是 _____ 财产,在中国,土地属于国家资源。

10. 他太 _____ 了,只想着自己的利益,完全不考虑别人的感受。

答案

练习一:
略

练习二:

(1) B   (2)D   (3)E   (4)A   (5)C

练习三:

1. 私自   2. 安稳   3. 终止   4. 摧残   5. 忠于

6. 摧毁   7. 袋   8. 终于   9. 私有   10. 自私

第9月,第4周的练习

练习一．根据词语给加点的字注音
1.( ) 2.( )   3.( )   4.( )   5.( )
闭塞   开幕   领袖   碍事   终止

练习二．根据拼音填写词语
  lín   lín   qū   qū   qū
1.( )国 2.( )时 3.( )势 4.( )服 5.( )折

练习三．辨析并选择合适的词填空
1. 他是我的( ),就住在我家前面的那座楼里。（邻居、隔壁）
2. 我家( )新搬进来了一户人家。（邻居、隔壁）
3. 大家强烈谴责当前的( )现象。（腐化、腐败）
4. 这个官员因为生活( )堕落而被调查。（腐化、腐败）
5. 政府每个月给失业人员发最低生活( )金。（保障、保证）
6. 他向老师( )以后再也不迟到了。（保障、保证）
7. 母亲打量着多年未见的儿子,眼里充满了( )。（慈爱、慈祥）
8. 我的姥姥生前总是对人笑嘻嘻的,很( )。（慈爱、慈祥）
9. 占领军对俘虏进行了各种可怕的( )。（摧毁、摧残）
10. 这里曾经确实有一座寺庙,不过,在战争期间被敌人( )了。（摧毁、摧残）

练习四．选词填空
热心   潮湿   爱护   爱戴   撤销
热潮   潮流   爱惜   取消   取代
1. 刚刚得知星期六还要加班,我们的约会只好( )了。
2. 和平与发展是当今世界的( ),谁也无法阻挡。
3. 他是位德高望重的学者,受到很多人( )。
4. 昨晚下了一场雨,今天空气很( )。
5. 如果他业绩不好,那么三年以后他的副经理的位置将被别人( )。
6. 父母从小教育孩子要( )粮食,因为这是农民辛勤劳动的成果。
7. 他的英语学习方法非常实用,中小学都采用了这种方法,并在全国掀起了一股学习英语的( )。
8. 校园意外事件发生后,校长的职务被( )了。
9. 大家要有( )公共财产的意识,不要在课桌上、教室的墙上乱写乱画。
10. 她总是很( )地帮助别人,因此她有很多朋友。

练习五．量词填空
滴   丸   艘   所   袋
1. 她想教留学生们做饺子,于是去超市买了一小( )面粉。

2. 这( )小学是全市的重点小学,升学率很高。
3. 探险家们在沙漠里行走,一( )水都没有了,他们希望能尽快找到水源。
4. 医生告诉她,这种中成药每次服一( ),一天两次。
5. 那( )轮船渐渐靠近了港口。

练习六．写出下列词语的同义词
1. 冷静( )   2. 摧残(   )
3. 开拓( )   4. 告别(   )
5. 腐化( )

练习七．写出下列词语的反义词
1. 冷却( )   2. 腐败(   )
3. 潮湿( )   4. 灵活(   )
5. 慈祥( )

 **答案**

练习一．
1.sè   2.mù   3.xiù   4.ài   5.zhōng
练习二．
1. 邻   2. 临   3. 趋   4. 屈   5. 曲
练习三．
1. 邻居   2. 隔壁   3. 腐败   4. 腐化   5. 保障
6. 保证   7. 慈爱   8. 慈祥   9. 摧残   10. 摧毁
练习四．
1. 取消   2. 潮流   3. 爱戴   4. 潮湿   5. 取代
6. 爱惜   7. 热潮   8. 撤销   9. 爱护   10. 热心
练习五．
1. 袋   2. 所   3. 滴   4. 丸   5. 艘
练习六．
1. 沉着   2. 迫害   3. 开创   4. 辞别   5. 堕落
练习七．
1. 加热   2. 廉洁   3. 干燥   4. 僵硬   5. 凶恶

10月 第1周的学习内容

星期一 Monday

zūnjìng
尊敬 （乙）动
respect; revere

常用搭配
尊敬老师 be respectful to the teacher
对她表示尊敬 show respect for her
尊敬的朋友们！ Esteemed Friends!

用法示例
学生们非常尊敬他们的历史老师。
The students have great respect for their history teacher.
所有了解他的人都很尊敬他。
He commands the respect from all who know him well.
这位牧师受到所有人的尊敬。
The clergyman is respected by everyone.

chōngmǎn
充满 （乙）动
be full of

常用搭配
她眼里充满了泪水。 Her eyes were full of tears.

用法示例
他的歌充满了忧伤。
His songs are full of sorrow.
我心中充满了胜利的喜悦。
I'm full of the joys of victory.

chōngfèn
充分 反缺乏 quēfá （乙）形
① full ② enough

常用搭配
充分利用 take full advantage of
充分准备 fully prepare
充分理解 fully understand

用法示例
她离婚的理由很充分。
She had adequate grounds for a divorce.
我们应充分利用人力资源。
We shall take full advantage of our human resources.

píngjià
评价 （丙）动／名
① evaluate ② evaluation

常用搭配
评价某人的工作 assess one's efforts
主观评价 subjective evaluation
恰当的评价 a proper estimation

用法示例
我们希望别人公正地评价我们的工作。
We like our work to be justly evaluated.
他在同事中受到很高的评价。
He is highly esteemed by his colleagues.
现在我认识到我对她性格的评价是片面的。
Now I've realized that my estimation of her character was biased.

zūnzhòng
尊重 （丙）动
esteem; respect

常用搭配
尊重别人的意见 respect the ideas of others
尊重他人的隐私 respect other's privacy

用法示例
他的朋友都很尊重他。
All his friends held him in high esteem.
我们应该尊重个性。
We should respect individuality.
你应该尊重长者。
You should show respect for your elders.

jiǎodù
角度 （丙）名
angle

常用搭配
从这个角度看 to look at from this angle

用法示例
试着从不同的角度来考虑这件事。
Try thinking of the affair from a different angle.
从这个角度来看,画中的女子面带微笑。
Seen from this angle, the woman in the picture is smiling.
从任何角度看,这座建筑物都很漂亮。
Looked at from any angle, the building is a handsome one.

jiǎoluò
角落 （丙）名
corner

常用搭配
房间的每个角落 every corner of the room
阴暗的角落 a dark corner

用法示例

喜讯传遍了祖国的各个角落。

The good news spread to every corner of the country.

角落里有一堆报纸。

There's a pile of newspapers in the corner.

她坐在角落里注视着我的一举一动。

She sat in the corner, watching my every move.

pìnqǐng

聘请 反 辞退 **cítuì** （丁）动

engage; hire (a lawyer, etc.)

常用搭配

聘请家庭教师 engage a private teacher

聘请厨师 employ a cook

用法示例

我们聘请他担任技术顾问。

We engage him as technical adviser.

他们聘请了最好的律师为他们的案子辩护。

They employed the best lawyer to plead their case.

pìnrèn

聘任 同 聘用 **pìnyòng** （丁）动

appoint (to a job or position)

常用搭配

聘任制 the appointment system

聘任委员会 an appointment committee

用法示例

委员会聘任她为公司的经营主任。

The committee appointed her to be chief operating officer of the company.

他是这家地方报纸最新聘任的新闻记者。

He is the new news hawk at the local newspaper.

píngxuǎn

评选 （丁）动

to choose

常用搭配

好新闻评选活动 selection of good news stories

被评选为劳动模范 be chosen as a model worker

用法示例

该片在第 73 届学院奖评选中获 4 项奥斯卡大奖。

It won four Oscars at the 73rd annual Academy Awards.

你们公司是《财富》杂志评选的 500 强之一。

Your company is a Fortune 500 company.

chōngpèi

充沛 同 充足 **chōngzú** （丁）形

bountiful; plentiful

常用搭配

精力充沛 be full of vigor

感情充沛 an abundance of heart

雨水充沛 abundant rainfall

用法示例

这个地区雨量充沛。

The rainfall is plentiful in this area.

他是一个精力充沛的运动员。

He is a vigorous player.

bù yán ér yù

不言而喻 （丁）

self-evident

常用搭配

这是不言而喻的事实。

It is a self-evident fact.

用法示例

她的聪颖是不言而喻的。

Her intelligence is self-evident.

他想成功,这是不言而喻的。

It is self-evident that he wants to be successful.

 词义辨析

尊重、尊敬

"尊敬"和"尊重"都是动词,都有恭敬的意思。"尊敬"的对象只能是人,有时候可以作定语,如尊敬的老师;"尊重"的对象可以是人,也可以是抽象的事物,比如:个性、风俗、历史、决定、劳动等,不能用作定语。例如:①我们都很尊敬/尊重这位钢琴家。②不能看别人的信,你要尊重别人的隐私。

Both 尊敬 and 尊重 are verbs, meaning "to show respect". The objects of 尊敬 are people, and sometimes it can function as an attributive, e.g. "尊敬的老师" (a respectable teacher); while the objects of 尊重 can be people or something abstract, such as "个性"(personality), "风俗"(customs), "历史" (history), "决定" (decision), "劳动" (effort), etc. It can not function as an attributive. For example: ① We all respect the pianist very much. ② Don't read other people's lettes. You should respect other's privacy.

 练习

练习一、根据拼音写汉字，根据汉字写拼音

( )xuǎn ( )luò pìn ( ) chōng ( ) zūn ( )
评( ) 角( ) ( )任 ( )分 ( )敬

练习二、搭配连线

(1) 精力   A. 模范
(2) 充分   B. 充沛
(3) 评选   C. 评价
(4) 尊重   D. 准备
(5) 客观   E. 隐私

练习三、从今天学习的生词中选择合适的词填空

1. 无论是成年人，还是小孩子，都要 _____ 他们的权利、想法和隐私。
2. 老板亲自拜访那位老专家，并 _____ 他为我们公司的技术顾问。
3. 她觉得她有足够的竞争力，对自己 _____ 了信心。
4. 他终于夺得了奥运会的冠军，他当时喜悦的心情是 _____ 的。
5. 他学习成绩特别好，年年都被 _____ 为优秀学生。
6. 我们有 _____ 的理由相信这条消息是可靠的。
7. 专家对这篇论文的 _____ 相当高。
8. 老法官以正直和公道赢得了当地人的 _____。
9. 现在很多大学都实行教授 _____ 制。
10. 他精力 _____，平均每天工作 12 个小时。

答案

练习一：
略
练习二：
(1) B   (2)D   (3)A   (4)E   (5)C
练习三：
1. 尊重   2. 聘请   3. 充满   4. 不言而喻   5. 评选
6. 充分   7. 评价   8. 尊敬   9. 聘任   10. 充沛

星期二 (Tuesday)

sànbù
散步 （乙）动
go for a walk

常用搭配
在公园散步 walk in a park   出去散步 go out for a walk

用法示例
咱们去散散步吧！
Let's go for a walk.
我经常在晚饭后散步。
I often take a walk after supper.

cónglái
从来 （乙）形
① always ② at all times

常用搭配
从来没 / 不 never

用法示例
我从来没听说过他。
I have never heard of him.
他从来不说谎！
He never tells lies！
我从来没去过那里。
I have never been there.

bìrán   ǒurán
必然 反偶然 （乙）形
① necessarily ② inevitable

常用搭配
必然要求 necessary requirements
必然规律 inexorable law

用法示例
这是过度放任的必然下场。
It is the inevitable result of overindulgence.
工资一高物价就高，这是必然的吗？
Is it a necessarily fact that higher wages will lead to higher prices?
战争带来的必然结果就是生产力下降。
The inevitable outcome of a war is a fall in production.

yīrán   réngrán
依然 同仍然 （丙）副
① still ② as before

常用搭配
依然年轻 as young as before
依然记得 still remember

用法示例
我的小学老师依然记得我的名字。
My teacher from primary school still remembers my name.

越狱犯依然在逃。
The escaped prisoner is still at large.
他的母亲去世了，但他父亲依然健在。
His mother is dead but his father is still alive.

gǎnshòu
感受 （丙）名/动
① feeling ② feel

常用搭配
顾客的感受 customers' feeling
感受到激情 feel the excitement

用法示例
他一点也不在乎我们的感受。
He doesn't care about our feelings at all.
他觉得很难说出自己的感受。
He finds it hard to say what he feels.
他的话使我感受到了来自朋友的温暖。
What he said made me feel the warmth of friendship.

sànbù
散布 （丙）动
spread; disseminate

常用搭配
散布消息 disseminate information

用法示例
谣言散布得很快。
The rumors spread fast.
种子随风散布。
The seeds were disseminated with the wind.

bìdìng   wèibì
必定   ⊗ 未必   （丙）副
be bound to; be sure to

常用搭配
必定会失败 be bound to fail
必定会成功 be sure to succeed

用法示例
增加成本必定使价格上涨。
The increase in costs is bound to send prices up.
建立在金钱基础上的婚姻必定会破裂。
Marriage for money is bound to break up.
我们教授非常有本事，必定能解决这一难题。
Our professor is so capable, he is bound to solve this difficult problem.

kǒngbù
恐怖 （丙）形
terrifying; horid

常用搭配
恐怖分子 terrorist   恐怖活动 campaigns of terror
恐怖电影 horror movies

用法示例
政府决定同国际恐怖主义作斗争。
The government is determined to combat international terrorism.
我们不会忘记战争的恐怖。
We won't forget the horrors of war.
业余时间她喜欢看恐怖小说。
She likes reading horror fiction in her spare time.

ràngbù
让步 （丁）动
① concede ② give in

常用搭配
对……让步 make a concession to
做些让步 make some concessions

用法示例
资方在与工人谈判中没有让步。
Employers made no concessions to the workers during negotiations.
为了和平我们做出了让步。
We made concessions for the sake of peace.
我一点儿也不让步。
I will not budge an inch.

yīlài
依赖 （丁）动
to depend on; to be dependent on

常用搭配
依赖别人 be dependent on others
依赖进口 depend on imports

用法示例
找个工作，别再依赖你的父母了。
Find a job and end your dependence on your parents.
现在人们越来越依赖计算机了。
Nowadays we rely increasingly on computers for help.

gǎnkǎi   gǎntàn
感慨   ⊜ 感叹   （丁）动
sigh with emotion

常用搭配
感慨万千 all sorts of feelings well up in oneself

用法示例
他感慨万千，用力握了一下她的手，离开了她。
Overcome with emotion, he pressed her hand and then left her.
最近她常常感慨青春易逝。
Lately, she often sighs for her lost youth.

bù zhī bù jué
不知不觉 （丁）
unconsciously; unwittingly

常用搭配
不知不觉睡着了 to unwittingly fall asleep

用法示例
他不知不觉地把车开进了沟里。
He drove into the ditch completely unawares.
不知不觉已经过了三个月。
Before we knew it, three months had passed.

 词义辨析

必定、必然

　　"必定"和"必然"都表示"一定会……"的意思,都可以用作状语。"必定"强调根据情况主观上判断一定会这样;"必然"强调根据客观规律判断事物发展的结果一定会这样,"必然"是形容词,可以作定语、谓语等;而"必定"是副词,只能在句子作状语。例如:①他是球迷,他必定会来看比赛。②不努力就会落后,这是必然的。③人会衰老、死亡,这是必然规律。

　　必定 and 必然 mean "certainly", "must be"; both can function as an adverbial. 必定 stresses the certainty based on one's subjective judgement; while 必然 stresses the certainty based on objective principles, meaning the things that will be developing as expected. 必然 is an adjective, and it can act as different functions such as an attributive, a predicate and so on. 必定 is an adverb, and can only function as an adverbial. For example: ① He is a football fan, so he will come to watch the match for sure. ② If you do not work hard, it is certain that you will fall behind. ③ It is a law of nature that man will get old and die.

 练习

练习一、根据拼音写汉字,根据汉字写拼音

yī ( )　　　sàn ( )　　( )bù ( )　　kǎi bì ( )
( )赖　　( )布　　恐( )　　感( )　　( )定

练习二、搭配连线

(1) 感慨	A. 电影
(2) 依赖	B. 消息
(3) 恐怖	C. 万千
(4) 散布	D. 规律
(5) 必然	E. 别人

练习三、从今天学习的生词中选择合适的词填空

1. 如果父母什么都帮孩子做了,那么孩子就会产生_____思想。

2. 他上大学四年,一直是全勤,_____没缺过课。

3. 我喜欢晚饭后到附近的公园_____。

4. 我们坚信正义_____会战胜邪恶。

5. 她保养得真好,十年后再次看到她时,她_____那么漂亮。

6. 时间过得真快,我是去年一月份来中国的,_____已经过了一年半了。

7. 谈判双方都不肯_____,因而没有达成任何协议。

8. 他们两个人性格不合,分手是_____的。

9. 这个旅行家写了不少旅行中的见闻和_____。

10. 政府宣布说,对于_____谣言、制造恐怖气氛的人一经发现就要严惩。

🔑 **答案**

练习一:
略

练习二:
(1) C　　(2)E　　(3)A　　(4)B　　(5)D

练习三:
1. 依赖　2. 从来　3. 散步　4. 必定　5. 依然
6. 不知不觉　7. 让步　8. 必然　9. 感受　10. 散布

星期三

悲痛 bēitòng　⊗ 欢乐 huānlè　（乙）形

sorrowfull; grieved

常用搭配

令人悲痛的消息 lamentable news
感到悲痛 feel grieved

用法示例

他对妻子的去世深感悲痛。
He deeply lamented the death of his wife.
她悲痛得精神恍惚,怎么安慰也没用。
She was distracted by grief and refused to be consoled.

尖锐 jiānruì　⊜ 锐利 ruìlì　（乙）形

sharp

常用搭配

尖锐的批评 sharp criticism　　尖锐地指出 point out sharply

用法示例

他的评语非常尖锐。
His remark is biting.
她对这个方案提出了尖锐的意见。
She gave her opinion on the project sharply.
他看问题很尖锐。
He sees things with a keen eye.

医疗 yīliáo　（丙）动

medical treatment

常用搭配

医疗器械 a medical instrument
医疗技术 medical technique
医疗保险 medical insurance

用法示例

所有工人都有公费医疗。
All the workers get free public health care.
这家医院有一些先进的医疗设备。
This hospital has some advanced medical equipment.

依据 yījù　（丙）动/名

① be in accordance with ② basis; foundation

常用搭配

依据法律 according to the law
以事实为依据 be based on facts

用法示例

依据交通法规,他将被罚款 50 元。
According to the traffic rules, he will be fined 50 yuan.

这一理论是以一系列错误的设想为依据的。
The theory is based on a series of wrong assumptions.
判断应该以事实为依据。
Judgment should be based on facts.

悲惨 bēicǎn　（丁）形

miserable; tragic

常用搭配

悲惨的景象 a woeful spectacle
悲惨的遭遇 a tragic experience
悲惨的结局 a tragic ending

用法示例

这部电影表现了过去穷人的悲惨生活。
The film represents the miserable lives of poor people in the past.
有十名旅客在这次悲惨的事故中遇难。
Ten passengers were killed in the tragic accident.
他们的结局非常悲惨。
They met with a terrible fate.

背诵 bèisòng　（丙）动

recite

常用搭配

背诵课文 recite the text　　背诵诗歌 recite poems

用法示例

老师让我们背诵这首诗。
Our teacher told us to recite this poem.
从头开始背诵这篇文章。
Recite the article from the beginning.
这首诗我才读了两遍,小女孩就会背诵了。
After I read the poem to her twice, the little girl could recite it.

背包 bèibāo　（丙）名

knapsack; rucksack

常用搭配

背背包 to shoulder a knapsack
旅行背包 traveling knapsack

用法示例

她背起背包出发了。
She shouldered her rucksack and set off.
这个军人背着一个背包。
The soldier carried a pack on his back.
那位旅行者从他的背包中拿出了一瓶水。
The traveler took out a bottle of water from his backpack.

悲剧 bēijù　⊗ 喜剧 xǐjù　（丁）名

tragedy

常用搭配

悲剧演员 tragic actor　　悲剧剧本 tragic plays

用法示例

他比较喜欢喜剧而不是悲剧。
He prefers comedies to tragedies.
事情以玩笑开始,以悲剧结束。
It began as a jest and ended as a tragedy.
莎士比亚的《哈姆雷特》是一部著名的悲剧。
Shakespeare's Hamlet is a famous tragedy.

jiānduān
尖端 （丁）名 / 形
① pointed end ② most advanced; sophisticated

常用搭配

叶子的尖端 cusp of a leaf
尖端武器 sophisticated weapons
尖端科学 the pinnacle of science

用法示例

他想学习最新最尖端的技术。
He wants to learn about the latest and most advanced technology.
去年,我们引进了新的尖端设备。
We introduced the sophisticated new equipment last year.

yīzhì
医治 *zhìliáo* 回 治疗 （丁）动
treat a sickness

常用搭配

接受医治 take a cure
医治烧伤 healing of burns

用法示例

医生应该能医治任何疾病的观念是错误的。
That a doctor has the ability to cure any disease is a misconception.
经过多年的研究,仍没找到医治这种疾病的疗法。
Years of research have failed to produce a cure for the disease.
老人因病医治无效,去世了。
The old man died of the illness after failing to respond to medical treatment.

gǎnrǎn
感染 （丁）动
to infect

常用搭配

细菌感染 bacterial infection
病毒感染 virus infection
轻度感染 light infection

用法示例

伤口很快就感染了。
The wound soon became infected.
她的笑声感染了全班同学。
She infected the whole class with her laughter.
这位年轻的老师以她的热诚感染了全班。
The young teacher infected the whole class with her enthusiasm.

bù bēi bù kàng
不卑不亢 （丁）
be neither overbearing nor servile

常用搭配

不卑不亢地说
said in neither an overbearing, nor servile manner

用法示例

这位秘书总是不卑不亢的。
The secretary is never overbearing, nor servile.
他不卑不亢地回答老板的问题。
He answered his boss' questions in neither an overbearing, nor servile manner.

词义辨析

悲惨、悲痛

"悲惨"和"悲痛"都是形容词。"悲惨"指凄惨的,令人感到不幸和痛苦的,一般作定语,用于某种不幸的情形,如悲惨的景象、悲惨的遭遇、悲惨的事故、悲惨的结局等;"悲痛"主要指非常伤心难过,一般用于人的感情,尤其是形容人因失去亲人或敬重的人而产生的情绪。例如:①母亲去世了,儿女们都十分悲痛。②他悲痛地告诉我,他的哥哥去世了。

Both 悲惨 and 悲痛 are adjectives. 悲惨 indicates "wretched", and it usually functions as an attributive, applied to describing miserable states, such as "悲惨的景象" (sorrowful spectacle), "悲惨的遭遇" (a tragic experience), "悲惨的事故" (a tragic accident), "悲惨的结局" (a miserable ending), etc. 悲痛 usually indicates "very sorrowful or grieved", and is mainly applied to describing one's feelings, especially when one's relative or a respected elder dies. For example: ① The children were greatly grieved by their mother's death. ② He told me with sorrow that his brother was dead.

 练习

练习一、根据拼音写汉字，根据汉字写拼音

(　　)ruì　(　　)liáo　(　　)cǎn　(　　)sòng　(　　)rǎn

尖(　　)　医(　　)　悲(　　)　背(　　)　感(　　)

练习二、搭配连线

(1) 医疗　　　　　　A. 遭遇
(2) 病毒　　　　　　B. 法律
(3) 尖端　　　　　　C. 感染
(4) 悲惨　　　　　　D. 器械
(5) 依据　　　　　　E. 武器

练习三、从今天学习的生词中选择合适的词填空

1. 这个故事的结局很_____，让人想哭。
2. 如果你再这样毫无_____地乱说，那我就会控告你诽谤。
3. 老师要求我们_____这篇课文，以便记住其中优美的句子。
4. 这项发明运用了目前最先进的设备，这项技术也已经达到了国际_____水平。
5. 由于没有及时对伤口作消毒处理，致使伤口大面积_____。
6. 他的腿因小时候生病没钱_____而终身残疾。
7. 虽然他家很穷，但他在家庭富裕的同学们面前总是_____的。
8. 记者提了一个非常_____的问题，那位名人说无可奉告。
9. 母亲得知儿子在战场上牺牲的消息后，感到万分_____。
10. 受害者家属公开了事件的过程，他希望这样的_____不要重演。

 答案

练习一：
略

练习二：
(1) D　　(2)C　　(3)E　　(4)A　　(5)B

练习三：
1. 悲惨　2. 依据　3. 背诵　4. 尖端　5. 感染
6. 医治　7. 不卑不亢　8. 尖锐　9. 悲痛　10. 悲剧

 星期四

tòngkǔ
痛苦　　　　　　　　　　　　（乙）形

miserable; painful; suffering

常用搭配

痛苦的经历 miserable experience
感到痛苦 feel miserable

用法示例

病人看上去很痛苦。
The patient looks miserable.
他的痛苦引起了我们的同情。
His sufferings aroused our sympathy.
她的话减轻了我的痛苦。
Her words alleviated my suffering.

yìnxiàng
印象　　　　　　　　　　　　（乙）名

impression

常用搭配

深刻的印象 a deep impression
给某人留下印象 make an impression on sb
第一印象 first impression

用法示例

主人的好客给我们留下了非常好的印象。
The host's hospitality left us with a very good impression.
你对伦敦的第一印象怎么样？
What were your first impressions of London?
那位年轻小姐给他留下了深刻的印象。
The young lady had made a deep impression on him.

xíngxiàng
形象　　　　　　　　　　（乙）名／形

① image ② vivid

常用搭配

形象思维 thinking in terms of images
形象的描述 vivid description

用法示例

我们该怎样来改善自己的形象呢？
How can we improve our image?
那丑闻极大地损害了他的形象。
The scandal detracted greatly from his image.
那位政治家在人民中的形象很差。
The politician has a very bad image amongst the people.

yíhàn
遗憾　　　　　　　　　　　　（丙）形

① regret ② sorry

对……表示遗憾 express regret for…
终身遗憾 a lifelong regret
十分遗憾地指出 point out with great regret

用法示例

听到这个消息我感到很遗憾。
I'm sorry to hear that.
很遗憾,你没有得到那份工作。
I'm sorry that you didn't get the job.
非常遗憾,我不能接受你的邀请。
Much to my regret, I'm unable to accept your invitation.

bēishāng
悲伤　📖悲痛 **bēitòng**　（丁）形

sad; sorrowful

常用搭配

悲伤的歌曲 a woeful song
悲伤地说 said sadly
悲伤得痛哭起来 sorrowful tears

用法示例

葬礼是令人悲伤的场合。
A funeral is a sorrowful occasion.
他悲伤地告诉我,他的母亲病得很厉害。
He told me with sorrow that his mother was very ill.

gāosù
高速　🔄慢速 **mànsù**　（丙）形

high speed

常用搭配

高速公路 express way
高速发展 develop by leaps and bounds
高速前进 advance at high speed

用法示例

我们的车正在公路上高速行驶。
Our car is going at a high speed on the road.
工厂里的所有机器都在高速运转。
All machines in the factory are operating at a high speed.

yíchǎn
遗产　（丙）名

heritage

常用搭配

文化遗产 cultural heritage
继承遗产 inherit one's fortune
历史遗产 a historical legacy

用法示例

他父亲给他留下了一笔遗产。
His father bequeathed him a fortune.
这些是文艺复兴时期的文化遗产。
These are the cultural legacies of the Renaissance.
那老人去世时留下二百万美元的遗产。
The old man left behind an estate of two million dollars when he died.

túxíng
图形　（丁）名

graph or figure

常用搭配

几何图形 geometric figure

用法示例

打印机也可以打印程序列表和图形图片。
Printers can also generate listings of programs and graphic images.
这是不规则图形。
It is an irregular figure.

túbiǎo
图表　📖表格 **biǎogé**　（丁）名

diagram; chart

常用搭配

设计图表 to design a chart
统计图表 a statistical chart

用法示例

他指着图表来说明他的论点。
He pointed at the diagram to illustrate his point.
他在设计图表。
He is designing a chart.

gāodàng
高档　🔄低档 **dīdàng**　（丁）形

① top quality ② high-grade

常用搭配

高档商品 high-grade goods
高档消费品 high-grade consumer goods

用法示例

高档家具总是很畅销。
There's always a market for high-quality furniture.
她总是在高档店铺里买首饰。
She always gets her jewels at highend stores.

túxiàng
图像　（丁）名

picture; image

常用搭配

三维图像 a three-dimensional picture
模拟图像 an analog picture
电视图像 a television picture

用法示例

从月球发来的电视图像很清晰。
The television pictures broadcast from the Moon are all very clear.
这台机器能够传送彩色图像。
The machine can transmit colored pictures.

bù xiāng shàng xià
不相上下　（丁）

be about the same

常用搭配

能力不相上下 of about the same ability

用法示例

我认为这两个选手不相上下。

I'd say the two players are pretty evenly matched.

那两个赛跑选手竞争激烈——在赛程中一直不相上下。

It was touch and go as to who would win the hotly contested race between the two runners.

 词义辨析

悲伤、痛苦

　　"悲伤"和"痛苦"都是形容词,都有由于遭受不幸或不如意的事儿伤心难过的意思。"悲伤"指内心悲痛而伤感,主要用于内心的感情和情绪,它的同义词是"悲痛";"痛苦"指身体或精神感到非常难受,难以忍耐,比如疼痛、焦虑、孤独、绝望等都可以称作"痛苦"。例如:①她丈夫在空难中去世了,她非常悲伤。②她嫁给了一个她并不喜欢的男人,她的心中非常痛苦。③他的伤使他很痛苦。

　　Both 悲伤 and 痛苦 are adjectives, meaning "grieved, sad". 悲伤 indicates "sorrowful", and is applied to describing one's feeling or mood, its synonymy is "悲痛"; while 痛苦 indicates mental or physical suffering, such as pain, anxiety, loneliness, despair. For example: ① Her husband was killed in the air crash and she was very grieved. ② She married a man whom she didn't love, and she had an anguished heart. ③ His wound caused him great suffering.

 练习

练习一、根据拼音写汉字,根据汉字写拼音

yìn（ 　）　hàn（ 　）　dàng（ 　）xiàng　bēi（ 　）

（ 　）象　遗（ 　）　高（ 　）　图（ 　）（ 　）伤

练习二、搭配连线

(1) 痛苦的　　　　　　　　A. 印象

(2) 形象的　　　　　　　　B. 图像

(3) 电视的　　　　　　　　C. 商品

(4) 高档的　　　　　　　　D. 描述

(5) 深刻的　　　　　　　　E. 经历

练习三、从今天学习的生词中选择合适的词填空

1. 这件体恤上印着很多几何 _____ 。

2. 这位民族英雄在人们心目中的 _____ 非常高大。

3. 很难说谁会得胜,因为这两个游泳选手的实力 _____ 。

4. 我很想去听明晚的音乐会,可是明晚我有事,真 _____ !

5. 我们宿舍的电视出毛病了, _____ 不清楚,还有杂音。

6. 汽车上了 _____ 公路以后,他开得很快。

7. 请把你的统计 _____ 附到论文的最后。

8. 第一次带女朋友回家,父母对他女朋友的 _____ 很好。

9. 长城被列为世界历史文化 _____ 。

10. 她喜欢穿 _____ 服装,衣服都是名牌。

答案

练习一:

略

练习二:

(1) E　　　(2)D　　　(3)B　　　(4)C　　　(5)A

练习三:

1. 图形　　2. 形象　　3. 不相上下　4. 遗憾　　5. 图像

6. 高速　　7. 图表　　8. 印象　　9. 遗产　　10. 高档

星期五

chéngkěn
诚恳 ≅ 恳切 （乙）形
sincere

常用搭配
诚恳的态度 a sincere attitude

用法示例
她为人诚恳，毫不造作。
She is sincere, without affectation.
他诚恳地向他的朋友道了歉。
He apologized to his friend sincerely.

chéngshí
诚实 ⊠ 虚伪 （乙）形
honest

常用搭配
诚实的人 an honest man

用法示例
我可以证明她是诚实的。
I can certify that she is honest.
他是一位诚实的商人。
He is an honest businessman.
他一向很诚实，我相信他。
He is always honest, so I believe him.

tíshì
提示 （丁）动
to hint; give clue

常用搭配
你能提示我一下吗？ Can you give me a clue?
谢谢你的提示。 Thanks for your hint.

用法示例
我又提示他一次，他还是不理解。
I gave him another clue, but he still didn't understand.
她没有记下台词，还需要提示。
She couldn't remember the lines, and needed to be prompted.
他不会做这道数学题，你能提示他一下吗？
He can not solve the math problem. Can you give him a clue?

chángshí
常识 （丙）名
common sense; general knowledge

常用搭配
生活常识 general knowledge of life
缺乏常识 be lacking in common sense

用法示例
她一点儿常识也没有。
She hasn't an ounce of common sense.

你应该了解更多的文学常识。
You should know more general knowledge about literature.
他们在学校学习了一些卫生常识。
They have gained a basic understanding of hygiene and sanitation in school.

tíxǐng
提醒 （丙）动
remind

常用搭配
提醒他回电话 remind him to call back
提醒大家注意 call everybody's attention to

用法示例
他提醒我带照相机。
He reminded me to bring my camera.
万一我忘了，请提醒我。
In case I forget, please remind me.
到快面试时请再提醒我一下。
Please remind me again when the interview is drawing near.

jiànjiě
见解 （丙）名
opinion; view

常用搭配
专家的见解 expert opinions
提出他的见解 put forward his views
持不同见解 have different views

用法示例
讲一讲你对这个问题的见解。
Tell us your views on the question.
他是个有固定见解的人。
He's a man of firm opinions.
这只是我个人的见解。
That's just my own opinion.

zhēnguì
珍贵 （丙）形
precious

常用搭配
珍贵的礼物 precious gifts   珍贵的照片 precious pictures

用法示例
熊猫是珍贵的动物。
Pandas are precious creatures.
这些罕见的邮票非常珍贵。
These stamps have great value because of their rarity.
那些旧书是我最珍贵的财产。
Those old books are my most precious possessions.

chánghuán
偿还 ≅ 归还 （丁）动
repay

常用搭配
偿还债务 repay a debt
偿还能力 capability of repayment

如数偿还 pay back the exact amount

用法示例

我破产了，不能偿还他的债务。
I was bankrupt, and unable to pay his debts.
银行催他偿还贷款。
The bank is pressing him for the repayment of his loan.
法院判决由他偿还债务。
The judge ruled that he should pay the debts.

chángshì
尝试 （丁）动／名
try; attempt

常用搭配

再次尝试 make another attempt
放弃尝试 abandon the attempts

用法示例

她曾尝试着自己完成实验，但是失败了。
She attempted to finish the experiment by herself, but she failed.
他做了一次成功的尝试。
His attempt was successful.
无力的尝试多半是要失败的。
A feeble attempt is liable to fail.

jiànjiē zhíjiē
间接 ⊗直接 （丁）形
indirect

常用搭配

间接宾语 indirect object   间接成本 indirect cost

用法示例

引发事故的间接原因是火车晚点。
The accident was the indirect result of the train being late.
这消息是我间接听来的。
I heard the news indirectly.

jiànshi
见识 （丁）名
knowledge and experience

常用搭配

增长见识 widen one's knowledge
有深远见识的人 a man of deep insight

用法示例

他身体好，有钱，又有见识。
He is possessed of health, wealth and good sense.
你应该多到各地走走以增长见识。
You should broaden your horizons by traveling more.

bù cí ér bié
不辞而别 （丁）
leave without saying good-bye

用法示例

她不辞而别了。
She left without saying goodbye.
自从她不辞而别以后，我再也没见过她。
I have not seen her since she left without saying goodbye.

词义辨析

诚实、诚恳

　　"诚实"和"诚恳"都是形容词，都可以作定语和谓语，都用于人，说明对象是可信的。"诚实"强调内心的想法与言行一致，不撒谎，不欺骗人，在句子中不常作状语。"诚恳"强调态度是真诚的，不是虚情假义，经常在句中作状语。例如：①我们没怀疑过他，他很诚实。②他诚恳地邀请我们参加他的婚礼。

　　Both 诚实 and 诚恳 are adjectives, and they can function as attributives or predicates, used to describe people, and meaning "be believable". 诚实 stresses "actions and words in accord with one's true thoughts", "no lying, not deceptive", and it rarely functions as an adverbial in a sentence; while 诚恳 stresses that the attitude is sincere, being without hypocrisy or pretense, and it usually functions as an adverbial in a sentence. For example: ① We have never doubted him; he is an honest man. ② He sincerely invited us to attend his wedding ceremony.

练习

练习一、根据拼音写汉字，根据汉字写拼音
（　）kěn cháng（　）cháng（　）jiàn（　）jiàn（　）
诚（　）　（　）试　（　）还　（　）接　（　）解

练习二、搭配连线
(1) 增长　　　　　　　　A. 常识
(2) 提出　　　　　　　　B. 见识
(3) 偿还　　　　　　　　C. 见解
(4) 生活　　　　　　　　D. 诚恳
(5) 态度　　　　　　　　E. 债务

练习三、从今天学习的生词中选择合适的词填空
1. 他的那种学习方法很有效，其他同学也可以 ＿＿＿＿ 一下。
2. 大人教育孩子一定要 ＿＿＿＿，可大人却经常用谎话来哄骗小孩。
3. 不要犯 ＿＿＿＿ 性错误，那会被人笑话的。
4. 大家都写不出这个汉字，于是老师给了一些 ＿＿＿＿，大家立刻知道怎么写了。
5. 参加会议的人都想听听这位教授的 ＿＿＿＿，因为在大家心目中，他的水平很高。
6. 他来北京玩时，在我房间住了三天，走时却 ＿＿＿＿，我很伤心。
7. 他们已经 ＿＿＿＿ 了买房子的大部分贷款。
8. 他认识到错误了，＿＿＿＿ 地给父母道了歉。
9. 通过在国外进修和考察，他学到了技术，也增长了 ＿＿＿＿。
10. 快九点的时候，秘书 ＿＿＿＿ 老板不要忘了九点半的会议。

答案

练习一：
略

练习二：
(1) B   (2)C   (3)E   (4)A   (5)D

练习三：
1. 尝试   2. 诚实   3. 常识   4. 提示   5. 见解
6. 不辞而别 7. 偿还   8. 诚恳   9. 见识   10. 提醒

第10月，第1周的练习

练习一. 根据词语给加点的字注音
1.(　)   2.(　)   3.(　)   4.(　)   5.(　)
充沛   尖锐   高档   恐怖   遗产

练习二. 根据拼音填写词语
cháng   cháng   cháng   xiàng   xiàng
1. (　)试 2. (　)还 3. (　)识 4. 图(　) 5. 印(　)

练习三. 辨析并选择合适的词填空
1. 最好不要随意评论宗教,我们要(　)人们的不同信仰。(尊敬、尊重)
2. 她是一位受人(　)的母亲,独自一人把三个孩子抚养成人。(尊敬、尊重)
3. 勤奋的学生不一定是最优秀的,但优秀的学生(　)是勤奋的。(必然、必定)
4. 你没有好好复习,考得不好是(　)的。(必然、必定)
5. 听说他的(　)遭遇后,我们都很同情他。(悲惨、悲剧)
6. 昨天的事故导致三人死亡,大家一定要注意安全,不要让这种(　)重演。(悲惨、悲剧)
7. 听到母亲去世的消息,她(　)地痛哭起来。(痛苦、悲伤)
8. 这种病折磨得他很(　),甚至有时候他都不想再活下去了。(痛苦、悲伤)
9. 他们的态度不够(　),所以我们不想跟他们合作。(诚恳、诚实)
10. 他很(　),他觉得不该撒谎,也没必要撒谎。(诚恳、诚实)

练习四. 选词填空
感染   感受   充沛   依然   依据
感慨   遗憾   充分   充满   依赖
1. 每当父母谈起年轻时的经历,就会十分(　)地劝我们要珍惜现在的幸福生活。
2. 她很独立,能够自己做的事就不(　)别人。
3. 这个男孩喜欢运动,浑身(　)了活力。
4. 他说这话毫无(　),不足以让人信服。
5. 观众们都被现场的气氛所(　),有的竟默默地流泪了。
6. 这个作家精力(　),一生写了很多作品。
7. 真(　)！妈妈没和我们一起来旅游,如果她来了,她肯定会特别喜欢这里的风景。
8. 二十年后再见我的小学老师,虽然明显老了,却(　)那么优雅。
9. 他们为了这次试验做了(　)的准备,我想他们一定能成功。
10. 他从小失去父母,老师的疼爱让他(　)到了家的温暖。

练习五. 成语填空
1. 不言(　)(　)   2. 不知(　)(　)   3. 不卑(　)(　)
4. 不相(　)(　)   5. 不辞(　)(　)

练习六. 写出下列词语的同义词
1. 偿还(　)   2. 悲伤(　)
3. 医治(　)   4. 依然(　)
5. 充沛(　)

练习七. 写出下列词语的反义词
1. 间接(　)   2. 悲剧(　)
3. 聘请(　)   4. 诚实(　)
5. 必然(　)

答案

练习一.
1. pèi   2.ruì   3.dàng   4.bù   5.yí
练习二.
1. 尝   2. 偿   3. 常   4. 像   5. 象
练习三.
1. 尊重   2. 尊敬   3. 必定   4. 必然   5. 悲惨
6. 悲剧   7. 悲伤   8. 痛苦   9. 诚恳   10. 诚实
练习四.
1. 感慨   2. 依赖   3. 充满   4. 依据   5. 感染
6. 充沛   7. 遗憾   8. 依然   9. 充分   10. 感受
练习五.
1. 而喻   2. 不觉／所措   3. 不亢   4. 上下
5. 而别／辛劳
练习六.
1. 归还   2. 悲痛   3. 治疗   4. 仍然   5. 充足
练习七.
1. 直接   2. 喜剧   3. 辞退   4. 虚伪   5. 偶然

10月 第2周的学习内容

星期一 Monday

chǔlǐ
处理 （乙）名／动
① treatment; disposal ② handle

常用搭配
污水处理 dispose of sewage
处理问题 handling problems
处理案件 handling a case

用法示例
我有重要的事要处理。
I have a matter of importance to deal with.
这种事情只能私下处理。
This sort of business can only be transacted in private.
垃圾处理一直是个难题。
The disposal of rubbish is always a problem.

yōuxiù
优秀 （乙）形
outstanding; excellent

常用搭配
优秀的教师 an excellent teacher
优秀的学生 an outstanding pupil
优秀作品 works of excellence

用法示例
他是个优秀的运动员。
He is an excellent athlete.
这个男孩决心成为一名优秀的建筑师。
The boy made up his mind to become an excellent architect.

tǐlì
体力 （丙）名
physical strength; physical power

常用搭配
体力劳动 physical labor

用法示例
多年以后,他的体力不如从前了。
His strength has diminished over the years.
病人的体力正在恢复。
The patient's beginning to get his strength back now.
女性在体力上而不是智力上比男性弱。
Woman is physically, but not mentally, weaker than man.

jiǎnglì **chéngfá**
奖励 反惩罚 （丙）名／动
reward (as encouragement)

常用搭配
物质奖励 material encouragement
奖励先进生产者 give awards to advanced workers

用法示例
他对国家有贡献,所以获得了奖励。
He received a reward for his services to the nation.
他因为研制了新产品而得到公司的奖励。
His company rewarded him for his development of new products.
每年政府都奖励先进工作者。
Every year, the government will reward advanced workers as encouragement.

tǐliàng **liàngjiě**
体谅 同谅解 （丁）动
consider（show understanding and sympathy for）

常用搭配
体谅他人 have consideration for others
体谅别人的难处 make allowance for others' difficulties

用法示例
你要多体谅他们。
You should treat them with more consideration.
老师没能体谅学生的心情。
The teacher failed to consider the feelings of the students.
你应该体谅他,因为他一直在生病。
You must make allowances for him because he has been ill.

chābié **chāyì**
差别 同差异 （丙）名
difference

常用搭配
颜色的差别 difference in colors
显著的差别 remarkable differences

用法示例
我比较了复印件和原件,但是差别不是很大。
I compared the copy with the original, but there was not much difference.
这两种计算机价格没多大差别。
There's not much difference in price between the two computers.
我看不出他们有什么大的差别。
I can't see much difference between them.

chājù
差距 （丁）名

gap; disparity

常用搭配

年龄差距 disparity in age
贫富差距 gap between the rich and the poor
缩小差距 to narrow the gap

用法示例

缩小贫富之间的差距是政府面临的主要难题之一。
Reducing the gap between the rich and the poor is one of the main challenges facing the government.
我们双方都作些让步来消除价格差距怎么样？
How about meeting each other halfway to bridge the price gap?

chācuò
差错 （丁）名

error; mistake; accident

常用搭配

出差错 make an error
小差错 a trivial mistake

用法示例

他不小心出了差错。
He made a careless error.
这件事对我们非常重要，任何人都不能出差错。
This is very important for us, no one is allowed to make a mistake.
那个差错使他付出了沉重的代价：他因此输掉了比赛。
That mistake cost him dearly; he lost the game because of it.

yōuzhì
优质 　　　⊗劣质 （丁）名
lièzhì

high quality

常用搭配

优质产品 products of a good quality
优质服务 high quality services

用法示例

他们想卖一批优质钢材。
They want to sell a batch of high quality steel.
这个商店有各种优质手表。
There are all kinds of high quality watches in the shop.

xīnshui
薪水 （丁）名

salary; wage

常用搭配

领薪水 draw one's salary
增加薪水 increase a salary

用法示例

有的人将会被解雇，因为公司负担不起那么多薪水了。
Some of you will be dismissed because the firm can not afford to pay such large salaries.

我想跟她谈谈我的薪水的事。
I want to speak to her about the matter of my salary.
她靠那么一点儿薪水怎么生活？
How does she live on such a small salary?

chǔzhì
处置 （丁）动

handle; punish

常用搭配

严厉处置 punish severely　处置不当 mismanage
公平的处置 a fair disposition

用法示例

老板打算怎么处置那个懒惰的工人？
How does the boss plan to punish the lazy worker?
他善于妥当地处置各种复杂情况。
He is good at handling complex situations.

chéngfá
惩罚 （丁）动

punish

常用搭配

惩罚措施 punitive measure
惩罚性制裁 punitive sanction

用法示例

他应该受到法律最严厉的惩罚。
He deserves to be punished by the full force of the law.
老师宣布她将惩罚那个坏学生。
The teacher declared she would punish the bad student.
他因迟到而受到惩罚。
He was punished for being late.

 词义辨析

差别、差距

　　"差别"和"差距"都是名词，都表示事物之间的不同。"差别"强调不同点和不同的方面；"差距"强调事物之间差异的程度和数量，通常用于表示与某种标准的差别程度。例如：①在这对孪生子之间看不出有什么明显的差别。②政府在努力缩小地区间的经济差距。

　　Both 差别 and 差距 are nouns, meaning "the difference". 差别 stresses the distinguishing factor, attribute, or characteristic. While 差距 indicates "gap or disparity", and stresses the degree or amount by which things differ. 差距 is usually used to indicate the gap or disparity that exists compared with the original. For example: ① There is no appreciable differerce between the twins. ② The government is trying to narrow the economic disparities between regions.

 练习

练习一、根据拼音写汉字，根据汉字写拼音

( )lì ( )liàng chā( ) xīn( ) ( )fá

奖( ) 体( ) ( )距 ( )水 惩( )

练习二、搭配连线

(1) 贫富　　　　　　　　A. 奖励
(2) 惩罚　　　　　　　　B. 体谅
(3) 相互　　　　　　　　C. 差距
(4) 体力　　　　　　　　D. 措施
(5) 物质　　　　　　　　E. 劳动

练习三、从今天学习的生词中选择合适的词填空

1. 到了比赛的下半场,运动员的 _____ 下降了,奔跑的速度明显变慢了。

2. 对于腐败官员,一经查实,将依法严肃 _____。

3. 年轻人工作中难免出 _____,这时应该用积极的态度去接受别人的意见。

4. 担任领导职务以后,一定要 _____ 好上下级的关系,多听听老员工的意见。

5. 这些都是用 _____ 不锈钢做的,所以价格比较贵。

6. 虽然我一直在努力,但和水平高的技术人员相比,仍然有 _____。

7. 这份工作 _____ 不高,还经常加班,所以他想换个工作。

8. 我们也要站在别人的立场上想想, _____ 一下别人,这样可以避免很多矛盾。

9. 孩子犯了错,但妈妈没有 _____ 他,而是耐心地给他讲道理。

10. 同学们在个性和能力方面存在 _____,这是正常的,所以老师要因材施教。

答案

练习一:

略

练习二:

(1) C　　(2)D　　(3)B　　(4)E　　(5)A

练习三:

1.体力　　2.处置　　3.差错　　4.处理　　5.优质

6.差距　　7.薪水　　8.体谅　　9.惩罚　　10.差别

星期二

xiángxì
详细　反粗略　cūlüè　(乙)形

① detailed ② in detail

常用搭配

详细的叙述 a detailed account

详细说明 illustrate in detail

用法示例

她详细地解释了她的方案。

She explained her proposal in detail.

请给我们公司寄一份详细的履历。

Please send a detailed resume to our company.

影评家对这部电影做了详细的分析。

The film has been minutely dissected by the critics.

hòuhuǐ
后悔　同懊悔　àohuǐ　(乙)动

repent; regret

常用搭配

没什么可后悔的 have nothing to repent of

后悔做了某事 regret doing sth

用法示例

他后悔错过了这么好的一次机会。

He repented missing such a good chance.

我后悔在一辆汽车上花了这么多钱。

I regret spending so much money on a car.

做出那样的决定,我并不后悔。

I do not regret having made that decision.

qiàdàng
恰当　(丙)形

suitable; appropriate

常用搭配

恰当的词 a suitable word

恰当的时机 appropriate time

用法示例

老师想通过恰当的例子来说明。

The teacher tried to illustrate the point by using appropriate examples.

秘书计划在恰当的时机汇报这件事。

The secretary planned to report it at an appropriate time.

你的这项提议不太恰当。

This proposal of yours hardly meets the criteria.

zǔchéng
组成　(丙)动

consist of; make up

常用搭配

组成篮球队 form a basketball team

由九人组成 be made up of 9 people
组成统一战线 form a united front

用法示例

公牛队是由十五名运动员组成的。
The Bull Team is made up of 15 players.
物质是由叫做分子的微粒组成的。
Substances consist of small particles called molecules.
这台机器是由 20 个部件组成的。
This engine is made up of 20 parts.

xiángjìn
详尽　　　jiǎnlüè　　　　（丙）形
　　　　　　　反简略

at large; in detail

常用搭配

详尽地介绍 a detailed introduction
详尽的调查 a thorough investigation

用法示例

我们以后再对此进行详尽探讨。
We will talk about it in more detail later.
这个问题无需详尽讨论。
The question needn't be discussed in detail.
这家报纸对体育赛事报导详尽。
This paper covers sports thoroughly.

zǔzhǐ
阻止　　　　　　　　　　（丙）动

prevent

常用搭配

阻止他离开 stop him leaving
阻止学生打架 stop students from fighting
阻止事态的恶化 prevent the situation from deteriorating

用法示例

没有人能够阻止他去冒险。
Nobody can prevent him from taking that risk.
谁也无法阻止社会的发展。
No one can hold back the development of society.
虽然他竭力阻止这桩婚姻，但还是成了事实。
He tried to prevent the marriage, but it still took place.

zǔlì
阻力　　　　　　　　　　（丙）名

resistance; hindrance

常用搭配

克服阻力 to overcome resistance
水的阻力 water resistance
发展的阻力 resistance to development

用法示例

飞机呈流线型以减少风的阻力。
The aircraft is streamlined to cut down wind resistance.
他在履行职责时遇到了许多阻力。
In the execution of his duties he had met with a great deal of resistance.

zǔxiān
祖先　　　　　　　　　　（丙）名

ancestor

常用搭配

祖先的智慧 ancestral wisdom

用法示例

据说我们的祖先是猴子。
It is said that our progenitors were monkeys.
他的祖先是美洲的早期移民。
His forefather was an early settler in America.
他的祖先来到英国的时候是难民。
His ancestors had come to England as refugees.

qìshì
气势　　　　　　　　　　（丁）名

look of great force or imposing manner

常用搭配

气势宏伟的阿尔卑斯山 the majestic Alps
气势雄伟的建筑 a grand building

用法示例

她单凭个人气势就镇住了会场。
She dominated the meeting through sheer force of character.
这幅画给人总的印象是很有气势。
The general effect of the painting is overwhelming.

huǐgǎi
悔改　　　　　　　　　　（丁）动

repent

常用搭配

决心悔改 be determined to mend one's ways
毫无悔改之意 have no intention of mending one's ways

用法示例

鉴于他们有悔改表现，他们的刑期缩短了。
In view of their repentance, their sentence was reduced.
他已经表示愿意悔改。
He has expressed his repentance and willingness to mend his ways.

qǐshì
启示　　　qǐdí　　　　　　（丁）动
　　　　　　同启迪

inspire

常用搭配

从……得到启示 draw inspiration from…
受到……的启示 be inspired by…

用法示例

也许他得到了某种神的启示。
Some divine inspiration had perhaps come to him.
侦探在嫌疑人的日记中得到启示，很快找到了一条重要线索。
The detective got inspiration from the suspect's diary and soon found an important clue.

qǐshì
启事　　　　　　　　　　（丁）名

public notice usually posted on a wall; announcement

常用搭配

张贴启事 put up a notice
招工启事 a notice of recruitment
一则重要启事 an important notice

用法示例

他们的结婚启事已见报了。
The announcement of their marriage appeared in the newspaper.
公司已经搬家了,而且在报上登了启事。
The company moved, and put a notice in the papers.

 **词义辨析**

后悔、悔改

"后悔"和"悔改"都是动词,都有懊悔的意思。"后悔"指对所做的或没有做成的事感到悔恨、歉疚或自责,可以带宾语从句;"悔改"指因为悔悟自己的行为而有所改正,不能带宾语。例如:①我后悔和他们一起来旅行,真没意思。②他意识到了自己的错误,并有所悔改。

后悔 and 悔改 are verbs, meaning "to repent". 后悔 indicates to feel remorse, contrition, or self-reproach for what one has done or failed to do, and it can be followed by an objective clause; while 悔改 indicates to make a change for the better as a result of remorse or contrition for one's behavior, and it can not be followed by objects. For example: ① I regret traveling with them as it's boring. ② He realized his mistakes and tried to mend his ways.

 **练习**

练习一、根据拼音写汉字,根据汉字写拼音

qǐ( ) ( )shì zǔ( ) qià( )( )huì ( )示 气( ) ( )止 ( )当 后( )

练习二、搭配连线

(1) 招聘   A. 阻力
(2) 气势   B. 启事
(3) 克服   C. 说明
(4) 感到   D. 雄伟
(5) 详细   E. 后悔

练习三、从今天学习的生词中选择合适的词填空

1. 大瀑布从高山上急流直下,从远处看很有_____。
2. 由于政府部门反应迅速,因此很快_____了事态的进一步恶化。
3. 跟父母吵架后,他有点_____,但他并没有道歉。
4. 关于这个项目的实施方案你能不能说得再_____一点儿?
5. 他们的恋爱遭到双方父母的反对,但他们最终冲破双方家庭的_____走到了一起。
6. 这件事给了我很大的_____,相信再遇到此类问题时,我能处理得更妥当一些。
7. 这支舞蹈队由 12 个热爱舞蹈的业余选手_____。
8. 老师说安娜造的句子非常好,句子中的比喻非常_____。
9. 那个报栏里贴着一张寻人_____,是一个母亲在寻找离家出走的孩子。
10. 如果犯人在服刑期间,确实有_____的表现,可以考虑减刑。

答案

练习一:
略

练习二:
(1) B   (2)D   (3)A   (4)E   (5)C

练习三:
1. 气势   2. 阻止   3. 后悔   4. 详细   5. 阻力
6. 启示   7. 组成   8. 恰当   9. 启事   10. 悔改

星期三

chéngrèn
承认 （乙）动

acknowledge; admit

常用搭配

承认错误 acknowledge one's mistake

承认自己有罪 confess one's guilt

用法示例

他从不承认自己错了。

He never admits that he is wrong.

在这么多的证据面前，他不得不承认错误。

With so much evidence against him he had to acknowledge his error.

她承认偷了钱。

She confessed to stealing the money.

xiǎngyìng
响应 回应 （乙）动

huíyìng

answer; respond to

常用搭配

响应某人的号召 answer sb's call

得到积极的响应 meet with an encouraging answer

用法示例

他的想法得到了热烈的响应。

His idea received an enthusiastic response.

千百万人响应救灾呼吁而捐款。

Millions of people responsed voluntarily to the call for disaster relief by donating.

他们迅速响应了号召。

They quickly responded to the call.

fǔshí
腐蚀 侵蚀 （丙）动

qīnshí

etch; erode

常用搭配

腐蚀作用 corrosive action   腐蚀剂 corrosive

金属的腐蚀 corrosion of metal

用法示例

酸腐蚀金属。

Acid erodes metal.

锈腐蚀了钢轨。

Rust corroded the steel rails.

糖会腐蚀牙齿。

Sugar can decay the teeth.

xiàngsheng
相声 （丙）名

① cross talk ② comic dialogue

常用搭配

相声演员 comedian

说相声 perform a comic dialogue

用法示例

在中国，人们喜欢听相声。

People enjoy comic dialogues talk in China.

相声是一门语言艺术。

Cross talks are an art form of language.

gānshè
干涉 干预 （丙）动

gànyù

interfere; intervene

常用搭配

干涉他的事 interfere in his business

武装干涉 armed intervention

互不干涉内政

non-interference in each other's internal affairs

用法示例

我不会干涉孩子们的事情。

I won't meddle in my children's business.

不要干涉别国内政。

Don't interfere with the internal affairs other countries.

她干涉得毫无道理。

Her interference was not warranted.

gānrǎo
干扰 （丙）动

disturb; interfere

常用搭配

干扰考试 to disturb an exam

噪声干扰 noise interference

雷达干扰 radar interference

用法示例

他在学习呢，别干扰他。

He is studying; don't disturb him.

工作的时候不要互相干扰。

Do not disturb each other while working.

他在为期末考试做准备，不要干扰他。

Don't interfere with him. He's preparing for the final exams.

fǔlàn
腐烂 腐朽 （丁）动

fǔxiǔ

① rot ② decompose

常用搭配

腐烂的食物 rotten food

木头腐烂了。 The wood had rotted.

用法示例

不要吃腐烂的苹果。

Don't eat rotten apples.

这只蜗牛已经在壳里腐烂了。

The snail has rotted in its shell.

这个地方有一股臭味，一定有东西腐烂了。

This place has an odious smell; something must be rotten.

dìngqī
定期 （丙）名

① regularly ② at regular intervals

常用搭配

定期存款 a fixed deposit

用法示例

所有汽车都需要定期检修。

All cars require regular servicing.

兼职音乐教师定期到校授课。

Part-time music teachers visit the school periodically.

医生定期来访,确保孩子没有问题。

The doctor made periodic visit to the house to see if the baby was all right.

xiāngbǐ
相比 （丁）动

compared to

常用搭配

与……相比 in comparison with…

用法示例

他们的房子和我们的相比简直太豪华了。

Compared to ours, their house is a palace.

我的书法不错,但与我父亲的相比,我的就很差了。

My handwriting is good, but it is poor compared to my father's.

农村的文化生活不能跟大城市的相比。

Cultural life in the country cannot compare to that in a large city.

xiāngyìng
相应 （丁）形

relevant; corresponding (reaction)

常用搭配

采取相应措施 take appropriate measures

作相应的改变 make corresponding changes

用法示例

我已经提供了所有的信息,你应该采取相应的行动。

I have provided you with all the information; you can act accordingly.

所有的权利都伴有相应的义务。

All rights have corresponding responsibilities.

chéngshòu
承受 （丁）动

to bear; to support

常用搭配

承受风险　take a risk

承受种种考验　endure every kind of trial

用法示例

这块地基不够牢固,无法承受房屋的重量。

The foundations were not strong enough to sustain the weight of the house.

冰太薄,承受不住你们的重量。

The ice is too thin to bear your weight.

每个人都要承受苦难。

We all have our crosses to bear.

xiǎngshēng
响声 （丁）名

noise; sound

常用搭配

沙沙的响声

rustling sound

空车响声大。

Empty wagons rattle the loudest.

用法示例

很小的响声也会吓着这个胆小的孩子。

The least noise would startle the timid child.

他听到身后有响声,便转过身来。

He turned around when he heard a noise behind him.

我听到隔壁房间里有奇怪的响声。

I heard a curious sound in the neighboring room.

 词义辨析

干涉、干扰

　　"干涉"和"干扰"都是动词,都有妨碍的意思。"干涉"指介入他人的事,强调强迫别人按照自己的意图办事,是贬义词,"干涉"的对象可能是别人的私事或别的国家、组织的事务。"干扰"指扰乱,可能是某人的活动,也可能是外界的因素,是中性词,"干扰"的对象可能是别人的正常工作、学习、谈话或电子信号。例如:①他想干涉我的私事。②不要干涉别国内政。③噪音干扰我工作。④因为有雷达干扰,所以我们的无线电收不到信号。

　　Both 干涉 and 干扰 are verbs, meaning "to interfere". 干涉 indicates to intervene or intrude in the affairs of others, and stresses "the intention to force others to act according to one's own wishes", so it has a derogatory sense. Its objects are the affairs or business of other peoples, organizations or countries. 干扰 indicates a disturbance or interference with somebody else by someone, or by some unintentional outside factors. It has a neutral sense, its objects may be others' normal behavior (such as work, study or talk) or an electronic signal. For example: ① He wanted to interfere in my private affairs. ② Don't interfere with the internal affairs of other countries. ③ The noise disturbed me when I was working. ④ Because there is radar interference, our radio can not receive a signal.

练习

练习一、根据拼音写汉字，根据汉字写拼音

（　）qī　　chéng（　）　xiǎng（　）　）shè　（　）shí
　定（　）　（　）受　（　）声　干（　）　腐（　）

练习二、搭配连线

(1) 相声　　　　　　　　A. 干扰
(2) 噪声　　　　　　　　B. 演员
(3) 定期　　　　　　　　C. 错误
(4) 承受　　　　　　　　D. 存款
(5) 承认　　　　　　　　E. 苦难

练习三、从今天学习的生词中选择合适的词填空

1. 对于一个国家的内部事务,其他国家不应该随意 _____。

2. _____ 是一种语言艺术形式,通常是两个人表演。

3. 你提的条件太高,超出了我的 _____ 能力,所以我不能答应。

4. 我们应根据形势发展变化的情况对计划进行 _____ 的调整。

5. 由于夏天气温高,食物容易 _____。

6. 我 _____ 他很有能力,但他的人品真的不怎么样。

7. 自从查出癌症后,叔叔每个月都要 _____ 去复查。

8. 与那个孩子 _____,我觉得这个孩子更勤奋。

9. 咸涩的海水 _____ 了轮船的底部,于是人们想了个办法,在船底涂上了油漆。

10. 每个人在学外语时总会或多或少地受到母语的 _____。

答案

练习一：
略

练习二：

| (1)B | (2)A | (3)D | (4)E | (5)C |

练习三：

| 1.干涉 | 2.相声 | 3.承受 | 4.相应 | 5.腐烂 |
| 6.承认 | 7.定期 | 8.相比 | 9.腐蚀 | 10.干扰 |

星期四

jiǎngxuéjīn
奖学金　　　　　　　　（乙）名

scholarship

【常用搭配】
获得奖学金 win a scholarship

【用法示例】
他获得一份到剑桥大学读书的奖学金。
He won a scholarship to Cambridge.
我们每年给三个学生奖学金。
We give three students fellowships every year.

yōujiǔ　　　　　　　　*jiǔyuǎn*
悠久　　　　　　回久远　　（乙）形

① long ② long-standing

【常用搭配】
历史悠久的城市 a city with a long history
悠久的传统 longstanding tradition

【用法示例】
中国是一个有着悠久历史的东方国家。
China is an eastern country with a long history.
中国具有五千年的悠久历史。
China has a long history of 5,000 years.

mǐngǎn
敏感　　　　　　　　　（丁）形

sensitive

【常用搭配】
敏感问题 sensitive issue　　敏感的皮肤 sensitive skin
过分敏感 oversensitive

【用法示例】
千万别笑话他,他很敏感。
Don't laugh at him; he's very sensitive.
别那么敏感,我不是在批评你。
Don't be so sensitive. I was not criticizing you.
这是一个非常敏感的问题,恐怕不应该告诉新闻界。
This is such a sensitive issue that perhaps the press should not be told.

jiǎngjīn
奖金　　　　　　　　　（丙）名

premium; award money

【常用搭配】
年终奖金 year-end bonus
奖金制度 bonus system

【用法示例】
她因没能获得奖金而深感不满。
She's very dissatisfied at not receiving a bonus.

这个月工人将得到额外的奖金。
The workers will get an extra bonus this month.
因为她工作努力,公司发给了她奖金。
The firm repaid her hard work with a bonus.

mǐnjié
敏捷 ⑩灵敏 （丙）形
nimble; quick

常用搭配

敏捷的思维 quick mind　行动敏捷 to act nimbly
反应敏捷 a quick response

用法示例

猴子敏捷地爬到了树上。
The monkey climbed the tree swiftly.
运动员敏捷地跨过了栏杆。
The athlete nimbly jumped over the railings.
他虽上了年纪,思维还很敏捷。
He's old but his mind is still sharp.

mǐnruì
敏锐 （丁）形
keen

常用搭配

敏锐的眼睛 sharp eyes　敏锐的嗅觉 a keen scent
敏锐的听觉 sharp hearing

用法示例

那个法官有敏锐的洞察力。
The judge has keen insight.
盲人有敏锐的触觉。
The blind have a keen sense of touch.
那个目光敏锐的警察发现了那辆被盗的汽车。
A sharp-eyed police officer spotted the stolen car.

fēnglì
锋利 ⑩尖利 （丙）形
sharp

常用搭配

锋利的刀 a sharp knife
锋利的牙齿 sharp teeth

用法示例

猫有锋利的爪子。
Cats have sharp claws.
我的手指被一块锋利的石头划破了。
I cut my finger on a sharp stone.

yuānwang
冤枉 ⑩屈枉 （丙）动/形
① to wrong (sb)② be wronged

常用搭配

我被冤枉了。I was wronged.
你不该冤枉他。You shouldn't do him an injustice.

用法示例

你这样说就确实冤枉她了。
In saying this you do her an injustice.

我冤枉了她,怎样才能补救呢?
How can I repair the wrongs I have done to her?
你说他说谎是冤枉了他。
You wronged him by saying that he had lied.

yōuxiān
优先 （丁）形
priority

常用搭配

女士优先　Lady first.
优先发展重工业
give priority to the development of heavy industry

用法示例

对于求职者,我们优先考虑有一定经验的人。
In considering people for jobs, we give preference to those with some experience.
他本来应该优先考虑自身的安全,而不是金钱的损失。
He should have given priority to his safety rather than to the loss of money.
应优先考虑国防。
National defense must take precedence over all other questions.

kēmù
科目 （丁）名
subject

常用搭配

考试科目 an examination subject
选修科目 elective subjects

用法示例

图书馆的书是按科目分类的。
The books in the library are classified by subject.
他历史考试不及格,其他科目都通过了。
He got a fail in history and a pass in other subjects.
物理和数学都是我喜欢的科目。
Physics and math are my favorite subjects.

jiǎngpǐn
奖品 （丁）名
prize; award

常用搭配

颁发奖品 present a prize
得到奖品 receive an award

用法示例

给优胜者颁发了奖品。
The trophy was bestowed upon the winner.
市长在学校运动会上颁发奖品。
The mayor gave away the prizes at the school sports day.
胜者有选择奖品的优先权。
The winner has first pick of the prizes.

yōuhuì
优惠 （丁）形
preferential; favorable

常用搭配

优惠待遇 preferential treatment
优惠价格 favorable prices
优惠政策 preferential policy

用法示例

我们给了那个国家特殊的贸易优惠。
We've granted that country special trade preferences.
中国的投资政策为外国投资者提供了优惠待遇。
China's investment policy gives preferential treatment to foreign investors.

 词义辨析

敏捷、敏锐

　　"敏捷"和"敏锐"都是形容词,都有反应灵敏的意思。"敏捷"多用于动作行为,常用于人或动物;"敏锐"多用于感官、感觉,常用于人、动物或机器。有时这两个词都可以用于同一个事物,但意义有所不同,如:"思维敏捷"强调反应迅速,"思维敏锐"强调考虑得精细而准确。例如:①猫敏捷地爬上了屋顶。②这个记者具有敏锐的观察力。③狗具有敏锐的嗅觉。

　　敏捷 and 敏锐 are adjectives, meaning "to react nimbly". 敏捷 is mostly applied to describing actions and behaviors of a person or animal; while 敏锐 is mostly applied to describing a sense organ or the perception of a person, animal or machine. Sometime both of them can be applied to describing the same thing, but with different emphasis. "思维敏捷" (quick mind), stresses to react quickly; "思维敏锐" (acute mind), stresses to react decidedly and precisely. For example: ① The cat jumped up the roof swiftly. ② The reporter has acute insight. ③ Dogs have a keen sense of scent.

 练习

练习一、根据拼音写汉字,根据汉字写拼音

yōu(　　) yōu(　　) yuān(　　) fēng(　　) (　　)jié
(　　)久 (　　)惠 (　　)枉 (　　)利 敏(　　)

练习二、搭配连线

(1) 悠久的　　　　　　　A. 问题
(2) 敏感的　　　　　　　B. 目光
(3) 敏捷的　　　　　　　C. 历史
(4) 敏锐的　　　　　　　D. 牙齿
(5) 锋利的　　　　　　　E. 动作

练习三、从今天学习的生词中选择合适的词填空

1. 他买彩票中了个二等奖,_____ 是一辆自行车。
2. 小猫的爪子非常 _____,一不小心就会被它抓破。
3. 这家商场的电器正在举办 _____ 展销活动,所有展品一律打八折。
4. 他的思维很 _____,分析也很到位,教授很欣赏这个学生,给了他全班最高分。
5. 她的学习成绩很好,每年都拿一等 _____。
6. 如果能超额完成今年的任务,年底除了工资以外,还将得到一笔 _____。
7. 这个话题很 _____,大家还是换个话题吧,以免影响聚会的气氛。
8. 中国是个有着五千年 _____ 历史的国家。
9. 这家公司在招聘工作人员时注明"有相关工作经验者 _____ 录用"。
10. 他的眼光很 _____,一下子就发现了犯罪嫌疑人。

答案

练习一:
略
练习二:
(1) C　　(2)A　　(3)E　　(4)B　　(5)D
练习三:
1. 奖品　　2. 锋利　　3. 优惠　　4. 敏捷　　5. 奖学金
6. 奖金　　7. 敏感　　8. 悠久　　9. 优先　　10. 敏锐

Friday 星期五

jìlù
记录 ⑤ 记载 （乙）动/名
jìzǎi
record

常用搭配
记录过去的事 to record past events
犯罪记录 criminal record
根据记录 according to records
世界记录（纪录）a world record

用法示例
他用照相的方式记录生活。
He records life through taking pictures.
这个医生保存了医院所有重病者的记录。
The doctor keeps a record of all the serious illnesses in the hospital.
去年冬天是北京有记录以来最寒冷的冬天。
Last winter was Beijing's coldest winter on record.
他在奥运会上创造了新的举重世界记录（纪录）。
He set a new world record in weightlifting at the Olympic Games.

chéngdān
承担 （丙）动
undertake; assume

常用搭配
承担责任 assume responsibility
承担医疗费 afford the fee of medical treatment
承担风险 acceptance of risk

用法示例
我错了，我愿为此承担责任。
I made a mistake and I will assume responsibility for it.
他是领导，但他拒绝承担责任。
He is our leader, but he refused to accept the responsibility.
公司将承担他留学的费用。
His company will pay his tuition to study abroad.

hùnxiáo
混淆 （丙）动
confuse; mix up

常用搭配
混淆是非 confuse right and wrong
混淆视听 mislead the public

用法示例
千万别把这两个词相混淆。
Never mix up these two words.
别把澳大利亚和奥地利混淆了。
Please don't confuse Australia with Austria.

不要混淆手段与目的。
Don't confound the means with the ends.

hùnluàn
混乱 ⑤ 整齐 （丙）形
zhěngqí
confusion; disorder

常用搭配
陷入混乱 fall into disorder

用法示例
电力供应中断了，城市陷于混乱。
After the failure of the electricity supply, the city was in chaos.
生日晚会之后，房间里一片混乱。
The room was in confusion after the birthday party.
你的房间混乱不堪，请把它打扫干净。
Your room is a mess. Please tidy it.

hùnhé
混合 （丙）动
to mix

常用搭配
混合双打 mixed doubles   混合物 mixture

用法示例
他把牛奶和水混合在一起了。
He mixed milk with water.
空气是气体的混合物。
Air is a mixture of gases.
他们把麦麸和玉米粉混合起来喂猪。
They mix the bran and corn powder together to feed the pigs.

hùnzhuó
混浊 ⑤ 洁净 （丁）形
jiéjìng
turbid; muddy

常用搭配
混浊的空气 foul or stale air
混浊的河流 muddy waters

用法示例
河水变混浊了。
The water in the river became turbid.
我的啤酒看上去混浊不清。
My beer looks cloudy.

jìzǎi
记载 （丙）动/名
① record; write down ② account

常用搭配
记载历史事件 record historic events
详细地记载 record in detail

用法示例
历史书中记载了这个事件。
The event was recorded in the history books.
这些档案记载了战争的全过程。
These files recorded the whole course of the war.

地方志中有关于这次旱灾的记载。
There is an account of this drought in the local chronicles.

xīnlǐ
心理　　　　　　　　　　（丙）名

psychological; mental

常用搭配

心理学 psychology　　心理测验 psychological tests
儿童的心理 the children's psychology

用法示例

我们应该注重心理健康。
We should pay more attention to our mental health.
多年来他一直在研究犯罪心理。
He has been studying criminal psychology for many years.
李教授是一位著名的心理学家。
Professor Li is a very famous psychologist.

chéngkè
乘客　　　　　　　　　　（丙）名

passenger

常用搭配

公共汽车上没有乘客。There were no passengers on the bus.

用法示例

公共汽车司机要求乘客买票。
The bus driver asked the passengers to buy tickets.
飞机失事了，所有乘客和机组人员都遇难了。
The plane crashed, killing all its passengers and crew.
所有乘客都必须出示车票。
All passengers are required to show their tickets.

jìhào
记号　　　　　　　　　　（丁）名

mark

常用搭配

做记号 put a mark
地图上的记号 mark on a map

用法示例

他把他书上的记号擦掉了。
He rubbed out the mark in his book.
他用粉笔在那棵树上做了记号。
He marked the tree with chalk.

chéngbàn
承办　　　　　　　　　　（丁）动

undertake; accept an assignment

常用搭配

承办人 undertaker
由……承办 be undertook by…

用法示例

这位律师免费承办那个案件。
The lawyer took on the case without a fee.
北京市政府将承办一个国际会议。
An international conference will be held by the Beijing government.

chéngbàn
惩办　　　　chéngchǔ
　　　　　　　⊜ 惩处　　　（丁）动

punish

常用搭配

依法惩办罪犯 punish criminals according to the law

用法示例

你们如何惩办偷窃者？
How would you punish somebody for stealing?
政府将严厉惩办贪污的官员。
The government will punish the corrupt officer severely.

 **词义辨析**

记载、记录

1. 作为动词"记载"和"记录"都有把发生的事情记下来的意思。"记载"比较正式，往往是用写文章的形式，其内容往往是一些重要的事件或现象；"记录"用得比较广泛，可以用多种形式，其内容可以是各种事，尤其指听到的话。如：①他的书记载了事件的全过程。②他用摄像机记录了他的留学生活。

As verbs, 记载 and 记录 mean "to record". 记载 is formal, usually meaning to record in an article; its objects are usually some important events or phenomena; while 记录 is used widely, and can be used in many kinds of ways, and its objects can be all kinds of things, especially what one has heard. For example: ① His book records the whole course of the event. ② He recorded his life study abroad using a video camera.

2. 作为名词，"记录"和"记载"都有记述事情的材料的意思。"记载"往往是书中的文字材料；"记录"可以是在纸上、笔记上、档案上、磁带、光盘中的各种文字或音像的资料。"记录"还有一个意思是在一定时期和范围内记载下来的最好成绩，也可以写作"纪录"。如：①会议记录；②世界记录(纪录)；③根据历史书中的记载……

As nouns, 记录 and 记载 mean materials that record something. 记载 indicates literal data in a book; while 记录 can be all kinds of records, such as literal records or photo-tapes and videotapes in all forms, such as papers, notebooks, files, tapes, and DVDs. 记录 has another meaning of "an unsurpassed measurement", and it is usually written as 纪录. For example: ① the minutes of a meeting; ② world record; ③ according to the records in the history books…

 **练习**

练习一、根据拼音写汉字，根据汉字写拼音

（　　）xiáo　（　　）zǎi　chéng（　　）（　　）bàn　chéng（　　）
混（　　）　记（　　）　（　　）客　惩（　　）　（　　）担

练习二、搭配连线

(1) 承担　　　　　　　　A. 是非
(2) 犯罪　　　　　　　　B. 罪犯
(3) 惩办　　　　　　　　C. 会议
(4) 承办　　　　　　　　D. 心理
(5) 混淆　　　　　　　　E. 责任

练习三、从今天学习的生词中选择合适的词填空

1. 今年北京市 _____ 中国大学生运动会。
2. 广播里询问哪位 _____ 是医生,火车里有位病人需要帮助。
3. 商家早就掌握了消费者的 _____,所以产品的包装做得很华丽。
4. 我和一个大学同学一起租了房子,所有费用共同 _____。
5. 罪犯没有得到应有的 _____,而举报人的生命却受到威胁。
6. 从录像上看,发生暴力事件时,大家都失去了理智,场面十分 _____。
7. 老师让学生们在不懂的地方打个 _____,下课后可以单独问她。
8. 这篇日记真实 _____ 了我当时的心情。
9. 留学生们很容易 _____ 这两个词,所以老师讲得很仔细。
10. 史书上对这座古城当时的情况有详细的 _____。

✸ 答案

练习一:
略
练习二:

(1) E　　　(2)D　　　(3)B　　　(4)C　　　(5)A

练习三:

1. 承办　　2. 乘客　　3. 心理　　4. 承担　　5. 惩办
6. 混乱　　7. 记号　　8. 记录　　9. 混淆　　10. 记载

第 10 月,第 2 周的练习

练习一 . 根据词语给加点的字注音

1.( )　2.( )　3.( )　4.( )　5.( )
冤枉　　腐蚀　　混淆　　优惠　　惩罚

练习二 . 根据拼音填写词语

　　lì　　　lì　　　　　zǔ　　zǔ
1.锋( )　2.奖( )　3.阻( )　4.( )先　5.( )成

练习三 . 辨析并选择合适的词填空

1. 中国是一个发展中国家,跟发达国家相比还有相当大的( )。（差别、差距）
2. 这两种颜色一个深一个浅,( )很大,根本就不是一种颜色。（差别、差距）
3. 杀人犯承认了自己的罪行,但他拒不( )。（后悔、悔改）
4. 她说,虽然出国留学很辛苦,但她不( )自己当初的选择。（后悔、悔改）
5. 这是我们两个人之间的事情,请你不要( )。（干涉、干扰）
6. 学校内的施工噪音严重( )了学生上课。（干涉、干扰）
7. 很多动物都有人类不具备的能力,比如狗的嗅觉就比人类的( )。（敏捷、敏锐）
8. 他虽然上了年纪,动作还很( )。（敏捷、敏锐）
9. 开会时,秘书对会议内容作了详细的( )。（记录、记载）
10. 这件事情在史书中没有( ),但在民间却有各种各样的传说。（记录、记载）

练习四 . 选词填空

承认　　承担　　惩办　　优秀　　优质
承受　　承办　　惩罚　　优惠　　优先

1. 在招聘职员时,我们将( )考虑有工作经验的男士。
2. 总统( )自己犯了错误,希望广大民众原谅他。
3.推销员说如果我再买100块钱的东西的话会得到更多的( )。
4. 公民在享有权利的同时应该自觉( )相应的义务。
5. 这是( )面粉,所以做出来的馒头口感特别好。
6. 每年,这个城市的大学都会轮流( )大学生运动会。
7. 他是一名非常( )的游泳运动员,在奥运会上曾夺得8枚金牌。
8. 检查机关没有( )所有的事故责任人,对此,市民很不满意。
9. 河面上的冰很薄,( )不了你的重量,不要去滑冰。
10. 孩子考试不及格,父母很生气,( )他抄写试卷。

练习五 . 写出下列词语的同义词

1. 干涉( )　　　　　2. 记录( )
3. 差别( )　　　　　4. 启示( )
5. 锋利( )

✸ 答案

练习一 .

1.yuān　　2.fǔ　　3.xiáo　　4.huì　　5.fá

练习二 .

1. 利　　2. 励　　3. 力　　4. 祖　　5. 组

练习三 .

1. 差距　　2. 差别　　3. 悔改　　4. 后悔　　5. 干涉
6. 干扰　　7. 敏锐　　8. 敏捷　　9. 记录　　10. 记载

练习四 .

1. 优先　　2. 承认　　3. 优惠　　4. 承担　　5. 优质
6. 承办　　7. 优秀　　8. 惩办　　9. 承受　　10. 惩罚

练习五 .

1. 干预　　2. 记载　　3. 差异　　4. 启迪　　5. 尖利

练习六 .

1. 劣质　　2. 整齐　　3. 简略　　4. 洁净　　5. 惩罚

练习六 . 写出下列词语的反义词

1. 优质( )　　　　　2. 混乱( )
3. 详尽( )　　　　　4. 混浊( )
5. 奖励( )

10月 第3周的学习内容

星期一

xiàoguǒ
效果 回 **chéngxiào 成效** （乙）名

effect

常用搭配
取得良好效果 to obtain good results
特技效果 special effects
效果显著 bring about a striking effect

用法示例
这种药立刻对病人产生了效果。
The drug has had an immediate effect on the patient.
惩罚对他没有什么效果。
Punishment had very little effect on him.
我试用了这种新型洗涤剂,效果很好。
I've tried this new detergent, the effect of which is excellent.

chénglì
成立 （乙）动

establish; set up

常用搭配
成立公司 establish a company
成立一个组织 set up an organization

用法示例
这家电脑公司是去年成立的。
This computer company was established last year.
成立了一个委员会来调查此事。
A committee was set up to look into the matter.

chéngyuán
成员 （丁）名

member

常用搭配
家庭成员 family members
主席团成员 members of a presidium

用法示例
所有的成员都同意这项提议。
All the members were in agreement with the proposal.
我是我们学校足球俱乐部的成员。
I am a member of our school football club.
他们是委员会的成员。
They are members of the committee.

bǐrú
比如 回 **lìrú 例如** （丙）动

for example; for instance

常用搭配
比如说北京吧 Take Beijing for example

用法示例
你可以在这里买水果,比如柑橘和香蕉。
You can buy fruit here — oranges and bananas, for example.
政府已经在几个方面削减了开支,比如高速公路的建设。
The government has reduced spending in several areas, for example in the construction of highways.

bǐlì
比例 回 **bǐlǜ 比率** （乙）名

proportion

常用搭配
进口与出口的比例 proportion of imports to exports
按比例分配 proportional allotment
按……的比例 in the proportion of

用法示例
这幅画比例失调。
This painting lacks proportion.
男生和女生人数的比例是 2 比 1。
The ratio of schoolboys to schoolgirls is 2 to 1.
她的头与身体大小不成比例。
Her head is out of proportion to the size of her body.

péiyǎng
培养 （丙）动

to train; foster

常用搭配
培养人才 foster a talented person
培养艺术才能 foster artistic talent

用法示例
培养儿童良好的习惯是很重要的。
It is important to train children into good habits.
这所学校培养出了一些一流的学者。
The school has turned out some first-rate scholars.
我小的时候,母亲就培养我对音乐的兴趣。
Mother fostered my interest in music when I was young.

péiyù
培育 （丙）动

cultivate; to breed

常用搭配
培育新一代 cultivate a new generation
培育水稻新品种 breed new varieties of rice

这些是农学院培育的改良品种。

These are improved strains bred by the Agricultural College.

他的工作是培育树苗。

His work is to grow saplings.

shèlì
设立　⑤建立　（丁）动

set up; establish

常用搭配

设立新的机构 set up a new organization

设立常务委员会 set up a standing committee

用法示例

大会设立了一个专门委员会对这个问题进行调查研究。

The Congress set up a special committee to investigate the matter.

这是专门为老年人设立的娱乐项目。

That is special recreational program for the elderly.

zhuóyuè
卓越　（丁）形

excellent; outstanding

常用搭配

卓越的贡献 outstanding contributions

卓越的人才 an eminently talented man

卓越的成就 remarkable achievements

用法示例

他是个卓越的音乐家。

He is a very fine musician.

没有人怀疑他在金融事务中的卓越成就。

No one doubted his superiority in financial matters.

莎士比亚是最卓越的戏剧家。

Shakespeare is an eminent playwright.

chāoyuè
超越　（丁）动

surpass; exceed; transcend

常用搭配

超越障碍 surmount an obstacle

超越边界 surpass the boundaries

用法示例

这位工作人员未经许可就这样做,显然,超越了他的职责范围。

It's clear that the clerk had acted above his station in doing so without authority.

他已经超越所有的对手了。

He has been risen above all his rivals.

péikuǎn
赔款　（丁）名

reparations

常用搭配

偿付赔款 pay reparations

战争赔款 reparation of war

用法示例

战胜国要求战败国交付巨额赔款。

The victorious nations are demanding huge indemnities from their former enemies.

她要求赔款遭到拒绝,原因是她事先没有交纳保险费。

Her claim was disallowed on the ground(s) that she had not paid her premium.

我认为你该向保险公司索取赔款。

I think you can claim money from the insurer.

jiā yù hù xiǎo
家喻户晓　（丁）

be known to all; widely known

常用搭配

家喻户晓的作家 a widely known writer

用法示例

这一产品非常成功,其名称已经家喻户晓。

The product was so successful that its name became a household word.

在中国,她是家喻户晓的明星。

She is a movie star who is known to all in China.

 词义辨析

培养、培育

　　"培养"和"培育"都是动词,都有养育的意思,都可以用于人或动植物。"培养"强调长期的教育和训练,多用于人;"培育"强调抚育并促其成长,多用于动物和植物。实际上,"培养"和"培育"有时可以交换使用,但是应注意这些固定搭配,如:①培养好习惯,②培养好的作风,③培养细菌,④培养接班人,⑤培育树苗,⑥培育英才,⑦培育市场等。

　　Both 培养 and 培育 are verbs, meaning "to foster"; they can be applied to people, animals or plants. 培养 stresses education and training in the long run, usually referring to people; while 培育 stresses "help to grow and develop", usually referring to animals or plants. In fact, 培养 and 培育 are interchangable sometimes, but please pay attention to the following collocations: ①培养好习惯 (develop a good habit), ②培养好的作风 (develop a good style of work), ③培养细菌 (culturing of bacteria), ④培养接班人 (cultivate a successor), ⑤培育树苗 (grow a sapling), ⑥培育英才 (cultivate the elite), ⑦培育市场 (develop markets),etc.

 **练习**

练习一、根据拼音写汉字，根据汉字写拼音

xiào ( ) ( )yuè péi ( ) péi ( )chéng ( )
( )果 卓( )( )款 ( )育 ( )员

练习二、搭配连线

(1) 效果 　　　　A. 人才
(2) 家庭 　　　　B. 赔款
(3) 成立 　　　　C. 成员
(4) 巨额 　　　　D. 显著
(5) 培养 　　　　E. 公司

练习三、从今天学习的生词中选择合适的词填空

1. 这个歌星在成名以前曾经是学校乐队的六名 ＿＿＿＿＿＿＿ 之一。
2. 这位企业家在很多大学 ＿＿＿＿＿＿＿ 了以他名字命名的奖学金。
3. 这位相声演员非常有名，在中国大陆是个 ＿＿＿＿＿＿＿ 的人物。
4. 打工赚了点钱后，他马上 ＿＿＿＿＿＿＿ 了自己的公司。
5. 我的车发生事故后，保险公司找了很多理由拒绝 ＿＿＿＿＿＿＿。
6. 她在处理事务过程中表现出来的 ＿＿＿＿＿＿＿ 才能引起了总裁的注意，并提升她为总经理。
7. 这种药治疗感冒的 ＿＿＿＿＿＿＿ 相当好。
8. 他以自己的聪明才智和勤奋努力 ＿＿＿＿＿＿＿ 了所有对手。
9. 她三岁开始学习舞蹈，父母想把她 ＿＿＿＿＿＿＿ 成一名舞蹈家。
10. 咱们学校欧洲留学生和亚洲留学生的 ＿＿＿＿＿＿＿ 是多少？

答案

练习一：
略

练习二：

(1) D　　(2)C　　(3)E　　(4)B　　(5)A

练习三：

1. 成员　　2. 设立　　3. 家喻户晓　4. 成立　　5. 赔款
6. 卓越　　7. 效果　　8. 超越　　9. 培养　　10. 比例

 星期二

yǒuguān
有关 （乙）动
to relate to; to concern

常用搭配
有关细节 relevant details
有关信息 relevant information

用法示例
无疑，她的死和政治有关。
No doubt her death is related to politics.
在有关钱的问题上，我总是尽量谨慎。
Where money is concerned, I always try to be very careful.
我要给有关人员发这份文件。
I will send the memorandum to those concerned.

cōngming yúchǔn
聪明 反愚蠢 （乙）形
intelligent; clever

常用搭配
聪明的男孩 a clever boy
他真聪明。He is so wise.

用法示例
他自以为聪明。
He thinks himself smart.
他并不聪明，但很勤奋。
He is not bright, but he always works hard.
据说海豚比其它动物聪明。
It is said that dolphins are more intelligent than other animals.

jiǎohuá
狡猾 （丙）形
sly; crafty

常用搭配
狡猾的商人 a crafty businessman
狡猾的老狐狸 a crafty old fox

用法示例
他像狐狸一样狡猾。
He is as cunning as a fox.
她对问题避而不答，显示出她很狡猾。
She showed her cunning in the way she avoided answering the question.
许多政客都是狡猾的诡辩家。
Many politicians are cunning sophists.

zhuīqiú
追求 （丙）动
pursue; seek

常用搭配

追求名誉 the quest for honor　追求享受 seek enjoyment
追求幸福 pursue happiness

用法示例

我们为追求幸福生活而努力工作。
We work hard in pursuit of a happy life.
他在千方百计地追求名利。
He is making every effort to court wealth and fame.
他已经追求李小姐六个月了。
He has been courting Miss Li for six months.

yúlè
娱乐　　　　　　　　　　（丙）动／名

① entertain ② entertainment

常用搭配

娱乐活动 recreational activities
娱乐设施 recreational facilities
娱乐中心 recreational centre

用法示例

象棋是他最喜欢的娱乐活动。
Chess is his favorite diversion.
电影院是公众娱乐场所。
A cinema is a public place of entertainment.
电视提供大众化的娱乐。
Television provides universal entertainment.

yǒujī
有机　　　　　　　　　　　（丁）形

organic

常用搭配

有机化学 organic chemistry
有机肥料 organic fertilizer
有机的组成部分 an organic part

用法示例

细菌会侵入有机体。
Germs may invade the organism.
我们应该把社会看作一个有机的整体。
We should consider the society as an organic whole.

shēngyù　　　　　míngyù
声誉　　　　◎名誉　　　　（丁）名

fame; repute

常用搭配

国际声誉 international fame
一家声誉好的旅馆 a hotel of repute
声誉扫地 fall into disrepute

用法示例

他赢得了钢琴家的声誉。
He won renown as a pianist.
他是一名享有国际声誉的科学家。
He is a scientist of international acclaim.
牛津大学享有很高的声誉。
The University of Oxford has a lot of prestige.

zhuījiū　　　　　　zhuīchá
追究　　　◎追查　　　　　（丁）动

① investigate ② look into

常用搭配

追究事故责任
investigate and affix the responsibility for an accident
概不追究……
no action will be taken to investigate…

用法示例

这场火灾应该追究谁的责任？
Who is to blame for starting the fire?
如果有人考试作弊，我们一定会追究。
If you cheat in the exam you'll be caught.
你要是道个歉，我们就不追究这件事了。
If you apologize we'll forget about the incident.

zhuīgǎn　　　　　　táotuō
追赶　　　◎逃脱　　　　　（丁）动

chase after; pursue

常用搭配

追赶世界先进水平
try to catch up with the advanced world

用法示例

狗喜欢追赶兔子。
Dogs like chasing rabbits.
他急忙下车去追赶小偷。
He quickly got off the bus and chased after the thief.
我因为追赶公共汽车，跑得上气不接下气。
I was out of breath while running after the bus.

yǒudài
有待　　　　　　　　　　　（丁）动

not yet (done)

常用搭配

有待改进 to have much room for improvement
有待解决 remains to be solved

用法示例

这个理论正确与否还有待证明。
Whether the theory is right or not remains to be seen.
我知道还有很多困难有待克服。
I know there are many difficulties to be overcome.

jù jīng huì shén
聚精会神　　　　　　　　　（丙）

concentrate one's attention

常用搭配

他聚精会神地听讲。
He is listening to the lecture with avid attention.

用法示例

他冷静沉着，聚精会神地判断如何打败对手。
He was calm and concentrated in working out how to
defeat his opponent.

孩子们聚精会神地观看演出。

The students zeroed in on the performance.

tiān cháng dì jiǔ

天 长 地 久 　　　　　　　　（丁）

a very long time; everlasting

用法示例

他说爱她,爱到天长地久。

He said he'd love her to the end of time.

愿我们的友谊天长地久。

I hope our friendship is everlasting.

词义辨析

追求、追赶

　　"追求"和"追赶"都是动词,都有努力接近或得到目标的意思。"追求"的对象一般是抽象的,如:进步、真理、幸福、享受、权力、利润等,"追求"也可以表示向异性求爱;"追赶"的对象一般是具体的,往往是移动或躲藏的人或物,或正在发展变化的事物,如:①追赶公共汽车,②追赶兔子,③追赶世界先进水平等。

　　Both 追求 and 追赶 are verbs, meaning "to follow in an effort to overtake or gain". The objects of 追求 are usually something abstract, such as progress, truth, happiness, enjoyment, power, profit, etc. and 追求 also means "to court; to try to win the love of a women"; while the objects of 追赶 are something concrete, such as somebody or something that is moving or escaping, or something that is developing or changing. For example: ① run after the bus, ② run after rabbits, ③ try to catch up with the advanced world, etc.

练习

练习一、根据拼音写汉字,根据汉字写拼音

jiǎo( )　　yú( )( )yù ( )jiū cōng ( )

( )猾　　( )乐 声( )　　追( )( )明

练习二、搭配连线

(1) 有待　　　　　　　　A. 设施

(2) 追究　　　　　　　　B. 改进

(3) 追求　　　　　　　　C. 化学

(4) 娱乐　　　　　　　　D. 名利

(5) 有机　　　　　　　　E. 责任

练习三、从今天学习的生词中选择合适的词填空

1. 老师讲课时,大家都在 _____ 地听讲。

2. 这个孩子又勤奋又 _____,反应特别快,尤其擅长数学。

3. 如果发现有人用我们公司的商标出售劣质产品,我们将 _____ 他的法律责任。

4. 他下了课就去打工,休息的时间都难以保证,更没有 _____ 的时间了。

5. 这个女孩性格特别好,而且非常优秀,_____ 她的男孩子很多。

6. 他的祖父在工商界享有很高的 _____,大家都对他十分敬重。

7. 双方都有合作的意愿,但合作的方式还 _____ 进一步商议。

8. 虽然犯罪分子很 _____,但警察还是找到了他们在现场留下的证据。

9. 与世界发展的脚步相比,中国还需要相当长的时间才能 _____ 得上。

10. 事故发生以后,政府立即派人调查 _____ 人员的责任。

答案

练习一:

略

练习二:

(1) B　　(2)E　　(3)D　　(4)A　　(5)C

练习三:

1. 聚精会神 2. 聪明　　3. 追究　　4. 娱乐　　5. 追求

6. 声誉　　7. 有待　　8. 狡猾　　9. 追赶　　10. 有关

星期三

流利 (乙)形
liúlì

fluent

常用搭配
说得流利 speak fluently

用法示例
他说一口流利的德语。
He speaks fluent German.
她能流利地说汉语。
She can speak Chinese fluently.
他的英语说得非常流利。
He speaks English with great fluency.

秩序 (乙)名
zhìxù

order

常用搭配
公共秩序 public order
秩序井然 in perfect order

用法示例
维护公共秩序是警察的职责。
It's the duty of the police to preserve the public order.
有些教师觉得课堂秩序很难维持。
Some teachers find it difficult to keep order in their classes.
法律和秩序对一个国家很重要。
Law and order are vital to a country.

欣赏 (丙)动
xīnshǎng

appreciate; enjoy

常用搭配
欣赏诗歌 appreciate poetry
欣赏音乐 enjoy music

用法示例
我很欣赏他对工作的专注精神。
I really appreciate his absorption in his work.
他太肤浅,无法欣赏这类文学巨著。
He is too superficial to appreciate great literature like this.
她对好音乐几乎没有欣赏能力。
She shows little appreciation of good music.

叙述 (丙)动
xùshù

narrate; recount

常用搭配
叙述事件的过程 to narrate the process of an event
叙述的技巧 narrative skill

用法示例
他详细叙述了那天发生的事情。
He recounted the happenings of the day.
探险者叙述他的冒险经历。
The explorer related his adventures.
叙述清楚比语言优美更重要。
The clarity of the statement is more important than the beauty of language.

软弱 ⊠坚强 (丙)形
ruǎnruò   jiānqiáng

weak; feeble

常用搭配
内心软弱 a weak heart
软弱的性格 a weak character

用法示例
他被看作是个软弱无能的领导。
He is considered a weak leader.
她双腿仍有些软弱无力,但总的情况尚好。
There is still some weakness in her legs, but her general condition is good.
怕这怕那的人是软弱的人。
A fearful person is a weak person.

勤劳 ⊜勤勉 (丙)形
qínláo   qínmiǎn

hardworking; industrious

常用搭配
勤劳的农夫 a hardworking farmer
勤劳的蜜蜂 laborious bees
勤劳的双手 an untiring pair of hands

用法示例
诚实、勤劳和善良是幸福生活的要素。
Honesty, industry and kindness are elements of a good life.
他靠勤劳而获得成功。
His success was achieved through hard work.
他的儿子已成长为一个健壮勤劳的小伙子。
His son has grown up into a sturdy, hardworking young man.

勤奋 ⊠懒惰 (丁)形
qínfèn   lǎnduò

diligent

常用搭配
勤奋的学生 diligent student
工作勤奋 be diligent in one's work

用法示例
这孩子比其他人都勤奋。
The boy is more diligent than anybody else.
他们的学生勤奋学习。
Their students are diligent about their studies.
勤奋通向成功。
Diligence is often the gateway to success.

85

gōngxù

工序 （丁）名

working procedure

常用搭配

生产工序 manufacturing process

用法示例

制造汽车要经过很多工序。

The process of building a car involves many steps.

刘师傅把每道工序演示给我们看，然后让我们自己干。

Master Liu demonstrated each process to us, and then let us do it ourselves.

shùnxù

顺序 ⊜次序 （丁）名

cìxù

sequence; order

常用搭配

按字母顺序 in alphabetical order

历史上的先后顺序 historical sequence

用法示例

该索引是按字母顺序排列的。

The index is arranged in alphabetical order.

他把书按顺序摆在书架上。

He placed the books on the shelf in order.

xùyán

序言 （丁）名

preface

常用搭配

书的序言 preface of a book

用法示例

这本书的序言非常简短。

The preface of this book is very brief.

他给这本日记写了序言，简述了日记发现的经过。

He prefaced the diaries with a short account of how they were discovered.

她以道歉的话作为书的序言。

She prefaced her book with an apology.

xīnqín

辛勤 （丁）形

hardworking; industrious

常用搭配

辛勤劳动 to work diligently

用法示例

辛勤劳动带来成功。

Hard work produces success.

他通过辛勤努力获得成功。

He succeeded by dint of hard work.

他靠自己辛勤劳动生活。

He earns his living by the sweat of his brow.

xiǎng fāng shè fǎ

想 方 设 法 （丁）

try every means; by hook or by crook

常用搭配

想方设法帮助他们 try every means to help them

用法示例

我们想方设法与他们取得联系。

We tried every means to get in touch with them.

他想方设法安慰她。

He tried to find ways of mollifying her.

当地的军人想方设法帮助地震灾民。

The local army used every means to help the victims of the earthquake.

 词义辨析

勤劳、勤奋

"勤劳"和"勤奋"都是形容词。"勤劳"指努力劳动，不怕辛苦，多用于日常的生活、工作中的体力劳动，不能作状语；"勤奋"指坚持努力进取，多用于学习、研究等脑力劳动，可以作状语。例如：①她是一个勤劳善良的女人。②同学们都在勤奋地学习。

Both 勤劳 and 勤奋 are adjectives. 勤劳 means "to strive painstakingly, and be hardworking". It is usually applied to daily life or work, mainly are manual labor, but it can not function as an adverbial; while 勤奋 means "to be persevering, painstaking and take enterprising effort". It is usually used to modify mental labor, such as study or research, and it can function as an adverbial. For example: ① She is an industrious and kind woman. ② The students are studying diligently.

 **练习**

练习一、根据拼音写汉字，根据汉字写拼音

zhì（   ） xù（   ） shǎng（   ） láo（   ） ruò
（   ）序 （   ）述 欣（   ） 勤（   ） 软（   ）

练习二、搭配连线

(1) 秩序　　　　　　　　A. 软弱
(2) 欣赏　　　　　　　　B. 井然
(3) 性格　　　　　　　　C. 音乐
(4) 工作　　　　　　　　D. 劳动
(5) 辛勤　　　　　　　　E. 勤奋

练习三、从今天学习的生词中选择合适的词填空

1. 请大家自觉地按 _____ 排队上车。
2. 父母用 _____ 的双手把我们两个孩子抚养成人，并给我们提供了受教育的机会。
3. 生产玩具的过程很复杂，最后一道 _____ 是把检验合格的玩具包装起来。
4. 农民的 _____ 劳动，换来了粮食的大丰收。
5. 他的母亲是中国人，所以他能说一口 _____ 的普通话。
6. 目击证人向法官 _____ 了那天下午发生的事情。
7. 现在的父母很溺爱孩子，总会 _____ 地满足孩子的要求。
8. 他请自己的导师为他即将出版的新书写了 _____。
9. 前方出现了交通事故，交警赶来维持交通 _____。
10. 这个孩子的性格有点 _____，所以别的孩子经常欺负他。

答案

练习一：
略
练习二：
(1) B　　　(2)C　　　(3)A　　　(4)E　　　(5)D
练习三：
1. 顺序　　2. 勤劳　　3. 工序　　4. 辛勤　　5. 流利
6. 叙述　　7. 想方设法 8. 序言　　9. 秩序　　10. 软弱

星期四

zhéxué
哲学　　　　　　　　　　　（乙）名

philosophy

常用搭配

哲学家 philosopher
教育哲学 educational philosophy
哲学思想 philosophic thinking

用法示例

他是一位哲学博士。
He is a Doctor of Philosophy.
她作了一次有关中国古代哲学的讲座。
She delivered a lecture on ancient Chinese philosophy.

xìjūn
细菌　　　　　　　　　　　（乙）名

germ; bacteria

常用搭配

细菌性疾病 bacterial diseases
细菌的传播 the spread of bacteria

用法示例

细菌太小，肉眼看不见。
Bacteria are too small to see with the naked eye.
这种消毒剂可以杀灭多种细菌。
This disinfectant can kill many kinds of germs.
许多疾病是由细菌引起的。
Many diseases are caused by bacteria.

xúnhuán
循环　　　　　　　　　　　（丙）动

circulate

常用搭配

血液循环 circulation of the blood
恶性循环 vicious circle

用法示例

四季循环交替。
The seasons follow each other in rotation.
循环小数" 3.999……" 亦作" 3.9 循环"。
The recurring decimal 3.999... is also described as 3.9 recurring.
我得有经验才能找到工作，可是没有工作我就无法获得经验——这真是个恶性循环。
I need experience to get a job, but without a job I can't get experience. It's a vicious circle.

zhémó
折磨　　　　　　　　　　　（丙）动/名

① persecute ② torment

常用搭配

折磨他 torture him

受病痛折磨 suffer severely from an illness

遭受折磨 suffer torment

用法示例

她正在经受牙痛的折磨。

She is being tormented by toothache.

他受尽了敌人的折磨。

He underwent all kinds of torture at the hands of the enemy.

对我来说,跟他一起工作是一种折磨。

Working with him is a torment to me.

yóuyù
犹豫　　　　　　　　　　　　　（丙）形

hesitate

常用搭配

毫不犹豫 without hesitation

犹豫不决 be hesitant

犹犹豫豫 shilly-shally

用法示例

不要犹豫,一有机会就抓住它!

Don't hesitate; seize the first opportunity that comes along!

她毫不犹豫地答应了。

She agreed without hesitation.

他在回答之前犹豫了一下,因为他不知道说什么。

He hesitated before he answered because he didn't know what to say.

chóuchú
踌躇　　　　⊠ guǒduàn 果断　　　（丁）动

① hesitate ② shilly-shally

常用搭配

踌躇不定 be hesitant

踌躇不安 be in fidgets

踌躇满志 be enormously proud of one's success

用法示例

他踌躇不定,又丧失了一次机会。

He hesitated and lost his chance again.

她踌躇不决,不知该怎样宣布这条坏消息。

She held back, not knowing how to break the terrible news.

我踌躇了好一阵,最后做了决定。

I dithered for quite a while, then finally made up my mind.

xúnwèn
询问　　　⊜ xùnwèn 讯问　　　（丁）动

inquire; ask

常用搭配

询问价格 inquire about prices

向某人询问某事 make inquiries of sb. about sth

用法示例

她询问我母亲的健康情况。

She inquired after my mother's health.

警察询问过路的人是否看到了事故发生的经过。

Police asked passers-by if they had seen the accident happen.

他询问李先生的手术是否成功。

He asked if Mr Li's operation had been successful.

xúnluó
巡逻　　　⊜ xúnchá 巡查　　　（丁）动

patrol

常用搭配

巡逻艇 patrol boat

执行巡逻任务 be on patrol duty

用法示例

晚上,警察在街道上巡逻。

Police patrol the streets at night.

恐怖分子袭击了两名正在巡逻的士兵。

Terrorists attacked two patrolling soldiers.

每隔一小时就有一名警察在我们这条街上巡逻。

Every hour a policeman patrolled our street.

zīxún
咨询　　　　　　　　　　　　　（丁）动

① consult ② advisory

常用搭配

咨询服务 consulting service

咨询公司 consulting corporation

咨询委员会 an advisory committee

用法示例

我向李先生咨询购买汽车的事。

I consulted Mr. Li about buying a car.

正常的咨询费是 50 美元。

The standard consultation fee is US $50.

xìjié
细节　　　⊠ gěnggài 梗概　　　（丁）名

particulars; detail

常用搭配

讨论细节问题 discuss the details

计划的细节 the details of a plan

用法示例

协议的细节尚未公布。

The full details of the agreement haven't been made public.

他非常仔细,把每一个细节都核对过了。

He was careful enough to check every detail.

任何细节都不得疏忽。

Not a single detail is to be omitted.

zhēng xiān kǒng hòu
争先恐后　　　　　　　　　　　（丁）

vie with each other in doing something

用法示例

她的追求者几乎是争先恐后地向她献殷勤。

Her admirers fell over each other with offers of hospitality.

同学们争先恐后地向他提问。
Students compete to be the first to ask the question.

gēn shēn dì gù
根 深 蒂 固 　　　　　　　（丁）

deep - rooted

【用法示例】

我们社会中普遍存在着根深蒂固的保守思想。
There is a deep-seated conservatism in our society.
这种思想在他的脑海里是根深蒂固的,不可能说服他。
The idea is deeply-rooted in his mind. It's impossible to persuade him otherwise.

 **词义辨析**

犹豫、踌躇

　　"犹豫"和"踌躇"都可以表示拿不定主意。"犹豫"是形容词,可以重叠使用,如"犹犹豫豫",可以作定语和状语。"踌躇"是动词,不可以重叠使用,不可以做定语或状语,主要用于书面语。另外"踌躇"还可以表示得意的样子,如"踌躇满志"。例如:①她对是否接受邀请犹豫不决。②他毫不犹豫地说出了他的想法。③在下定决心前,他踌躇了一下。

　　Both 犹豫 and 踌躇 mean "to hesitate". 犹豫 is an adjective, and it can be used in a repeated form such as 犹犹豫豫 . It can function as an attributive or an adverbial. 踌躇 is a verb, can not be used in a repeated form, and functions as an attributive or an adverbial; it is mainly used in writing. 踌躇 also means "being smug", e.g. 踌躇满志 (be enormously proud of one's success). For example: ① She was hesitant about accepting the invitation. ② He spoke his opinion without hesitation. ③ He hesitated for a while before he made up his mind.

 **练习**

练习一、根据拼音写汉字，根据汉字写拼音

( )jūn　zhé( )　chóu( )( )yù　xún( )
细( )　( )磨　( )踌　犹( )　( )环

练习二、搭配连线

(1) 毫不　　　　　　　　A. 折磨
(2) 恶性　　　　　　　　B. 犹豫
(3) 消灭　　　　　　　　C. 不安
(4) 遭受　　　　　　　　D. 循环
(5) 踌躇　　　　　　　　E. 细菌

练习三、从今天学习的生词中选择合适的词填空

1. 如果您想进一步了解情况,可以打我们公司的_____电话。
2. 重男轻女的思想在有些人心里_____,很难改变。
3. 我租住的房子很安全,因为小区里有保安夜间_____。
4. 要不要告诉对方真相呢,她对此显得有点_____不决。
5. 老师让大家比赛爬山,看谁最先爬到山顶,老师的话刚说完,学生们就_____地往山顶跑去。
6. 运动可以使血液流动的速度加快,促进血液_____。
7. 我丈夫在外地工作,不能经常回家,但他常给家里打电话,_____我和女儿的情况。
8. 我的姥姥长期受病痛的_____,去世时瘦得只有80斤了。
9. 总的来说,我同意你们制订的活动方案,但是,有些_____还需要考虑得更周到。
10. 上大学时他_____满志,可是工作后,热情一天天消退了。

答案

练习一:
略

练习二:
(1) B　　　(2)D　　　(3)E　　　(4)A　　　(5)C

练习三:
1. 咨询　　2. 根深蒂固3. 巡逻　　4. 犹豫
5. 争先恐后6. 循环　　7. 询问　　8. 折磨
9. 细节　　10. 踌躇

星期五

yùjiàn
遇见 （乙）动
meet
常用搭配
偶然遇见 to meet by chance
遇见一位同学 meet a classmate
用法示例
真想不到在这儿遇见你。
Fancy seeing you here.
我今天在街上遇见了我的老师。
I ran into my teacher in the street today.
昨天我在火车上遇见一位朋友。
I came across a friend on the train yesterday.

xìtǒng
系统 （乙）名
system
常用搭配
系统工程 systematic engineering
消化系统 the digestive system
神经系统 the nervous system
用法示例
你知道怎么登录这个系统吗？
Do you know how to log into the system?
这个街区的供暖系统不太好。
The heating system in this block doesn't work well.
我们有一个庞大的铁路系统。
We have a large system of railways.

xiézuò
协作 （丙）动
cooperate; coordinate
常用搭配
商业协作 commercial coordination
协作精神 cooperative spirit
用法示例
感谢你们的协作。
Thank you for your cooperation.
为了提高效率，我们要加强协作。
Our efforts need to be further coordinated for greater efficiency.
社会公益服务机构和当地医生应该加强协作。
There should be more interaction between social services and local doctors.

yùbào
预报 （丙）动/名
forecast
常用搭配
天气预报 weather forecast
预报交通情况 forecast the traffic condition
地震预报 earthquake forecast
用法示例
专家预报火山将在本周爆发。
The expert forecasted that the volcano would erupt this week.
这次地震早在几个月以前就发布了预报。
Notice of this earthquake had been issued several months before it occurred.
天气预报说明天是晴天。
The weather forecast says it will be sunny tomorrow.

yǐncáng
隐藏 ⑩ 隐蔽 yǐnbì （丁）动
hide; lurk
常用搭配
隐藏逃犯 to hide an escaped criminal
隐藏在大树后边 lurk behind a big tree
用法示例
海关查出了隐藏在货物中的海洛因。
Customs have found heroin hidden in the freight.
森林中隐藏着危险。
Danger lurked in the forest.
她把字条隐藏在衣服里。
She concealed the note in her dress.

yǐnbì
隐蔽 ⊗ 暴露 bàolù （丁）动/形
① conceal ② covert
常用搭配
隐蔽起来 to be concealed
隐蔽的敌人 a covert enemy
公开的和隐蔽的活动 overt and covert activities
用法示例
那里没有树木，军队无法隐蔽。
The land was bare and provided no cover for the troops.
他们想找个地方隐蔽起来。
They wanted to find a place to take cover.
拐角处有个隐蔽的入口。
There is a hidden entrance of concealment just around the corner.

yùyán
寓言 （丁）名
fable
常用搭配
《伊索寓言》Aesop's Fables   讲寓言故事 tell a fable
用法示例
寓言常以动物为主角。
Fables often have animals as their main characters.
他经常给学生读寓言故事。
He often reads fables to his students.

yùjiàn
预见

yùzhī
⑥ 预知

（丁）动／名

① foresee ② foresight

常用搭配

预见到有问题 to foresee trouble
这是可以预见的。This can be predicted.

用法示例

这些困难是无法预见的。
The difficulties could not have been foreseen.
他预见到做这件工作需要很长时间。
He foresaw that the job would take a long time.
她声称能预见未来。
She claims to see into the future.

yùwàng
欲望

（丁）名

lust; desire

常用搭配

满足某人的欲望 satisfy sb's desire
受欲望驱使 be stung with desire

用法示例

拥有越多，欲望越高。
The more you have, the more you want.
他是个没什么欲望的人。
He is a man of few wants.
他对财富没有欲望。
He has no desire for wealth.

xiéshāng
协商

（丁）动

negotiate; talk things over

常用搭配

与某人协商 negotiate with sb.
协商解决 settle sth through negociation
民主协商 democratic consultation

用法示例

双方之间的任何争议都应通过友好协商来解决。
Any dispute between the two parties shall be settled by friendly consultation.
参加协商的人花了十个小时才敲定这笔生意。
It took the negotiator ten hours to nail down the deal.

xièlòu
泄露

bǎomì
⑥ 保密

（丁）动

divulge; leak (information)

常用搭配

泄露机密 let out a secret　燃料泄露 fuel leak

用法示例

辐射泄露的消息引起了公众的普遍恐慌。
The news of the radiation leak caused widespread public alarm.
是谁把消息泄露给新闻界的？
Who leaked the news to the press?

这些细节原属秘密，可是不知怎么给泄露出去了。
The details were supposed to be secret but somehow leaked out.

jīng dǎ　xì suàn
精打细算

（丁）

calculate carefully; budget strictly

常用搭配

为节约能源而精打细算 calculate carefully to save energy

用法示例

我们精打细算就能买辆新汽车了。
If we budget carefully, we'll be able to afford a new car.
爸爸没工作了，妈妈不得不精打细算地过日子。
My father lost his job and my mother had to budget strictly in everyday life.

 词义辨析

隐藏、隐蔽

　　"隐藏"和"隐蔽"都是动词，都有防止被看到的意思。"隐藏"是及物动词，可以带宾语；"隐蔽"是不及物动词，不能带宾语。"隐蔽"还是形容词，"隐藏"不是。例如：①有一个可疑的人隐藏／隐蔽在暗处。②母狮子在浓密的草丛中隐藏幼崽。③他是从一个隐蔽的出口逃走的。

　　Both 隐藏 and 隐蔽 are verbs, meaning "to keep from being seen or found". 隐藏 is a transitive verb, and it can be followed by objects; while 隐蔽 is an intransitive verb, and it can not be followed by objects. 隐蔽 is also an adjective; 隐藏 is not. For example: ① There is a suspicious man lurking in the shadows. ② The lioness concealed her cubs in the tall grass. ③ He escaped through a hidden exit.

 练习

练习一、根据拼音写汉字，根据汉字写拼音

yù（　）（　）bì　xié（　）　xiè（　）（　）yán
（　）望　隐（　）（　）商　（　）露　寓（　）

练习二、搭配连线

(1) 满足　　　　　　　　A. 机密
(2) 民主　　　　　　　　B. 预报
(3) 泄露　　　　　　　　C. 欲望
(4) 系统　　　　　　　　D. 协商
(5) 天气　　　　　　　　E. 工程

练习三、从今天学习的生词中选择合适的词填空

1. 强烈的求知 _____ 激励他刻苦学习。
2. 父母相继失业，我们不得不 _____ 地过日子。
3. 这是一则 _____ 故事，故事的主角是大灰狼和小白兔。
4. 经过 _____，厂家和消费者达成了赔偿协议。

5. 玩捉迷藏时,有个孩子藏到了一个非常 _____ 的角落里,谁都没找到他。

6. 对方公司知道了我们的销售计划,肯定是有人 _____ 了消息。

7. 总经理要求各个部门要相互 _____,提高工作效率。

8. 天气 _____ 说今天有雨,可是到现在也没下。

9. 法官提醒说: _____ 证据是违法的,要负法律责任。

10. 这个人很英明,他 _____ 到了这个行业前景不好,所以毅然转行了。

答案

练习一:
略

练习二:
(1) C   (2)D   (3)A   (4)E   (5)B

练习三:

1. 欲望	2. 精打细算	3. 寓言	4. 协商	5. 隐蔽
6. 泄露	7. 协作	8. 预报	9. 隐藏	10. 预见

第10月,第3周的练习

练习一 . 根据词语给加点的字注音
1.( ) 2.( )   3.( )   4.( )   5.( )
娱乐   秩序   巡逻   细菌   赔款

练习二 . 根据拼音填写词语
      yù   yù   yù   yù   yù
1. 声( ) 2. 养( ) 3.( )报 4. 犹( ) 5.( )望

练习三 . 辨析并选择合适的词填空
1. 这种水稻新品种是研究人员经过两年时间( )的。(培养、培育)

2. 父母从她儿童时代起就开始( )她对艺术的兴趣。(培养、培育)

3. 作为一家知名企业,他们不仅( )利润,还十分重视社会效益。(追求、追赶)

4. 他知道自己基础比较差,于是每天努力学习,希望能( )上其他同学。(追求、追赶)

5. 每个人都用自己( )的双手创造着幸福生活。(勤奋、勤劳)

6. 这个年轻人( )好学,很快就成为了公司里的技术骨干。(勤奋、勤劳)

7. 丈夫让她很失望,可想到离婚她又有些( ),她担心离婚对孩子不好。(犹豫、踌躇)

8. 他( )满志地去参加比赛了,对获得冠军充满了信心。(犹豫、踌躇)

9. 这个犯罪集团的作案方式非常( ),警察调查了很长时间才找到证据。(隐蔽、隐藏)

10. 在她冷漠的外表背后,( )着一颗火热的心。(隐蔽、隐藏)

练习四 . 选词填空
卓越   秩序   工序   有关   有待
超越   顺序   协商   协作   有机
1. 遇到意外事件,要与厂家好好( ),不能擅自作主。

2. 大脑是人体的( )组成部分之一。

3. 这种电池,性能( ),使用寿命是普通电池的三倍。

4. 阿里喜欢旅行,房间里摆着很多( )旅游的书籍。

5. 食堂里,同学们都自觉排队,按( )打饭。

6. 这个业务员进我们公司的第二年,业务量就( )了其他人。

7. 生产这种产品的( )十分复杂,从选择原料到产品包装最少要两个月才能完成。

8. 军营里的生活每天都紧张而有( )。

9. 大家在参加野外探险活动时,一定要有通力( )的精神,互相照顾,互相帮助。

10. 当前的经济形势发生了很大的变化,而相应的政策法规( )更新。

练习五 . 成语填空
1. 家( )户( )   2.( )长( )久   3.( )方( )法
4. 根( )蒂( )   5.( )打( )算   6.( )精( )神

练习六 . 写出下列词语的同义词
1. 比如( )   2. 隐藏( )
3. 巡逻( )   4. 勤劳( )
5. 声誉( )

练习七 . 写出下列词语的反义词
1. 隐蔽( )   2. 梗概( )
3. 勤奋( )   4. 聪明( )
5. 软弱( )

答案

练习一 .

1.yú	2.zhì	3.luó	4.jūn	5.kuǎn

练习二 .

1. 誉	2. 育	3. 预	4. 豫	5. 欲

练习三 .

1. 培育	2. 培养	3. 追求	4. 追赶	5. 勤劳
6. 勤奋	7. 犹豫	8. 踌躇	9. 隐蔽	10. 隐藏

练习四 .

1.协商	2. 有机	3. 卓越	4. 有关	5. 顺序
6. 超越	7. 工序	8. 秩序	9. 协作	10. 有待

练习五 .

1. 喻／晓	2. 天／地	3. 想／设	4. 深／固	5. 精／细
6. 聚／会				

练习六 .

1. 例如	2. 隐蔽	3. 巡查	4. 勤勉	5. 名誉

练习七 .

1. 暴露	2. 细节	3. 懒惰	4. 愚蠢	5. 坚强

10月 第 4 周的学习内容

星期一 Monday

xīnqíng
心情 　　同 情绪 （乙）名

① mood ② state of mind

常用搭配
愉快的心情 a merry mood　　心情不好 in a bad mood

用法示例
她太累了,没有心情跳舞。
She's tired, and in no mood for dancing.
阳光明媚的早晨使我心情愉快。
The beautiful sunny morning put me in a happy mood.
我没心情和你聊天。
I am in no mood to chat to you.

qíngxù
情绪 （乙）名

emotion; feeling

常用搭配
情绪低落 be in poor spirits
情绪高涨 be in high spirits

用法示例
她总是那样情绪低沉。
She is always in that gloomy mood.
他今天在闹情绪。
He's in a temper today.
听到那个消息后,他们的情绪很稳定。
They displayed an unruffled appearance after hearing the news.

zhuàng
幢 （丙）量

measure word for houses

常用搭配
一幢摩天大楼 a skyscraper

用法示例
他最近买了一幢新房子。
He bought a new house recently.
邮局就在那幢白楼的对面。
The post-office is opposite the white building.

nándé
难得 （丙）形／副

seldom; rare

常用搭配
难得的机会 a rare chance

用法示例
他难得称赞我一句。
Only on very rare occasions does he give me a word of praise.
他们难得清闲。
They're seldom at their leisure.
她难得一笑。
She seldom, if ever, smiles.

kǎoyàn
考验 　　同 检验 （丙）动／名

test

常用搭配
经得起考验 stand trial
时间的考验 test of time
经受严峻的考验 stand the ordeal

用法示例
长距离比赛考验了运动员的耐力。
The long race tested the athletes' endurance.
这次危难是对他的勇气和技能的考验。
The crisis put his courage and skill to the test.
他经受住了战争的考验。
He has stood the test of war.

yóubāo
邮包 （丙）名

postal parcel

常用搭配
航空邮包 air mail parcel
收到邮包 receive a parcel

用法示例
她用邮包把礼物寄给了我。
She sent me the present by parcel post.
邮包一定投递错了,因为她一直没有收到。
The parcel must have been misdirected, for she never received it.

nánguài
难怪 （丙）动／连

(it's) no wonder that...; (it's) not surprising

用法示例
难怪找不到人,都开会去了。
No wonder you can't find anybody here, they're all away at a meeting.
难怪她不高兴,她考试不及格。
No wonder she's unhappy, she failed the exam.

母亲整夜守着她生病的孩子，难怪她这么疲倦！

Mother sat by her sick baby all night, small wonder she was so tired!

他总是乱放东西——难怪他什么都找不到。

He just strews his stuff around—no wonder he can never find anything!

kǎohé
考核 回 考评^{kǎopíng} （丁）动

① examine ② check up on

常用搭配

考核干部 check on cadres

定期考核 routine check

建立考核制度 set up a check-up system

用法示例

实习生顺利地通过了考核。

The trainees checked out all right.

有多少受训的飞行员没有通过上次考核而被淘汰？

How many pilots in training were washed out in the last examination?

yóujì
邮寄 （丁）动

send by post

常用搭配

邮寄贺卡 post a card

邮寄证书 mail a certificate

用法示例

他邮寄给我一个包裹。

He sent me a package by post.

我们将用快递邮寄这些货。

We'll send the goods by express post.

商店可以免费邮寄商品。

The store posts articles free of charge.

yóugòu
邮购 （丁）动

buy by mail order

常用搭配

邮购服务 mail order service

用法示例

你可以邮购，但是你得先付款。

You can purchase by mail order but you have to pay first.

邮购这些商品需要一个星期的时间。

It takes one week to purchase the articles by mail order.

xīnyuàn
心愿 回 愿望^{yuànwàng} （丁）名

wish

常用搭配

美好的心愿 a nice wish

用法示例

除了要通过考试之外，我没有别的心愿。

I have no wish other than to pass the examination.

这个姑娘最大的心愿就是嫁个有钱人。

This girl's most fervent wish is to marry a rich man.

duàn duàn xù xù
断 断 续续 （丁）

intermittently; off and on manner

常用搭配

断断续续地说 speak disjointedly

断断续续上了四年学

have four years of schooling off and on

用法示例

他小时候只断断续续地接受过初等教育。

He only attended primary school off and on during his childhood.

他断断续续地给我们写信已经有好几年了。

He has been writing to us off and on for several years.

整个下午断断续续地下着雨。

It showered off and on all afternoon.

 词义辨析

心情、情绪

　　"心情"和"情绪"都是名词，都指一种心理或情感的状态。"心情"强调内在的感情；"情绪"强调情感的外在表现，尤其指心理激动或不稳定的状态。要注意一些固定搭配及其不同的意思，如：心情好、心情舒畅、没心情，有情绪、情绪高涨、情绪低落、闹情绪。在以上搭配中，"情绪"和"心情"都不能相互替换。

　　Both 心情 and 情绪 are nouns, indicating "a state of mind or emotion". 心情 emphasises the internal mood; while 情绪 emphasises the external expression of the emotion, specially indicating states of mental agitation or disturbance. Please pay attention to the following collocations and their meanings: 心情好 (a good mood), 心情舒畅 (a cheerful mood), 没心情 (be in no mood to; be unwilling to), 有情绪 (be discontented with), 情绪高涨 (in high spirits), 情绪低落 (in poor spirits), 闹情绪 (in a bad temper), etc. 心情 and 情绪 are not to be interchanged in these collocations.

 **练习**

练习一、根据拼音写汉字，根据汉字写拼音
（　）hé　（　）guài　（　）yuàn　（　）gòu　（　）xù
考（　）　难（　）　心（　）　邮（　）　情（　）

练习二、搭配连线
(1) 美好的　　　　　A. 心情
(2) 严峻的　　　　　B. 心愿
(3) 难得的　　　　　C. 情绪
(4) 愉快的　　　　　D. 机会
(5) 低落的　　　　　E. 考验

练习三、从今天学习的生词中选择合适的词填空
1. 雨 _____ 地下了一个星期，房间里的东西都是潮乎乎的。
2. 这个孩子最大的 _____ 是将来能考上北京大学。
3. 在恶劣的天气条件下，登山运动员面临着一场严峻的 _____。
4. 这本书在书店已经买不到了，于是我通过邮局 _____ 了一本。
5. 孩子受了惊吓，_____ 很不稳定，你们先让她好好休息休息。
6. 单位每年对工作量都有 _____，如果达不到要求就会扣奖金。
7. 下午我要去邮局取 _____，是我妈妈给我寄的好吃的。
8. 他住在那 _____ 白色的楼里。
9. 工作没做好，被领导批评了一顿，他现在的 _____ 很不好。
10. 新年时，他从国外给我 _____ 了一张明信片。

答案

练习一：
略
练习二：
(1) B　(2)E　(3)D　(4)A　(5)C
练习三：
1. 断断续续　2. 心愿　3. 考验　4. 邮购　5. 情绪
6. 考核　7. 邮包　8. 幢　9. 心情　10. 邮寄

 星期二

tǐhuì
体会　◎领会　（乙）动／名
① understand; taste (through learning or by experience) ② understanding
常用搭配
体会生活的艰辛 taste the hardships of life
学习体会 reflections on the study
用法示例
参加了那次活动之后，他体会到了学习外语的重要性。
I realized the importance of learning a foreign language after attending the activity.
请你谈一点个人体会好吗？
Will you please say a few words about your personal experiences?

zhèn
阵　（乙）名／量
① disposition of troops ② measure word for a short period of time
常用搭配
方阵 square formation　列阵 display a battle array
一阵炮火 a burst of gunfire
一阵咳嗽 a spasm of coughing
用法示例
预计今天下午有阵雨。
Showers are expected this afternoon.
他们爆发出阵阵笑声。
They burst into peals of laughter.
一阵风把窗子吹开了。
A blast of wind blew the window open.

xiǎnshì
显示　（丙）动
show; display
常用搭配
显示能力 to show one's ability
显示力量 make a show of force
用法示例
高度表显示那架飞机正在下降。
The altimeter showed that the plane was descending.
钟上显示的时间是两点二十分。
The clock showed 20 past 2.
他颤抖的双手显示出他内心的恐惧。
His shaking hands showed his inner fear.

zhuāngshì
装饰　　　◎ zhuāngdiǎn 装点　　　（丙）动／名
① decorate ② ornament ③ decoration

常用搭配
用花装饰房间 decorate a room with flowers
装饰圣诞树 adorn a Christmas tree
室内装饰 interior decoration

用法示例
他们用画装饰大厅。
They adorned the hall with paintings
她佩戴了一把小梳子作为装饰。
She wore a small comb as an ornament.
房间里摆满了各种装饰品。
The room is crowded with all kinds of ornaments.

tǐyàn
体验　　　（丁）动
experience (for oneself) ; taste

常用搭配
体验生活 to experience and observe real life

用法示例
这个奴隶从未体验过自由的乐趣。
The slave has never experienced the sweetness of freedom.
他们将在农村生活一个月,体验那里的生活。
They will live in the countryside for one month to experience the life there.

zhuāngbèi
装备　　　（丙）动／名
① equip ② equipment

常用搭配
装备精良 be well equipped
军事装备 military equipment
探险家的装备 explorer's equipment

用法示例
水手们装备船只准备出航。
The seamen equipped a ship for a voyage.
士兵们装备着最新式的武器。
The soldiers were equipped with the latest weapons.
这位旅行家装备齐全。
The traveler was well equipped.

xiétiáo
协调　　　（丁）动
coordinate; harmonize

常用搭配
与……协调一致 be in harmony with...
协调各部门的职能 coordinate the function of departments

用法示例
优秀运动员的动作都非常协调。
The movements of a top athlete are perfectly coordinated.

这些村舍与周围风景十分协调。
The cottages are in harmony with the landscape.
他是个优秀的运动员,他所有的动作都非常协调。
He is an excellent athlete; all his movements are perfectly coordinated.

huìlù
贿赂　　　◎ ézhà 讹诈　　　（丁）动
bribe

常用搭配
贿赂法官 to bribe the judge
收受贿赂 to accept a bribe
贿赂罪 bribery crime

用法示例
他贿赂他的领导来巩固他在公司的地位。
He bribed his leader to ensure his position in the company.
那位官员接受了商人的贿赂。
The official took bribes from businessmen.

zhuāngpèi
装配　　　◎ chāixiè 拆卸　　　（丁）动
assemble

常用搭配
装配机器 assemble a machine
装配车间 assembly plant

用法示例
他一块块地装配飞机模型。
He assembled the model aircraft piece by piece.
机器人逐渐代替了装配线上的工人。
Robots are replacing people on assembly lines.
汽车一般由机器装配。
The assembly of cars is often done by machines.

pèifāng
配方　　　（丁）名
formulation

常用搭配
香料配方 spice formula

用法示例
他们正在研制新的颜料配方。
They are working on the new formula for paint.
有人盗走了我们新药的秘密配方。
Someone has stolen the secret formula for our new drug.

xiányí
嫌疑　　　（丁）名
suspicion

常用搭配
有同谋的嫌疑 be suspected of being accomplice
有间谍嫌疑 be suspected of being a spy
嫌疑分子 suspected person

用法示例
警察调查了嫌疑分子时常出没的所有酒吧。
The police visited all the bars that the suspect frequented.

那个嫌疑人被带到警察局问话。
The suspect was taken to the police station for questioning.
警方正在审讯两个嫌疑犯。
The police are interrogating two suspects.

xīn xīn xiàng róng
欣 欣 向 荣 （丁）

① blossoming (said of flowers in spring) ② flourishing (said of business, etc.)

常用搭配

一派欣欣向荣的景象 a picture of prosperity
欣欣向荣的事业 a prosperous business

用法示例

那些植物长得欣欣向荣。
Those plants are flourishing.
过去荒凉的山村已发展成为欣欣向荣的城镇。
The once deserted mountain village has grown into a flourishing town.

 **词义辨析**

体验、体会

"体会"和"体验"都是动词,意思是通过实践认识事物。"体验"强调亲身经历,通过实践、行动去认识和理解事物,它的对象往往是一种具体的实践活动;"体会"强调对事物的认识和理解,把体验和感想上升为理性的思考,"体会"的对象往往是一种抽象的认识。另外,"体会"还是名词,指所体会到的内容。例如:①他体验过各种艰难困苦。②他深深体会到了经验的重要性。③他写了一篇参加军训课程的体会。

Both 体会 and 体验 are verbs, meaning "to learn something through practical experience". 体验 stresses "personal experience", and "to learn from the experience", and its objects are usually concrete practical activities. 体会 stresses the knowledge and understanding of something", and trying to form rational knowledge on the basis of personal experience. the objects of 体会 are usually abstract knowledge. 体会 is also a noun, meaning "what one understands and realizes". For example: ① He experienced all sorts of difficulties and hardships. ② He deeply felt the importance of experience. ③ He wrote an article about his idea to attend the military training course.

 **练习**

练习一、根据拼音写汉字,根据汉字写拼音
xiǎn（　　）（　　）shì　xié（　　）（　　）lù　xián（　　）
（　　）示　装（　　）（　　）调　贿（　　）（　　）疑

练习二、搭配连线
(1) 收受　　　　　　　　　　A. 生活
(2) 装配　　　　　　　　　　B. 机器
(3) 军事　　　　　　　　　　C. 装饰
(4) 体验　　　　　　　　　　D. 贿赂
(5) 室内　　　　　　　　　　E. 装备

练习三、从今天学习的生词中选择合适的词填空
1. 妻子突然失踪了,邻居认为她的丈夫有杀害妻子的_____。
2. 这个房间内的墙壁颜色和家具颜色有点不_____,所以令人感到有些压抑。
3. 开学以后,我们开会交流了暑期社会实践的_____。
4. 指导员让我们蒙上双眼,_____盲人在黑暗世界的感受。
5. 圣诞节时,每家都_____一新,到处都洋溢着节日的气氛。
6. 春天来了,天气变暖了,草木也发出了嫩芽,一切都显得_____。
7. 这种食物使用了12种调料,但厨师对具体的调料_____保密。
8. 这位法官清正廉洁,从不接受任何_____。
9. 我接到一个神秘的电话,对方的电话号码没有在我手机上_____。
10. 新机器运回来时,是散装的,工人们不一会儿就按照图纸把机器的各个部分_____起来了。

答案

练习一:
略
练习二:
(1) D　　　(2)B　　　(3)E　　　(4)A　　　(5)C
练习三:
1. 嫌疑　　2. 协调　　3. 体会　　4. 体验　　5. 装饰
6. 欣欣向荣　7. 配方　　8. 贿赂　　9. 显示　　10. 装配

星期三

xiàng
项 （乙）量
① item ② measure word for itemized things

常用搭配
一项任务 a task
一项协议 an agreement
一项规定 a regulation

用法示例
所有的成员都同意这项提议。
All the members were in agreement with the proposal.
一些委员会成员不同意这项决定。
Some members of the committee didn't agree to the decision.

wàijiāo
外交 （乙）名
① diplomacy ② diplomatic

常用搭配
外交关系 diplomatic relations
外交官 diplomat

用法示例
他有外交豁免权。
He has diplomatic immunity.
外交官通过谈判解决了那个国际问题。
The diplomat solved the international problem through negotiation.
她大学毕业后就到外交部门工作了。
She worked for the Ministry of Foreign Affairs after her graduation from university.

xiàngzhēng
象征 （丙）动／名
① symbolize; signify ② symbol; emblem

常用搭配
友谊的象征 symbol of friendship
火炬象征光明。A torch symbolizes brightness.

用法示例
橄榄枝象征着和平。
The olive branch signifies peace.
这枚戒指是他们爱情的象征。
The ring was an emblem of their love.
中国人把莲花看作是纯洁的象征。
Chinese people regard the lotus as an emblem of purity.

xiàngdǎo
向导 （丙）名
guide

常用搭配
当地的向导 local guide

用法示例
向导带领我们到河边。
The guide led us to the river.
要不是这位好心的向导,我可能就在山中迷路了。
Had it not been for the kind guide, I might have got ten lost in the mountains.
我熟悉那地方,我来当你们的向导。
I know the place well, so let me be your guide.

yǎnhù
掩护 （丙）动
cover; to shield

常用搭配
掩护他逃脱 provide the cover for his escape
在……的掩护下 under cover of...

用法示例
我前进时你掩护我。
Cover me while I move forward.
炮火掩护步兵前进。
The infantry advanced under the cover of gunfire.
我们在夜幕的掩护下行进。
We traveled under cover of darkness.

yǎnshì
掩饰 反揭穿 jiēchuān （丁）动
① conceal ② gloss over

常用搭配
掩饰缺点 conceal a fault
掩饰错误 gloss over one's mistakes
掩饰真实的意图 conceal one's true intentions

用法示例
他假装忙碌,以掩饰内心的不安。
He conceals his anxiety behind an energetic mask.
他尽量掩饰他的自卑感。
He tried to mask his feelings of inferiority.
她从不掩饰自己的感情。
She never hides her feelings.

xiàngyàng
像样 同体面 tǐmiàn （丙）形
presentable; decent

常用搭配
一份像样的礼物 a presentable gift
一所像样的房子 a decent house

用法示例
他有几十套衣服,却没有一套像样的。
He's got dozens of suits but not one of them is presentable.
这家医院没有像样的设备。
The hospital has no decent equipment.
他的第一部小说如昙花一现,此后他再没写出像样的东西。
His first novel was a flash in the pan, and he hasn't written anything decent since.

wàizī
外资 （丁）名
foreign investment

常用搭配

外资企业 foreign-owned enterprise

吸引外资 attract foreign funds

利用外资 make use of foreign capital

用法示例

我们利用外资的水平明显提高了。

We have markedly improved our ability to use foreign investment.

中国鼓励外资参与西部开发。

China encourages foreign investment in its western areas.

wàibiǎo　　　　 nèixīn
外表 反 内心 （丁）名
① outside ② outward appearance

常用搭配

从外表看 judge by appearance

外表美观 have a fine exterior

用法示例

他外表粗鲁，内心善良。

He has a rough exterior, but a good heart.

她的外表引起了我的注意。

Her appearance caught my attention.

斯文的外表掩盖着的是一个火暴脾气的人。

Beneath that seemingly calm surface is a man of fierce temper.

wàishì
外事 （丁）名
foreign affairs

常用搭配

外事部门 foreign affairs department

外事服务单位 service unit for foreigners

用法示例

我来介绍一下郑先生，他是外事办公室的负责人。

Let me introduce Mr. Zheng, who is in charge of the foreign affairs office.

处理外事工作一定要尽量考虑周到。

We must deal with foreign affairs as thoughtfully as possible.

wàixíng　　　　 xíngzhuàng
外形 同 形状 （丁）名
shape; figure

常用搭配

外形为金字塔形 the general shape is pyramidal

用法示例

这个岛的外形呈三角形。

This island is triangular in shape.

他买了一张外形不规则的咖啡桌。

He bought an irregularity shaped coffee table.

jīn jīn yǒu wèi
津津有味 （丁）
do something with keen pleasure

常用搭配

津津有味地吃 eat with relish

津津有味地读 read with relish

用法示例

我津津有味地品尝了我妈妈做的鱼。

I relished tasting the fish my mother cooked.

他们开始津津有味地大吃起来。

They fell to eating with great gusto.

他讲了一个冒险故事，孩子们听得津津有味。

He told us a tale of adventure, as the children avidly listened.

 词义辨析

掩护、掩饰

　　"掩护"和"掩饰"都是动词。"掩护"的意思是用身体或武力保护，使免遭伤害，多用于军事行动，它的对象是人或军队；"掩饰"的意思是设法掩盖真实的情况或感情，"掩饰"的对象通常是抽象的事物。例如：①战舰在战斗机的掩护下驶近战区。②她设法掩饰自己的感情。③她用微笑来掩饰尴尬。

　　Both 掩护 and 掩饰 are verbs. 掩护 means "to protect with body or armed force against an attack". It is mostly used to describe military action; the objects of it are people or troops. 掩饰 means "to try to conceal feelings or something true, and its objects are usually something abstract. For example: ① The battleship approached the combat zone under the cover of fighter planes. ② She tried to hide her feelings. ③ She smiled to hide her embarrassment.

 **练习**

练习一、根据拼音写汉字，根据汉字写拼音

yǎn（　　）（　　）zī xiàng（　　）xiàng（　　）xiàng（　　）
（　　）护　外（　　）（　　）样　（　　）征（　　）导

练习二、搭配连线

(1) 外表　　　　　　A. 有味
(2) 外资　　　　　　B. 缺点
(3) 掩饰　　　　　　C. 关系
(4) 外交　　　　　　D. 企业
(5) 津津　　　　　　E. 美观

练习三、从今天学习的生词中选择合适的词填空

1. 这座体育馆的 _____ 很别致，远远看去，像一只巨大的鸟巢。
2. 可能太饿了，大家都觉得不好吃的饭他却吃得 _____。
3. 他精通日语和英语，希望毕业后能去从事 _____ 工作。
4. 玫瑰花 _____ 爱情，所以男孩给喜欢的女孩送玫瑰。
5. 为了改善国际形象，提高国际地位，这个国家制定了新的 _____ 政策。
6. 他家境贫寒，工作之前，他没买过一套 _____ 的西服。
7. 在中国境内的 _____ 企业，也要遵守中国的相关法律。
8. 军官安排我们在山头阻击敌人，以便 _____ 另一支部队安全过江。
9. 妈妈说找对象不能光看 _____，更重要的是要看人品怎么样。
10. 她笑了笑，转过头去，看着窗外，以 _____ 内心的不安。

答案

练习一：
略

练习二：

(1) E	(2) D	(3)B	(4)C	(5)A

练习三：

1. 外形	2. 津津有味	3. 外事	4. 象征	5. 外交
6. 像样	7. 外资	8. 掩护	9. 外表	10. 掩饰

 星期四

pī
批
（乙）量

measure word for batches, lots

常用搭配

一批货物 a batch of goods
一批游客 a group of travelers

用法示例

这所学院接待了一批来访的外国科学家。
The college received a group of visiting foreign scientists.
我们是看展览的第一批观众。
We are the first group of visitors to see the exhibition.

kēyán
科研
（乙）名

scientific research

常用搭配

科研项目 scientific research project
科研人员 researcher
科研成果 achievements in scientific research

用法示例

大学的任务是教学和科研。
The mission of a university is to educate, and conduct research.
他为自己在科研方面所取得的巨大成就而自豪。
He is proud of his great success in scientific research.
他在一个科研机构工作。
He works in a scientific research department.

xiàjiàng　　　　　shàngshēng
下降　　反 上升
（丙）动

decline; drop; fall

常用搭配

下降十米 a drop of 10 meters
出生率下降 a decline in the birth rate
持续下降 decline continuously

用法示例

雨后气温下降了。
There was a drop in temperature after rain.
我希望物价下降。
I wish prices would fall.
产品的质量正在下降。
The quality of the products is declining.

shàngshēng
上升
（丙）动

ascend; rise

常用搭配

犯罪率在上升。Crime is on the increase.

逐年上升 rise with years

稳步上升 rise steadily

用法示例

温度正在上升。

The mercury is rising.

英国货币可能贬值,如果果真如此,利率就会上升。

The sterling may fall, if so, interest rates will rise.

我们的生产稳步上升。

Our production is increasing steadily.

dàidòng

带动　　　　　　　　　　　（丙）动

to provide impetus

常用搭配

先进带动后进。

The strong drive the weak.

用法示例

在他的带动下,战士们斗志昂扬。

His example kept the soldiers in high spirits.

我们试着用柴油机来带动水泵。

We experimented with diesel engines to drive the pumps.

dàilǐng

带领　　　　　　　　　　　（丙）动

lead; guide

常用搭配

带领学生 lead students

带领一支部队 lead an army

用法示例

导游带领游客参观宫殿。

A guide conducted the visitors round the palace.

他带领我们开发新产品。

He led us to develop new products.

教练带领我们队取得了胜利。

The coach led our team to victory.

shūhu

疏忽　　　　　　　　　　　（丁）动

neglect

常用搭配

疏忽大意 be neglectful and careless

用法示例

这是由于你疏忽引起的。

This comes from your carelessness.

这个问题被我疏忽了。

The point slipped my mind.

疏忽能引发事故。

Accidents can arise from carelessness.

xiàdá　　　　　　chuándá

下达　　⊜ 传达　　　　　　（丁）名

① send down ② make known to lower levels

常用搭配

下达任务 to assign a mission

下达指示 give instructions

用法示例

军官用无线电向士兵下达命令。

The officer communicated his orders to the men by radio.

已下达撤离该城的命令了。

The order to leave the city has been given.

jiànglín　　　　　　láilín

降临　　⊜ 来临　　　　　　（丁）动

befall

常用搭配

夜色降临。Night falls.

用法示例

一场灾难降临到他的头上。

A great misfortune befell him.

我们都有大祸降临的感觉。

A sense of disaster has befallen us all.

死亡对每个人都一视同仁,它会降临到每个人的身上。

Death does not discriminate; it comes for us all.

shēngtài

生态　　　　　　　　　　　（丁）名

ecology

常用搭配

生态系统 ecosystem

生态学 ecology

生态学家 ecologist

用法示例

他开始研究生态学,并决心献身于这门科学。

He started to study ecology, and then decided to devote his whole life to the science.

人类采用各种手段保持生态平衡。

Mankind has been trying by every means to maintain the balance of nature.

这座工厂排出的化学物质改变了整个地区的生态环境。

Chemicals in the factory's sewage system have changed the ecology of the whole area.

shēngshū　　　　　　shúxī

生疏　　⊜ 熟悉　　　　　　（丁）形

① unfamiliar; disaccustomed ② out of practice

用法示例

我在这儿人地生疏。

I'm unfamiliar with the place, and the people here.

我对这里的路很生疏。

I am unfamiliar with the roads here.

我的棋艺生疏了。

I'm rusty at chess.

我板球曾打得很好,可惜现在已生疏了。

I used to be good at cricket, but now I'm out of practice.

jīng jīng yè yè

兢兢业业　　　　　　　　　（丁）

be cautious and conscientious

常用搭配

兢兢业业工作的典型 a prime example of the work ethic

兢兢业业地工作 to work conscientiously

用法示例

他对所有工作都兢兢业业。

He shows great assiduity in all his work.

这位老工人一直兢兢业业地工作了三十年。

The old worker has worked meticalously and conscientiously for 30 years.

词义辨析

带动、带领

"带动"和"带领"都是动词,都有带头做某事的意思。"带动"强调带头的人(通常是榜样)通过自身的行动,影响或发动其他人进行某项工作或活动。"带领"指带头的人让后边的人跟随着,还表示带头的人(通常是领导或指挥人员)引导、领导、指挥其他人进行某项工作或活动。例如:①在他的带动下,我们也跟着早起锻炼了。②我们的向导带领着我们穿过一个又一个的洞穴。③军官带领他的部队取得了胜利。

Both 带动 and 带领 are verbs, meaning "to take the lead in doing something". 带动 stresses the leader(who is usually the model) who influences or mobilizes other people to do works or activities, while 带领 indicates to act as a commander, director, or guide. For example: ① His example spurred us on to do morning exercise too. ② Our guide led us through a series of caves. ③ The officer led his army to victory.

练习

练习一、根据拼音写汉字,根据汉字写拼音

shū (　　) (　　)lín (　　)tài (　　)lǐng (　　)yán

(　　)忽　　降(　　)　生(　　)　带(　　)　科(　　)

练习二、搭配连线

(1) 科研　　　　　　　　A. 大意

(2) 疏忽　　　　　　　　B. 环境

(3) 下达　　　　　　　　C. 成果

(4) 生态　　　　　　　　D. 上升

(5) 稳步　　　　　　　　E. 命令

练习三、从今天学习的生词中选择合适的词填空

1. 有人第一次买彩票就中了大奖,我常常买彩票,好运却一直没有_____到我的头上。

2. 为了做好这项工作,他认真调研,周密安排,任何细节都不敢_____。

3. 父亲一辈子一直_____地工作,一心想着国家的利益。

4. 根据上级_____的命令,我们立即做好了各项准备工作。

5. 由于这里的_____系统遭到了严重破坏,鸟的种类减少了很多。

6. 孩子三年没见爸爸,跟爸爸有点_____,过了几天就好了。

7. 他每天都早起锻炼身体,在他的_____下,宿舍的其他人也不睡懒觉了。

8. 经济形势不好,城市人口的失业率从2%_____到了4%。

9. 在他的_____下,这个小工厂逐渐成了全国有名的大企业。

10. 发达国家的人口出生率在逐年_____,因此政府鼓励生育。

答案

练习一:

略

练习二:

(1) C　　　　(2)A　　　　(3)E　　　　(4)B　　　　(5)D

练习三:

1. 降临　　2. 疏忽　　3. 兢兢业业　4. 下达　　5. 生态

6. 生疏　　7. 带动　　8. 上升　　9. 带领　　10. 下降

星期五

套 （乙）量

measure word for a set of something

常用搭配

一套家具 a set of furniture
一套酒杯 a set of wine cups
一套工具 a set of tools

用法示例

他穿着一套黑西装。
He is wearing a black suit.
这套古瓷器非常珍贵。
This set of ancient china is invaluable.
他有两套住房。
He has two houses.

贸易 mào yì （乙）名

trade

常用搭配

对外贸易 foreign trade
双边贸易 bilateral trade
贸易壁垒 trade barriers

用法示例

他们从事国际贸易。
They are engaged in international trade.
近年来我们的对外贸易有所扩大。
Our foreign trade has expanded during recent years.
我国在努力扩大与其他国家的贸易往来。
Our country is trying to broaden its commerce with other nations.

无情 wú qíng （丙）形

pitiless; ruthless

常用搭配

无情的行为 ruthless behavior
无情地杀戮 to kill ruthlessly
无情地打击 merciless blow

用法示例

他是个冷酷无情的对手。
He is a cold and ruthless adversary.
事实是无情的。
Facts are inexorable.
他们是最残酷无情的敌人。
They were the most ruthless enemies.

信念 xìn niàn （丙）名

belief; faith

常用搭配

坚定的信念 a firm belief   动摇信念 to shake a conviction

用法示例

她始终坚持自己的信念。
She always holds to her convictions.
我有一个信念——几分耕耘，几分收获。
I have a belief — no pain, no gain.
这坚定了我的信念。
It confirmed my beliefs.

忧虑 yōu lù   圆 忧愁 yōu chóu （丁）动

worry; be anxious

常用搭配

过度忧虑 be excessively worried
对前途的忧虑 worries concerning the future
深感忧虑 feel extremely anxious

用法示例

我们都为他的前途而忧虑。
We are all anxious about his future.
一些经济学家对失业的程度表示忧虑
Some economists showed their anxiety over the level of unemployment.
忧虑损害了她的健康。
Worries preyed upon her health.

忧郁 yōu yù   圆 忧伤 yōu shāng （丁）形

melancholy; sullen

常用搭配

忧郁的心情 a melancholy mood
忧郁的神情 a sullen look

用法示例

一个面色忧郁的年轻女人独自坐在长凳上。
A young woman of sullen aspect was sitting alone on the bench.
他的性格有些忧郁。
There is a vein of melancholy in his character.
她似乎很忧郁。
She seems rather melancholy.

冒险 mào xiǎn （丁）动

take a risk

常用搭配

冒险家 adventurer
冒险做某事 take the risk of doing sth.

用法示例

他冒险把孩子从火中救了出来。
He risked his life saving the child from the fire.

尽管有暴风雨,他们还是冒险驾车赶路。
They took the risk in driving on in spite of the storm.

mào shèng
茂盛　　 🔄 繁茂　　　　（丁）形
lush

常用搭配

草木茂盛 flourishing vegetation
茂盛的庄稼 flourishing crops

用法示例

这一带山区是很好的牧羊场,羊吃了茂盛的青草会长得肥肥的。
The hilly areas make good sheep pastures; sheep will fatten themselves up feeding on the lush grass.
这种花在温暖的气候中长得很茂盛。
This species of flower flourishes in a warm climate.
植物在这个地区生长得很茂盛。
Plants flourish in this area.

xìn yù
信誉　　　　　　　　（丁）名
prestige; reputation

常用搭配

讲信誉的银行 reputable bank
信誉第一 credit first

用法示例

公司的信誉已大大受损。
The firm's reputation has been badly damaged.
信誉是消费界的生命。
Credit is the life-blood of the consumer society.

xìn yǎng
信仰　　 🔄 信奉　　　（丁）动／名
① believe in ② firm belief; conviction

常用搭配

捍卫自己的信仰 defend one's faith
宗教信仰 religious belief

用法示例

我信仰基督教。
I believe in Christianity.
困境中,他坚定的信仰支撑着他。
The firmness of his his belief supported him through difficulties.
我们不应该嘲笑别人的宗教信仰。
We should not mock other people's religious beliefs.

wú liáo
无聊　　　　　　　　（丁）形
① nonsense ② bored

常用搭配

无聊的故事 a silly story
无聊的表演 a boring performance

用法示例

继续这种无聊的争辩是没用的。
It's useless to continue such a nonsensical argument.

我的周末过得很无聊——只是看看电视。
My weekend was boring; I just watched TV.
我敢说你在家里会感到无聊。
I dare say you're dull at home.

tāo tāo bù jué
滔滔不绝　　　　　　　（丁）
talk fluently and endlessly

常用搭配

【谚】智者沉默寡言,愚者滔滔不绝。
Wise men are silent; fools talk.

用法示例

她说话滔滔不绝,我们都插不上嘴。
She talks so much that the rest of us can never get a word in.
他的话滔滔不绝。
His words gushed out.

 词义辨析

信念、信仰

　　"信念"和"信仰"都是名词,都可以表示在思想上接受的观念。"信念"强调对真理、事实在思想上接受或深信不疑;"信仰"一般指非基于逻辑或物质证明的坚定信念,往往与宗教有关。"信仰"还是动词,表示坚定地相信,尤其是宗教方面的观念,可以作谓语,可以带宾语;"信念"只是名词,没有这种用法。例如:①他有一个信念——有志者事竟成。②她不喜欢谈论宗教信仰。③那个男人虔诚地信仰上帝。

　　Both 信念 and 信仰 are nouns, meaning "belief". 信念 emphasizes a conviction in the truth and reality. 信仰 indicates a belief that does not rest on logical proof or material evidence; it usually relates to religion. 信仰 is also a verb, indicating to have firm faith, especially religious faith. It can function as a predicate, and can be followed by an object; while 信念 is just a noun, and can not be followed by an object. For example: ① He has a belief that where there is a will, there is a way. ② She doesn't like talking about religious beliefs. ③ That man has a strong belief in God.

 **练习**

练习一、根据拼音写汉字，根据汉字写拼音

( )liáo ( )yù mào ( )( )lù mào ( )

无( ) 信( ) ( )盛 忧( ) ( )易

练习二、搭配连线

(1) 国际 A. 无情

(2) 冷酷 B. 忧虑

(3) 动摇 C. 贸易

(4) 宗教 D. 信仰

(5) 深感 E. 信念

练习三、从今天学习的生词中选择合适的词填空

1. 周末我感到 _____ 时就独自去看电影。

2. 这家商场的 _____ 很好，从不销售劣质产品。

3. 孩子整天玩电脑游戏，还跟父母说谎，父母对孩子的这种状态深感 _____ 。

4. 他自己的游泳技术并不高，但还是 _____ 去救落水的孩子了。

5. 地里的庄稼长得很 _____ ，今年又将是一个丰收年。

6. 他很健谈，说起话来 _____ ，讨论变成了他一个人的演说。

7. 她 _____ 地望着窗外，一定是又想起了在狱中的儿子。

8. 我们要尊重他人的宗教 _____ ，并要谨慎对待。

9. 今年我国的对外 _____ 发展得很快，出口额比去年增长了 40%。

10. 他有好几 _____ 西服，但他喜欢穿休闲款式的衣服。

答案

练习一：

略

练习二：

(1) C (2)A (3)E (4)D (5)B

练习三：

1. 无聊 2. 信誉 3. 忧虑 4. 冒险 5. 茂盛

6. 滔滔不绝 7. 忧郁 8. 信仰 9. 贸易 10. 套

第10月,第4周的练习

练习一.根据词语给加点的字注音

1.( ) 2.( ) 3.( ) 4.( ) 5.( )
贿赂 嫌疑 生疏 装饰 考核

练习二.根据拼音填写词语

xiàng xiàng xiàng mào mào
1.( )征 2.( )导 3.( )样 4.( )险 5.( )盛

练习三.辨析并选择合适的词填空

1. 刚知道这件事时,妻子的( )非常激动,过了一会儿才渐渐平静下来。(心情、情绪)

2. ( )不好时,李华总是一个人在房间里听音乐。(心情、情绪)

3. 座谈会上,大部分同学都谈了自己学汉语的( )。(体会、体验)

4. 有的演员为了演好角色专门到农村( )生活。(体会、体验)

5. 虽然她竭力( ),我还是能感觉到她内心的不安。(掩护、掩饰)

6. 这个小战士为了( )他的战友而不幸牺牲了。(掩护、掩饰)

7. 没有办法的情况下,我们试着用柴油机来( )水泵。(带动、带领)

8. 他大学毕业后,( )一帮同学创业,最终成就了今天的辉煌。(带动、带领)

9. 是坚定的( )使他不畏艰险,坚持真理。(信念、信仰)

10. 中国人有的有宗教( ),有的没有,不管有没有,大家都互相尊重。(信念、信仰)

练习四.选词填空

外交 外资 疏忽 降临 忧虑
外表 生疏 生态 下降 忧郁

1. 孩子的突然去世好像夺走了她的全部欢乐和希望,从此,她的神情总是很( )。

2. 从( )来看,他长得像亚洲人。

3. 由于自然灾害频繁,近年的 GDP 有所( )。

4. 因为很久没有弹钢琴了,他感到自己的琴艺有些( )了。

5. 世界上的很多事故都是( )大意造成的,所以我们工作时要尽量认真。

6. 地区之间的冲突尽量采用( )途径解决,以免冲突升级。

7. 这个专业的就业前景让学生们感到( ),于是大家纷纷考了第二学位。

8. 由于滥砍滥伐,这个地区的( )环境受到了破坏。

9. 专家认为中国对引进( )应有所选择,高新技术应受重视,而高污染的制造业应受限制。

10. 走在长安街上,不知不觉间夜色( ),我发现北京的夜景也十分迷人。

练习五.量词填空

套 批 项 阵 幢

1. 医生说,还有一( )没检查完,检查完了再来找他。

2. 一( )大风把天空中的乌云都吹散了。

3. 我们的学校就在那( )塔楼后边。

4. 暑假,北京语言大学迎来了一( )短期进修汉语的留学生。

5. 他在秀水街定做了一( )西服。

练习六.成语填空

1. 断断( )( ) 2. 欣欣( )( ) 3. 津津( )( )
4. 兢兢( )( ) 5. 滔滔( )( )

练习七.写出下列词语的同义词

1. 外形( ) 2. 下达( )
3. 信仰( ) 4. 考核( )
5. 装饰( )

练习八.写出下列词语的反义词

1. 下降( ) 2. 装配( )
3. 外表( ) 4. 显示( )
5. 生疏( )

 **答案**

练习一.

| 1.huì | 2.yí | 3.shū | 4.shì | 5.hé |

练习二.

| 1. 象 | 2. 向 | 3. 像 | 4. 冒 | 5. 茂 |

练习三.

| 1. 情绪 | 2. 心情 | 3. 体会 | 4. 体验 | 5. 掩饰 |
| 6. 掩护 | 7. 带动 | 8. 带领 | 9. 信念 | 10. 信仰 |

练习四.

| 1. 忧郁 | 2. 外表 | 3. 下降 | 4. 生疏 | 5. 疏忽 |
| 6. 外交 | 7. 忧虑 | 8. 生态 | 9. 外资 | 10. 降临 |

练习五.

| 1. 项 | 2. 阵 | 3. 幢 | 4. 批 | 5. 套 |

练习六.

| 1. 续续 | 2. 向荣 | 3. 有味 | 4. 业业 | 5. 不绝 |

练习七.

| 1. 形状 | 2. 传达 | 3. 信奉 | 4. 考评 | 5. 装点 |

练习八.

| 1. 上升 | 2. 拆卸 | 3. 内心 | 4. 隐藏 | 5. 熟悉 |

第 1 周的学习内容

jùjué
拒绝　　　　反接受　　　（乙）动
jiēshòu
refuse; repulse

常用搭配

遭到拒绝 meet with refusal

拒绝她的要求 refuse her request

用法示例

他拒绝了他们的邀请。

He rejected their invitation.

她拒绝帮助我。

She refused to help me.

她要求赞助却遭到拒绝。

Her request for a donation was turned down.

zájì
杂技　　　　　　　　　（乙）名
acrobatics

常用搭配

杂技演员 acrobat　　杂技表演 acrobatic performance

用法示例

他五岁就开始学习杂技了。

He started to learn acrobatics when he was five years old.

据说中国杂技在俄罗斯很受欢迎。

It is said that Chinese acrobatics is very popular in Russia.

zázhì
杂质　　　　　　　　　（丙）名
impurity

常用搭配

去除杂质 remove impurities

杂质含量 impure content

用法示例

工人们正去除银中的杂质。

Workers are removing impurities from the silver.

水中有杂质。

There were impurities in the water.

zázhì
杂志　　　　　　　　　（丙）名
magazine; journal

常用搭配

订阅杂志 subscribe to a magazine

医学杂志 a medical journal

杂志撰稿人 magazine winter

用法示例

这本杂志的发行量很大。

This magazine has a large circulation.

这本杂志登载优秀的小说。

This magazine published excellent stories.

我订阅了几份杂志。

I have subscribed to several magazines.

xièjué
谢绝　　　　　　　　　（丁）动
politely refuse; decline

常用搭配

谢绝参观 Not open to visitors.

婉言谢绝 politely decline

用法示例

他提出送送她，但她谢绝了。

He offered to be her escort, but she declined him.

我因有约在先，所以只好谢绝你的邀请。

I shall have to refuse your invitation due to of a prior engagement.

我邀请她和我们在一起，可是她婉言谢绝了。

I invited her to join us, but she declined.

zhǒnglèi
种类　　　　同类别　　　（丙）名
lèibié
kind; species; sort

常用搭配

种类繁多 a great variety

用法示例

家禽的种类很多。

There are many kinds of fowl.

杂货商有种类繁多的存货。

The grocer's has a variety of goods in stock.

zhèngyì
正义　　　　反邪恶　　（丙）名／形
xiéè
justice; righteousness

常用搭配

主持正义 uphold justice

为正义而战 fight for justice

正义感 a sense of justice

用法示例

正义最终将会获胜。

Justice triumphs in the end.

我们拥护自由和正义。

We stand up for the cause of liberty and justice.

他很有正义感。
He has a great sense of justice.

guīzhāng
规章　　　　　◉ 规定　　　（丁）名
regulations; rules

常用搭配
规章制度 rules and regulations
废除旧的规章 abolish the old regulations

用法示例
这些规章制度旨在防止事故发生。
These regulations are intended to prevent accidents.
新规章对我们大家都会大有好处。
The new regulations will be of great benefit to us all.

guīfàn
规范　　　　　　　　（丁）名／动／形
① standard ② be specified ③ without variation

常用搭配
合乎规范 conform to the standard
技术规范 technical standard
不符合规范 fall short of the specification

用法示例
他们制定了新的规定来规范粮食市场。
They made a new regulation to standardize the grain market
这个词的用法不规范。
This is not the usual way of using this word.
他的普通话说得不规范。
He doesn't speak standard Mandarin.

zhǒngzú
种族　　　　　　　　　　（丁）名
race; ethnicity

常用搭配
种族隔离 racial segregation
种族歧视 racial discrimination
种族主义 racism

用法示例
他反对种族歧视。
He is against racial prejudice.
法律适用于所有的人，不分种族、信仰或肤色。
The laws apply to everyone irrespective of race, creed or colour.
种族关系是敏感的问题。
Race relations is a sensitive issue.

záluàn
杂乱　　　　　　　　　　（丁）形
① mess ② mixed and disorderly

常用搭配
杂乱的房间 a messy room

用法示例
因为房间十分杂乱，她不好意思请我进去。
Her room is in such an untidy state that she is ashamed to ask me in.

桌子上堆满了杂乱的文件。
There are piles of papers all over the desk with no semblance of order.
她的想法杂乱无章。
Her thoughts were all jumbled together.

gè zhǒng gè yàng
各 种 各 样　　　　　　　　（丁）
various sorts and varieties

常用搭配
各种各样的水果 all kinds of fruit

用法示例
夏天这条河里有各种各样的鱼。
The river teems with all kinds of fish in summer.
桌子上摆着各种各样的物品。
Various objects were on the table.

 词义辨析

谢绝、拒绝

"谢绝"和"拒绝"都是动词，都可以接宾语，都有不接受的意思。"谢绝"比"拒绝"礼貌、委婉。"谢绝"表示感谢好意但不能接受，如邀请、拜访、礼物、合作、帮助等；"拒绝"的态度比较强硬，表示不愿意做、不愿意接受、不愿意给予或不允许的意思，"拒绝"的事情可能是好意的，也可能是恶意的。例如：①我谢绝了他们提供的帮助。②他们拒绝帮助我们。

Both 谢绝 and 拒绝 are verbs, and can be followed by objects, meaning "to refuse". 谢绝 is more polite and euphemistic. 谢绝 indicates that a person is thankful for the good wishes, but doesn't accept them. It may be an invitation, visit, gift, cooperation or help, etc. 拒绝 is a strong and firm refusal, indicating someone is "unwilling to do, accept, give, or allow" something. The objects of 拒绝 may be of good intention, or may not be. For example: ① I declined their offer of help. ② He refused to help us.

 练习

练习一、根据拼音写汉字，根据汉字写拼音
( )yì zá ( ) guī ( ) ( )lèi ( )jué
正( ) ( )乱 ( )章 种( ) 拒( )

练习二、搭配连线
(1) 遭到 　　　　A. 参观
(2) 去除 　　　　B. 歧视
(3) 种族 　　　　C. 拒绝
(4) 杂技 　　　　D. 杂质
(5) 谢绝 　　　　E. 表演

练习三、从今天学习的生词中选择合适的词填空
1. 新领导一来,重新修订了 _____ 制度,并要求大家严格遵守。
2. 他想请我吃饭,被我 _____ 了,因为我跟他不是很熟。
3. 昨天晚上我们去剧场看了场 _____,演员们表演得非常精彩。
4. 打开灯一看,房间里非常 _____,好像有一两个月没收拾过似的。
5. 圣诞节前夕,这家商店里摆满了 _____ 的玩具。
6. 黑人和白人属于不同的 _____,但大家同样热爱和平和自由。
7. 她在一家 _____ 社工作,是一位编辑。
8. 通过不断健全经济领域的法律,可以逐步 _____ 商家的交易行为。
9. 他被带到警察局以后 _____ 回答任何问题,他说等他的律师来了再说。
10. 通过过滤,可以去除水中的大部分 _____。

🔑 **答案**

练习一：
略
练习二：
(1) C 　　(2)D 　　(3)B 　　(4)E 　　(5)A
练习三：
1. 规章　　2. 谢绝　　3. 杂技　　4. 杂乱　　5. 各种各样
6. 种族　　7. 杂志　　8. 规范　　9. 拒绝　　10. 杂质

 星期二

zhēnglùn
争论　　🔄 争辩　　（乙）动
argue; debate
常用搭配
与她争论某事 dispute with her about sth
用法示例
他们为这件事争论了几个小时。
They argued the case for hours.
他和她为去哪里度假而争论。
He argued with her about which place to go to for a holiday.
让争论到此为止吧,因为我们的意见永远不会一致。
Let the argument rest there, because we shall never agree.

zuòkè
做客　　（乙）动
to be a guest or visitor
常用搭配
欢迎你来做客! You are welcome to be my guest!
用法示例
下星期来我们家做客吧?
Would you care to visit us next week?
他请我到他家做客。
He invites me to be a guest at his home.

zhěngtǐ
整体　　🔄 部分　　（丙）名
① as a whole ② entirety
常用搭配
从整体上看 view the situation as a whole
整体方案 overall plan　　整体结构 overall structure
用法示例
从整体来看 , 这两幢楼是相似的。
On the whole, the two buildings are similar.
自然界是一个整体。
The completeness of nature.

wǎnjiù
挽救　　🔄 拯救　　（丙）动
save; rescue
常用搭配
挽救病人的生命 save the patient's life
挽救失足青年 redeem juvenile delinquents
用法示例
他就是那名挽救溺水儿童的警察。
He is the policeman who saved a child from drowning.
我们应该竭尽全力挽救濒临灭绝的生物。
We should do our best to save endangered species.

这种药挽救了许多人的生命。
This medicine has saved many lives.

jiānshì
监视 （丙）动

① oversee ② watch over

常用搭配

监视嫌疑犯 watch suspects
严密监视…… keep a close watch on…
监视敌人的行动
keep a watch on the movements of the enemy

用法示例

犯罪嫌疑人的处所已处于警方的严密监视之下。
The suspect's house has been closely watched by policeman.
警方一直监视着他的一举一动。
The police have been observing his movements.
他受到警方监视。
He was under observation by the police.

jiāndū
监督 （丙）动

supervise

常用搭配

监督他学习 supervise him studying
政府监督 government supervision
安全监督员 safety supervisor

用法示例

公务员应该受到舆论的监督。
Civil servants should be guided by public opinion.
我监督工人把货物装上卡车。
I supervised the workers loading the lorry.
老人的遗嘱是在律师的监督下执行的。
The old man's will was executed under the supervision of the lawyer.

xìnhào
信号 （丙）名

signal

常用搭配

信号灯 signal light   求救信号 signal for help
发信号 give a signal

用法示例

铁路的信号标志显示火车可以通过。
The railway signal showed that the train could pass.
红灯常常是危险的信号。
A red lamp is often a danger signal.
灯塔每分钟发出两次信号。
The lighthouse flashes signals twice a minute.

zhēngyì
争议 （丁）动

controvert; dispute

常用搭配

有争议的地区 a disputed area
有争议的条款 a contentious clause
一个有争议的历史人物 a controversial historical figure

用法示例

许多新税种都是有争议的。
Many of the new taxes are controversial.
他的诚实是无可争议的。
His honesty is beyond dispute.
事故的真正起因仍有争议。
The exact cause of the accident is still being disputed.

wǎnxī
惋惜 （丁）动

to feel sorry

常用搭配

为……感到惋惜 I feel sorry for…

用法示例

她看着照片，为她逝去的青春而惋惜。
She looked at the photo, sighing for her lost youth.
不知为什么，我为你感到惋惜。
I'm not sure why, but I feel kind of sorry for you.
他批评同事，并非出于气愤而是为他惋惜。
It was more in sorrow than in anger that he criticized his colleague.

jiùjì
救济 （丁）动

relieve

常用搭配

救济金 a relief fund   救济粮 relief grain
紧急救济 emergency relief

用法示例

政府已经制定出了救济贫民的计划。
The government has worked out a plan to assist the needy.
老人靠救济金生活。
The old man lives on benefits.
我们将尽力救济难民。
We will try our best to relieve the refugees.

xìnlài
信赖 　反 怀疑 （丁）动

trust

常用搭配

信赖某人 trust in sb.

用法示例

我完全信赖我的朋友。
I have perfect trust in my friend.
你过于信赖你的记忆力了。
You trust to your memory too much.
这里没有一个让我信赖的人。
There's no one here I can confide in.

gè háng gè yè
各行各业

(saying) all kinds of occupations

常用搭配

各行各业的专家 experts from all fields

用法示例

他们采访过各行各业的人。
They interviewed people from all walks of life.
各行各业都繁荣兴旺。
Every trade is thriving.

 **词义辨析**

监督、监视

　　"监督"和"监视"都是动词,都有察看别人举动的意思。"监督"一般是公开的,它的对象可以是从事各种工作的人,可以作谓语、主语、宾语和定语;"监视"一般是隐蔽的,它的对象主要是敌人或犯罪嫌疑人。例如:①经理正在监督工人工作。②警察严密监视他,惟恐他会逃脱。

　　Both 监督 and 监视 are verbs, meaning "to keep a watch on an other's actions". 监督 is usually to the public. The objects of it can be people in all kinds of industries, and it can function as a predicate, a subject, an object or an attributive. 监视 is usually referring concealed behavior. Its objects are mainly enemies or suspects. For example: ① The manager is superintending the staff's work. ② The police watched him closely in case he tried to escape.

 **练习**

练习一、根据拼音写汉字,根据汉字写拼音

zuò(　) wǎn(　)(　)lài (　)dū wǎn(　)
(　)客 (　)惜 信(　) 监(　) (　)救

练习二、搭配连线

(1) 挽救　　　　　A. 信号
(2) 救济　　　　　B. 惋惜
(3) 求救　　　　　C. 监视
(4) 感到　　　　　D. 生命
(5) 严密　　　　　E. 难民

练习三、从今天学习的生词中选择合适的词填空

1. 进入大山后手机就没有 _____ 了,电话一直打不出去。
2. 他一向正直诚实,我觉得他是一个值得 _____ 的人。
3. 他和爱人为去哪里购物而 _____ 不休,其实,他们可以两个地方都去。
4. 在没有人 _____ 的情况下,人们很可能会滥用职权。
5. 他是个聪明好学的学生,老师们听说他不上学了,都为他感到 _____。
6. 参加国庆招待会的有劳模,有专家,还有来自于 _____ 的代表。
7. 伤员被抬到医院时,已经太晚了,最好的医生也无法 _____ 他的生命了。
8. 很多穷人和残疾人依靠政府的 _____ 维持生计。
9. 我们班的 _____ 水平不错,同学们之间的水平差距不大。
10. 这个间谍暴露了身份,警察一直在 _____ 他的一举一动。

答案

练习一:
略

练习二:
(1) D　　(2)E　　(3)A　　(4)B　　(5)C

练习三:
1. 信号　2. 信赖　3. 争论　4. 监督　5. 惋惜
6. 各行各业 7. 挽救　8. 救济　9. 整体　10. 监视

星期三

zhuāngyán
庄严　　同 zhuāngzhòng 庄重　　（乙）形
stately

常用搭配
庄严的仪式 a grand ceremony
庄严的国歌 the stately national anthem

用法示例
风琴奏出庄严的乐曲。
The organ produced a stately melody.
人民大会堂看上去非常庄严。
The Great Hall of the People looks very magnificent.

huìtán
会谈　　（乙）动／名
① talk formally ② negotiation

常用搭配
与部长会谈 to talk with a minister
举行会谈 hold a talk

用法示例
两国总理将在下个月举行会谈。
The talks between the two premiers will be held next month.
我们的会谈已经取得了令人满意的进展。
We have made pleasing progress in our talks.
会谈的结果很可能是妥协。
The probable outcome of the talks is a compromise.

zhènyā
镇压　　（丙）动
suppress; quell

常用搭配
镇压叛乱 put down a rebellion
镇压反革命 suppress counterrevolutionaries

用法示例
所有的抗议活动都遭到了政府的野蛮镇压。
All protests are brutally repressed by the government.
叛乱分子很快都被镇压下去了。
The rebels were quickly brought to order.
警方把暴乱镇压了下去。
The police succeeded in quelling the riot.

zhènjìng
镇静　　（丙）形
calm; cool

常用搭配
镇静剂 tranquillizer
保持镇静 remain calm

用法示例
遇到紧急情况要镇静。
Keep calm in an emergency.
镇静！别慌。
Keep calm! Don't get flustered.
她心里非常害怕，但表面上显得很镇静。
Though badly frightened, she appeared outwardly calm.

zhēnchéng
真诚　　（丁）形
① sincere ② sincerely

常用搭配
真诚的话 sincere words
真诚地合作 sincerely cooperate

用法示例
我可以非常真诚地说,你一直是我最好的朋友。
I say in all sincerity that you have been my best friend.
我肯定他是真诚的。
I'm certain of his sincerity.
我真诚地希望他能接受别人的批评。
I sincerely hope that he can accept criticism.

zhēnzhì
真挚　　（丁）形
① sincerity ② sincere

常用搭配
真挚的友谊 sincere friendship
真挚的问候 sincere regards

用法示例
请向你全家转达我真挚的问候。
Please give my sincere regards to all your family members.
他的话听起来是真挚的,工人们都很信任他。
His words rang true, and the workers trusted him.

tuōyán
拖延　　同 tuīchí 推迟　　（丁）动
① delay ② put off

常用搭配
拖延 1 小时 a delay of one hour
不得拖延！ Don't delay!

用法示例
她老是拖延着不去看牙病。
She keeps putting off going to the dentist.
限期快到了,不能再拖延了。
The deadline is drawing near, so we can't delay any more.
今天能够做的事,就别拖延到明天。
Never put off till tomorrow what you can do today.

zhuāngzhòng
庄重　　反 qīngfú 轻浮　　（丁）形
grave; solemn

常用搭配
表情庄重 look serious
庄重的神情 solemn expression

【用法示例】

他庄重地宣布了这则消息。

He announced the news gravely.

你不能穿那种衣服出席招待会,不太庄重。

You can't wear that to the reception; it's not dressy enough.

zhùzhòng

注重 （丁）动

① pay attention to ② emphasize

【常用搭配】

不注重外表 put little emphasis on appearance

注重实效 emphasize practical results

【用法示例】

我们应该更注重心理健康。

We should pay more attention to our mental health.

有些学校十分注重语言学习。

Some schools put great emphasis on language study.

美国人的性格是注重实际。

The American people are pragmatic by nature.

zhènxīng　　　shuāibài

振兴 ⊠ 衰败 （丁）动

develop vigorously

【常用搭配】

振兴中华 rejuvenate China

【用法示例】

政府正在采取措施来振兴贸易。

The government is taking measures to revive trade.

我们致力于振兴民族工业。

We are working vigorously at developing national industry.

zhēnchá

侦察 （丁）动

scout; detect

【常用搭配】

侦察部队 scouting force

侦察机 reconnaissance plane

侦察卫星 reconnaissance satellite

【用法示例】

在发动进攻前,派一个排去侦察。

The platoon was sent to explore the area before the attack.

侦察员们两人一组,开始在这个地区巡逻。

The scouts paired off and began to patrol the area.

这个空军中队在执行一项侦察任务。

The squadron is flying on a reconnaissance mission.

rèn láo rèn ruàn

任劳任怨 （丁）

do something without complaint despite hardships and criticism

【常用搭配】

任劳任怨地工作

to work hard without any complaint

【用法示例】

妈妈任劳任怨地照顾我们三个孩子。

My mother looks after our three children without any complaint.

即使工作特别繁忙,我的秘书也是任劳任怨。

My secretary never complains despite sometimes having a lot of work.

他在公司任劳任怨,在家里却脾气暴躁。

In his company, he works hard and is not upset by criticism, but he is irritable at home.

 词义辨析

真诚、真挚

　　"真诚"和"真挚"都是形容词,都含有褒义,都可以作定语。"真诚"多用于态度,可以作状语。"真挚"多用于感情,不可以作状语,常用于书面语。例如:①他真诚地祝愿我们成功。②这些诗篇充满真挚的感情。

　　Both 真诚 and 真挚 are adjectives, with commendatory senses, and can function as an attributive. 真诚 is mostly applied to expressing attitudes, and can function as an adverbial. While 真挚 is mostly applied to emotions, but can not function as an adverbial. It is often used in the written form. For example: ① He sincerely wishes us success. ② These poems are infused with sincerity.

 练习

练习一、根据拼音写汉字，根据汉字写拼音

zhèn（　　）（　　）chá（　　）yán zhèn（　　）（　　）zhì
（　　）兴　侦（　　）　拖（　　）　（　　）静　真（　　）

练习二、搭配连线

(1) 拖延　　　　　　　　　A. 庄重
(2) 真诚　　　　　　　　　B. 时间
(3) 表情　　　　　　　　　C. 合作
(4) 举行　　　　　　　　　D. 叛乱
(5) 镇压　　　　　　　　　E. 会谈

练习三、从今天学习的生词中选择合适的词填空

1. 他的病需要马上手术治疗,如果再＿＿＿＿＿＿时间的话,可能会有生命危险。
2. 我们派了三个人到敌人的营地附近＿＿＿＿＿＿情况。
3. 母亲一辈子勤勤恳恳,＿＿＿＿＿＿,为我们几个孩子的成长付出了全部。
4. 他当时的态度特别＿＿＿＿＿＿,我们谁都没有意识到他在骗我们。
5. 为＿＿＿＿＿＿农业,政府一连推出了几项优惠政策。
6. 举行升国旗仪式时,在场的人都起立,注视着国旗,表情非常＿＿＿＿＿＿。
7. 这个姑娘好像不太＿＿＿＿＿＿仪表,我从没见她化过妆。
8. 暴徒的活动被政府＿＿＿＿＿＿下去了,城市又恢复了平静。
9. 看着＿＿＿＿＿＿的国旗徐徐升起的时候,我的心情非常激动。
10. 读着他写的信,我被他那深沉而＿＿＿＿＿＿的感情打动了。

🔑 答案

练习一:
略

练习二:
(1) B　　(2)C　　(3)A　　(4)E　　(5)D

练习三:
1. 拖延　2. 侦察　3. 任劳任怨　4. 真诚　5. 振兴
6. 庄重　7. 注重　8. 镇压　9. 庄严　10. 真挚

 星期四

qīpiàn
欺骗　　　　　　　　　（乙）动

deceive; cheat

常用搭配
欺骗自己 deceive oneself
欺骗顾客 cheat customers

用法示例
他故意欺骗我们。
He has deliberately deceived us.
你如果还相信她爱你,你就是在欺骗自己。
You are deceiving yourself if you still believe that she loves you.
欺骗孩子是不光彩的。
It's not honorable to deceive children.

jiānqiáng
坚强　　　　cuìruò 反 脆弱　　（乙）形

strong; staunch

常用搭配
坚强的意志 strong will

用法示例
一个坚强的人会忍受艰辛而不抱怨。
A strong man will bear hardships without complaining.
小男孩的性格很坚强,他受伤的时候也没哭。
The little boy has a strong personality; he didn't cry when he was hurt.

gùdìng
固定　　　　　　　　　（丙）形/动

① regular; fixed ② set

常用搭配
固定职业 regular occupation
固定汇率 fixed（exchange）rate
固定资产 fixed capital

用法示例
我可以用铆钉把这些金属板固定在一起吗?
Can I fasten these metal plates with rivets?
把灯座固定在车床上。
Fix the lamp-stand on the lathe.
要正式提出投诉是有固定程序的。
There is a set procedure for making formal complaints.

jiāngù
坚固　　　　　　　　　（丙）形

solid; firm

常用搭配
坚固的基础 a solid foundation
坚固耐用 sturdy and durable

用法示例

这座桥造得很坚固。
This bridge is very sturdily built.
新建的写字楼非常坚固。
The new office building is a very solid construction.
房屋必须建造在坚固的土地上。
Houses must be built on solid ground.

zhàpiàn
诈骗 (丁)动

cheat; bilk

常用搭配

诈骗犯 swindler   诈骗罪 crime of fraud
诈骗财物 defraud of money and property

用法示例

她因涉嫌诈骗而受审。
She was put on trial for fraud.
她被判犯有诈骗罪。
She was convicted of fraud.
新的法规旨在杜绝诈骗行为。
The new regulations were deliberately conceived to make cheating impossible.

dǎoméi   zǒuyùn
倒霉 反 走运 (丙)动

① have bad luck ② be out of luck

常用搭配

倒霉死了！ What horribly bad luck!

用法示例

每个人都可能碰上倒霉的事。
Every one strikes a bad patch occasionally.
真倒霉,我的钥匙丢了。
I was unfortunate enough to lose my keys.

pàiqiǎn
派遣 (丁)动

send (on a mission); dispatch

常用搭配

派遣一名使者 dispatch a messenger

用法示例

派遣了一些士兵守卫城堡。
A number of men were sent to guard the castle.
我们向受灾最重的地区派遣了一个医疗小组。
We're sending a group of doctors to the most badly affected areas.
那个国家派遣了部队去中东。
That country sent troops into the Middle East.

gùzhí   wángù
固执 同 顽固 (丁)形

obstinate; stubborn

常用搭配

别这么固执！ Don't be so obstinate!
固执的孩子 a stubborn child

用法示例

她不按我的要求去做,她真固执。
She won't do what I ask —— she's really stubborn.
她很固执,是不会改变主意的。
She is very obstinate and won't change her mind.
他爷爷是个固执的老人。
His grandfather is a stubborn old man.

dìngyì
定义 (丁)名

definition

常用搭配

下定义 give a definition   确切的定义 an exact definition

用法示例

给一个词下定义比举例说明它的用法困难。
To give a definition of a word is more difficult than to give an illustration of its usage.
根据定义,首都是一个国家的政治文化中心。
By definition, the capital is the political and cultural center of a country.

yúlùn
舆论 (丁)名

public opinion

常用搭配

国际舆论 world opinion
舆论监督 supervised by public opinion

用法示例

舆论对他不利。
Public opinion is against him.
一个正直的法官不能一味顺从舆论。
An honest judge cannot be a slave to public opinion.
政府并未向舆论让步。
The government has not yielded to public opinion.

fěibàng   dǐhuǐ
诽谤 同 诋毁 (丁)动

slander; libel

常用搭配

恶毒的诽谤 a wicked slander
对他的恶意诽谤 a malignant slander upon him

用法示例

他在我的朋友面前诽谤我。
He slandered me in front of my friend.
他写了篇文章来诽谤她的人格。
He wrote a libel against her character.
我要以诽谤罪控告你。
I'll sue you for libel.

quán xīn quán yì
全心全意

whole - heartedly

常用搭配

全心全意为人民服务 serve the people with heart and soul

用法示例

重要的是,我们必须全心全意为人民服务。

Above all, we must serve the people wholeheartedly.

全心全意投身到工作中,你的生活就会充实而快乐。

If you set your whole mind and heart on your work, your life will be full and happy.

 词义辨析

欺骗、诈骗

　　"欺骗"和"诈骗"都是动词,都有使人上当的意思,都含有贬义。"欺骗"强调隐瞒真相,使人上当,宾语多是人。"诈骗"强调讹诈骗取钱财,宾语多是钱财。"诈骗"的程度比"欺骗"深,"诈骗"已经构成犯罪。例如:①他欺骗了我,总有一天我要跟他算账。②他因诈骗罪而被捕。

　　Both 欺骗 and 诈骗 are verbs, meaning "cheat, deceive", and have a derogatory sense. 欺骗 stresses to cheat somebody by concealing the truth. Its objects are mostly people. 诈骗 stresses to deprive someone of money or property by trickery, its objects are mostly money or property. 诈骗 has a stronger meaning than 欺骗, 诈骗 is a kind of crime. For example: ① He cheated me but I'll get even with him one day! ② He was arrested for fraud.

 练习

练习一、根据拼音写汉字,根据汉字写拼音

qī(　)　(　)méi　(　)qiǎn　yú(　)　fěi(　)

(　)骗　倒(　)　派(　)　(　)论　(　)谤

练习二、搭配连线

(1) 坚强的　　　　　A. 老人
(2) 固定的　　　　　B. 意志
(3) 坚固的　　　　　C. 职业
(4) 固执的　　　　　D. 诽谤
(5) 恶毒的　　　　　E. 基础

练习三、从今天学习的生词中选择合适的词填空

1. 大家都十分爱戴这位市长,认为他是_____为老百姓服务的好领导。

2. 社会_____普遍反对调高税率,这使政府的压力很大。

3. 我真_____,考试差一分就及格。

4. 我决定找她面对面地谈一谈,问问她是误解了我,还是故意_____我。

5. 我能用用你的《大百科全书》吗?我想查查这个概念的确切_____。

6. 孩子们都有稳定的工作,有了_____收入,在经济上就可以独立了。

7. 这座桥虽然不大,但是很_____,你可以放心过。

8. 她很_____,一旦决定了就很难改变。

9. 军官_____了两名精明能干的士兵去侦察敌军的情况。

10. 他们伪造了假证明,并用它向基金会申请资金,这种行为已经构成了_____罪。

答案

练习一:
略

练习二:
(1) B　　(2)C　　(3)E　　(4)A　　(5)D

练习三:
1. 全心全意 2. 舆论　3. 倒霉　4. 诽谤　5. 定义
6. 固定　7. 坚固　8. 固执　9. 派遣　10. 诈骗

星期五

jìnhuà
进化 　　　　　　　　　　　（乙）动
① evolve ② evolution

常用搭配
人类的进化 the evolution of man
进化论 evolution any theory

用法示例
据说人是由低级生物进化而来的。
It is said that Man has evolved from lower life forms.
他的工作就是研究鱼类的进化。
His work is to study the evolution of fish.
社会发展史告诉我们人是从类人猿进化来的。
The developmental history of society tells us that man has evolved from apes.

jìngōng
进攻 　　　　　　　　　　　（乙）动
attack

常用搭配
向……进攻 make an attack on
发起进攻 start an attack

用法示例
进攻是最好的防御。
Attack is the best form of defense.
我们必须加强防御以抵御进攻。
Our defenses must be strengthened against attack.
我们的军队击退了敌人的进攻。
The army repelled the enemy's attack.

jiǎnbiàn
简便　　　　反 繁琐　　　（丙）形
fánsuǒ
simple and convenient

常用搭配
简便的方法 a simple and convenient method
操作简便 easy to operate

用法示例
对他来说开张支票是个十分简便的手续。
Writing a check is quite a simple procedure for him.
我想找个更简便的方法来解决这个问题。
I want to find an easier way to solve the problem.

cáifù
财富 　　　　　　　　　　　（丙）名
① riches ② wealth

常用搭配
物质财富 material wealth
累积财富 accumulate wealth

用法示例
一般人都相信健康重于财富。
It is believed that health is greater than wealth.
财富并不一定带来幸福。
Money doesn't always bring happiness.
他的作品是我们民族的精神财富。
His works are the spiritual wealth of our nation.

cáichǎn
财产　　　　同 资产　　　（丙）名
zīchǎn
property

常用搭配
公共财产 public property
私人财产 private property
财产保险 property insurance

用法示例
他打算把财产转让给儿子。
He intends to transfer the property to his son.
法律是为保卫人民的权利和财产而制定的。
Laws are created to protect individual rights and properties.
他把这个女人的财产骗走了。
He defrauded the woman of her property.

jìnqǔ
进取 　　　　　　　　　　　（丁）动
forge ahead; go forward

常用搭配
不思进取 be against progress
有进取心的学生 an enterprising student
进取精神 spirit of progress

用法示例
我们要想克服困难,就要有进取精神。
We need to have a spirit of enterprise if we are to overcome our obstacles.
我希望你永远保持谦虚和进取的精神。
I hope you always remain modest, and keep forging ahead.
那些有进取心的年轻人学得很认真。
The enterprising young men study carefully.

biāotí
标题 　　　　　　　　　　　（丁）名
title; headline

常用搭配
文章的标题 headline of an article

用法示例
我没看整版报纸,只是浏览了一下大标题。
I didn't read the whole paper, I only glanced at the headlines.
标题是用大号字体印刷的。
Headlines are written in large print.
这一章的标题是"我早年的生活"。
This chapter was entitled *My Early Life*.

jiǎnhuà
简化　　　　　　　　　　（丁）动
simplify

常用搭配
简化手续 simplify the procedure
简化工序 simplify work processes
简化字 simplified Chinese characters

用法示例
她简化了指令以便于儿童理解。
She simplified the instructions so that the children could understand them.
政府将简化审批手续。
The government will simplify the procedure of examination and approval.

yuēshù
约束　　　　⊜限制　　　（丁）动／名
① restrict ② limit to ③ restraint

常用搭配
自我约束 self-discipline
受到……的约束 under the restraint of

用法示例
你得学会约束自己。
You must learn to restrain yourself.
我受这项协议的约束。
I am bound by this agreement.
协议对双方具有约束力。
The agreement is binding to both parties.

shùfù
束缚　　　　　　　　　　（丙）动
restrict; bind

常用搭配
打破习惯的束缚 break the shackles of habit
受传统束缚 be fettered by tradition

用法示例
我可不想束缚你的思想；你尽管自己动脑筋。
I don't want to restrict you; feel free to use your own ideas.
今天，人们已经摆脱了一些习俗的束缚。
Nowadays, people have shaken off the constraints of convention.
年轻人不受传统观念的束缚。
The youth are not bound by traditional ideas any more.

háohuá
豪华　　　⊝简陋　　　（丁）形
luxurious

常用搭配
豪华的游轮 a luxury ocean liner
豪华的旅馆 a luxurious hotel

用法示例
他买了一辆豪华轿车。
He bought a luxury car.

他们住在一所豪华的大房子里。
They live in a very big, luxurious house.
这个酒店看上去很豪华。
The hotel seems very luxurious.

tǎo jià huán jià
讨价还价　　　　　　　（丁）
haggle over price

常用搭配
与某人讨价还价 bargain with sb. about the price

用法示例
推销员拒绝讨价还价。
The salesman refused to bargain over the price.
她和卖水果的人讨价还价，直到他把水果便宜地卖给了她。
She bargained with the trader till he sold her the fruit cheaply.
你跟他们讨价还价，他们可能会把价钱降低。
If you bargain with them they might reduce the price.

 词义辨析

财富、财产

　　"财富"和"财产"都是名词，表示大量有价值的资产或资源，有时候可以相互替换。"财富"比较抽象，多用于精神方面；"财产"比较具体，多用于物质方面。例如：①健康是我们最宝贵的财产／财富。②这座房子是我的私人财产。③李白的诗歌是我们民族的精神财富。

　　Both 财富 and 财产 are nouns, meaning "an abundance of valuable possessions or resources". Sometimes they are interchangble. 财富 means "wealth", is relatively abstract, and mostly applied to spiritual aspects; while 财产 means "property", is relatively concrete, and is mostly applied to material aspects. For example: ① Our health is our most valuable wealth. ② This house is my private property. ③ The poetry of Li Bai is part of our valuable cultural heritage.

 练习

练习一、根据拼音写汉字，根据汉字写拼音
（　　）gōng　jiǎn（　　）（　　）fù　háo（　　）cái（　　）
进（　　）（　　）便　束（　　）（　　）华　（　　）富

练习二、搭配连线
(1) 反应　　　　　　　A. 进攻
(2) 发起　　　　　　　B. 约束
(3) 进取　　　　　　　C. 手续
(4) 受到　　　　　　　D. 精神
(5) 简化　　　　　　　E. 冷淡

练习三、从今天学习的生词中选择合适的词填空
1. 根据老人的遗嘱,他的所有 _____ 都将捐献给慈善机构。
2. 他们的新房装修得特别 _____,肯定花了很多钱。
3. 比赛结束前的最后三分钟,对方发起猛烈 _____,连进两球,取得了最后的胜利。
4. 她的汉语水平提高很快,现在都能用汉语跟小贩 _____ 了。
5. 做这道数学题有两种方法,第一种方法比较麻烦,第二种比较 _____。
6. 他整天不思 _____,怎么能有进步呢!
7. 一个国家在创造物质 _____ 的同时,也要注意在文化和艺术方面有所创新。
8. 我们应该尊重传统,但不被传统所 _____。
9. 这篇文章的内容其实比较一般,但是 _____ 特别吸引人,容易引起读者的兴趣。
10. 有些行为我们在法律里找不到依据,这时应用道德来 _____。

 **答案**

练习一:
略
练习二:
(1) E   (2)A   (3)D   (4)B   (5)C
练习三:
1. 财产   2. 豪华   3. 进攻   4. 讨价还价 5. 简便
6. 进取   7. 财富   8. 束缚   9. 标题   10. 约束

第 11 月 ,第 1 周的练习

练习一 . 根据词语给加点的字注音

1.(　) 　2.(　) 　3.(　) 　4.(　) 　5.(　)
简便   　束缚   　侦察   　豪华   　种族

练习二 . 根据拼音填写词语

　　wǎn　　　wǎn　　　qiǎn　　　yì　　　　yì
1.(　)救 2.(　)惜 3.派(　)4.争(　) 5. 正(　)

练习三 . 辨析并选择合适的词填空
1. 学生们想请老师去饭店吃饭,但被老师(　)了。(拒绝、谢绝)
2. 这家咖啡店门口挂了一块牌子(　)宠物进入。(拒绝、谢绝)
3. 孩子放在姥姥家,没人(　)他学习,所以成绩明显下降了。(监督、监视)
4. 这个议员的行为受到(　),电话也被监听,他自己一点都不知道。(监督、监视)
5. 他在读作文的时候,感情非常(　),感染了所有的听众。(真诚、真挚)
6. 希望我们能够(　)合作,取得双赢。(真诚、真挚)
7. 虽然这是一件很小的事,但是你应该诚实,不能(　)你的父母。(欺骗、诈骗)
8. 他因(　)巨额财产罪被判处有期徒刑15年。(欺骗、诈骗)

9. 这位老人临终前写下遗嘱把(　)都留给了他的保姆。(财富、财产)
10. 年轻时的苦难是一笔巨大的精神(　)。(财富、财产)

练习四 . 选词填空
坚固　　　坚强　　　简便　　　镇静　　　规章
固定　　　固执　　　简化　　　镇压　　　规范
1. 在操练的时候,军官要求士兵的每一个动作都要(　),不能有任何松懈。
2. 他这个人非常(　),只要自己认为正确的事情一定坚持到底。
3. 面对记者的责难,他显得非常(　)。
4. 为了加强两国交往,双方都进一步(　)了签证手续。
5. 母亲告诉孩子,一个人在异国他乡生活一定要(　)。
6. 那些人企图推翻现在的政府,不过很快就被军队(　)了。
7. 这种照相机操作特别(　),连小孩子都会用。
8. 这座教堂修建得十分(　),别的建筑物都在地震中遭到了破坏,只有它依然完好。
9. 这个有名的导演成名前没有(　)收入,靠他妻子养家。
10. 老师在给新来的留学生开会时一再强调要遵守学校的(　)制度。

练习五 . 成语填空
1. 各种(　)(　) 　2. 各行(　)(　) 　3. 任劳(　)(　)
4. 全心(　)(　) 　5. 讨价(　)(　)

练习六 . 写出下列词语的同义词
1. 财产(　)　　　　　　 2. 诽谤(　)
3. 种类(　)　　　　　　 4. 挽救(　)
5. 拖延(　)

练习七 . 写出下列词语的反义词
1. 豪华(　)　　　　　　 2. 庄重(　)
3. 拒绝(　)　　　　　　 4. 信赖(　)
5. 倒霉(　)

 **答案**

练习一 .
1.biàn   2.fù   3.zhēn   4.háo   5.zhǒng
练习二 .
1. 挽   2. 惋   3. 遣   4. 议   5. 义
练习三 .
1. 谢绝   2. 拒绝   3. 监督   4. 监视   5. 真挚
6. 真诚   7. 欺骗   8. 诈骗   9. 财产   10. 财富
练习四 .
1. 规范   2. 固执   3. 镇静   4. 简化   5. 坚强
6. 镇压   7. 简便   8. 坚固   9. 固定   10. 规章
练习五 .
1. 各样   2. 各业   3. 任怨   4. 全意   5. 还价
练习六 .
1. 资产   2. 诋毁   3. 类别   4. 拯救   5. 推迟
练习七 .
1. 简陋   2. 轻浮   3. 接受   4. 怀疑   5. 走运

11月 第2周的学习内容

星期一 Monday

xiāngtóng
相同　　　　**xiāngfǎn** 反 相反　　　　（乙）形

same; identical

常用搭配

和／与……相同 be identical with…
相同的处境 the same situation

用法示例

这两种式样几乎完全相同。
These two designs are almost identical.
我的意见和他的意见相同。
My opinion is identical to his.
她的名字与我的相同。
Her name and mine are the same.

guīdìng
规定　　　　（乙）动／名

① prescribe ② provision

常用搭配

管理规定 administrative provisions
根据规定 according to regulations

用法示例

这是合同中所规定的。
It is provided for in the contract.
这些规定仅适用于儿童。
This directive only applies to children.
我们应该依照规定行事。
We should act in accordance to the rules.

quánlì
权力　　　　（丙）名

power; authority

常用搭配

无限的权力 measureless power
权力斗争 power struggle

用法示例

你们没有权力进入这所房子,这是私人住宅。
You don't have the authority to enter this house. It's private property.
人们有集会和发表言论的权利。
People have the right of assembly, and of expression.

你一定要维护自己的权利。
You must stand up for your rights.

shèngyú
剩余　　　　（丙）动／名

① remain ② remnant; surplus

常用搭配

剩余的钱 the remainder of the money
剩余利润 surplus profit

用法示例

剩余的财产属于他的儿子。
The remainder of the estate belongs to his son.
客人都挤在剩余的几个房间里了。
Guests were crowded into the few remaining rooms.

xiāngtōng
相通　　　　**xiānggé** 反 相隔　　　　（丁）动

① communicate ② have a connection

常用搭配

人类的感情是相通的。
The emotions of mankind are interwoven.

用法示例

这个房间与那个房间相通。
This room communicates with the other room.
这座山里有许多相通的洞穴。
Under the mountain there is a network of caves.
这两个大厅有门相通。
The two halls open onto each other.

guīzé
规则　　　　（丙）名／形

① regulation ② regular

常用搭配

交通规则 traffic regulations
遵守规则 follow the procedures
违反规则 go against the rules
规则图形 regular pattern

用法示例

不合理的规则被废除了。
The unreasonable rules were revoked.
安全驾驶的规则适用于每个人。
The rules of safe driving apply to everyone.
他的脉搏不很规则。
His pulse is not very regular.

shěngde
省得　　　　**miǎnde** 同 免得　　　　（丙）连

① (so as to) save ② so as not to

用法示例

到了就来信,省得我挂念。

Send me a letter as soon as you arrive so that I won't worry.

写在本子上,省得你忘了。

Write it down in your notebook so that you won't forget.

dǎobì
倒闭 （丁）动

① bankrupt ② close down

常用搭配

企业倒闭 bankruptcy of an enterprise

用法示例

那家公司因经营不善倒闭了。

The company went bankrupt because of its poor management.

在这次经济危机中,几家银行倒闭了。

Several banks folded during the economic crisis.

在经济萧条期间,公司很可能倒闭。

In a depression companies are liable to fail.

shěnglüè
省略 （丁）动

omit

常用搭配

省略号 ellipsis   省略句 elliptical sentence

用法示例

第二段可以省略。

The second paragraph can be omitted.

这句话的主语被省略了。

The subject of the sentence is omitted.

quányì
权益 （丁）名

rights and benefits

常用搭配

维护合法权益 safeguard lawful rights and interests

权益转让 subrogation of rights and interests

用法示例

人们的权益是受法律保护的。

The rights of the people are protected by law.

法庭宣判不承认我对这片土地的权益。

The court ruled against my claim to the land.

sāhuǎng
撒谎　　shuōhuǎng
🔘 说谎 （丁）动

tell a lie

常用搭配

当面撒谎 to tell a barefaced lie

他在撒谎。He is lying.

用法示例

我马上察觉出那人在撒谎。

I soon discerned that the man was lying.

谁能信任这样一个撒谎的人?

Who can rely on a man lies?

撒谎违反我做人的原则。

Lying goes against my principles.

chuān liú bù xī
川 流不息 （丁）

(of traffic, people etc.) a constant flow

常用搭配

川流不息的车辆 the flow of cars

用法示例

游客川流不息地来长城参观。

A stream of visitors came to the Great Wall.

川流不息的车辆在高速公路上飞驰。

Streams of cars were racing along the superhighway.

汽车在干道上川流不息地驶过。

The cars flowed in a steady stream along the main road.

 词义辨析

相通、相同

"相通"是动词,意思是相互贯通;"相同"是形容词,意思是彼此一样或一致,没有区别。它们不能相互替换。例如:①这两条道路是相通的。②这两封信笔迹相同,肯定是一个人写的。

相通 is a verb, meaning "to communicate or have a connection"; while 相同 is an adjective, meaning "to be identical or the same, with no difference". These two can not be interchanged. For example:　① This road communicates with the other road. ② The handwriting of these letters is the same, and must have been written by the same person.

练习

练习一、根据拼音写汉字，根据汉字写拼音

shèng（ ） shěng（ ） （ ）bì （ ）yì sā（ ）
（ ）余 （ ）得 倒（ ） 权（ ） （ ）谎

练习二、搭配连线

(1) 规则的   A. 企业
(2) 倒闭的   B. 权利
(3) 公民的   C. 图形
(4) 相同的   D. 产品
(5) 剩余的   E. 看法

练习三、从今天学习的生词中选择合适的词填空

1. 这是城市主干道，每天都有各种车辆 _____。
2. 最近经济不景气，很多小企业 _____ 了。
3. 他家离公司比较远，他想在公司附近租套房子，_____ 每天在上班路上花那么多时间。
4. 制定这部法律的目的是为了维护妇女和儿童的 _____，使她们免遭伤害。
5. 既然参加比赛，就要遵守比赛 _____。
6. 他是董事长，他的 _____ 比总经理大。
7. 虽然这两件事情不一样，但道理都是 _____ 的。
8. 不管怎么样，我都希望你说实话，不要对我 _____。
9. 由于时间有限，他在讲这件事时 _____ 了很多细节。
10. 她得到了 1 万块钱的奖金，她用一部分钱买了化妆品，_____ 的钱都存到了银行。

答案

练习一：
略

练习二：
(1) C   (2)A   (3)B   (4)E   (5)D

练习三：
1. 川流不息 2. 倒闭 3. 省得 4. 权益 5. 规则
6. 权力 7. 相通 8. 撒谎 9. 省略 10. 剩余

星期二 Tuesday

侵略 qīnlüè （乙）动
invade

常用搭配
侵略者 invader   文化侵略 cultural invasion
抵御侵略 repel an invasion

用法示例
我们绝不会向侵略者屈服。
We will never yield to invaders.
侵略军被消灭了。
The invading force was annihilated.
敌军准备侵略我国。
The enemy troops are ready to invade our country.

无数 wúshù ⊠ 有限 yǒuxiàn （乙）形
countless; innumerable

常用搭配
无数颗星星 countless stars

用法示例
海滩上有无数沙粒。
There are innumerable grains of sand on the beach.
我告诉过她无数次了。
I've told her countless times.

无比 wúbǐ ◎ 无上 wúshàng （丙）形
matchless

常用搭配
无比自豪 infinitely proud

用法示例
她无比喜悦。
Her joy was beyond measure.
你们年轻人都有无比光明的前途。
There is an infinitely bright future ahead of you young people.

用品 yòngpǐn （丙）名
articles for use

常用搭配
日用品 a daily commodity
体育用品 sporting goods
盥洗用品 toiletries

用法示例
被大雪隔绝的村庄需要生活用品。
The villages that still isolated by the snow need daily necessities.

难民苦于缺少食物和医疗用品。

The refugees are suffering from the shortage of food and medical supplies.

这家商店供应各种野营用品。

The shop sells all kinds of equipment and items for camping.

qīnfàn
侵犯　　　回 进犯 jìnfàn　　　（丙）动

violate; to infringe on

常用搭配

侵犯人权 infringe upon human rights

侵犯著作权 infringement of copyright

侵犯隐私 invasion of privacy

用法示例

任何国家都不能侵犯别国的领土和主权。

No country should violate an other country's territorial integrity and sovereignty.

他们侵犯了她的权力。

They infringed up on her rights.

看我的日记是一种不可原谅的侵犯隐私的行为。

Reading my diary is an inexcusable invasion of privacy.

yòngxīn
用心　　　（丙）形

① motive; intention ② diligently; attentively

常用搭配

用心学习 concentrate on one's studies

别有用心 have ulterior motives

用法示例

他终于露出了他那邪恶的用心。

He showed his sinister motives at last.

他用心解决这个难题。

He applied his mind to the problem.

要格外用心地把这事做好。

Take great care to do it properly.

qīnhài
侵害　　　（丁）动

to encroach on; to infringe on

常用搭配

减少风沙的侵害 prevention of sandstorms

防止蝗虫侵害农作物

prevent the encroachment of locusts on the crops

用法示例

律师说这一裁决侵害了他的委托人。

The attorney argued that the decision involved prejudice towards his client.

我意识到我们的名誉受到了侵害。

I realized that our reputation was being infringed upon.

土豆易受几种害虫的侵害。

The potato is vulnerable to several pests.

qīnshí
侵蚀　　　（丁）动

erode; corrode

常用搭配

风雨的侵蚀 erosion by wind and rain

受到侵蚀 be eroded

用法示例

河水侵蚀着两岸。

The river is eating away at the bank.

海水侵蚀岩石。

The sea erodes the rocks.

锈侵蚀了钢轨。

Rust corroded the steel rails.

yòngyì
用意　　　（丁）名

purpose; intention

常用搭配

好的用意 with good intentions

用法示例

她的用意是好的，但不符合实际。

She is a well-meaning person, but she's completely unreal.

他的用意很好，但他做起来却不令人满意。

His intention was good, but his execution of the plan was unsatisfactory.

你这是什么用意？

What's your game?

wúcháng
无偿　　　回 有偿 yǒucháng　　　（丁）形

① free ② gratuitous

常用搭配

无偿援助 non-reimbursable assistance

无偿转让 voluntary conveyance　　无偿使用 free use

用法示例

所有的书都无偿赠送。

All the books were given away free of charge.

他们想无偿地为这些学生提供援助。

They wanted to render their free assistance to these students.

wúchǐ
无耻　　　（丁）形

① without any sense of shame ② unembarrassed

常用搭配

无耻之徒 a shameless person

无耻的谎言 brazen lies　　无耻的背叛 a shameless betrayal

用法示例

他这样说真是无耻！

It was brazen of him to say so!

他是一个无耻的骗子。

He is a shameless liar.

别那么无耻！

None of your impudence!

dé bù cháng shī
得不偿失 （丁）
the loss outweighs the gain

常用搭配

不干得不偿失的活

avoid the work in which we lose more than we gain

用法示例

迪克一开始舍不得花钱去看医生,因此,他的心脏病越来越严重。这真是得不偿失。

Dick's heart trouble became serious after he didn't spend money to see a doctor when it began; he was indeed penny wise and pound foolish.

犯罪是得不偿失的。

Crime doesn't pay.

 **词义辨析**

侵略、侵犯

"侵略"和"侵犯"都是动词,都有用武力强行进入别的国家的意思,都含有贬义。"侵略"的行为主体一定是国家,对象是另一个国家。在固定搭配"经济侵略"、"文化侵略"中"侵略"是渗透的意思。"侵犯"的行为主体和对象不一定是国家,它也指非法占有、干涉别人的权益,它的对象通常是抽象的。例如:①敌军准备侵略我国。②你的行为已经侵犯了我们的隐私。

Both 侵略 and 侵犯 are verbs, meaning "to invade another country by force", with a derogatory sense. The subject of 侵略 is a country, and its object is another country. In the collocation—经济侵略 (economic invasion), 文化侵略 (cultural invasion), 侵略 here means "infiltration"; while the subject and object of 侵犯 are not always a country. It also means "to violate the rights or interests of other people or organizations". Its objects are usually something abstract. For example: ① The enemy troops are ready to invade our country. ② What you did has violated our privacy.

 **练习**

练习一、根据拼音写汉字,根据汉字写拼音

( )fàn ( )cháng ( )yì ( )chǐ ( )shí
侵( ) 无( ) 用( ) 无( ) 侵( )

练习二、搭配连线

(1) 侵犯   A. 用品

(2) 侵略   B. 隐私

(3) 侵害   C. 学习

(4) 医疗   D. 名誉

(5) 用心   E. 邻国

练习三、从今天学习的生词中选择合适的词填空

1. 在沙漠的边缘地带,我们种上了树,这样可以减少风沙对庄稼的_____。

2. 我没想到他会说出这么_____的话,真是太令人气愤了。

3. 海浪拍打着海岸,岸边的礁石都被海水_____了。

4. 他把那幅名画_____捐献给国家美术馆。

5. 谈起她儿子的时候,她总是感到_____自豪,好像她儿子是世界上最完美的人。

6. 现在学习是你最主要的事,要是为打工耽误了学习,那就_____了。

7. 去旅行时,她总是把洗漱_____装在一个小包里。

8. 我不知道他说这些话的_____是什么,他为什么要告诉我这些事呢。

9. 你不应该看孩子的日记,你这种做法_____了他的隐私权。

10. 如果你_____观察,你会发现几乎每一片树叶的形状都有所不同。

 **答案**

练习一:
略

练习二:
(1) B   (2)E   (3)D   (4)A   (5)C

练习三:
1. 侵害   2. 无耻   3. 侵蚀   4. 无偿   5. 无比
6. 得不偿失   7. 用品   8. 用意   9. 侵犯   10. 用心

星期三

huìkè
会客 （乙）动
receive a visitor

常用搭配

会客室 reception room

用法示例

她现在病得厉害,不能会客。
She's too ill to see anyone at present.
他经常在下午会客。
He often receives visitors in the afternoon.

mǎimai
买卖 shēngyì 生意 （乙）名
① transactions ② business dealings

常用搭配

小买卖 small trading
做买卖 to do business

用法示例

我不跟这种不诚实的商人做买卖。
I won't do business with this dishonest merchant.
她参与了不正当的买卖。
She took part in dishonest business deals.

zhōngduàn
中断 zhōngzhǐ 中止 （丙）动
① interrupt ② break off

常用搭配

中断谈判 break off the negotiations
中断节目 interrupt the program

用法示例

大雨使我们的棒球比赛中断了。
The heavy rain interrupted our baseball game.
交通中断了几小时。
Traffic was held up for a few hours.
两国间的贸易因战争而中断了。
Trade between the two countries was interrupted by the war.

zhōngnián
中年 （丙）名
middle - aged

常用搭配

中年人 middle-aged person
中年教师 middle-aged teacher

用法示例

这人已到了中年。
The man has reached middle age.

她中年以后才结婚。
She didn't get married until she was well into middle age.
一位中年妇女走了进来,后面跟着一群孩子。
A middle-aged woman came over, followed by a group of children.

lùnshù
论述 chǎnshù 阐述 （丁）动
① discourse ② dissertate

常用搭配

精辟的论述 brilliant exposition
论述国际形势 expound upon the international situation

用法示例

演讲者头头是道地论述了一系列问题。
The speaker spoke knowledgeably on a variety of subjects.
她的新书是论述残疾人问题的。
Her latest book discusses the problems of the disabled.
那位学者详细论述了李白的诗歌风格。
The scholar talked at great length on the poetic style of Li Bai.

lùnzhèng
论证 （丁）动
demonstrate or prove (through argument)

常用搭配

论证方式 a way of argumentation
论证过程 process of argumentation

用法示例

你怎样论证地球是圆的？
How do you demonstrate that the earth is round?
哥白尼论证了地球绕着太阳转。
Copernicus reasoned that the earth revolved around the sun.
他的推理不符合逻辑,因而论证无效。
This non sequitur invalidates his argument.

zhōngshēn
终身 （丙）名
lifelong

常用搭配

终身事业 one's lifework
终身大事
a great event in one's life(usu. Referring to marriage)

用法示例

婚姻是终身大事。
Marriage is for life.
她在意外事故中获救了,但却终身残废,再也不能行走了。
She survived the accident, but she was maimed for life and will never walk again.
一个算命的告诉她,她将在二十多岁时遇到自己的终身伴侣。
A fortune-teller told her that she will meet her soulmate in her twenties.

zhōngnián
终年 （丁）名

① all the year round ② age at death

常用搭配

终年积雪的高山 mountains perennially covered with snow

用法示例

山顶上终年积雪。

The mountain peaks are covered with snow all year round.

撒哈拉的大部分地区终年无雨。

Most of the Sahara receives almost no rain at all.

他终年 78 岁。

He died at the age of seventy-eight.

zhōngtú
中途 （丁）名

midway

常用搭配

中途停留 stop halfway

中途下车 get off the car midway

用法示例

她中途退出了比赛。

She dropped out in the middle of the competition.

我可以中途下车吗？

Can I make a stop-over on the way?

不要在开会时中途退场。

Don't leave before the meeting is over.

huìwù
会晤 （丁）动

① meet ② conference

常用搭配

两国外长定期会晤。

The foreign ministers of the two countries meet regularly.

用法示例

你们会晤的结果怎么样？

What was the outcome of your meeting?

我们做了非正式的会晤。

We had an informal meeting.

两国首相昨天在日内瓦会晤。

The premiers of the two countries met in Geneva yesterday.

huíbì
回避 **duǒbì** 躲避 （丁）动

evade; shun; avoid

常用搭配

回避困难 avoid difficulties

回避关键问题 evade the key question

用法示例

你不必回避这个问题。

You needn't evade the question.

我们大家不要回避棘手的问题。

Let's not skirt round the awkward questions.

这个讲话回避了所有的敏感问题。

The speech avoided addressing the sensitive questions.

cóng róng bú pò
从 容不迫 （丁）

calm and unflustered

常用搭配

她从容不迫地讲话。 She spoke with an unruffled calm.

用法示例

他从容不迫地回答警察的提问。

He answered the policeman's questions calmly.

他在舞台上表现得从容不迫。

He performed very calmly on the stage.

 词义辨析

论述、论证

　　"论述"和"论证"都是动词，都有分析说明的意思。"论述"强调详细叙述，使其更加清晰或易懂；"论证"强调验证一个假设或命题的正确性，通过提出论据或证据来确立其论点。例如：①那位学者论述了老年人的一系列问题。②你怎样论证能量守恒的原理？

　　Both 论 述 and 论 证 are verbs, meaning "to analyze and expound". 论述 stresses to give a detailed statement and to make something clear and easier to understand; while 论证 stresses to demonstrate the validity of a hypothesis or proposition and to establish the truth or validity by the presentation of arguments. For example: ① The scholar discoursed on a series of problems of the old. ② How do you demonstrate the theory of energy conservation？

 **练习**

练习一、根据拼音写汉字，根据汉字写拼音

mǎi（　　）zhōng（　　）zhōng（　　）（　　）wù（　　）bì（　　）
（　　）卖　（　　）身　（　　）断　会（　　）回（　　）

练习二、搭配连线

(1) 中年　　　　　　　　A. 大事
(2) 终身　　　　　　　　B. 妇女
(3) 中途　　　　　　　　C. 会晤
(4) 定期　　　　　　　　D. 矛盾
(5) 回避　　　　　　　　E. 下车

练习三、从今天学习的生词中选择合适的词填空

1. 他在一次交通事故中失去了右腿，造成了_____残疾。
2. 在这篇文章中，作者详细_____了改革面临的各种问题。
3. 现场很混乱，但是医生非常镇静，_____地为伤员处理伤口。
4. 要是你报名参加这项活动就必须坚持到底，不能_____退出。
5. 前年，我的同学搬到另一个城市居住，从此我们的联系就_____了。
6. 听到他们俩聊私事，他很知趣地_____了。
7. 远处那座高山的山顶上_____积雪，夏天都能看到皑皑白雪。
8. 他提出的观点十分新颖，但_____过程不太严密，缺乏逻辑性。
9. 他想跟几个朋友做_____，一起到南方采购商品，再到北方来卖。
10. 董事长正在_____，据说来的那个人是公司的重要客户。

 答案

练习一：
略

练习二：

(1) B　　　(2)A　　　(3)E　　　(4)C　　　(5)D

练习三：

1. 终身　　2. 论述　　3. 从容不迫　4. 中途　　5. 中断
6. 回避　　7. 终年　　8. 论证　　9. 买卖　　10. 会客

星期四 Thursday

zhùzuò
著作　　　　　　　　（乙）名

works of literature

常用搭配

著作权 copyright
学术著作 academic books

用法示例

这是有关这个问题的权威著作之一。
This is one of the authoritative books on this subject.
这部著作已是第三次重印了。
The work is into its third reprint.

xiāngfǎn
相反　　　　　　　　（乙）形

opposite; contrary

常用搭配

相反的方向 opposite directions
相反的意见 contrary opinions
恰恰相反 quite the contrary

用法示例

反义词是指意思相反的词。
Antonyms are words that have opposite meanings.
从这些事实中可能得出两种截然相反的结论。
It is possible to infer two completely opposite conclusions from this set of facts.
我没有病；恰恰相反，我健康极了。
I'm not sick; on the contrary, I'm in the prime of health.

yǔzhòu
宇宙　　　　　　　　（丙）名

universe; outer space

常用搭配

宇宙飞船 spaceship
宇宙的演变 the evolution of the universe

用法示例

我们的世界只是宇宙的一小部分。
Our world is but a small part of the universe.
我们开始探索宇宙的奥秘。
We have begun to plumb the mysteries of the universe.
宇宙无限深广。
The depth of the universe is immeasurable.

zhùshì　　　　　　**níngshì**
注视　　　　近 凝视　　　　（丙）动

watch attentively

常用搭配

注视着她的眼睛 gaze into her eyes

用法示例

她睁大了眼睛注视着他。

She stared at him with wide eyes .

她注视着夕阳。

She stared at the setting sun.

雷达兵目不转睛地注视着屏幕。

The radar man's eyes were glued to the screen.

yúmèi
愚昧 （丁）形

ignorant

常用搭配

愚昧落后 ignorant and backward

愚昧无知 unenlightened

用法示例

贫穷和愚昧是进步的敌人。

Poverty and ignorance are the enemies of progress.

要是没有书,我们就会愚昧无知。

If there had been no books, we would have been ignorant.

yúchǔn
愚蠢 （丙）形

silly; stupid

常用搭配

愚蠢的行为 stupid behavior

愚蠢的问题 stupid question

用法示例

他的坦白简直是愚蠢!

His frankness is just stupid!

试图说服他未免太愚蠢了。

It is a great folly to try to persuade him.

他对自己的愚蠢行为感到懊恼。

He is repentant of his folly.

xiāngduì
相对 （丙）动／形

① opposite; face to face ② relatively

常用搭配

相对论 the theory of relativity

相对真理 relative truth

用法示例

两山遥遥相对。

The two hills stand far apart, facing each other.

相对而言,这事并不重要。

Relatively speaking, this matter is unimportant.

相对来说,我喜欢那个蓝色的。

Comparatively speaking, I like the blue one.

zhùshì
注释 　　zhùjiě
　　　　同注解 （丁）动／名

① annotate ② annotation

常用搭配

见注释 see the notes 　 注释栏 comment column

注释部分 interpretation section

用法示例

这些注释有助于弄清文中最难懂的部分。

The notes help to elucidate the most difficult parts of the text.

课后有详细的注释。

There are some detailed annotations at the end of the text.

xuānshì
宣誓 （丁）动

swear an oath

常用搭配

请跟着我宣誓。Repeat the oath after me.

宣誓就职 swearingin

用法示例

总统宣誓维护宪法。

The President swore to uphold the constitution.

他宣誓要为他的国家而战。

He took the oath to fight for his country.

士兵们宣誓效忠于他们的祖国。

The soldiers swore allegiance to their motherland.

gòngjì
共计 　　héjì
　　　同合计 （丁）动

sum up to; total up to

常用搭配

共计多少? What does the total come to?

用法示例

金额共计 230 美元。

The sum came to 230 dollars.

我们共计 20 人。

We numbered 20 (ie There were 20 of us) in all.

两项开支共计 30 元。

These two items come to 30 yuan.

dǎoluàn
捣乱 　　dǎoguǐ
　　　同捣鬼 （丁）动

cause a disturbance; intentionally bother

常用搭配

捣乱分子 troublemaker

别跟我捣乱! Don't make trouble with me!

用法示例

他如果再来这里捣乱,我就会教训他一顿。

If he comes here to make trouble again, I will teach him a lesson.

把这些捣乱分子赶出去。

Let's get rid of out the troublemakers.

他存心捣乱。

He means (to cause) trouble.

měi zhōng bù zú
美中不足 （丁）

a flaw in an otherwise perfect thing

用法示例

那是一个非常好的聚会,美中不足的是,主人喝醉了。

It was a very good party. The only fly in the ointment was that the host got drunk.

我们队表现很好,而且赢了。美中不足的是,我的腿受伤了。

Our team performed well, and finally won. The only problem was that my leg was hurt.

 **词义辨析**

愚蠢、愚昧

　　"愚蠢"和"愚昧"都是形容词,都有不明事理的意思。"愚蠢"强调脑子笨,不聪明,有时候有荒谬可笑的意思,可以作状语,可以用于人也可以用于事,很少作主语或宾语;"愚昧"强调缺乏知识和教导,不开明,一般用于人,不能作状语,有时作主语或宾语。例如:①她愚蠢地相信了他的谎言。②他提出了一个愚蠢的问题。③她不喜欢那些贫穷而愚昧的村民。

　　Both 愚蠢 and 愚昧 are adjectives, meaning "unwise". 愚蠢 means "foolish, silly". Sometimes it also means "absurd or ridiculous", and can function as an adverbial. It is applied to expressing of somebody or something, but seldom functions as a subject or an object; while 愚昧 stresses "uneducated, ignorant, unenlightened", and is usually applied to people. It can not function as an adverbial. Sometime it can function as a subject or an object. For example: ① She foolishly believed his lie. ② He raised a stupid question. ③ She dislikes those poor and ignorant villagers.

 **练习**

练习一、根据拼音写汉字,根据汉字写拼音

zhù(　　) (　　)zhòu(　　)shì　　yú(　　) zhù(　　)

(　　)作　　宇(　　)　宣(　　)(　　)蠢(　　)视

练习二、搭配连线

(1) 学术　　　　　　　　　A. 无知

(2) 宇宙　　　　　　　　　B. 著作

(3) 愚昧　　　　　　　　　C. 相反

(4) 宣誓　　　　　　　　　D. 飞船

(5) 恰恰　　　　　　　　　E. 就职

练习三、从今天学习的生词中选择合适的词填空

1. 经济和教育的发展逐渐改变了那个地区 _____ 落后的旧观念。

2. 全国的商品房都在涨价,这里的房价 _____ 合理,我们那里更贵。

3. 这个学生总爱在课堂上 _____,老师们和同学都不喜欢他。

4. 他们在国旗下庄严 _____ 永远效忠自己的祖国。

5. 这个词在课文的最后有 _____,不明白的同学仔细看看。

6. 两位老人觉得生活很幸福,_____ 的是孩子在外地工作,不能常陪在他们身边。

7. 这个月的交通费、洗衣费和通讯费 _____ 两千元。

8. 大家都笑话他,认为他的想法很 _____。

9. 猎狗目不转睛地 _____ 着前方,它好像发现了猎物。

10. 我的观点正好与你 _____,我认为他们一定能赢。

答案

练习一:

略

练习二:

(1) B　　　(2)D　　　(3)A　　　(4)E　　　(5)C

练习三:

1. 愚昧　　2. 相对　　3. 捣乱　　4. 宣誓　　5. 注释

6. 美中不足 7. 共计　　8. 愚蠢　　9. 注视　　10. 相反

星期五

gòngtóng
共同 反 单独 dāndú （乙）形

common

常用搭配

共同利益 common interest
共同的特点 common characteristics
共同的目标 common objectives

用法示例

两姐妹没有什么共同之处。
The two sisters have nothing in common.
共同的爱好使两人成为朋友。
Common tastes form a bond between the two men.
他们联合起来抵御共同的敌人。
They made an alliance against the common enemy.

yǐnqǐ
引起 （乙）动

cause; arouse

常用搭配

引起怀疑 arouse suspicion
引起注意 draw attention

用法示例

大雨引起了洪水。
The heavy rain caused the flood.
他鬼鬼祟祟的行为引起了我的怀疑。
His surreptitious behavior aroused my suspicion.
他的病是工作过度引起的。
His illness was brought on by overwork.

mángmù
盲目 （丙）形

① blindly ② aimless

常用搭配

盲目乐观 unrealistically optimistic
盲目追随某人 follow sb. blindly

用法示例

你不能盲目相信他。
You shouldn't blindly believe him.
你最好亲自调查一下，别盲目下结论。
You'd better investigate yourself, don't just draw a conclusion blindly.

dàng'àn
档案 （丙）名

file; record

常用搭配

保管档案 to keep archives

档案室 archives office

用法示例

她是我们公司的档案员。
She is the filing clerk of our company.
警方正在查阅类似案件的档案。
The police are trawling through their files for similar cases.
我们将把你的简历存入档案。
We will keep your resume on file.

tóngshì
同事 （丁）名

colleague; co-worker

常用搭配

老同事 an old colleague
公司的同事 a colleague in a company

用法示例

他总能和同事们和睦相处。
He always gets on well with his colleagues.
我代表我的同事和我本人向你表示感谢。
On behalf of my colleagues, and myself, I thank you.
他在同事中受到很高的评价。
He is highly esteemed among his colleagues.

yǐnjìn
引进 同 引入 yǐnrù （丙）动

introduce from elsewhere

常用搭配

引进人才 to introduce talent
引进外资 introduction of foreign investment
引进先进技术 importation of advanced technology

用法示例

政府认为引进新技术至关重要。
The government saw the introduction of new technology as vital.
在澳洲，兔子是引进的动物。
The rabbit is a new introduction to Australia from overseas.
她把来访者引进屋子里。
She ushered the visitor into the room.

yǐnyuē
隐约 （丙）形

vague; indistinct

常用搭配

隐约可见 can be indistinctly seen

用法示例

他隐隐约约地觉得以前曾经见过她。
In the back of his mind was the vague idea that he had met her before.
我隐约记得他。
I remember him vaguely.
我隐约听到有人叫我。
I vaguely heard somebody call me.

tónghàng
同行 （丁）名
person in the same business or occupation

常用搭配

我们是同行。We are of same profession.

用法示例

她是同行的光荣。
She is an honor to her profession.

【谚】同行是冤家。
Two of a trade can never agree.

他们是同行，但他们不是同事，因为他们在不同的学校工作。
They are in the same occupation. But they are not colleagues because they work in different schools.

yǐnyòng
引用 回 援引 （丁）动
quote; cite

常用搭配

引用《圣经》的话 quote the Bible

引用谚语 quote a proverb

用法示例

他喜欢在作文中引用谚语。
He likes to quote proverbs in his compositions.

对不信上帝的人引用《圣经》的话是没用的。
It's no use citing the Bible to somebody who doesn't believe in God.

作者经常引用莎士比亚作品里的话。
The author frequently quoted the works of Shakespeare.

yǐnmán   tǎnbái
隐瞒 反 坦白 （丁）动
hide; conceal

常用搭配

隐瞒事实 hide the truth

隐瞒错误 conceal one's mistakes

毫不隐瞒 hold back nothing

用法示例

你不该对警察隐瞒实情。
You shouldn't conceal the facts from police.

她试图隐瞒真相。
She tried to conceal the truth.

他说出了一些事情，但也隐瞒了一些事。
He told part of the truth, but he also kept something back.

yínhuì
淫秽 （丁）形
bawdy; salacious; obscene

常用搭配

淫秽读物 salacious books   淫秽的图片 obscene pictures

用法示例

那本书中有很多淫秽的语言。
There is a lot of obscene language in the book.

那本杂志属于淫秽出版物，已被海关没收了。
The magazine is classified as an obscene publication and has been seized by the customs officers.

wēi bù zú dào
微不足道 （丁）
too trivial or insignificant to mention

常用搭配

微不足道的事情 trivial matters

用法示例

比率虽有下降，但下降的数量微不足道。
The rate has fallen by an insignificant amount.

这次选举后该党已沦为微不足道的少数党。
The election reduced the Party to insignificance.

最微不足道的小事也会使他紧张。
The merest little thing makes him nervous.

 词义辨析

同事、同行

"同事"和"同行"都是名词，都表示工作中的人事关系。"同事"表示在同一单位工作的人，他们可能从事不同工作。"同行"表示在同一行业工作的人，他们可能不在同一个单位。例如：①他是我的同事，他是我们公司的设计师，我是经理的秘书。②我们是同行，但他所在的公司离我们公司很远。

Both 同事 and 同行 are nouns, indicating human relations at work. 同事 indicates colleagues, or the fellow members in the unit (but maybe they do different job). While 同行 indicates the persons of one trade (but maybe they work in different units). For example: ① He is my colleague, a designer in our company, and I work for the manager as a secretary. ② We are of the same occupation, but the company he works in is far from mine.

 练习

练习一、根据拼音写汉字，根据汉字写拼音

yín（ ） yǐn（ ） yǐn（ ） tóng（ ）（ ）àn
（ ）秽 （ ）瞒 （ ）进 （ ）行   档（ ）

练习二、搭配连线

(1) 引用   A. 事实
(2) 引进   B. 读物
(3) 淫秽   C. 外资
(4) 查阅   D. 档案
(5) 隐瞒   E. 谚语

练习三、从今天学习的生词中选择合适的词填空

1. 我 _____ 看见那儿站着一个人，可是再仔细一看，是树的影子。

2. 他是我的_____,我们两个人在同一间办公室工作。

3. 为了_____优秀人才,他们制定了几项非常吸引人的优惠政策。

4. 调查表明,这次森林火灾是由闪电_____的,不是人为事故。

5. 警察捣毁这个窝点时,发现大量_____书籍和录像带,全都现场销毁了。

6. 你也是老师啊?原来我们是_____。

7. 他的文章_____了很多资料,数据翔实,很有说服力。

8. 孩子怕父母责备,就_____了自己的考试成绩。

9. 我所做的这些都是_____的小事,你就别表扬我了。

10. 你要根据自己的情况认真考虑,别_____地追赶潮流。

答案

练习一:
略

练习二:
(1) E　　(2)C　　(3)B　　(4)D　　(5)A

练习三:
1. 隐约　2. 同事　3. 引进　4. 引起　5. 淫秽
6. 同行　7. 引用　8. 隐瞒　9. 微不足道　10. 盲目

第11月,第2周的练习

练习一.根据词语给加点的字注音

1.(　)　2.(　)　3.(　)　4.(　)　5.(　)
　捣乱　　回避　　同行　　著作　　侵蚀

练习二.根据拼音填写词语

　　shì　　　shì　　　yǐn　　　yǐn　　　yín
1.同(　)　2.宣(　)　3.(　)用　4.(　)瞒　5.(　)秽

练习三.辨析并选择合适的词填空

1. 这个城堡和那个宫殿是(　)的,有一条秘密通道连接着它们。(相同、相通)

2. 他们都是篮球迷,(　)的爱好使他们成了好朋友。(相同、相通)

3. 这个国家对邻国发动了一场(　)战争。(侵略、侵犯)

4. 这家公司因(　)商标权而被告上了法庭。(侵略、侵犯)

5. 他的精辟的(　)使论文增色不少。(论述、论证)

6. 他花了十年时间收集资料,用事实来(　)自己的观点。(论述、论证)

7. 政府决定在那些偏远地区大力发展教育,用科学知识战胜(　)落后。(愚昧、愚蠢)

8. 她其实很(　),被那个男人骗了好几次,居然还肯相信他。(愚昧、愚蠢)

9. 他善于处理人际关系,跟单位的每个(　)都相处得很融洽。(同事、同行)

10. 我也是搞室内设计的,咱们是(　),以后有空多交流。(同事、同行)

练习四.选词填空

权力　　中途　　无比　　无数　　引进
权益　　中断　　无偿　　引起　　引用

1. 这篇经济学论文(　)了很多经典案例。

2. 当得知儿子成为世界冠军后,这位母亲感到(　)自豪。

3. 消费者协会的宗旨是要维护广大消费者的(　)。

4. 风刮断了电线,一时间,这个城市(　)了与外界的联系。

5. 当失主知道自己钱包被偷时才发现小偷已经(　)下车了。

6. 他在当地政府有很大的(　),所以找他办事的人很多。

7. 他的异常举动(　)了警察的注意。

8. 男女老少都很喜欢这位影星,她在世界各地有(　)的影迷。

9. 对于残疾人,学校可以(　)提供技术培训。

10. 这个印刷厂不惜巨资(　)了两台进口设备。

练习五.成语填空

1.(　)(　)不息　2. 得不(　)(　)　3.(　)(　)不迫
4.(　)(　)不足　5. 微不(　)(　)

练习六.写出下列词语的同义词

1. 侵犯(　)　　　　2. 撒谎(　)
3. 回避(　)　　　　4. 注视(　)
5. 引进(　)

练习七.写出下列词语的反义词

1. 隐瞒(　)　　　　2. 无数(　)
3. 无偿(　)　　　　4. 相通(　)
5. 相同(　)

答案

练习一.
1.dǎo　2.bì　3.háng　4.zuò　5.shí

练习二.
1. 事　2. 誓　3. 引　4. 隐　5. 淫

练习三.
1. 相通　2. 相同　3. 侵略　4. 侵犯　5. 论述
6. 论证　7. 愚昧　8. 愚蠢　9. 同事　10. 同行

练习四.
1. 引用　2. 无比　3. 权益　4. 中断　5. 中途
6. 权力　7. 引起　8. 无数　9. 无偿　10. 引进

练习五.
1. 川流　2. 偿失　3. 从容　4. 美中　5. 足道

练习六.
1. 进犯　2. 说谎　3. 躲避　4. 凝视　5. 引入

练习七.
1. 坦白　2. 有限　3. 有偿　4. 相隔　5. 相反

11月 第3周的学习内容

星期一

休息 xiūxi ⊗ 劳动 láodòng （甲）动

to rest

常用搭配
休息休息 to take a rest

用法示例
出去以前我休息了一个小时。
I had one hour of rest before I went out.
咱们休息一会儿吧。
Let's have a break.
休息一会儿后,比赛继续进行。
After a short break the match continued.

结合 jiéhé （乙）动

combine; integrate

常用搭配
理论与实践相结合 combine theory with practice
A 和 B 结合起来。 A integrates with B.

用法示例
他的性格是刚与柔的结合。
His character is a combination of strength and tenderness.
他的作品是技艺和想象力的完美的结合。
His work is the perfect union of craftsmanship and imagination.

挑选 tiāoxuǎn ⊜ 选择 xuǎnzé （丙）动

select; choose

常用搭配
认真挑选 choose carefully
挑选首饰 select jewelry

用法示例
她从收藏品中挑选了一枚钻石戒指。
She selected a diamond ring from the collection.
我花了几个小时的时间挑选窗帘。
I spent several hours choosing curtains.
我挑选了一件红衬衣,因为我喜欢红颜色。
I picked a red shirt because I like red.

通常 tōngcháng （丙）形

① ordinary; normal ② usually

常用搭配
通常情况下 in normal conditions

用法示例
她按照通常的习惯,在海滨别墅度过了星期天。
She followed her usual custom of spending Sunday at her seaside villa.
他通常在附近的超市购物。
He usually goes shopping in the nearby supermarket.
老年人通常比年轻人保守。
Old people are usually more conservative than young people.

提议 tíyì ⊜ 建议 jiànyì （丙）名／动

① proposal; suggestion ② to propose

常用搭配
一项提议 a proposal
我提议…… I suggest that …

用法示例
他提议根据新形势的要求,修改工作计划。
He suggested that the work plan should be tailored to the new situation.
这项提议已提交大会了。
The motion was put to the assembly.
经过慎重的考虑,我们决定接受他们的提议。
After careful consideration, we've decided to accept their offer.

体面 tǐmiàn （丙）名／形

① face; dignity ② honorable; respectable

常用搭配
有失体面 a loss of face
体面的外表 a respectable appearance

用法示例
他希望改邪归正,过体面的生活。
He wishes to straighten himself out, and lead an honorable life.
太太先生们的举止应该总是十分体面的。
Ladies, and gentlemen, should always act with great dignity.

条例 tiáolì （丙）名

rule; regulation

常用搭配
安全条例 safety regulations
组织条例 organizational rules

本条例自公布之日起施行。

These regulations come into force upon promulgation.

他因违犯绝密条例，而成了嫌疑人。

By breaking the rule of absolute secrecy, he became a marked man.

tōngsú
通俗　　　　　　反 深奥 shēnào　　（丁）形

common; popular

常用搭配

通俗歌曲 popular song

通俗读物 popular literature

用法示例

他善于用通俗的语言说明深刻的道理。

He is good at expressing a profound truths in simple language.

他的小说生动有趣，通俗易懂。

His novels are interesting and easy to understand.

tōngyòng
通用　　　　　　　　　　　（丁）动

① common (use) ② interchangeable

常用搭配

通用插座 utility socket

通用电气公司 General Electric Company(GE)

用法示例

渐渐地，这种货币不再通用了。

Gradually, this kind of currency fell into disuse.

英语现在通用于全世界。

English is used all over the world today.

tìdài
替代　　　　　　　　　　　（丁）动

be a substitute for

常用搭配

用茶替代咖啡 substitution of tea for coffee

替代作用 substitution effect

用法示例

塑胶有时可以替代皮革。

Plastic is sometimes used instead of leather.

人和机器不同，人是不可替代的。

A person, unlike a machine, is not replaceable.

帆船已被汽船所替代。

The sailing ships were superseded by the steamships.

tìhuàn
替换　　　　　　　　　　　（丁）动

shift; replace

常用搭配

让 3 号替换 8 号 replace player No.8 with No. 3

用法示例

带上一套替换的衣服。

Take a change of clothes with you.

他们应该把他替换下来。

They should get a replacement for him.

shí quán shí měi
十全十美

be perfect in every way

常用搭配

使事物达到十全十美 bring sth to perfection

用法示例

别想找十全十美的工作了——那简直是幻想。

Stop looking for a perfect job—it's just a fantasy.

那种工作不可能做到十全十美。

Perfection is impossible to achieve with that kind of work.

 词义辨析

替代、替

"替代"和"替换"都是动词，都表示更换。"替代"强调代替或取代，以 A 换 B，A 起 B 的作用，但是 B 几乎不可能再换 A；"替换"则强调轮换，A 和 B 交替进行，A 和 B 可能发挥相同的作用，也可能发挥不同的作用。例如：①教练在比赛即将结束时频繁地替换球员。②如果没有煤，可以用石油来替代。

Both 替代 and 替换 are verbs, indicating "to replace". 替代 stresses "to take the place of", "A replaces B, and functions as B". But there is little possibility that B will replace A in return; 替换 stresses "to alternate", A and B do, or execute, in turns. The function of A may be the same as B, or different from B. For example: ① The coach rotates her players frequently near the end of the game. ② If there is no coal, oil can be used instead.

 **练习**

练习一、根据拼音写汉字，根据汉字写拼音

tiáo（　　）tì（　　）（　　）sú xiū（　　）（　　）xuǎn
（　　）例 （　　）换 通（　　）（　　）息 挑（　　）

练习二、搭配连线

(1) 挑选　　　　　　　A. 提议
(2) 一项　　　　　　　B. 歌曲
(3) 安全　　　　　　　C. 货币
(4) 通用　　　　　　　D. 首饰
(5) 通俗　　　　　　　E. 条例

练习三、从今天学习的生词中选择合适的词填空

1. 这是全国 _____ 的银行卡,在任何一个城市都能使用。
2. 世界上根本就没有 _____ 的人,但有些人就是喜欢追求完美。
3. 我喜欢听 _____ 歌曲,而他喜欢听美声。
4. 这个骗子穿得很 _____,在出入高档场所时保安根本没有怀疑他。
5. 出差前,他特意回家拿了两套 _____ 的衣服。
6. 报考大学的时候,不要盲目地追求大学的名气,而是应该 _____ 自己的特长和兴趣,选择适合自己的院校。
7. 这些礼物是我和爱人精心 _____ 的,但愿他们会喜欢。
8. 工作的时候,一定要严格遵守安全 _____。
9. 在科学发展史上,爱因斯坦的地位是不可 _____ 的。
10. 我周末 _____ 会逛逛街、收拾收拾房间、洗洗衣服什么的。

答案

练习一：
略

练习二：
(1) D　　(2)A　　(3)E　　(4)C　　(5)B

练习三：
1. 通用　　2. 十全十美　3. 通俗　　4. 体面　　5. 替换
6. 结合　　7. 挑选　　8. 条例　　9. 替代　　10. 通常

 星期二

bùmén
部门　　　　　　　　　　　（乙）名

department; division

常用搭配

人事部门 HR department
教育部门 educational department

用法示例

他在政府的行政部门工作。
He works for the executive branch of the government.
环保部门要求我们使用无烟煤。
We are required by the environmental protection department to use anthracite.
你在这个公司的哪个部门工作?
Which division of the company do you work in?

jígé
及格　　　　　　　　　　　（乙）动

to pass a test

常用搭配

考试不及格 fail to pass the exam
他(考试)及格了。He passed (an examination).

用法示例

他历史考试不及格,其他科目都通过了。
Except for history, he passed all his other subjects.
如果你作弊,考试及格也没什么价值。
There is little merit in passing the examination if you cheated.
她每一项测试都及格了。
She passed every test.

guīgé
规格　　　　　　　　　　　（丁）名

specification

常用搭配

规格标准 specification standards
规格齐全 complete the specifications
不符合规格 fall short of the specifications

用法示例

不知你们有没有这种规格的产品?
Have you got a product of this specification?
你能给我一份有规格说明的价目单吗?
Can you give me a price list with the specification listed?

shōují　　　　　sōují
收集　　🔄 搜集　　　　　（丙）动

gather; collect

常用搭配

收集邮票 collect stamps

收集资料 gather information

用法示例

你收集到的大部分信息没有实用价值。

Much of the information you have gleaned is of no practical use.

为了收集数据我们发给他们一些调查表。

We gave them some questionnaires to collect data.

收集这些邮票花了我一百块钱。

It cost me 100 yuan to collect the stamps.

zītài

姿态 姿势 （丙）名

posture; stance

常用搭配

各种不同姿态的泥塑 clay figurines in various postures

采取强硬的姿态 take a strong posture

用法示例

他把叔叔的声音和姿态模仿得惟妙惟肖。

He mimicked his uncle's voice and gestures perfectly.

为了合作,我们公司向那家公司表示出友善的姿态。

Our company made a show of goodwill to that company for its cooperation.

你是领导,姿态要高一些。

You are the leader, and you should be tolerant.

zīshì

姿势 （丙）名

posture; position

常用搭配

直立的姿势 an erect posture

姿势优美 have a graceful posture

姿势端正 have a regular posture

用法示例

那位画家要求她摆好姿势。

The artist asked her to pose for him.

他用一只手臂围住她,做出保护的姿势。

He put his arm round her in a protective gesture.

bùwèi

部位 （丁）名

position; place

常用搭配

发音时舌的部位

the position of the tongue when speaking

受伤部位 an injured part

用法示例

我们得防止敌人从防守不严的部位逃走。

We should lead the enemy away from the weaker areas.

医生检查了他受伤的部位。

The doctor examined the part which was wounded.

jiǎntǎo

检讨 （丁）动/名

① examine one's own mistakes ② self-criticism

常用搭配

检讨书 self-criticism

作检讨 make a self-criticism

用法示例

我将深刻检讨自己的行为。

I will deeply examine my behavior.

在总结今年的工作之前,我们的总经理先作了检讨。

Before summarizing this year's work, our general manager made a self-criticism.

jiānchá

监察 监督 （丁）动

supervise

常用搭配

监察员 supervisor

监察委员会 supervision commission

监察制度 supervisory system

用法示例

他负责监察我们部门的工作。

He is in charge of supervising our department.

他在一家工厂作安全监察员。

He works in a factory as a safety supervisor.

jiǎncè

检测 检验 （丁）动

detect

常用搭配

检测设备 monitoring equipment

检测仪器 detecting instrument

用法示例

他的职责就是检测产品的质量。

His duty is to monitor the quality of products.

他们正在检测这些仪器。

They are detecting these instruments.

zīchǎn

资产 （丁）名

assets; property

常用搭配

资产净值 net value 资产总额 gross assets

国有资产 national assets

用法示例

如果你所负的债务超过了你的资产,你就会破产。

If your liabilities exceed your assets, you may go bankrupt.

这些厂房和设备只是他的部分资产。

These workshops and this equipment are just a part of his assents.

chéng qiān shàng wàn

成 千 上 万 （丙）

thousands upon thousands

常用搭配
成千上万的观众 an audience of thousands
成千上万只鸟 thousands of birds

用法示例
暴风给成千上万的人带来了灾难。
The cyclone brought misery to thousands of people.
成千上万的牲畜正在挨饿。
Thousands of cattle are starving.
在内战期间成千上万的人逃离了这个国家。
During the civil war thousands of people fled the country.

 **词义辨析**

姿态、姿势
　　"姿态"和"姿势"都是名词,都可以表示体态。"姿态"强调内涵,包括神情、态度和气度。"姿势"只是身体外在的具体样子。例如:①画面上少女的姿态/姿势十分端庄优雅。②她摆好姿势,准备照相。③警察对绑架者采取了温和的姿态。

　　Both 姿态 and 姿势 are nouns, meaning "posture". 姿态 stresses "connotation, including manner and bearing," while 姿势 only indicates a position of the body. For example: ① The posture of the girl in the picture is very graceful. ② She posed for a photograph. ③ The police took a moderate stance towards abductors.

 **练习**

练习一、根据拼音写汉字,根据汉字写拼音
zī ( ) ( )tǎo ( )chá zī ( ) ( )gé
( )势 检( ) 监( ) ( )产 规( )

练习二、搭配连线
(1) 收集　　　　　A. 仪器
(2) 检测　　　　　B. 部门
(3) 姿势　　　　　C. 齐全
(4) 行政　　　　　D. 优美
(5) 规格　　　　　E. 邮票

练习三、从今天学习的生词中选择合适的词填空
1. 我们一定要加强 _____ 工作,保证工程质量。
2. 这个小岛被称为鸟岛,每年春天都会有 _____ 的鸟光顾这里。
3. 你们做这套试卷时不要看书、查资料,_____ 一下自己的实际水平。
4. 打太极拳可以锻炼身体的各个 _____。
5. 他喜欢 _____ 车模,现在已经有两千多件了。
6. 他考了 57 分,很遗憾,没 _____。
7. 在照相之前,摄影师要帮模特摆好 _____,并选择合适的摄影角度。
8. 由于尺寸不合 _____,买来的零件不能用。
9. 事情被发现后,他对自己的所作所为作了深刻的 _____。
10. 随着音乐响起,他们跳起了舞蹈,_____ 非常优美。

 **答案**

练习一:
略
练习二:
(1) E　　(2)A　　(3) D　　(4)B　　(5)C
练习三:
1. 监察　　2.成千上万　3.检测　　4.部位　　5.收集
6.及格　　7.姿势　　8.规格　　9.检讨　　10.姿态

星期三

zhuānjiā
专家 （乙）名
expert; specialist

常用搭配
法律专家 legal expert
金融专家 expert in finance

用法示例
她是个有声望的专家。
She is a reputable expert.
她是著名的幼儿教育专家。
He's a well-known expert in primary education.
专家们正在勘查这个岛。
The experts are exploring the island.

jīnshǔ
金属 （乙）名
metal

常用搭配
金属零件 metal parts
金属制品 metal products

用法示例
铜和金都是金属。
Copper and gold are both metals.
铝是一种轻的银色的金属。
Aluminum is a kind of light silvery metal.

bùzhòu
步骤 （丙）名
measure; step

常用搭配
解决问题的步骤 moves towards solving a problem

用法示例
换轮胎的第一个步骤是卸下车轮。
The first step in changing a car tire is to loosen the wheel.
我们将有计划有步骤地进行工作。
We will carry on the work step by step in a planned way.
他们遵照指示中的每一个步骤。
They followed every step of the instructions.

lúnkuò
轮廓 （丙）名
outline

常用搭配
轮廓清晰 clear-cut
脸的轮廓 the contour of a face
山的轮廓 profile of the mountain

用法示例
那座大山的轮廓看上去像一条龙。
The outline of that mountain looks like a dragon.
雕塑平滑的轮廓线简直太美了。
The smooth contour of the sculpture is wonderful.
先画轮廓，再画细部。
Draw an outline before you fill in the details.

tōngbào
通报 回 通知 **tōngzhī** （丁）动/名
① circulate information ② bulletin

常用搭配
通报批评 to make one's malpractice, etc. known to all as a criticism
通报人 notifier

用法示例
客人来时你通报一声好吗？
Would you give me notice when the guests come in?
你看那份通报了吗？
Have you read the correspondence?

tōnggào
通告 回 公告 **gōnggào** （丁）动/名
① announce; give notice ② notice; announcement

常用搭配
发出通告 give out a notice
张贴通告 put up a notice

用法示例
该通告将于明日见报。
The announcement will appear in tomorrow's newspaper.
有些报纸刊登出生、婚姻、死亡的通告。
Announcements of births, marriages and deaths appear in some newspapers.
这项通告证明了我的猜测是对的。
The announcement confirmed my suspicions.

liánméng
联盟 反 决裂 **juéliè** （丙）名
federation; alliance

常用搭配
工农联盟 alliance of the workers and peasants
国际联盟 the League of Nations
与……结成联盟 make an alliance with…

用法示例
其他国家正在结成联盟。
The other nations are forming a federation.
他们中止了联盟。
They broke up the alliance.
哪个国家在联盟中居于支配地位？
Which country is the predominant member of the alliance?

zhuānlì
专利 （丁）名
patent

常用搭配

专利产品 patented product　专利技术 patent technology
专利申请 patent application

用法示例

他获得了这项发明的专利权。
He got a patent for this invention.
这项专利期限为 3 年。
The patent runs out in three years time.
那是我的专利发明。
It is my patent device.

zhuāncháng
专长　反弱项 （丁）名

specialty

常用搭配

学术专长 academic aptitude
没有专长 have no special skill

用法示例

你的专长是什么？
What's your specialty?
可别问我怎么摊鸡蛋，烹饪不是我的专长。
Don't ask me how to make an omelette; cooking isn't my forte.
她把与顾客讨价还价看作自己的专长。
She regards negotiating prices with customers as her special preserve.

bùjú
布局 （丁）名

layout; arrangement; composition

常用搭配

国民经济的布局 layout of the national economy
工业的合理布局 rational distribution of industry
布局巧妙的画 a painting masterful in composition

用法示例

他为我们介绍了花园中对称的布局。
He introduced to us the symmetrical arrangement of the garden.
她的画有功力，但布局欠佳。
Her drawing is competent, but her composition is poor.
他们正在了解房屋的布局。
They are getting to know the geography of the house.

liánxiǎng
联想 （丁）动

associate

常用搭配

联想记忆 associative memory
联想思维 associative thinking
联想学习 associative learning

用法示例

她把幸福和有钱联想到一起。
She associated happiness with having money.

我总是由他联想到猴子。
I always associate him with a monkey.
你能从大海联想到什么？
What associations does the sea have for you?

qī zuǐ bā shé
七嘴八舌 （丁）

everybody talking at the same time

常用搭配

别七嘴八舌的！　Don't all talk at once.

用法示例

听到这个决定后，工人们开始七嘴八舌地议论。
After having heard the decision, the workers all began to discuss it at once.
报社记者七嘴八舌地高声向他提问时，他表现得很镇定。
He was as cool as a cucumber when the newspaper reporters bombarded him with questions.

 词义辨析

通报、通

1. 作为名词，"通报"和"通告"都是一种通知的形式。"通报"指上级机关把有关情况传达给下级机关，通常是文件的形式，只限于相关单位或人员；"通告"指公开的通知，为了让大家都知道，往往会张贴在公共场所。例如：①会上，我们讨论了总部的通报。②你看报纸上的政府通告了吗？

As nouns, 通报 and 通告 are two kinds of notifications. 通报 indicates that a superior unit imparts information to a junior unit, usually in the form of a formal document, and is just given to related units or people concerned; while 通告 indicates an open notice that is given to the public. Usually it is posted in a public place. For example: ① We discussed the circulated notification from headquarters at the meeting. ② Did you read the government's announcement in the newspaper?

2. 作为动词，"通报"和"通告"都有通知的意思，"通报"指把信息告诉上级或主管，"通告"指普遍地通知。例如：①立即把这个消息通报给总部。②政府定期向公众通告有关情况。

As verbs, 通报 and 通告 all mean "to inform". 通报 indicates to report information to a superior unit or director; 通告 indicates to inform the public generally. For example: ① Report this information to headquarters at once. ② The government regularly notifies the public of important information.

 **练习**

练习一、根据拼音写汉字，根据汉字写拼音

( )kuò ( )zhòu ( )shǔ lián ( ) bù ( )
轮( ) 步( ) 金( ) ( )盟 ( )局

练习二、搭配连线

(1) 专利   A. 专家
(2) 国际   B. 产品
(3) 张贴   C. 联盟
(4) 通报   D. 通告
(5) 教育   E. 批评

练习三、从今天学习的生词中选择合适的词填空

1. 上级领导认为我们改革的成果十分显著,并在大会上对我们进行了 _____ 表扬。

2. 在各门功课中,数学是他的 _____ ,英语和体育则比较差。

3. 这几个国家组成了 _____ 来共同对抗敌国。

4. 今天有点薄雾,远处的山只能看个大概的 _____ 。

5. 他是这个领域的 _____ ,一定要重视他的意见。

6. 这是一个大型实验,为了确保实验成果,这位专家亲自检查实验的每一个 _____ 。

7. 市政府发出了在公共场所禁烟的 _____ ,希望全体市民共同维护环境。

8. 请别着急,大家按顺序发言,不要在下面 _____ 地议论。

9. 专家确认了这项发明的成果,并为发明者颁发了 _____ 证书。

10. 所有的 _____ 都有导电的特性,金子也不例外。

答案

练习一:
略

练习二:

(1) B	(2)C	(3)D	(4)E	(5)A

练习三:

1. 通报	2. 专长	3. 联盟	4. 轮廓	5. 专家
6. 步骤	7. 通告	8. 七嘴八舌	9. 专利	10. 金属

星期四 Thursday

biǎomiàn
表面 反 实质 （乙）名

surface; appearance

常用搭配

地球的表面 the surface of the earth
家具的表面 surface of the furniture

用法示例

这张桌子的表面很光亮,可是它的背面却很粗糙。
The table had a shiny surface, but underneath it was rough.
他只是表面诚实而已。
He is only honest on the surface.
不要根据表面现象来判断。
Do not judge by appearances.

jízhōng
集中 反 分散 （乙）动/形

① concentrate; get together ② concentrated

常用搭配

集中精力 concentrate one's energy
集中供暖 central heating

用法示例

大家的目光都集中在发言人身上。
All eyes were focused on the speaker.
你应该把心思集中在学习上。
You should focus your mind on study.
紧张和疲劳常使人精神不集中。
Stress and tiredness often result in a lack of concentration.

jítuán
集团 （丙）名

bloc; group

常用搭配

军事集团 a military bloc
集团公司 group companies

用法示例

该公司隶属于一个国际金融集团。
The company belongs to an international financial group.
警方在调查瞒税案件时意外地发现了一个贩毒集团。
Police investigating tax fraud stumbled across a drug ring.

tújìng
途径 （丙）名

way; channel

常用搭配

外交途径 diplomatic channels
非法途径 illegal ways

【用法示例】

他们探索过各种途径,但是没有找到解决的办法。

They explored every avenue but could not find a solution.

你的意见必须通过正当途径投诉。

Your complaint must be made through the proper channels.

成功的唯一途径是勤奋。

The only way to succeed is to work hard.

jìnsì
近似　　　　　　　　　　　　（丁）动

approximate; be similar to

【常用搭配】

和……近似 be similar to…

以近似的方式 in a similar way

【用法示例】

西班牙语与拉丁语近似。

Spanish is akin to Latin.

我的看法跟你的近似。

My opinion is similar to yours.

目前的危机与大战前夕的形势近似。

The present crisis is analogous with the situation immediately before the war.

lèisì
类似　　　　　　　　　　　　（丙）形

similar; analogous

【常用搭配】

类似于…… is similar to…

类似的产品 similar products

类似的经历 similar experience

【用法示例】

大蕉类似于香蕉。

A plantain is similar to a banana.

类似的原因往往产生类似的结果。

Similar causes tend to produce similar results.

这项提案与上次会议上我们讨论过的那份类似。

This proposal was analogous with the one we discussed at the last meeting.

róngxǔ
容许　　　　　　　　　　　　（丙）动

permit; allow

【常用搭配】

如条件容许 if conditions permit

容许他解释 permit him to explain

【用法示例】

这条河很宽可容许大船航行。

The river can be used by big ships because of its width.

情况不容许有任何耽搁。

The situation does not permit for any delay.

我们不容许有这种事情发生。

We don't allow such things to be done.

nàshuì
纳税　　　　　反　征税zhēngshuì　　　（丁）动

pay taxes

【常用搭配】

纳税人 taxpayer

纳税对象 object of taxation

纳税的义务 duty to pay taxes

【用法示例】

法律使我们负有纳税的义务。

The law obliges us to pay taxes.

不纳税就可能被起诉。

Failure to pay your taxes will make you liable to prosecution.

你有什么要申报纳税的吗?

Do you have anything to declare tax wise?

róngnà
容纳　　　　　　　　　　　　（丁）动

accommodate; contain

【常用搭配】

这间房能容纳几个人?

How many people does the room hold?

【用法示例】

这间大厅最多容纳 70 人。

This hall holds a maximum of seventy people.

这家戏院只能容纳 250 名观众。

The theatre admits an audiences of only 250.

一套单元房可容纳一个五口之家。

One flat can accommodate a family of five.

miànróng
面容　　　　　　　　　　　　（丁）名

facial appearance; face

【常用搭配】

面容憔悴 look haggard

面容消瘦 look emaciated

【用法示例】

我就是想不起他的面容。

I just can't call his face to mind.

他的面容让人永生难忘。

His face is never forgotten.

她罩的面纱遮掩了她的面容。

The veil she wore obscured her features.

biǎozhāng
表彰　　　　　反　惩处chéngchǔ　　　（丁）动

cite (in dispatches); commend

【常用搭配】

表彰劳模 to commend model workers

表彰先进集体 give commendation to the advanced units

【用法示例】

公司发给他一笔额外奖金以表彰他出色的工作。

The firm recognized his outstanding work by giving him an extra bonus.

所有的英勇的战士都受到了表彰。
All the soldiers were commended for bravery in battle.
政府授予他勋章,以表彰他的卓著功绩。
The government recognized his outstanding service by giving him a medal.

sān fān wǔ cì
三番五次 　　　　　　　　　　　(丁)
time and again

常用搭配
三番五次地强调 to stress again and again
三番五次地邀请她 to invite her time and again

用法示例
我三番五次地告诉过你,不要做那种事。
I've told you again and again not to do that.
我三番五次请她来,她都断然拒绝了。
I asked her several times to come, but she categorically refused.
他三番五次地问问题惹得我回答时也没有好气。
His persistent questions finally goaded me into an angry reply.

词义辨析

类似、近似

"类似"和"近似"都是形容词,都有相似、相像的意思,都可以与"跟"、"与""和"搭配。"类似"强调属于同类的或可类比的,有时候可以带动词。"近似"常用于书面语,强调形式或情况比较接近,不能带动词。例如:①写文章类似于建房子,需要好的材料和周密的设计。②他们用不同的试验方法,得出了近似的结论。

Both 类似 and 近似 are adjectives, meaning "similar". They are usually used in collocation with 跟 , 与 and 和 . 类似 stresses something being of the same kind, comparable, and sometimes it can be followed by a verb; while 近似 is quite literary, stressing similarity in form or condition, which can not be followed by a verb. For example: ① Writing an article, like building a house, needs good material and a deliberate design. ② They did the experiment in a different way, but got approximate results.

练习

练习一、根据拼音写汉字,根据汉字写拼音
( )jìng　nà( )　( )zhāng　( )róng　( )sì
途( )　( )税　表( )　面( )　类( )

练习二、搭配连线
(1) 集中　　　　　　A. 憔悴
(2) 非法　　　　　　B. 劳模
(3) 面容　　　　　　C. 精力
(4) 表彰　　　　　　D. 集团
(5) 军事　　　　　　E. 途径

练习三、从今天学习的生词中选择合适的词填空
1. 大病一场后再见她,她的 _____ 有点憔悴。
2. 警察捣毁了一个国际走私 _____ ,其中涉及到了好几个国家的 100 多名犯罪分子。
3. 老百姓要求政府对 _____ 人的税款用途进行详细通报。
4. 鱼类的鳃与人类的肺功能相 _____ 。
5. 这个音乐厅能 _____ 一万人。
6. 这两个城市的物价水平 _____ ,可工资水平却存在很大差距。
7. 中方认为两国的矛盾还是尽量通过外交 _____ 解决,以免事态进一步恶化。
8. 我不想接受采访,可是那名记者 _____ 地给我打电话。
9. 大会对各行各业的先进工作者进行了 _____ 。
10. 他想搬出去一个人住,可是父母不 _____ 。

答案

练习一:
略
练习二:
(1) C　　　(2)E　　　(3)A　　　(4)B　　　(5)D
练习三:
1. 面容　　2. 集团　　3. 纳税　　4. 类似　　5. 容纳
6. 近似　　7. 途径　　8. 三番五次 9. 表彰　　10. 容许

星期五 Friday

kěpà
可怕 (乙)形
fearful; frightful; horrible

常用搭配
可怕的声音 a fearful sound
可怕的灾难 terrible catastrophe
可怕的怪物 a grisly monster

用法示例
昨天在这里发生了一起可怕的事故。
There was a horrible accident here yesterday.
那座房子是个多么可怕的地方啊！
What a ghastly place that house is!
那是一次可怕的经历。
That was a terrible experience.

wènhòu
问候 ⑩ 问好 (乙)动
wènhǎo

send a greeting

常用搭配
亲切的问候 warm greeting
向她表示问候 say hello to her

用法示例
我向他表达了诚挚的问候。
I send him my earnest regards.
他要我问候你。
He asked me to inquire after you.
他每次来信都向你表示问候。
He always asks after you in his letters.

jiěfàng
解放 (乙)动/名
① liberate ② liberation

常用搭配
解放思想 emancipate the mind
解放奴隶 emancipate slaves
中国人民解放军 the Chinese People's Liberation Army

用法示例
解放前,他们一家住在农村。
The family lived in a village before liberation.
军队解放了这些地区。
The army had liberated these occupied areas.
她对妇女解放运动的历史很感兴趣。
She is interested in the history of the women's liberation movement.

tóuxiáng
投降 ⑩ 反抗 (丙)动
fǎnkàng

surrender

常用搭配
无条件投降 unconditional surrender
向敌人投降。Surrender to the enemy.

用法示例
我们宁死也不投降。
We would rather die than surrender.
他们向敌人投降了。
They surrendered to the enemy.
士兵们被迫投降了。
The soldiers had to yield.

mányuàn
埋怨 ⑩ 抱怨 (丁)动
bàoyuàn

complain; blame

常用搭配
互相埋怨 blame one another
别埋怨他。Don't blame it on him.

用法示例
我们对他没完没了的埋怨感到厌烦。
We are tired of his incessant complaining.
她埋怨他马虎。
She complained of his carelessness.
我们输了比赛以后没有互相埋怨。
We didn't blame each other after we lost the game.

tóujī
投机 (丙)形
① speculate ② opportunistic

常用搭配
投机分子 opportunist
投机市场 speculative market
投机取巧 speculate and take advantage of an opportunity

用法示例
他们投机购买粮食是不合法的。
Their speculative buying of grain is illegal.
他是金融领域的投机者。
He is an adventurer in the financial field.
做投机买卖是很危险的。
It's dangerous to speculate.

bàoyuàn
抱怨 (丁)动
complain; grumble

常用搭配
没什么可抱怨的 nothing to grumble about
抱怨坏天气 complain about the bad weather

用法示例
游客抱怨说房间太脏了。
The tourist complained that the room was too dirty.
这个女孩总是抱怨没有合适的衣服。
The girl always complains about lacking suitable raiment.
他们抱怨工资过低。
They complained that the wages were too low.

kěqiǎo
可巧 （丙）副

by a happy coincidence

用法示例

大家正念叨他,可巧他来了。

We were just talking about him when he turned up.

可巧他们都在那儿。

It so happened that they were all there.

他来访时,可巧我刚回来。

I happened to be back when he called.

wènshì
问世 （丁）动

to be published; come out

常用搭配

新产品即将问世。The new product will come out soon.

用法示例

自从原子动力问世以来,工业发生了巨大的变化。

Since the advent of atomic power, there have been great changes in industry.

经过千辛万苦这部词典才终于得以问世。

It's been a long haul, but at last this dictionary is published.

他的新书将于春季问世。

His new book will be appearing in the spring.

jiěsàn
解散 反 集合 jíhé （丁）名

dissolve; disband

常用搭配

解散国会 dissolve parliament

用法示例

网球俱乐部已经解散了。

The tennis club has disbanded.

总统宣布解散国会。

The president announced the dissolution of parliament.

士兵在列队行进之后,很快便解散了。

The men fell out quickly after their march.

shìfàng
释放 （丁）动

release

常用搭配

释放电流 release a current

释放犯人 release a prisoner

刑满释放

be released upon completion of a sentence

用法示例

植物可以吸收二氧化碳释放氧气。

Plants can absorb carbon dioxide and release oxygen.

有些罪犯被释放后有可能重新犯罪。

Some criminals are likely to offend again when they are released.

只要交了罚款,他就会被释放。

He will be set free as soon as the fine is paid.

qiān fāng bǎi jì
千方百计 （丙）

use every conceivable means

常用搭配

千方百计地劝说他 make every attempt to persuade him

用法示例

他一定会千方百计地阻止你。

He'll use any trick in the book to stop you.

她千方百计地想逃跑。

She made every attempt to escape.

 词义辨析

抱怨、埋

　　"抱怨"和"埋怨"都是动词,都有表达不满的意思。"抱怨"强调不满意的感受,它的对象可以是事物,也可以是人,但通常不是自己。"埋怨"有责备的意思,它的对象一般是人,可以是自己。例如:①他们抱怨书太贵了。②她埋怨自己太马虎了。

　　Both 抱怨 and 埋怨 are verbs, meaning "to complain". 抱怨 stresses to express feelings of dissatisfaction. Its objects may be something or somebody (but not oneself); while 埋怨 has the sense of blame. Its objects are somebody (including oneself). For example: ① They complained that books were too expensive. ② She complained about her own carelessness.

 练习

练习一、根据拼音写汉字,根据汉字写拼音

tóu（　）（　）yuàn　shì（　）（　）sàn（　）hòu

（　）降　埋（　）（　）放　解（　）问（　）

练习二、搭配连线

(1) 释放　　　　　　　　A. 别人

(2) 解散　　　　　　　　B. 问候

(3) 投机　　　　　　　　C. 犯人

(4) 埋怨　　　　　　　　D. 国会

(5) 亲切　　　　　　　　E. 取巧

练习三、从今天学习的生词中选择合适的词填空

1. 生活中遇到不顺心的事时不要总_____,要想办法解决问题。

2. 他们俩有共同的兴趣爱好,说话很_____。

3. 我昨天晚上做了一个_____的梦,梦到自己从山上掉了下来。

4. 起床起晚了,他_____妈妈没有及时叫醒他。

5. 那个推销员说了很多好话,_____就是想把东西推销出去。

6. 我们把敌军包围了起来,敌军看没有冲出去的可能,就被

迫 _____ 了。

7. 留学生篮球队曾经有 20 多人,后来大家陆续回国了,篮球队也就只好 _____ 了。

8. 这种物质燃烧后 _____ 出的气体有毒。

9. 我去她家的时候, _____ 另外两个朋友也在。

10. 听说他正在写一部长篇小说,我们都期待着他的作品尽快 _____。

答案

练习一:
略

练习二:
(1) C   (2)D   (3)E   (4)A   (5)B

练习三:
1. 抱怨   2. 投机   3. 可怕   4. 埋怨   5.千方百计
6. 投降   7. 解散   8. 释放   9. 可巧   10. 问世

第 11 月 ,第 3 周的练习

练习一 . 根据词语给加点的字注音
1.( )   2.( )   3.( )   4.( )   5.( )
专长   投降   埋怨   纳税   轮廓

练习二 . 根据拼音填写词语
bù   bù   bù   jí   jí
1.( )骤   2.( )局   3.( )位   4.( )格   5.( )团

练习三 . 辨析并选择合适的词填空
1. 教练让 3 号上场( )体力不支的 7 号。（替代、替换）
2. 为了减轻高能耗和高污染,人们一直在寻找石油的( )能源。（替代、替换）
3. 她跟你吵架,你就摆个高( ),让着她点不就行了吗?（姿态、姿势）
4. 长期在电脑前保持一个( )、较少运动的人很容易得颈椎疾病。（姿态、姿势）
5. 为了缓解交通压力,政府发了个( ),号召市民尽量乘坐公共交通工具。（通报、通告）
6. 政府的财政支出情况应该向纳税人( )。（通报、通告）
7. 他算出了这道题的( )值。（近似、类似）
8. 如果认真检查,这种事故是可以避免的,希望以后不要再发生( )的事。（近似、类似）
9. 你总是为了那件事而( )我,这不公平。（埋怨、抱怨）
10. 这个人特别爱( ),总是唠叨个没完,就像谁都欠他的似的。（埋怨、抱怨）

练习四 . 选词填空
通常   检查   检测   容许   表面
通俗   通用   监察   容纳   面容

1. "账号"和"帐号"都是一个意思,这两个字在这个词中( )。

2. 你讲得太高深了,听不懂,能不能讲得( )一点?

3. 丈夫的去世对她的打击非常打,几天不见,变得( )消瘦,头发花白。

4. 无聊的时候,你( )怎么打发时间?

5. 经( ),这个牌子的矿泉水含有对人体有害的物质,不适合长期饮用。

6. 我在上大学以前,晚上一超过七点,父母就不( )我出门。

7. 这对明星夫妻在( )上装得非常恩爱,其实他们正在办理离婚手续。

8. 你知道世界上最大的音乐厅能同时( )多少人一起听音乐吗?

9. 老师对我们很严格,每次上课都要( )我们的家庭作业。

10. 近日,有关部门进一步加强了劳动( ),监督企业履行法律责任。

练习五 . 成语填空
1. 十( )十( )   2. 七( )八( )   3. 千( )百( )
4. ( )千( )万   5. 三( )五( )

练习六 . 写出下列词语的同义词
1. 姿态( )   2. 收集( )
3. 挑选( )   4. 通报( )
5. 埋怨( )

练习七 . 写出下列词语的反义词
1. 集中( )   2. 表彰( )
3. 通俗( )   4. 专长( )
5. 解散( )

答案

练习一 .
1.cháng   2.xiáng   3.mán   4.shuì   5.kuò

练习二 .
1. 步   2. 布   3. 部   4. 及   5. 集

练习三 .
1. 替换   2. 替代   3. 姿态   4. 姿势   5. 通告
6. 通报   7. 近似   8. 类似   9. 埋怨   10. 抱怨

练习四 .
1. 通用   2. 通俗   3. 面容   4. 通常   5. 检测
6. 容许   7. 表面   8. 容纳   9. 检查   10. 监察

练习五 .
1. 全,美   2. 嘴,舌   3. 方,计   4. 成,上   5. 番,次

练习六 .
1. 姿势   2. 搜集   3. 选择   4. 公告   5. 抱怨

练习七 .
1. 分散   2. 惩处   3. 深奥   4. 弱项   5. 集合

11月 第 4 周的学习内容

星期一

rénwù 人物 （乙）名

characters; figure

常用搭配

小说中的人物 the characters in novels
历史上的大人物 the great figures of history
重要人物 a person of importance

用法示例

这本书中的人物都是虚构的。
All the characters in this book are imaginary.
国王是一个王国中最重要的人物。
The king is the most important person in a kingdom.

rénlèi 人类 （乙）名

human race; mankind

常用搭配

人类的弱点 human foibles
人类环境 human environment
人类社会 human society

用法示例

疾病是人类的敌人。
Disease is an enemy of mankind.
这个新发现将对全人类做出贡献。
This new discovery will contribute to all humanity.
据说同情心是人类特有的感情。
It's said that sympathy is a special feeling characteristic of mankind.

kǒngpà 恐怕 ◎ 也许 yěxǔ （乙）副

(I'm) afraid (that)

常用搭配

恐怕你错了。I'm afraid you're wrong.
恐怕要下雨了。I'm afraid it's going to rain.

用法示例

恐怕我得走了。
I'm afraid I need to go.
恐怕我们不能答应这件事。
I am afraid we can not permit that.

这台旧收音机恐怕不能修了。
I'm afraid this old radio is beyond repair.

lèixíng 类型 ◎ 种类 zhǒnglèi （丙）名

type

常用搭配

机器的类型 type of machine
各种类型 all kinds of

用法示例

这个地区有两种类型的岩石。
There are two types of rocks in this area.
我不熟悉这种类型的计算机。
I'm unfamiliar with this type of computer.
这两种类型的狗可以杂交繁殖。
These two types of dogs can interbreed.

shēngpà 生怕 ◎ 惟恐 wéikǒng （丁）副

① fearful ② fear

常用搭配

生怕失败 for fear of failure
生怕吵醒某人 be fearful of wakening sb

用法示例

他赶忙躲进一间屋里，生怕让我瞧见。
He ducked into a room for fear I would see him.
他越狱后，时时如惊弓之鸟，生怕再次被捕。
Since he escaped from prison, he has been living on the razor's edge, terrified of recapture.

sōují 搜集 （丙）动

collect; gather

常用搭配

搜集标本 collect specimens
搜集情报 gather information
搜集民歌 collect folk songs

用法示例

他正在为写书搜集素材。
He is collecting materials for a book.
他搜集的邮票是我的三倍多。
He has collected more than three times as many stamps as I (have).
她喜欢搜集小摆设。
She likes collecting bric-a-brac.

bēi 杯 （甲）名/量

glass; cup

常用搭配

塑料杯 plastic cup
一杯咖啡 a cup of coffee
三杯啤酒 three glasses of beer

用法示例

我需要买几个咖啡杯。
I need to buy some tea cups.
他每天早晨喝一杯牛奶。
Every morning he drinks a glass of milk.

sōusuǒ
搜索　　　　⊜搜寻　　（丁）动
sōuxún
search

常用搭配

四处搜索 search everywhere for
仔细搜索 search carefully

用法示例

飞机被彻底搜查了一遍。
The plane was searched thoroughly.
士兵们在山上搜索失事的飞机。
The soldiers combed the hills for the site of the plane crash.
警察搜索了周围六英里以内的树林。
The police searched all the woods within a six-mile radius.

rénxìng
人性　　　　　　　　（丁）名
human nature; humanity

常用搭配

探讨人性 discuss human nature
人性的光辉 excellence of human nature

用法示例

人性的弱点之一是懒惰。
One of the frailties of human nature is laziness.
没有什么能使他丧失对人性的信心。
Nothing could extinguish his faith in human nature.
他的残忍表明他没有人性。
His cruelty suggests that he is less than human.

rénquán
人权　　　　　　　　（丁）名
human rights

常用搭配

人权法 Human Rights Act
人权外交 human rights diplomat
人权委员会 Human Rights Commission

用法示例

他就人权问题提出的抗议听起来很有道理。
His protests on human rights sound reasonable.
他的新书是有关人权发展的。
His new book is on the development of human rights.

xínghào
型号　　　　　　　　（丁）名
① model number ② type

常用搭配

各种型号 all kinds of...
打印机的型号 type of printer

用法示例

这种最新型号的洗衣机目前正在你们的商店中出售。
The latest model of this washer is now on sale in your shops.
汽车展览会上展出了今年所有的新型号。
All this year's new models are displayed at the motor show.
这是在所有产品中最受欢迎的型号。
This is the most popular model in our whole range.

chéng xīn chéng yì
诚心诚意　　　　　　　（丁）
with heart and soul

常用搭配

诚心诚意地致歉 to make heart-felt apologies

用法示例

他是诚心诚意地请你原谅。
He cries for your mercy with all his heart.
我们诚心诚意地帮助他们，可他们不接受。
We sincerely wish to help them, but they won't accept our offer.

 词义辨析

恐怕、生

"恐怕"和"生怕"都是副词,都有担心的意思。"恐怕"表示为可能发生的事而担心,还有也许或认为可能的意思,可以用于句首。"生怕"表示为可能发生的事感到很不安和害怕,语气比"恐怕"重,有特别不愿意发生某事的意思,不能用于句首。例如:①快点走,恐怕要下雪。②恐怕,他也不知道怎么办。③他悄悄地跟我说话,生怕别人听到。

Both 恐怕 and 生怕 are adverbs, meaning "to be afraid". 恐 怕 indicates "be afraid that something maybe happen", and it also means "probably or consider probable", and can be used at the beginning of a sentence. While 生怕 indicates being fearful and uneasy about something that maybe happen. The degree of uneasiness is higher than 恐怕 . It has the sense of "being unwilling to see something happen very much". It can not be used at the beginning of a sentence. For example: ① Come on, I'm afraid it is going to snow. ② I am afraid he doesn't know how to deal with it either. ③ He said it to me in a very low voice for fear that someone would hear.

练习

练习一、根据拼音写汉字，根据汉字写拼音

sōu（　）（　　）xíng kǒng（　）（　　）wù（　　）bēi
（　）索　类（　）（　　）怕　人（　）酒（　）

练习二、搭配连线

(1) 搜集　　　　　　　A. 搜索
(2) 各种　　　　　　　B. 情报
(3) 四处　　　　　　　C. 社会
(4) 人类　　　　　　　D. 人权
(5) 维护　　　　　　　E. 类型

练习三、从今天学习的生词中选择合适的词填空

1. 请接受我 _____ 的道歉，我为自己的行为感到惭愧。
2. 你要是不知道，就去网络上 _____ 一下吧，肯定能找到相关信息。
3. 孔子是一位有名的历史 _____，中国人民都十分尊敬他。
4. 我点了三个菜，他又要了两 _____ 饮料。
5. 科技的进步可能使我们的世界更美好，也可能彻底毁掉 _____。
6. 她悄悄地下床，连灯都不打开，_____ 吵醒孩子。
7. 这两个女孩的性格不一样，是两种不同 _____ 的人。
8. 前方有车祸，交通堵塞特别严重，今天 _____ 要迟到了。
9. 我们公司销售各种 _____ 的打印机，欢迎大家前来选购。
10. 他是个球迷，_____ 了很多足球明星的资料。

答案

练习一：
略
练习二：
(1) B　　　(2)E　　　(3)A　　　(4)C　　　(5)D
练习三：
1. 诚心诚意 2. 搜索　3. 人物　4. 杯　5. 人类
6. 生怕　7. 类型　8. 恐怕　9. 型号　10. 搜集

星期二

cǎigòu
采购　　　　　　　　（乙）动

① purchase ② make purchases for an organization

常用搭配

采购员 purchasing clerk
图书采购 purchase of books

用法示例

她负责采购原材料。
She was responsible for buying raw materials.
你得填写一张采购清单。
You should fill in a list of things to purchase.
她每学期都为学生采购课本。
She buys textbooks for the students every term.

yìngyòng
应用　　　　　　　　（乙）动

use; apply

常用搭配

计算机应用 a computer application
广泛应用 extensive use
把理论应用于实践 apply a theory to practice

用法示例

这项研究成果能应用于新的技术开发。
The results of this research can be applied to new developments in technology.
一本好的学生字典应该既提供词语的含义，又举出应用这些词语的例子。
A good learner's dictionary should give both the meanings of the words; and examples of the constructions in which they are used.

jīngfèi
经费　　　　　　　　（丙）名

funds; expenditure

常用搭配

科研经费 expenditure of scientific research
行政经费 administrative expenditure

用法示例

我们如果要增加教育经费就必须加税。
We must increase taxation if we are to spend more on education.
他总是叹息研究经费不足。
He always bemoans the shortage of funds for research.
我们手头没有经费。
We have no funds in our hands.

qiānxū
谦虚　　　⊠ 傲慢　　　（丙）形
àomàn

modest

常用搭配

别那么谦虚。Don't be so modest.

谦虚的学者 a modest scholar

用法示例

我们应该谦虚谨慎。

We should be modest and prudent.

他很谦虚，乐于接受意见。

He is very modest and open to advice.

谦虚是一种美德。

Modesty is a virtue.

lúnliú
轮流　　　⊜ 轮番　　　（丙）动
lúnfān

① alternate ② take turns

常用搭配

轮流值日 take turns to be on duty

轮流放牧 rotational grazing

用法示例

孩子们在操场上轮流滑滑梯。

The children were taking turns on the slides in the playground.

店员要轮流休息。

The shop assistants had to take their days off in rotation.

他俩轮流值夜班。

They alternately work on night shifts.

lúnhuàn
轮换　　　（丁）动

① rotate ② take turns

常用搭配

定期轮换 take turns according to a fixed schedule

轮换种植 shifting cultivation

用法示例

在交通信号轮换到绿灯以前不要穿过马路。

Don't cross the street before the traffic signal turns to green.

教练在比赛即将结束时频繁地让球员轮换上阵。

The coach rotates her players frequently at the end of the game.

pán
盘　　　（乙）名/量

tray; plate

常用搭配

托盘 bracket tray

一盘食物 a plate of food

一盘鱼 a plate of fish

用法示例

她要我帮忙把菜盛到盘子里。

She asked me to help her dish up dinner.

这个瓷盘是从中国进口的。

This porcelain plate is imported from China.

桌子上有一盘草莓和一盘花生。

There is a plate of strawberries and a plate of peanuts on the table.

cǎijí
采集　　　（丁）动

gather; collect

常用搭配

采集标本 collect specimens

采集种子 collecting seeds

用法示例

蜜蜂采集花粉时会使花授粉。

The bees may fertilize flowers when they collect nectar.

他采集各种岩石和矿物的标本。

He collects all kinds of rock and mineral specimens.

qiānzhèng
签证　　　（丁）动/名

visa

常用搭配

出境签证 exit visa

过境签证 transit visa

入境签证 entry visa

用法示例

他办出国签证时遇到了很大的麻烦。

He experienced great difficulty in getting a visa to leave the country.

他申请延长签证有效期。

He asked for an extension of his visa.

他正向领事申请签证。

He is applying to the Consul for a visa.

qiānjiù
迁就　　　⊜ 将就　　　（丁）动
jiāngjiu

① yield ② adapt to

常用搭配

迁就姑息 excessively accommodating

互相迁就 give in to each other

用法示例

他对他的同事太迁就了。

He indulges his colleague too much.

他不得不迁就他的弟弟。

He has to appease his young brother.

要使婚姻美满，双方必须懂得互相迁就。

For a marriage to succeed, both partners must learn to give and take.

jīngshòu
经受　　　（丁）动

① endure ② withstand

常用搭配

经受各种考验 experience all sorts of trials

在斗争中经受锻炼 be tempered in the struggle
经受风雨侵蚀的岩石 rocks weathered by wind and water

用法示例

新产品经受了严格的考验。
The new product has been subjected to stringent tests.
船经受住了暴风雨,安全抵达了。
The ship weathered the storm, and arrived safely.
我认为他们经受不住任何严峻的考验。
I don't think they can stand up to any serious test.

tàn tóu tàn nǎo
探头探脑 (丁)
to stick one's head and look around

用法示例

他正在乘凉,只见一个人探头探脑在那里张望。
He was enjoying the cool breeze, when all at once he saw a man stealthily spying on him.
他发现有个人在门前探头探脑的。
He saw a man pop up his head, and look out from the gate.

词义辨析

采购、采

"采购"和"采集"都是动词。"采购"指大量选购,对象是大量的实物,强调购买和挑选;"采集"是指收集材料,往往指到现场或产地获取某物或搜罗资料,对象可能是各种各样的材料或资料,也可能是一种或一类材料或资料。例如:①他负责为实验室采购设备。②他上山去采集草药了。③法医去现场采集了死者血液的样本。

Both 采购 and 采集 are verbs. 采购 indicates to purchase. Its objects are a lot of commodities, stressing "buy" and "choose"; while 采集 means "to gather or to collect", usually indicating to gather things or information on the spot or in a production area. Its objects are all kinds materials (data), one sort of material (data) or just one material (datum). For example: ① He is responsible for purchasing equipment for the lab. ② He went up the mountain to collect herbs. ③ A legal medical expert went to the scene of death to collect the blood sample.

练习

练习一、根据拼音写汉字,根据汉字写拼音

qiān ( ) qiān ( ) qiān ( ) ( ) gòu ( ) fèi
( )证 ( )就 ( )虚 采( ) 经( )

练习二、搭配连线

(1) 采购   A. 值日
(2) 采集   B. 考验
(3) 入境   C. 设备
(4) 经受   D. 标本
(5) 轮流   E. 签证

练习三、从今天学习的生词中选择合适的词填空

1. 他想去美国工作,但美国大使馆拒绝给他 _____。
2. 老师带着孩子们到乡间去 _____ 植物标本。
3. 这个人可能是个小偷,因为他总是 _____ 朝开着门的那家张望。
4. 从今天开始,大家 _____ 擦黑板。
5. 他诚恳地向老同事请教问题,态度非常 _____。
6. "团购"的意思是很多人组成一个团体一起去 _____,因为量大,价格可能会便宜。
7. 他给了我三 _____ 空白磁带。
8. 他的技术很好,但是脾气很坏。为了工作,我们不得不 _____ 他。
9. 政府专门为这个项目拨了专项 _____。
10. 我和同屋两个人 _____ 着打扫房间,一人一星期。

答案

练习一:
略
练习二:
(1) C   (2)D   (3)E   (4)B   (5)A
练习三:
1. 签证   2. 采集   3. 探头探脑   4. 轮流   5. 谦虚
6. 采购   7. 盘   8. 迁就   9. 经费   10. 轮换

星期三

cǎisè
彩色 （乙）名
① color ② multi-colored
常用搭配
彩色电视机 a color TV set
彩色的旗帜 colored flags
用法示例
那里有些彩色的气球。
There are some colored balloons.
我喜欢那家餐厅的彩色的餐巾纸。
I like the colored napkins in that restaurant.
那顶帽子上装饰着彩色的珠子。
The hat was decorated with colored beads.

réncái
人才 （乙）名
talented person
常用搭配
聘用人才 employ a person of ability
管理人才 person with administrative ability
用法示例
他们最需要的是高级管理人才。
What they need most is advanced administrative talent.
这个国家最优秀的人才在外流。
This country is being drained of its best talents.

cáizhèng
财政 （丙）名
finances
常用搭配
财政补贴 financial subsidies
财政部长 the Minister of Finance
财政赤字 financial deficits
用法示例
这家公司陷入严重的财政困难。
This company was in serious financial difficulties.
英国财政大臣是负责该国财政的部长。
The Chancellor of the Exchequer is the minister in charge of finance in Britain.

pínqióng
贫穷 回 富有 **fùyǒu** （丙）形
poor; impoverished
常用搭配
贫穷落后的面貌 in a poor and backward state
贫穷的农民 poor peasant
贫穷的家庭 a poor family

用法示例
那里的人们过着贫穷的生活。
People in that area are living in penury.
我们不应该漠视贫穷的孩子们。
We should not show apathy towards poor children.
她是如此贫穷，以致看不起病。
She is so poor that she can not afford the cost of seeing a doctor.

tūpò
突破 （丙）动/名
① break through ② breakthrough
常用搭配
突破敌人的防线 break through the enemy's defences
医学上的突破 a medical breakthrough
用法示例
示威群众企图突破警察的封锁线。
Demonstrators tried to break through the police cordon.
我方坦克突破了敌人的防线。
Our tanks have breached the enemy defenses.
外科医生们在肾移植方面取得了重大突破。
Surgeons have made a great breakthrough in kidney transplantation.

chōngpò
冲破 回 打破 **dǎpò** （丁）动
break through
常用搭配
冲破重重障碍 break through one barrier after another
冲破经济界限 break down the economic boundaries
用法示例
河水冲破了堤岸。
The river broke its banks.
汹涌而来的示威者冲破了围栏。
A surge of demonstrators broke through the fence.

jīn
斤 （甲）量
① half kilogram ② jin
常用搭配
二斤苹果 one kilo of apples　一斤米 half kilo of rice
用法示例
1000 公斤是 1 吨。
1000 kilos is a ton.
她一天能吃 2 斤草莓。
She can have two jin of strawberries per day.
我买了 6 斤盐。
I bought six jin of salt.

cǎifǎng
采访 （丁）动/名
① cover (a news story) ② interview
常用搭配
采访某人 interview sb.　电话采访 telephone interview

用法示例

记者正在采访他。

A reporter is interviewing him.

记者们缠住获胜者进行采访。

Reporters besieged the winner asking for interviews.

由于无可奉告,他拒绝了记者的采访。

As he had nothing to tell, he refused to give any interviews to the journalists.

pínmín
贫民　　　　　fùháo
　　　　　反 富豪　　　　　（丁）名

poor people

常用搭配

贫民区 slum area

城市贫民 the urban poor

用法示例

补助津贴一削减,最倒霉的就是那些老人和贫民。

It's the old and the poor who suffer the most when subsidies are cut.

他最后沦落到了贫民窟。

He ended up on skid row.

yòuhuò
诱惑　　　　　yǐnyòu
　　　　　同 引诱　　　　　（丁）动

tempt; entice

常用搭配

受诱惑 fall into temptation

抵御诱惑 resist the temptation

用法示例

我抵挡不了诱惑。

I can't resist temptation.

她禁不住诱惑,又吃了一块巧克力。

She yielded to temptation and had another chocolate.

桌上那包糖果对那孩子是个难以抗拒的诱惑。

The bag of sweets on the table was too strong a temptation for the child to resist.

cáizhì
才智　　　　　（丁）名

ability and wisdom

常用搭配

天生的才智 innate wit

增长聪明才智 grow in wisdom

用法示例

他是一个才智超群的人。

He is a man of great wisdom.

她很聪明,可谓才智过人。

She is a kind of intellectual superwoman.

发挥你的聪明才智,你一定能取得成就。

Use your intelligence, and you're sure to achieve something.

huò duō huò shǎo
或多或少　　　　　（丁）

more or less

用法示例

希望我们的说明或多或少有些帮助。

We hope our explanation will prove more or less helpful.

我们是同学,所以我们或多或少地了解对方。

We are classmates, so we more or less know each other.

 词义辨析

突破、冲

　　"突破"和"冲破"都是动词,都有强行穿过的意思。"突破"还有取得重要发现或发展的意思,其对象往往是敌人的防线或科学研究、产品开发、技术或制度创新等,还可以用作名词;"冲破"的对象往往是敌人的防线、河岸或限制、束缚、障碍等。例如:①敌人想要冲破/突破包围圈。②那些内科医生在同心脏病的斗争中取得了突破。③她冲破了传统观念的束缚,和她的情人私奔了。

　　Both 突破 and 冲破 are verbs, meaning "to break through". 突破 also means "to make new and important discoveries or developments". Its objects are usually enemy defenses, scientific research, developments of new products, skills or systems; and it is also a noun. The objects of 冲破 are usually enemy defenses, a bank of a river, a limitation, restriction, obstacle and so on. For example: ① The enemy wanted to breach the line of encirclement. ② Those physicians made a break through in their fight against heart disease. ③ She broke through the chains of traditional thinking, and eloped with her lover.

 练习

练习一、根据拼音写汉字，根据汉字写拼音

cái（ ）cái（ ）pín（ ）chōng（ ）yòu（ ）
（ ）智（ ）政（ ）穷（ ）破（ ）惑

练习二、搭配连线

(1) 聪明　　　　　　　　A. 防线
(2) 抵御　　　　　　　　B. 人才
(3) 冲破　　　　　　　　C. 赤字
(4) 招聘　　　　　　　　D. 诱惑
(5) 财政　　　　　　　　E. 才智

练习三、从今天学习的生词中选择合适的词填空

1. 来中国以前，他们都对中国 _____ 地有些了解。
2. 年轻人应该把自己的聪明 _____ 用在学业和事业上。
3. 在金钱和美女的 _____ 下，他终于说出了军事机密。
4. 昨天我买了三 _____ 苹果。
5. 这座城市的中心地带是有钱人居住的地方，而多数 _____ 住在城市的西部地区。
6. 这个市的经济比较发达，政府一年的 _____ 收入是我们那个市的好几倍。
7. 他们俩 _____ 种种阻碍，最终组成了幸福的家庭。
8. 这张照片是 _____ 的，我想洗一张黑白的。
9. 在这次运动会中，他在原有成绩的基础上又有了新的 _____。
10. 关于这件事，记者 _____ 了当事人。

答案

练习一：
略
练习二：
(1) E　　　(2)D　　　(3)A　　　(4)B　　　(5)C
练习三：
1. 或多或少　2. 才智　　3. 诱惑　　4. 斤　　　5. 贫民
6. 财政　　　7. 冲破　　8. 彩色　　9. 突破　　10. 采访

 星期四

xíngróng
形容　　　　　　　　　　　　（乙）动
describe

常用搭配
形容词 an adjective
难以形容 beyond description

用法示例
无法形容她的美貌。
Her beauty is beyond description.
你能给我形容一下那个小偷的模样吗？
Can you give me a description of the thief?
难以用语言形容这美丽的景色。
Words cannot describe this beautiful scene.

wēndù
温度　　　　　　　　　　　　（乙）名
temperature

常用搭配
温度计 thermometer　　温度调节 temperature adjustment

用法示例
在夏天，温度变得很高。
In summer the temperature gets very high.
七月份最高温度可能达到 38 摄氏度。
The maximum temperature in July may be 38℃ degrees elsius.
铅会在相当低的温度下熔化。
Lead will fuse at quite a low temperature.

pínkǔ
贫苦　　　　　　　　　　　　（丙）形
poverty - stricken; poor

常用搭配
过着贫苦的生活 live in poverty
贫苦地区 poverty stricken area

用法示例
在旧社会老百姓的生活是贫苦的。
In the olden days the common people led lives of poverty.
许多伟人曾经是贫苦、平凡的小孩。
Many great men were once poor and unimportant boys.
他出身于贫苦的家庭。
He comes from a poor family.

píjuàn　　　　　　　　　píbèi
疲倦　　🔘 疲惫　　　　　　（丙）形
tired

常用搭配
觉得疲倦 feel tired　　疲倦的笑容 a weary smile

用法示例

我下班后感到疲倦。

I felt weary after work.

病人容易疲倦。

The patient is easily fatigued.

他疲倦得很快就睡着了。

He soon fell asleep with weariness.

zhànlǐng
占领   回 占据 **zhànjù**   （丙）动

to occupy (a territory)

常用搭配

占领城市 seize a city

占领要塞 capture a fort

用法示例

恐怖分子占领了大使馆。

The terrorists have seized the Embassy.

军队占领了敌国首都。

The army occupied the enemy's capital.

机场被敌军占领了。

The airfield was seized by enemy troops.

zhànyǒu
占有   （丙）动

to occupy; to possess

常用搭配

占有生产资料 have the means of production

占有剩余价值 possession of surplus value

用法示例

他占有公司 30% 的股份。

He has a 30% stake in of the company.

李白的诗在中国古代文学中占有重要的地位。

Li Bai's poems occupy an important place in Chinese ancient literature.

xiāng
箱   （丙）量／名

trunk; box

常用搭配

三箱鸡蛋 three cartons of eggs

一箱衣物 a chest of clothes

保险箱 coffer

垃圾箱 dustbin

用法示例

他买了一箱水果。

He bought a box of fruit.

这个信箱每天开两次。

This letterbox is checked twice a day.

这个箱子有多重？

How heavy is this box?

piānpì
偏僻   回 偏远 **piānyuǎn**   （丁）形

far from the city; remote

常用搭配

偏僻的村庄 an obscure village

偏僻的地方 an out-of-the-way place

偏僻的小镇 A small and insignificant city

用法示例

这个农舍坐落在偏僻的地方，离最近的村庄也有五英里。

The cottage was situated in an out-of-the-way place, five miles from the nearest village.

这件事发生在河南一个偏僻的村子里。

The thing happened in an out-of-the-way village in Henan.

邮车每周只到这个偏僻的地方一次。

Mail only comes to this remote place once a week.

móuqiú
谋求   （丁）动

seek; strive for

常用搭配

谋求解决办法 try to find a solution

谋求好职位 try to find a good position

用法示例

他在千方百计地谋求这份差使。

He is angling for the job.

他一直在谋求合作的机会。

He is always seeking for an opportunity to cooperate.

piānjiàn
偏见   回 成见 **chéngjiàn**   （丁）名

prejudice

常用搭配

对某人有偏见 have a prejudice against sb.

消除偏见 dispel prejudice

用法示例

这种仇恨是由种族偏见引起的。

This hatred was caused by racial prejudice.

我要声明我对你没有偏见。

I want to make it clear that I have no prejudice against you.

他对所有的外国人都有偏见。

He has a prejudice against all foreigners.

piànkè
片刻   （丁）名

short period of time

常用搭配

稍等片刻。Wait a moment.

用法示例

我们一个星期都在工作，没有片刻空闲。

We've been working all week without a moment's nest.

他想了片刻，然后说。

He thought for a moment, and then spoke.

她犹豫了片刻。

She hesitated for an instant.

yǒu shēng yǒu sè
有 声 有 色 （丁）
vivid and dramatic (said of a description)

常用搭配
有声有色的描写 a vivid description

用法示例
聚会搞得有声有色。
The party went off with a bang.
她有声有色地讲述她的经历。
She told her story vividly.

 **词义辨析**

占领、占

"占领"和"占有"都是动词。"占领"的原意是强占领地，也常用于军事、政治、商业等领域。"占有"是拥有的意思，其对象可以是财产、名声、地位等各方面的事物，使用范围很广。例如：①敌军占领了我们的城市。②民主党在议院中占有大部分席位。

Both 占领 and 占有 are verbs. The original meaning of 占领 is "to occupy territory with force". It is usually applied to military, political or commercial aspects. 占 有 means "to possess or own", and its objects can be property, reputation, status, and many other things. It can be widely applied. For example: ① The enemy's army occupied our city. ② Most of the members in parliament are Democratic party members.

 练习

练习一、根据拼音写汉字，根据汉字写拼音
( )juàn ( )pì piàn ( ) móu ( )( ) lǐng
疲( ) 偏( )( )刻 ( )求 占( )

练习二、搭配连线
(1) 消除　　　　　　　　A. 发展
(2) 觉得　　　　　　　　B. 偏僻
(3) 谋求　　　　　　　　C. 片刻
(4) 稍等　　　　　　　　D. 偏见
(5) 位置　　　　　　　　E. 疲倦

练习三、从今天学习的生词中选择合适的词填空
1. 那个地方很 _____，晚上不要一个人去那儿。
2. 对于国际争端，我国政府主张通过谈判来 _____ 和平解决。
3. 无论是男人还是女人，也无论是黑人还是白人，我们都应公平对待，不要存有 _____。
4. 连着两天没睡觉，他看起来很 _____。
5. 她非常兴奋，简直无法用语言 _____ 她当时的心情。
6. 这一家人过着 _____ 的生活，父亲失业后靠捡垃圾、卖废品养活一家人。
7. 新的学生会主席很有能力，在他的带领下，学生的课外活动搞得 _____。
8. 对于记者的提问，这位发言人想了 _____ 才回答。
9. 昨天他在超市买了一 _____ 方便面，一共有10袋，够他吃一个星期的。
10. 今天的 _____ 比昨天的低，多穿点衣服，小心感冒。

答案

练习一：
略

练习二：
(1) D　　(2)E　　(3)A　　(4)C　　(5) B

练习三：
1. 偏僻　2. 谋求　3. 偏见　4. 疲倦　5. 形容
6. 贫苦　7. 有声有色 8. 片刻　9. 箱　10. 温度

星期五

qiángdù
强度 （乙）名
intensity; strength

常用搭配
工作强度 work intensity
训练强度 intensity of training
铁丝的强度 the strength of a wire

用法示例
强度是金属的重要性能之一。
Strength is one of the important properties of metal.
工人认为这个工厂的劳动强度适中。
Workers think the intensity of labor in this factory is appropriate for them.

qiángdào
强盗 （乙）名
robber

常用搭配
他是强盗。He is a robber.

用法示例
强盗在警察到来之前逃走了。
The robbers escaped before the police arrived.
昨晚他们被强盗洗劫一空。
Last night, they were cleaned out by robbers.
我的手表被两个强盗抢走了。
I had my watch stolen by two robbers.

fēnjiě
分解 反 合成 **héchéng** （丙）动
① resolve ② decompose

常用搭配
水可分解为氢和氧。
Water can be broken down into hydrogen and oxygen.

用法示例
糖和淀粉在胃里被分解了。
Sugar and starch are broken down in the stomach.
这种混合物会分解成两种物质。
This mixture resolves into two substances.
你可以通过加热来分解有机化合物。
You can apply heat to decompose organic compounds.

fēngōng
分工 （丙）动
① divide the work ② division of labor

常用搭配
社会分工 social division of labor
专业分工 division of labor based on specialization

用法示例
蚂蚁间有明确的分工。
There is a clear division of labor among ants.
根据分工,我们负责开发新产品。
According to the division of labor, we are in charge of developing new products.

yǒuyì
有益 反 有害 **yǒuhài** （丙）形
helpful; good

常用搭配
有益于健康 be good for one's health
读书对你有益。Reading books is good for you.

用法示例
生活要有规律,因为规律对健康有益。
It is good to lead a regularly life, as it is very conducive to one's health.
蜂蜜对你身体有益。
Honey is good for you.
良好的饮食有益于健康。
A good diet leads to good health.

yǒuài
友爱 （丙）形/名
① friendly affection ② friendship

常用搭配
团结友爱 togetherness

用法示例
愿新年为你带来快乐、友爱和宁静。
May the coming New Year bring you joy, love and peace.
我永远也不会忘记同学间的友爱。
I never forget the strong friendship among classmates.

dòng
栋 （丁）量
roof beam

常用搭配
一栋楼房 a building   两栋别墅 two villas

用法示例
那栋旧房子的屋顶塌了。
The roof of the old house caved in.
她的父亲很富有,他在英国有几栋房子。
Her father is as rich as Croesus. He owns several houses in England.

qiánjǐng
前景 同 前途 **qiántú** （丁）名
prospects

常用搭配
美好的前景 good prospects
公司的前景 prospect of company

用法示例
我们公司有好的前景。
Our company has good prospects.

我认为前景并不乐观。
I don't think the prospect is brilliant.
今年的葡萄酒产量前景不佳。
The prospects for this year's wine production are poor.

yǒuhài
有害 （丁）形
harmful; damaging

常用搭配
有害气体 harmful gas
对……有害 do harm to…

用法示例
吸烟有害健康,这是大家公认的。
It is generally accepted that smoking is harmful to our health.
过量饮酒对你的身体有害。
It is harmful to your health to drink too much.
这是一种有害物质。
It is a harmful substance.

yuǎnjǐng
远景 （丁）名
① prospect ② long-range view

常用搭配
远景规划 a far-reaching plan

用法示例
从这座山上可以拍摄远景。
A fine long range picture can be taken from the hill.
他们制定了行业的远景发展规划。
They made a long term plan for the development of industry.

qīnpèi
钦佩 ⑩ 敬佩 jìngpèi （丁）动
① admire ② have great respect for sb

常用搭配
钦佩他的正直 to admire him for his righteousness
令人钦佩的运动员 admirable athlete

用法示例
他的勇气令人钦佩。
His bravery is admirable.
我钦佩这位牧师的奉献精神。
I admire the priest's dedication.
考虑到那种困难的情况,我认为他的表现令人钦佩。
I think he conducted himself admirably, considering the difficult circumstances.

suí shí suí dì
随时随地 （丁）
whenever and wherever possible

用法示例
在参观访问的过程中,我们随时随地都能学到很多东西。
Over the course of our trip, we have learned a great deal about all the places we have visited.

如果你愿意,你可以在北京随时随地练习汉语。
If you want to, you can practice your Chinese at anywhere and any time.

 词义辨析

前景、远景
　　"前景"和"远景"都是名词,都可以表示前途。"前景"的原意是前面的景色,可以指将要出现的景象,强调在较近的将来;"远景"的原意是远处的景物,可以指很长时间以后会出现的景象,强调在较远的将来。例如:①史密斯先生被选为议员的前景并不乐观。②我们为公司制定了远景发展规划。

　　Both 前景 and 远景 are nouns, indicating "future". The original meaning of 前景 is "foreground". It indicates "a prospective, or expected condition in near future"; while the original meaning of 远景 is "distant view", indicating "a long-range prospective or expected condition in the future". For example: ① There's not much prospect of Mr Smith's being elected as Congressman. ② We made a longterm plan for our company.

 练习

练习一、根据拼音写汉字,根据汉字写拼音
(　　)dào　yǒu(　　)　yǒu(　　)qīn(　　)(　　)jǐng
　强(　)(　)爱　(　)益　(　)佩　远(　)

练习二、搭配连线
(1) 远景　　　　　A. 强度
(2) 有害　　　　　B. 友爱
(3) 团结　　　　　C. 规划
(4) 社会　　　　　D. 气体
(5) 劳动　　　　　E. 分工

练习三、从今天学习的生词中选择合适的词填空
1. 我知道吸烟对人体 _____ ,可是戒不掉,没办法。
2. 我和丈夫之间有明确的 _____ ,我做饭,他洗碗。
3. 他非常善于处理紧急情况,我对他的勇气和胆识十分 _____ 。
4. 政府对开发区作了一个十五年的 _____ 规划。
5. 我每天和中国朋友在一起, _____ 都能跟他们学习汉语。
6. 教练增加了训练的 _____ ,有的队员累得受不了了。
7. 适当的参加体育运动 _____ 身心健康。
8. 我们班是一个团结 _____ 的集体,就像一个温暖的大家庭。
9. 那 _____ 大楼有 60 米高,是我们那里最高的建筑物。
10. 环保行业受到了政府的大力扶植,有很好的发展 _____ 。

答案

练习一：
略
练习二：
(1) C　　(2)D　　(3)B　　(4)E　　(5)A
练习三：
1. 有害　　　2. 分工　　　3. 钦佩　　　4. 远景
5. 随时随地　6. 强度　　　7. 有益
8. 友爱　　　9. 栋　　　　10. 前景

第11月，第4周的练习

练习一．根据词语给加点的字注音
1.（　）2.（　）3.（　）4.（　）5.（　）
　疲倦　　钦佩　　强盗　　贫穷　　片刻

练习二．根据拼音填写词语
　qiān　　qiān　　qiān　　cǎi　　cǎi
1.（　）虚 2.（　）就 3.（　）证 4.（　）色 5.（　）访

练习三．辨析并选择合适的词填空
1. 因为有过一次迟到的经历，这次他提前四小时去机场，（　）再错过飞机。（恐怕、生怕）
2. 小王，这个周末的聚会我（　）不能参加了。（恐怕、生怕）
3. 这家饭店的肉类、蔬菜都是定点（　），以防发生意外时无法追踪。（采购、采集）
4. 科学家利用月球探测器从月球上（　）岩石和土壤样本进行研究。（采购、采集）
5. 这种新的治疗方法是癌症研究上的一项重大（　）。（突破、冲破）
6. 她最终（　）传统世俗的观念走出了属于自己的一条人生之路。（突破、冲破）
7. 他在公司（　）51% 的股份。（占领、占有）
8. 这个公司在亚洲的策略是第一年不赚钱，目的是快速（　）亚洲市场。（占领、占有）
9. 随着人们对环保越来越重视，环保产业的（　）非常可观。（前景、远景）
10. 政府对城市的发展做了一个十年（　）规划。（前景、远景）

练习四．选词填空
人才　　搜集　　偏见　　经费　　类型
人物　　搜索　　偏僻　　经受　　型号
1. 你喜欢什么（　）的女孩，文静的还是泼辣的?
2. 这个小村庄地处（　）的山区，跟外界的交流很少。
3. 这个项目还没有完成，但项目的活动（　）就已经花完了。
4. 要充分合理地利用各类（　），使每个人都能发挥出良好的水平。
5. 不要对少数民族的人有（　），他们也是这个国家的公民，

也为社会做出了贡献。
6. 在这个小镇上，林老板是个大（　），是小镇居民的骄傲。
7. 为了给儿子治病，这位父亲（　）了很多病例资料。
8. 意志不坚定的人（　）不住各种诱惑的考验。
9. 厂家说这个（　）的空调已经不生产了,所以没有办法配零件。
10. 这类资料很容易查找，只要上网（　）一下，马上就会出来很多这类信息。

练习五．量词填空
　　箱　　　栋　　　斤　　　盘　　　杯
1. 除了这里的房子以外，他在郊区还有一（　）别墅。
2. 他们两个人点了六（　）菜，太多了，肯定吃不了。
3. 在昨天的宴会上，他至少喝了五（　）白酒。
4. 请问，草莓多少钱一（　）?
5. 他买了一大（　）苹果，分给我们每个人五个。

练习六．成语填空
1. 诚（　）诚（　）　2. 探（　）探（　）　3. 或（　）或（　）
4. 有（　）有（　）　5. 随（　）随（　）

练习七．写出下列词语的同义词
1. 生怕(　　)　　　　2. 诱惑(　　)
3. 疲惫(　　)　　　　4. 钦佩(　　)
5. 搜索(　　)

练习八．写出下列词语的反义词
1. 谦虚(　　)　　　　2. 分解(　　)
3. 贫穷(　　)　　　　4. 有益(　　)
5. 贫民(　　)

答案

练习一．
1.pí　　　　2.pèi　　　3.dào　　　4.qióng　　5.kè
练习二．
1. 谦　　　2. 迁　　　3. 签　　　4. 彩　　　5. 采
练习三．
1. 生怕　　2. 恐怕　　3. 采购　　4. 采集　　5. 突破
6. 冲破　　7. 占有　　8. 占领　　9. 前景　　10. 远景
练习四．
1. 类型　　2. 偏僻　　3. 经费　　4. 人才　　5. 偏见
6. 人物　　7. 搜集　　8. 经受　　9. 型号　　10. 搜索
练习五．
1. 栋　　　2. 盘　　　3. 杯　　　4. 斤　　　5. 箱
练习六．
1. 心,意　2. 头,脑　3. 多,少　4. 声,色　5. 时,地
练习七．
1. 唯恐　　2. 引诱　　3. 疲倦　　4. 敬佩　　5. 搜寻
练习八．
1. 傲慢　　2. 合成　　3. 富有　　4. 有害　　5. 富豪

第 1 周的学习内容

sùliào
塑料　　　　　　　　　　（乙）名
plastic

常用搭配

塑料碗 a plastic bowl
塑料杯 plastic cups

用法示例

很多日常生活用品是用塑料制成的。
Many items in daily use are made of plastic.
这些塑料盘子非常便宜。
These plastic plates are very cheap.

jīngzhì
精致　　　　　　反 粗糙　　（丙）形
cūcāo
delicate

常用搭配

精致的花边 exquisite lace
做得精致 be delicately made

用法示例

她穿了一件带有精致花边的裙子。
She wears a dress with delicate lace.
这张古老的羊皮纸是在一个精致的铁盒子里发现的。
This ancient parchment was discovered in a delicate iron box.
这本小册子做得很精致。
This booklet is delicately made.

dàfang
大方　　　　　反 小气　　（丙）形
xiǎoqì
generous; decent

常用搭配

他花钱大方。 He is generous with his money.
大方的衣服 a dress that looks decent
举止大方 to be decent in manner

用法示例

她很大方,捐助了这么多钱。
It was generous of her to contribute such a large sum.
是什么原因使他如此大方呢?
What prompted him to be so generous?
她穿了套漂亮的长裙,看上去很大方。
She wore a pretty dress and looked very decent.

dàyì
大意　　　　　　　　（丙）名/形
① main idea ② careless

常用搭配

文章的大意 general idea of an article
粗心大意 very careless

用法示例

我听懂了他们谈话的大意,但没有听懂某些细节。
I understood the tenor of their conversation but not the details.
他因疏忽大意而断送了前途。
He ruined his prospects by carelessness.
他是个粗心大意的司机。
He drives with carelessness.

zhàngài
障碍　　　　　　　　（丙）名/动
① hindrance ② obstacle ③ obstruct

常用搭配

清除障碍 clear away obstacles
制造障碍 create obstacles
改革的障碍 an impediment to reform

用法示例

一棵倒下的树横在大路上成了障碍。
The fallen tree lying across the road is an obstacle.
发展的主要障碍是这个国家人口太多。
The main impediment to development is the country's large population.
我认为大多数障碍都是可以克服的。
I think most of these obstacles can be surmounted.

fángài
妨碍　　　　　　　　　　（丙）动
hamper; impede

常用搭配

妨碍公务 interfere with the public function
不要妨碍我。 Don't hinder me.

用法示例

不要妨碍我工作。
Don't hinder me in my work.
一个人不应该妨碍他人进步。
One shouldn't impede others' progress.
在阅览室里不要大声说话,以免妨碍别人。
Talk quietly in the reading room in order not to disturb others.

huāngmáng
慌忙　　　　　　　　　　（丙）形
in a great rush; in a flurry

常用搭配

慌忙赶到现场 rush to the spot
慌忙离去 leave hurriedly

用法示例

警察来到时，他慌忙逃走了。
When the police arrived he bolted for the door.
不必慌忙，时间多的是。
Don't rush; there is plenty of time.
我走进他房间时，他慌忙地把一大包东西藏到书桌底下了。
When I went into his room, he hurriedly hid a large parcel under his desk.

huāngzhāng
慌张 （丁）形

flustered

常用搭配

神色慌张 look flurried

用法示例

她慌慌张张地走下楼梯。
She went down the stairs in a panic.
不要慌张！没有危险。
Don't panic! There is no danger.
他很慌张，赶快跑到安全的地方去了。
He panicked and ran as fast as he could to safety.

huāngtáng huāngmiù
荒唐 ⑩ 荒谬 （丁）形

absurd; ridiculous

常用搭配

荒唐透顶 absolutely ridiculous
荒唐的生活 a dissipated life

用法示例

我们认为你的建议很荒唐。
Your suggestion seems like an absurd one to us.
在这么恶劣的天气里出去太荒唐了。
It is absurd to go out in such terrible weather.
信任他简直是荒唐。
It is ridiculous to trust him.

huāngliáng huāngwú
荒凉 ⑩ 荒芜 （丁）形

desolate

常用搭配

荒凉的景色 desolate scenery
荒凉的土地 desolate land
一片荒凉 a scene of desolation

用法示例

看到战争造成的荒凉，他感到触目惊心。
He was shocked when he saw the desolation caused by war.
这个地方看上去很荒凉。
The place looks barren and wild.

jīngtōng
精通 （丁）动

be proficient in

常用搭配

精通汉语 be proficient in Chinese
精通本职业务 be proficient in one's professional work

用法示例

我们的经理精通会计制度。
Our manager is conversant with the accounts system.
他精通中国历史和文化。
He is proficient in Chinese history and culture.
精通日语要花几年时间。
It takes years to gain a mastery of Japanese.

zì yán zì yǔ
自言自语 （丙）

think aloud

用法示例

这个精神病人老是自言自语地说："是我不好，是我不好。"
The mad man is always thinking aloud and saying: "It was my fault. It was my fault."
这个老太太有时自言自语。
The old woman sometimes talks to herself.

 词义辨析

障碍、妨碍

"障碍"和"妨碍"都有阻碍的意思，都是动词。"妨碍"的宾语可以是工作、学习、进步、发展、交通等，"障碍"的宾语通常只有视线和眼睛，这两个词也可以作为"妨碍"的宾语。"障碍"可以是名词，通常作主语和宾语，"妨碍"不用作名词。例如：①那棵树障碍/妨碍了我的视线。②噪音妨碍了我写作。③他的身体不好，这是他完成计划的一个障碍。

Both 障碍 and 妨碍 are verbs, meaning "to hinder". The objects of 妨碍 can be 工作 (work), 学习 (study), 进步 (progress), 发展 (develop), 交通 (traffic) and so on; the objects of 障碍 are usually 眼睛 (eyes) and 视线 (view). These two words can also be the objects of 妨碍. 障碍 is also a noun, and it is usually used as a subject or an object, while 妨碍 is not a noun. For example: ① The tree obstructs our view. ② The noise hindered me in my writing. ③ His poor health is an obstacle to the fulfillment of his plan.

练习

练习一、根据拼音写汉字,根据汉字写拼音

( )zhì huāng( ) huāng( ) sù ( ) ( )ài
精( ) ( )张 ( )唐 ( )料 障( )

练习二、搭配连线

(1) 荒凉的　　　　　　　A. 神情
(2) 荒唐的　　　　　　　B. 景色
(3) 慌张的　　　　　　　C. 相册
(4) 精致的　　　　　　　D. 障碍
(5) 巨大的　　　　　　　E. 想法

练习三、从今天学习的生词中选择合适的词填空

1. 工作时一定要仔细,不能马虎 _____。
2. 我以为他是在跟我说话呢,原来是在 _____。
3. 他是个慷慨的人,出手很 _____。
4. 保安看见有个陌生人神色 _____ 地走出电梯,就拦住了他,要求他出示证件。
5. 我们要请的这位专家 _____ 机械制造的各个环节。
6. 看见一辆警车开了过来,那个抢劫犯就扔下东西 _____ 逃跑了。
7. 在图书馆里,不要大声说话,以免 _____ 别人。
8. 这里现在是高楼林立,一派繁华,二十年前可是非常 _____ 的郊区。
9. 这件工艺品不大,但是非常 _____,我要把它摆在客厅。
10. 他为年轻时做过的 _____ 事感到惭愧,并希望能得到受害者的原谅。

答案

练习一:
略
练习二:
(1) B　　　(2)E　　　(3)A　　　(4)C　　　(5)D
练习三:
1. 大意　　2. 自言自语　3. 大方　　4. 慌张　　5. 精通
6. 慌忙　　7. 妨碍　　8. 荒凉　　9. 精致　　10. 荒唐

星期二

shēnhòu
深厚　　　　⊗ 淡薄　　　　　（乙）形
dànbó
profound; deep

常用搭配

深厚的友谊 profound friendship
深厚的感情 deep feelings

用法示例

作曲家用音乐表达深厚的感情。
Through music the composer expressed his deepest feelings.
他对祖国的爱十分深厚。
He has a deep and profound love for his motherland.

shénmì
神秘　　　　　　　　　　　　（丙）形
mysterious

常用搭配

神秘人物 a mystery person
神秘的符号 mysterious symbols

用法示例

他们举行了一个神秘的宗教仪式。
They held a mystical religious ceremony.
对他来说,非洲是一片神秘的土地。
Africa is a mysterious land to him.
关于他们的度假计划,他们显得很神秘。
They're being very mysterious about their holiday plans.

àomì
奥秘　　　　　　　　　　　　（丙）名
mystery

常用搭配

大自然的奥秘 the secrets of nature
探究奥秘 probe into mysteries

用法示例

那是无法解释的奥秘。
It's an unexplainable mystery.
我们开始探索宇宙的奥秘。
We have begun plumb the mysteries of the universe.
他们用很多时间探讨生命的奥秘。
They spend their time philosophizing about the mysteries of life.

shènzhòng
慎重　　　⊜ 谨慎　　　　　（丙）形
jǐnshèn
prudent; cautious

常用搭配

为慎重起见 for caution's sake
采取慎重的态度 adopt a prudent policy

用法示例

经过慎重的考虑，我们决定接受他们的提议。

After careful consideration, we've decided to accept their offer.

他说："我希望他们今后能更慎重一些"。

"I hope they'll be more cautious in future," he observed.

宗教是一个必须慎重处理的问题。

Religion is a subject that must be approached with great delicacy.

tiānrán
天然 (丙)形

natural

常用搭配

天然食品 natural food

天然气 natural gas

天然产品 natural produce

用法示例

这个港口是天然港。

This harbor is a natural harbor.

撒哈拉沙漠是北非与中非之间的天然屏障。

The Sahara Desert is a natural barrier between Northern and Central Africa.

这是天然珍珠做成的项链。

The necklace is made of natural pearls.

zhàojiù
照旧 (丁)形

① as before ② as in the past

常用搭配

一切照旧。Everything remains unchanged.

用法示例

所有东西都涨价，只有薪水照旧。

Everything went up except salaries.

老板警告过他，可是他照旧迟到。

The boss warned him, but he arrived late as usual.

yījiù
依旧 （照旧 zhàojiù） (丙)形

as before

常用搭配

山河依旧 The landscape remains unchanged.

用法示例

她依旧是那个老样子。

She still looks like her old self.

书房的陈设依旧未变。

The study is furnished as it was before.

对于我们老百姓来说，生活依旧。

Life goes on for those of us who remain here.

shēnào
深奥 （反 浅显 qiǎnxiǎn） (丁)形

profound; recondite

常用搭配

深奥的理论 a profound theory

深奥的书 a profound book

用法示例

哲学对我来说太深奥了。

Philosophy is too profound for me.

现在教给孩子的知识都过于深奥。

The child is being taught things that are beyond his ability to grasp.

他们在讨论一个深奥的问题。

They are discussing a deep question.

wánjù
玩具 (丁)名

toy

常用搭配

玩具卡车 a toy truck

玩具商店 a toy shop

用法示例

那小孩玩着新玩具快乐极了。

The child was in seventh heaven with his new toys.

她给儿子买了一把玩具手枪。

She bought a toy gun for her son.

我给她买了一个玩具马。

I bought a toy pony for her.

shèzhì
设置 (丁)动

set up

常用搭配

设置专门机构 set up a special organization

课程设置 curriculum design

用法示例

警方在广场的入口处设置了路障。

The police barricaded the entrance to the square.

这座剧院是为儿童设置的。

This theatre is set up for children.

shèshī
设施 (丁)名

facilities; installation

常用搭配

公用设施 pubilic facilities

医疗设施 medical facilities

军事设施 military installations

用法示例

这个城市的体育设施是一流的。

The sports facilities in this city are superb.

我们学校里几乎没有什么娱乐设施。

There are few recreational facilities in our school.

zì shǐ zhì zhōng
自始至终 (丙)

① from start to finish ② from beginning to end

用法示例

那会议自始至终都很无聊。
The meeting was boring from start to finish.
在辩论中,他自始至终都保持冷静。
He remained calm throughout the discussion.
那件事我自始至终都知道。
I've known that all along.

词义辨析

依然、照旧、依旧

　　三个词都有像以前一样的意思,都可以做状语,有时候可以相互替换。"依然"是副词,不能作定语或谓语;"照旧"和"依旧"是形容词,可以作定语或谓语。"依旧"和"照旧"更口语化,一般可以互换使用,但强调按老规矩、老样子行事时,只能用"照旧",而"依然"多用于书面语。例如:①大病痊愈以后,他依然/依旧/照旧努力工作。②他回到家,发现一切依旧/照旧。③工作计划将照旧进行。

　　The three words mean "as before", and they can function as an adverbial; sometimes they are interchangeable. 依然 is an adverb, and it can not function as an attributive or a predicate; while 照旧 and 依旧 are adjectives, and they can function as an attributive or a predicate. 依旧 and 照旧 are colloquial, and they usually can be interchanged. But they can't be changed when 照旧 emphasizes "to act according to the old rules or patterns," 依然 is usually applied in written language. For example: ① After recovering from a serious illness, he works hard as before. ② He went home and found everything remained unchanged. ③ The work plan will be carried out as scheduled.

练习

练习一、根据拼音写汉字,根据汉字写拼音
(　)jù　(　)shī　yī(　)　shèn(　)　ào(　)
玩(　)　设(　)　(　)旧　(　)重　(　)秘

练习二、搭配连线
(1) 深厚的　　　　　　A. 仪式
(2) 深奥的　　　　　　B. 食品
(3) 漂亮的　　　　　　C.感情
(4) 神秘的　　　　　　D. 理论
(5) 天然的　　　　　　E. 玩具

练习三、从今天学习的生词中选择合适的词填空
1. 你讲的化学知识对于小学生来说太 _____,他们可能听不懂。
2. 我小时候玩过的 _____ 妈妈都收藏着。
3. 他的电脑别人用不了,因为他 _____ 了密码。
4. 虽然来了新的领导,但是我们工作的方法还是 _____ 进行。
5. 这个小区的教育、医疗、商业等 _____ 还不完善。
6. 这个决定将影响你今后的前途,你一定要 _____ 考虑。
7. 过了十年再见面,他 _____ 是老样子,一点都没变。
8. 虽然离开家乡的时候很小,但他对家乡的感情非常 _____。
9. 妈妈到现在也不知道我发生车祸的事,我怕她担心, _____ 都瞒着她。
10. 我接到了一封 _____ 的信,信封里只装着两张婴儿的旧照片,一个字都没写。

答案

练习一:
略
练习二:
(1) C　　(2)D　　(3)E　　(4)A　　(5)B
练习三:
1. 深奥　2. 玩具　3. 设置　4. 照旧　5. 设施
6. 慎重　7. 依旧　8. 深厚　9. 自始至终　10. 神秘

星期三

jīlěi
积累　回积攒　（乙）动

accumulate

常用搭配
积累资料 accumulate data
积累经验 accumulate experience
积累词汇 build up a vocabulary

用法示例
他每月买十本书,不久便积累了很多。
By buying ten books every month, he soon accumulated a good library.
他已在这所学校工作了十年,积累了丰富的教学经验。
He has worked in this school for ten years. And he acquired rich experience in teaching.

jīyā
积压　反脱销　（丁）动

overstock; having more than can be managed

常用搭配
积压物资 materials kept too long in stock
产品积压 overstocking of products

用法示例
经理想把仓库里所有积压的存货清理掉。
The manager wants to clear out all the old stock in the warehouse.
小商店要注意防止积压商品。
It is important for small shops to avoid overstocking their goods.

jīngyíng
经营　（丙）动

operate (a business)

常用搭配
经营一家企业 operate a business
改善经营管理 improve management and marketing
经营不善 poor operation

用法示例
没有良好的经营管理,事业就不会兴旺发达。
A business cannot thrive without good management and marketing.
挽救该公司的唯一办法是彻底改变其经营方式。
The only thing that will save the company is a thorough shake-up of the way it is run.
我们只经营硬件,不经营软件。
We deal in hardware, but not software.

shēnqǐng
申请　（丙）动

apply

常用搭配
申请补助 apply for an allowance
申请调动工作 apply for a transfer
入学申请 application for a school

用法示例
这个工人申请调换工作岗位。
The worker applied for a transfer to another post.
你应该向领事申请签证。
You should apply to the consul for a visa.
经理收到了二十份求职申请书。
The manager received twenty applications for the post.

shēngmíng
声明　回申明　（丙）动/名

declare; statement

常用搭配
公开声明 state openly
联合声明 joint declaration
发表一项声明 issue a statement

用法示例
我在会上声明我不支持他。
I declared at the meeting that I did not support him.
他声明他决不再与他们合作。
He avowed that he would never cooperate with them again.
他对这个事件发表了公开声明。
He made his public statement about the affair.

hǎnjiàn
罕见　反常见　（丁）形

① rare ② rarely seen

常用搭配
罕见的动物 rare animals　罕见的现象 rare phenomena

用法示例
那种鸟在这个国家十分罕见。
That bird is very rare in this country.
该国对汽车工业严加保护,外国汽车很罕见。
The country's car industry is so strongly protected that foreign cars are rarely seen there.
这种野生金鱼越来越罕见了。
This kind of wild golden fish is becoming rare.

diàodòng
调动　（丙）动

transfer

常用搭配
调动工作 transfer sb. to another post

用法示例
他已从北京调动到上海了。
He has been transferred from Beijing to Shanghai.

你听说这次谁要被调动到什么地方了吗?

Have you heard anything about who will be transferred, and to where?

diàodù
调度　　　　　　　　　　(丁) 动

dispatch

常用搭配

列车调度员 train dispatcher

调度公共汽车 dispatch buses

用法示例

她负责在终点站调度公共汽车。

She is in charge of dispatching buses at the terminal.

他是电车公司的调度员。

He is a dispatcher at the trolleybus company.

shēnbào
申报　　　　　　　　　　(丁) 动

report or declare (to customs or other authority)

常用搭配

申报表 declaration form

申报关税 make a customs declaration

用法示例

请书面申报你在国外购买的全部商品。

Please make a written declaration of all the goods you bought abroad.

你必须申报去年的总收入。

You must declare everything you have earned in the last year.

huòqǔ
获取　　　　　　　　　　(丁) 动

gain; obtain

常用搭配

获取暴利 reap staggering profits

获取信息 get information

用法示例

军官获取了敌人的重要情报。

The officer learned important information about the enemy's plans.

那位新闻记者偶然获取了这些重要的资料。

The journalist obtained these important facts by chance.

jīngshāng
经商　　　　　　　　　　(丁) 动

① be in business ② do commerce

常用搭配

他善于经商。He is good at doing business.

用法示例

他在经商方面没有经验。

He is inexperienced in business.

我叔叔给了我一些钱让我开始经商。

My uncle gave me some money to start me out in a trade.

他已经商多年。

He was engaged in trade for many years.

zì xiāng máo dùn
自相 矛 盾　　　　　　　　(丙)

self-contradictory

常用搭配

自相矛盾的言论 self-contradictory statements

用法示例

她觉察到他的论点有几处自相矛盾。

She noticed several minor inconsistencies in his argument.

我们都认为那个发言自相矛盾。

We all thought it was a paradoxical speech.

 **词义辨析**

积累、积压

"积累"和"积压"都是动词,都表示物品被储存得(越来越)多。"积累"表示有意识地积攒,它的对象可以是具体的,也可以是抽象的,是褒义词。"积压"表示因为无法销售或运送而增多,它的对象是具体的物品,是贬义词。例如:①这名老专家积累了很多有价值的资料和丰富的经验。② 我们该怎么处理仓库积压的产品呢?

Both 积累 and 积压 are verbs, meaning "to keep a lot of things, to pile up". 积累 indicates "to gather intentionally", and its objects can be something abstract or concrete, and it has a commendatory sense; while 积压 indicates "excessive goods in stock which can not be sold or transported in a timely manner", Its objects are something concrete, and it has a derogatory sense. For example: ① The old expert accumulated a lot of valuable data and many rich experiences. ② How can we deal with the excess stock in warehouse?

 **练习**

练习一、根据拼音写汉字，根据汉字写拼音

jī（   ） diào（   ）（   ）yíng hǎn（   ） huò（   ）
（   ）累 （   ）度 经（   ） （   ）见 （   ）取

练习二、搭配连线

(1) 积累   A. 工作
(2) 积压   B. 暴利
(3) 入学   C. 产品
(4) 调动   D. 申请
(5) 获取   E. 经验

练习三、从今天学习的生词中选择合适的词填空

1. 他是通过互联网 _____ 这些资料的。
2. 他肯定是在说谎，因为我发现他的话有些 _____。
3. 这家工厂因 _____ 不善而倒闭。
4. 每天记住几个生词，坚持一年，你会发现你已经 _____ 了很多词汇。
5. 老张负责 _____ 咱们单位的卡车，如果你需要送货，你最少提前一天告诉他。
6. 她想 _____ 工作，因为现在的单位离她家太远了，另外她对这份工作也不太满意。
7. 仓库里堆满了 _____ 的产品，我们得想办法把它们处理掉。
8. 这种动物非常 _____，甚至有人认为它已经灭绝了。
9. 他很有商业头脑，如果学习 _____，将来一定前途无量。
10. 你应该如实向税务局 _____ 你的年收入。

答案

练习一：
略
练习二：

(1) E	(2)C	(3)D	(4)A	(5)B

练习三：

1. 获取	2. 自相矛盾	3. 经营	4. 积累	5. 调度
6. 调动	7. 积压	8. 罕见	9. 经商	10. 申报

 星期四

huòdé
获得   （乙）动

obtain; receive

常用搭配
获得奖励 obtain a prize
获得胜利 gain a victory

用法示例
他获得了建筑专业的学位证书。
He received a diploma in architecture.
他获得了领导的赏识。
He gained recognition from leaders.
这个国家在 1972 年获得了独立。
The country attained its independence in 1972.

jízào   nàixīn
急躁   反 耐心   （丙）形

irritable; irascible; impetuous

常用搭配
性情急躁 irritable disposition

用法示例
年轻人常比老年人急躁。
Youngsters are usually more impetuous than older people.
老板脾气急躁，经常对我们大喊大叫。
Our boss is irritable, and often shouts at us.
他急躁的脾气使他很讨厌。
His quick temper made him offensive.

jíbìng   bìngtòng
疾病   同 病痛   （丙）名

sickness; disease

常用搭配
预防疾病 prevent disease
治疗疾病 cure disease

用法示例
许多疾病是由细菌引起的。
Many diseases are caused by bacteria.
水痘是一种常见的儿童期疾病。
Chicken pox is a common childhood illness.
我们怎么防止这种疾病蔓延呢？
What can we do to prevent the disease from spreading?

èhuà   hǎozhuǎn
恶化   反 好转   （丙）形

worsen

常用搭配
使事情恶化 aggravate a matter
形势恶化了。The situation worsened.

【用法示例】

病人的情况在夜间恶化了。

The patient's condition worsened during the night.

他的健康状况迅速恶化。

His health is rapidly deteriorating.

暴风雨使燃料的缺乏状况更加恶化。

Heavy storms made the fuel shortages worse.

róngxìng
荣幸 （丙）形

honored

【常用搭配】

我荣幸地通知您……

I have the honor to inform you that…

如蒙光临，不胜荣幸。

We will be greatly honored by your presence.

【用法示例】

我认为能应邀参加晚宴是很大的荣幸。

I consider it a great honor to have been invited to the dinner.

他的到来是我们的荣幸。

He has honored us with his presence.

我很荣幸能介绍我们的州长。

I have the honor of presenting the governor.

xìngyùn
幸运 （丁）形

lucky; fortunate

【常用搭配】

幸运儿 luck fellow

幸运数字 a lucky number

【用法示例】

你有这样一位通情达理的父亲，真是幸运。

You are fortunate to have such a reasonable father.

有些人似乎总是幸运的。

Some people seem to be always lucky.

我在最后一分钟赶上了今天最后一班车，真是幸运。

I was fortunate enough to catch today's last bus, at the last minute.

èliè
恶劣 （丙）形

vile

【常用搭配】

恶劣的气候 very bad climate

恶劣的行径 adverse circumstances

【用法示例】

我们不顾恶劣的天气而去钓鱼。

In spite of the abominable weather, we went fishing.

凶杀是最恶劣的罪行。

Murder is the most abominable crime.

lèqù
乐趣 （丁）名

joy; pleasure

【常用搭配】

人生的乐趣 joys of life

工作中的乐趣 delight in work

【用法示例】

她感到了写作的乐趣。

She discovered the joys of writing.

和她谈话是一种乐趣。

It is a pleasure to converse with her.

我们并不总是能在工作中享受到乐趣。

We can't always combine work with pleasure.

lèyì
乐意 （丁）动/形

① be willing ② happy (to do)

【常用搭配】

乐意去农村工作 be willing to work in the countryside

不乐意跟他们去 be unwilling to go with them

【用法示例】

我乐意为你做任何事情。

I am willing to do anything for you.

如果有空，我很乐意跟他们见面。

I'll be happy to meet with them when I have time.

jídù
嫉妒 ◎ 妒忌 dùjì （丁）动

① envy ② be jealous

【常用搭配】

嫉妒他的名声 be jealous of his fame

出于嫉妒 out of envy

【用法示例】

他嫉妒他们的成就。

He is jealous of their success.

他嫉妒她挣的比他多。

He grudges her earning more than he does.

你的话引起了他的嫉妒。

Your remark excited his jealousy.

jièkǒu
借口 （丙）动/名

① on the excuse of ② excuse

【常用搭配】

找借口 find an excuse

【用法示例】

那淘气的男孩借口头疼，离开了教室。

The naughty boy left the classroom under the pretext of having a headache.

工作太忙不能成为不学习的借口。

Having too much work is no excuse for not studying.

她的借口是说她没看见信号。

Her excuse was that she did not see the signal.

zì lì gēng shēng
自力更生 （丁）

stand on one's own feet

常用搭配

自力更生的精神 the spirit of independence

用法示例

那个大富翁捐出了大部分财产,他希望他的孩子能够自力更生。

The millionaire gave away most of his property; because he hoped his children could stand on their own feet.

不要依赖任何人,你要学会自力更生。

Don't depend on anybody; you should learn to stand on your own feet.

词义辨析

荣幸、幸运

"荣幸"和"幸运"都是形容词,都表示运气好。"荣幸"比较正式,强调感到幸运而光荣,一般作状语、谓语,不作定语。"幸运"比较口语化,可以作状语、谓语和定语。例如:①我在餐厅遇到了那个电影明星,并且跟她合影,我感到很幸运/荣幸。②我很荣幸能参加王子的婚礼。③我的幸运数字是8,你的呢?

Both 荣幸 and 幸运 are adjectives, meaning "lucky". 荣幸 is formal, and it stresses to feel lucky and honored; it can function as an adverbial or a predicate, but it can't function as an attributive. 幸运 is colloquial, and it can function as an adverbial, a predicate or an attributive. For example: ① I was very lucky to have met the movie star in the restaurant and have my picture with her. ② I have the honor to attend the prince's wedding ceremony. ③ My lucky number is eight. What is yours?

练习

练习一、根据拼音写汉字,根据汉字写拼音

jí ( ) jí ( ) ( )liè ( )qù ( )xìng

( )躁 ( )病 恶( ) 乐( ) 荣( )

练习二、搭配连线

(1) 性情   A. 恶劣
(2) 获得   B. 急躁
(3) 病情   C. 疾病
(4) 预防   D. 胜利
(5) 条件   E. 恶化

练习三、从今天学习的生词中选择合适的词填空

1. 他的脾气有点 _____ ,遇事不够冷静。

2. 由于没有钱治病,他的病情进一步 _____ 了。

3. 你要知道,医生并不能治疗所有的 _____ ,你自己应该注意保养。

4. 李教授是全国知名的专家,能当他的学生,我感到很 _____ 。

5. 尽管那里环境异常 _____ ,他们还是按时完成了勘探的任务。

6. 如果需要帮助,您尽管说,我很 _____ 帮忙。

7. 他的成功引起了别人的 _____ ,甚至有人诽谤他,说他有贪污行为。

8. 他特别喜欢钻研,他说在科学研究的过程中充满了 _____ 。

9. 作文比赛中,田中 _____ 了一等奖。

10. 很 _____ ,我赶上了最后一趟班车。

答案

练习一:

略

练习二:

(1) B   (2)D   (3)E   (4)C   (5)A

练习三:

1. 急躁   2. 恶化   3. 疾病   4. 荣幸   5. 恶劣

6. 乐意   7. 嫉妒   8. 乐趣   9. 获得   10. 幸运

Friday
星期五

shōuhuò
收获 ⊜ 损失 （乙）名／动
① acquirement ② harvest

常用搭配
收获的季节 harvest season
收获粮食 harvest grains

用法示例
现在是收获期，所以我们都很忙。
We are all very busy because it's the harvest time.
不付出就没有收获。
No gain without pain.
你能谈谈你参观那所大学的收获吗？
Can you talk about what you gained from visiting the university?

dàilǐ
代理 （丙）动

常用搭配
代理费 agent fee   代理机构 agency
代理人 deputy

用法示例
我得找一个人，在我离开期间代理我的职务。
I must find someone to act as a deputy for me during my absence.
要进一步了解情况，请与本地代理商联系。
For further information, contact your local agent.
我不在时，张谋将是我的代理人。
Zhang Mou will be my deputy while I am away.

dàijià
代价 （丙）名
cost

常用搭配
不惜任何代价 at any cost
付出很高代价 pay a high price for

用法示例
他们为取得胜利付出了沉重的代价。
They paid a heavy price for the victory.
这个集邮迷决心不惜任何代价得到那枚稀有的邮票。
The stamp collector decided to get that rare stamp at any costs.
我相信取得成功的代价就是努力工作。
I believe that the price of success is hard work.

diàochá
调查 ⊜ 调研 （乙）名／动
① investigation; survey ② investigate

常用搭配
调查报告 investigative report
调查问卷 questionnaire
调查一件事情 look into an affair

用法示例
警方开始调查事故的原因。
The police instituted an inquiry into the cause of the accident.
他们答应对这次飞机失事进行彻底的调查。
They've promised a thorough inquiry into the plane crash.
根据最近的一项调查，仅上海就有 250 多万外来民工。
According to a recent survey, in Shanghai alone there are more than 2.5 million migrant workers.

cāozuò
操作 （丙）动
operate; handle

常用搭配
易于操作 easy to handle   操作板 operation panel
操作机器 operate a machine

用法示例
我能够熟练操作计算机。
I am skilled in operating a computer.
我是一名计算机操作人员。
I am a computer operator.
工人要提高操作水平。
The workers should improve their operating skills.

cāozòng
操纵 （丙）动
operate; control

常用搭配
无线电操纵 radio control
操纵他人 manipulate others
被操纵着……manipulated into doing…

用法示例
这台机器由电子脉冲信号操纵。
The machine is operated by an electronic pulse.
这些商人试图操纵股票价格。
These traders tried to manipulate stock prices.

hùzhù
互助 （丙）形
help each other

常用搭配
互助组 support group
互助合作 mutual aid and cooperation

用法示例
在任何困难时期，我们都能友好互助。
In times of trouble, we always help each other.
他懂得互助的重要性。
He understands the importance of mutual aid.

diàohuàn
调换 (丁)动
exchange; change places

常用搭配
与……调换座位 exchange seats with…
调换职位 change one's position

用法示例
我和你调一下座位好吗？
May I exchange seats with you?
我想调换一下工作,可是他劝我还是干老本行好。
I wanted to change my job, but he advised me to stay where was.
请遵守我们的协议,给我们调换损坏的货物。
Please honor our agreement by exchanging the damaged goods.

shōucheng
收成 (丁)名
harvest

常用搭配
好收成 good harvest

用法示例
由于收成不好,成千上万的人在挨饿。
Thousands are going hungry because of the failure of the harvest.
尽管遭受干旱,还是获得了好收成。
A good harvest was obtained in spite of the drought.

hùlì
互利 同 互惠 (丁)动
hùhuì
be mutually beneficial

常用搭配
在平等互利的基础上
on the basis of equality and mutual benefits
以互利为目的 for mutual benefit

用法示例
中国希望在平等互利的基础上同所有国家开展贸易。
China wishes to trade with all countries on the basis of equality and mutual benefits.
我相信通过双方的努力,交易往来定会朝着互利的方向发展。
I am convinced that with our joint efforts, business between us will be mutually beneficial.

fánhuá
繁华 反 萧条 (丁)形
xiāotiáo
① flourishing ② bustling

常用搭配
城里最繁华的地区 the busiest section of town

用法示例
好莱坞的虚荣与繁华似乎强烈吸引着这个女孩。
The glitz and glamor of Hollywood were fascinating to the girl.

这一带越来越繁华了。
This district is getting more and more prosperous and bustling.

zì sī zì lì
自私自利 (丁)
① selfish ② self-contered

常用搭配
自私自利的人 a selfish man

用法示例
所有这些说明一点——他是一个自私自利的人。
It all adds up to this—he is a selfish man.
他特别自私自利,从不帮助别人。
He is very selfish and will never help others.

词义辨析

操作、操纵

　　"操作"和"操纵"都是动词,都有控制的意思。"操作"强调按照一定的技巧和方法进行控制或处理,对象一般是机器或事物;"操纵"也可以表示控制机器的意思,还表示为达到个人目的,用不正当的手段进行控制,对象可能是人或组织。例如:①我能够熟练操作电脑。②他是一个善于操纵舆论的精明的政客。

　　Both 操作 and 操纵 are verbs, meaning "to operate". 操作 stresses to deal with an affair or to operate a machine in a certain way, or with certain skills, and its objects are usually affairs or machines. 操纵 can indicate to operate a machine, and it also means to control somebody or something by unfair means for personal gain. Its objects are people or organizations. For example: ① I am skilled in operating a computer. ② He is a clever politician who knows how to manipulate public opinion.

练习

练习一、根据拼音写汉字,根据汉字写拼音
( )zòng shōu( ) fán( ) ( )chá dài( )
操( ) ( )成 ( )华 调( ) ( )价

练习二、搭配连线
(1) 收获　　　　　　A. 代价
(2) 付出　　　　　　B. 问卷
(3) 调查　　　　　　C. 职位
(4) 操作　　　　　　D. 粮食
(5) 调换　　　　　　E. 机器

练习三、从今天学习的生词中选择合适的词填空
1. 王府井是北京非常_____的地段,这里的房价当然很高。
2. 这个人_____,没有一点团队精神,我们都不愿意跟他打交道。
3. 这次到国外进修的_____很大,我不仅学到了先进的技术,还学到了先进的管理经验。

4. 我们公司在中国的大城市都有_____,您可以直接和他们联系。

5. 趁观众不注意,魔术师在转身的时候_____了两个杯子的位置。

6. 这几个大财团想联合起来_____市场的物价,结果受到了有关部门的惩罚。

7. 根据_____,现在中国男性在总人口中的比例比女性高,而且差距还在不断增大。

8. 新买了一台洗衣机,我需要看看说明书才能正确_____。

9. 今年发生了自然灾害,影响了_____。

10. 他两岁的女儿丢了,他决心不惜任何_____也要找到她。

答案

练习一:
略
练习二:
(1) D　　(2)A　　(3)B　　(4)E　　(5)C
练习三:
1. 繁华　　2. 自私自利　3. 收获　　4. 代理　　5. 调换
6. 操纵　　7. 调查　　8. 操作　　9. 收成　　10. 代价

第12月,第1周的练习

练习一.根据词语给加点的字注音
1.(　)　2.(　)　3.(　)　4.(　)　5.(　)
慎重　　积累　　乐趣　　繁华　　恶劣

练习二.根据拼音填写词语
　　jí　　　jí　　　jí　　　zhì　　　zhì
1.(　)病 2.(　)躁 3.(　)妒 4.精(　) 5.设(　)

练习三.辨析并选择合适的词填空
1. 我们应该在不伤害他人而且不(　)他人的前提下享受自由。(障碍、妨碍)
2. 这两个国家的人交流没有(　),他们使用同一种语言。(障碍、妨碍)
3. 明天是妇女节,女职员放假半天,男职员(　)工作。(依旧、照旧)
4. 这个明星是我父母那一辈的偶像,都过了二十年了,她风采(　)。(依旧、照旧)
5. 他做这一行已经有十年了,(　)了一定的经验。(积累、积压)
6. 如果再不把(　)的产品卖出去,这些产品就超过保质期了。(积累、积压)
7. 刚刚大学毕业就找到了这样一份好工作,她觉得非常(　)。(荣幸、幸运)
8. 能够代表公司在大会上演讲,并与众多企业家交流,我感到很(　)。(荣幸、幸运)
9. 这道工序(　)起来相当难,需要有丰富的实践经验才能

做好。(操作、操纵)
10. 民众怀疑政府的决策受到了某些利益集团的(　)。(操作、操纵)

练习四.选词填空
慌忙　　荒唐　　调查　　调动　　神秘
慌张　　荒凉　　调换　　调度　　奥秘
1. 商店发生火灾时,很多顾客显得很(　),不知道安全出口在哪里。
2. 考试的时候,每个人都要坐在指定的座位上,不能随意和别人(　)位置。
3. 列车几点出发几点进站都要听铁路部门的统一(　)。
4. 他做事向来很(　),甚至连家人都不清楚他每天在忙什么。
5. 要想做成这件事,必须充分(　)大家的积极性。
6. 由于环境的恶化,那片美丽的草原,已经变成了(　)的沙漠。
7. 人类通过各种努力正在不断探索宇宙的(　)。
8. 有人揭发他有贪污行为,警方准备对此进行(　)。
9. 小偷听到有人在用钥匙开门,便(　)藏到了窗帘后边。
10. 孩子是认真的,而他的父母却觉得他的想法(　)可笑。

练习五.成语填空
1. 自言(　)(　)　2. 自相(　)(　)　3. 自私(　)(　)
4. 自始(　)(　)　5. 自力(　)(　)

练习六.写出下列词语的同义词
1. 互利(　)　　　　2. 慎重(　)
3. 积累(　)　　　　4. 嫉妒(　)
5. 荒凉(　)

练习七.写出下列词语的反义词
1. 积压(　)　　　　2. 深奥(　)
3. 恶化(　)　　　　4. 繁华(　)
5. 精致(　)

答案

练习一.
1.zhòng　2.lěi　　3.lè　　4.fán　　5.è
练习二.
1. 疾　　2. 急　　3. 嫉　　4. 致　　5. 置
练习三.
1. 妨碍　　2. 障碍　　3. 照旧　　4. 依旧　　5. 积累
6. 积压　　7. 幸运　　8. 荣幸　　9. 操作　　10. 操纵
练习四.
1. 慌张　　2. 调换　　3. 调度　　4. 神秘　　5. 调动
6. 荒凉　　7. 奥秘　　8. 调查　　9. 慌忙　　10. 荒唐
练习五.
1. 自语　　2. 矛盾　　3. 自利　　4. 至终　　5. 更生
练习六.
1. 互惠　　2. 谨慎　　3. 积攒　　4. 妒忌　　5. 荒芜
练习七.
1. 脱销　　2. 浅显　　3. 好转　　4. 萧条　　5. 粗糙

12月 第 2 周的学习内容

星期一 Monday

cèyàn
测验 ⊜ 测试 cèshì （乙）名／动
① exam ② test

常用搭配
智力测验 intelligence test
测验的结果 result of the test

用法示例
我们明天早晨要进行一个小测验。
We will have a quiz tomorrow morning.
教师测验了学生上星期的功课。
The teacher quizzed the students on last week's work.

zhùyuàn
住院 （乙）动
be in hospital

常用搭配
医疗保险 hospital insurance
住院病人 inpatient

用法示例
他病了，已住院一个星期了。
He is ill, and has been in the hospital for a week.
她住院了，要做一个切除阑尾的手术。
She's gone into hospital to have her appendix taken out.

hàoqí
好奇 （丙）形
curious

常用搭配
好奇的目光 a curious glance
对……感到好奇 be curious about…
好奇地问 ask curiously

用法示例
对周围的世界感到好奇是件好事。
It is good to be curious about the world around you.
好奇是儿童的天性。
Curiosity is part of a child's nature.
她对别人的事情很好奇。
She is inquisitive about other people's affairs.

wěiqu
委屈 （丙）动／形
① wrong (sb) ② feel wronged

常用搭配
受委屈 suffer a wrong
诉委屈 pour out one's grievances

用法示例
她觉得有点委屈。
She feels rather hard done by.
她诉说她受到的委屈。
She complained of the wrongs she had suffered.
我工作时间是别人的两倍，可拿的钱却比谁都少，我感到十分委屈。
I felt very hard done by when I got less money than anybody else, even though I'd worked twice as long.

wěituō
委托 （丙）动
entrust

常用搭配
把某事委托给某人 entrust sth. to sb.
委托书 deed of trust
委托人 client

用法示例
我能把这些秘密计划委托给他吗？
Can I entrust him with the secret plans?
他把部门的管理工作委托给助手了。
He deputized the running of the department to an assistant.
被告的律师辩称其委托人是无辜的。
Counsel for the defendant submits that his client is innocent.

cèshì
测试 （丙）名／动
① measure and test ② test the performance of

常用搭配
参加测试 take a test
运动员耐力测试 a test of an athlete's endurance
测试某人的能力 test sb's ability

用法示例
我们正在测试新药的功效。
We are testing the efficacy of a new drug.
研究人员正在对食品的酸含量进行测试。
The researchers are testing the acid content of the food.
这种新型赛车在道路测试中时速达 100 英里。
The new sports model achieved 100 miles an hour in road tests.

sìyǎng
饲养 ⊜ 喂养 wèiyǎng （丙）动
raise; rear

常用搭配
饲养牲畜 raise livestock
饲养家禽 raise poultry
用法示例
饲养员正在喂动物。
The keeper is feeding the animals.
我饲养了 12 只小鸡。
I had bred a dozen chickens.
我把现有的家禽饲养方面的书全都读过了。
I've read all the available literature on poultry-farming.

hàokè
好客 （丁）形
hospitable
常用搭配
好客的主人 a cordial host
用法示例
李太太以好客闻名。
Mrs Li is known for her hospitality.
好客的主人很快为尊贵的客人腾空了闲置着的房间。
The courteous host had his spare room quickly cleaned out for the honoured guest.
当地人十分热情好客。
The local people are very warm and hospitable.

sìliào
饲料 （丁）名
fodder; feed
常用搭配
精饲料 fine fodder
猪饲料 pig feed
用法示例
那儿有很多喂牛的饲料。
There is much feed for the cattle.
母鸡的饲料不够了。
There isn't enough feed left for the hens.
鸭子和鹅都已经喂过饲料了。
The ducks and geese have been fed.

hūluè
忽略 ⓠ 忽视 hūshì （丁）动
neglect; overlook
常用搭配
不要忽略细节。Don't neglect the details.
忽略了他的错误。Overlook his mistakes.
用法示例
他们忽略了其中的巨大风险。
They overlooked the enormous risks involved.
他忽略了他的姑姑,因而得罪了她。
He neglected his aunt, and it displeased her.
你忽略了火车或许晚点的可能性。
You left out the possibility that the train might be late.

bēibǐ
卑鄙 ⓠ 卑劣 bēiliè （丁）形
① mean ② contemptible
常用搭配
卑鄙的伎俩 a mean trick
卑鄙的家伙 a contemptible man
用法示例
我认为他的行为卑鄙而自私。
I think his behavior mean and selfish.
做出那种事真够卑鄙无耻的!
That was a mean and dirty thing to do!
用那样的花招欺负一个老太太,真卑鄙。
That was a horrible trick to play on an old lady.

běnnéng
本能 （丁）名
instinct
常用搭配
本能反应 instinctive reaction
保护孩子的本能 an instinct to protect her children
用法示例
鸟类学习飞翔是出于本能。
Birds learn to fly by instinct.
遇到危险时,我们的本能反应就是跑开。
Running away is our instinctive reaction when we meet with danger.
哺乳是哺乳动物的本能。
Suckling is an instinct in mammals.

 词义辨析

测试、测验

作为动词,"测试"和"测验"都有检验能力的意思,作为名词都可以表示小型的或非正式的考试。"测试"强调用仪器或其它办法检验性能或功效,它的对象通常是人、机器、仪器等。"测验"强调用考试或其它方式检验学习效果,它的对象一般是学生或学员。例如:①我们每周一上午要进行一次小测验/测试。②他们正在对新汽车的性能进行测试。③士兵们最终完成了耐力测试。④教师测验了学生的基础知识。

As verbs, both 测试 and 测验 mean "to examine"; as nouns, they mean "a test that may be informal or on a small-scale". 测试 stresses to test the performance or efficacy by using instruments or other means, and its objects are people, machines, instruments, etc. 测验 stresses to test one's learning, and its objects are usually students or learners. For example: ① We have a quiz every Monday morning. ② They are testing the performance of the new car. ③ The soldiers eventually completed the endurance tests. ④ The teacher quizzed the students on their basic knowledge.

 **练习**

练习一、根据拼音写汉字，根据汉字写拼音

( )qu sì( ) ( )kè bēi( ) hū( )

委( ) ( )养 好( ) ( )鄙 ( )略

练习二、搭配连线

(1) 本能的   A. 目光

(2) 卑鄙的   B. 结果

(3) 好客的   C. 反应

(4) 好奇的   D. 伎俩

(5) 测试的   E. 主人

练习三、从今天学习的生词中选择合适的词填空

1. 每上两课，老师都会给我们做一个小 _____。

2. 他和妻子都很 _____，经常邀请我们到他家玩。

3. 我马上要出差，所以我只好 _____ 同事帮我处理那件事。

4. 出于妒忌，他诽谤我，甚至还诽谤我的妻子，这个人可真 _____。

5. 孩子对学习越来越不感兴趣了，可他的父母整天忙于工作，_____ 了孩子的这种变化。

6. 小孩子的 _____ 心特别强，每天问我各种各样的问题。

7. 在正式使用前，我们还要进一步 _____ 这种机器的性能。

8. 金智恩生病 _____ 了，我们要去医院看她。

9. 养这么多牛，光一天的 _____ 就消耗不少。

10. 她以为自己做了件好事，结果没有人理解她，她 _____ 得哭了。

答案

练习一：

略

练习二：

(1) C   (2)D   (3)E   (4)A   (5)B

练习三：

1. 测验   2. 好客   3. 委托   4. 卑鄙   5. 忽略

6. 好奇   7. 测试   8. 住院   9. 饲料   10. 委屈

 星期二

shāmò

沙漠   （乙）名

desert

常用搭配

撒哈拉大沙漠 the Sahara desert

沙漠化 desertification

用法示例

大片的土地已经变成了沙漠。

Vast areas of land have become deserted.

这种仙人掌生长在沙漠地区。

This kind of cactus lives in the desert.

xùnliàn

训练   （乙）动

train

常用搭配

体育训练 physical training

军事训练 military training

用法示例

这位冠军正在为下一场比赛进行训练。

The champion is in training for his next fight.

他的母亲已经把他训练成为了一名优秀的钢琴家。

His mother has trained him to be an excellent pianist.

毕业前，我们将要接受一些职业训练。

We will have some vocational training before graduating.

fěngcì   **wākǔ**

讽刺   回 **挖苦**   （丙）动

satire

常用搭配

讽刺画 satirical cartoon

讽刺诗 satirical poem

辛辣的讽刺 piercing satire

用法示例

讽刺往往是一种抗议的形式。

Satire is often a form of protest.

最具讽刺意味的是：尽管他竭力解释，可没一个人相信他。

The great irony is that despite all his explanations, nobody believed him.

政客当然是被讽刺的对象。

Politicians are legitimate targets for satire.

dàiyù   **bàochou**

待遇   回 **报酬**   （丙）名

treatment; salary

常用搭配

优惠的待遇 preferential treatment

政治待遇 political treatment
国民待遇 citizen's treatment

用法示例

我对受到这样的待遇表示抗议。
I object to being treated like this.
其他地方的更优厚的待遇使他离开了公司。
He was lured away from the company by the offer of higher pay elsewhere.
他的工资待遇很好,但他总是向朋友借钱而且从来不还。
He gets a good salary, yet he always borrows money from his friends and never pays it back.

wéinán
为难　　　chéngquán 反 成全　　　（丙）动

① feel awkward ② make things difficult for

常用搭配

为难的事 an awkward matter
使人为难 put sb. in an awkward situation

用法示例

有人要给我一份更好的工作,但薪水较低,我很为难,不知如何是好。
I've been offered a better job, but at a lower salary. I'm in a quandary as to what to do.
你的拒绝让我十分为难。
Your refusal puts me in an awkward position.
你使我非常为难。
You place me in a very difficult position.

cāoliàn
操练　　　（丁）动

practice; drill

常用搭配

步枪操练 rifle drill　　阅兵操练 parade drill

用法示例

新兵每天要操练三个小时。
New recruits have three hours of drills a day.
操练了半天之后,他让这个班解散了。
At the end of a long drill he told the squad to fall out.
士兵在军营里操练。
The soldiers are doing drills in the barrack-yard.

wéichí
维持　　　（丙）动

maintain; preserve

常用搭配

维持现状 maintain the status quo
维持原判 affirm the original judgment
维护秩序 preserve order

用法示例

那位老师无法维持课堂纪律。
The teacher can't preserve discipline in her class.
我们的钱只能勉强维持到周末。
We had barely enough money to last us through the weekend.

警察在街上维持秩序。
Policemen keep the peace in the street.

ěxin
恶心　　　（丙）形

sick; disgusting

常用搭配

感到恶心 to be sickened
你真让我恶心! You make me sick!

用法示例

他奉承雇主的拍马屁的嘴脸令我恶心。
His servile praise for his employer was disgusting to me.
我一想到吃生贝就恶心。
The idea of eating raw shellfish nauseates me.
你觉得恶心吗?
Do you feel nauseous?

éwài
额外　　　fènnèi 反 分内　　　（丁）形

extra

常用搭配

额外费用 extra charges
额外负担 added burden
额外开支 extra expenses

用法示例

这个旅馆对有洗澡间的房间额外收费。
This hotel charges extra for a room with a bath.
我们不因为额外的工作而要求额外的报酬。
We do not ask for extra pay for extra work.
为获得额外收入,她决定租出一个房间。
She decided to rent out a room to make some extra income.

dàikuǎn
贷款　　　（丁）名／动

① loan ② to (provide a) loan

常用搭配

消费贷款 loan for consumption
无息贷款 interest-free loans
专项贷款 special-purpose loan

用法示例

他为申请贷款而不得不抵押土地。
He will have to mortgage his land for a loan.
他们贷款收多少利息?
How much interest do they charge on loans?
银行拒绝再贷款给这家公司。
The bank refused any further loans to the company.

wéixiū
维修　　　（丁）动

① protect and maintain ② repair

常用搭配

维修汽车 service a car
维修设备 upkeep of equipment

维修手册 servicing manual

用法示例

这些机器需要经常保养维修。

The machines require constant maintenance and repair.

我对电脑的维修保养很在行。

Maintaining of a PC is my forte.

shātān

沙滩　　　　　　　　　　　　　　（丁）名

① beach ② sand bank

常用搭配

金色的沙滩 a golden beach

用法示例

我喜欢沙滩,不喜欢遍布小石子的海滩。

I prefer a sandy beach to a rocky one.

沙滩上挤满了晒太阳的人。

The beach was crowded with sunbathers.

退潮时,一只蟹被留在沙滩上了。

A crab was left stranded on the beach when the tide went out.

 **词义辨析**

操练、训练

　　"操练"和"训练"都是动词,都有培训的意思。"操练"还指训练士兵行进和使用武器以及队列演练,它的对象一般是一组人。"训练"强调用指导和实践的方法系统地进行技能或行为的培训,它的对象可以是很多人,也可以是一个人,还可以是动物。例如:①他在训练这只狗用两条腿站立。②士兵在操练队列。

　　Both 操练 and 训练 are verbs, meaning "to train". 操练 also means to train soldiers to march, use arms or to perform in formation; its objects are a group of people. 训练 stresses to train people to master a skill, or to perform actions with a systematic method that combines instructions and practices, its objects can be a lot of people, or one person, or even animal(s). For example: ① He is training his dog to stand on two legs. ② The soldiers are having a formation drill.

 **练习**

练习一、根据拼音写汉字,根据汉字写拼音

( )cì ( )yù wéi ( ) dài ( ) é ( )

讽( ) 待( ) ( )持 ( )款 ( )外

练习二、搭配连线

(1) 维修　　　　　　　　A. 秩序

(2) 无息　　　　　　　　B. 电脑

(3) 额外　　　　　　　　C. 训练

(4) 维持　　　　　　　　D. 贷款

(5) 体育　　　　　　　　E. 负担

练习三、从今天学习的生词中选择合适的词填空

1. 他和妻子已经分居了,恐怕他们的婚姻难以继续_____下去了。

2. 周围化工厂的污水都排放到这条河里了,每次经过,都能闻到_____的臭味。

3. 有的人躺在_____上晒太阳,有的人在海里游泳。

4. 如果您在这里购买的电器出现故障,我们将负责为您免费_____。

5. 他们的房子是_____买的,所以每个月的大部分工资要还贷。

6. 老师对学生要有耐心,一定不能嘲笑或_____他们。

7. 由于长期干旱,那片草原变成了_____,已经没有人在那里居住了。

8. 除了每个月的工资,他还有_____的收入吗?

9. 他们公司的_____特别好,不仅工资高,而且每年还有一个月的带薪假期。

10. 经过严格的_____,这只警犬已经开始执行搜捕任务了。

答案

练习一:

略

练习二:

(1) B　　　(2)D　　　(3)E　　　(4)A　　　(5)C

练习三:

1. 维持　　2. 恶心　　3. 沙滩　　4. 维修　　5. 贷款

6. 讽刺　　7. 沙漠　　8. 额外　　9. 待遇　　10. 训练

星期三

wùzhì
物质　⊗ 精神　（乙）名
substance
【常用搭配】
营养物质 nutritional substance
物质财富 material wealth
有害物质 harmful substance
【用法示例】
这种物质能够溶解在酒精中。
This substance is soluble in alcohol.
石墨是一种软而黑的物质。
Graphite is a soft black substance.
过敏是身体对某些物质的不良反应。
An allergy is an adverse reaction of the body to certain substances.

wǎngqiú
网球　（乙）名
① tennis ball ② tennis
【常用搭配】
网球场 a tennis court
网球鞋 tennis shoes
【用法示例】
他善于打网球。
He is good at playing tennis.
我想买几个网球。
I want to buy some tennis balls.
我哥哥是网球运动员。
My elder brother is a tennis player.

jìmò
寂寞　（丙）形
① lonesome ② lonely
【常用搭配】
感到寂寞 feel lonely
寂寞的夜晚 a lonesome evening
【用法示例】
他一个人呆在家里感到寂寞。
He felt lonesome at home by himself.
在这座陌生的城市里，她感到很寂寞。
She feels rather lonely in the strange town.

láogù
牢固　⊜ 稳固　（丙）形
firm
【常用搭配】
牢固的基础 solid foundation
牢固的碉堡 a secure fortress
【用法示例】
攀登的人脚踩的地方要很牢固。
A climber needs secure footholds.
卡车上的货物已经绑得很牢固了。
The lorry's load had been securely strapped down.

wùzī
物资　（丙）名
goods and materials
【常用搭配】
物资储备 material reserve
战略物资 strategic materials
【用法示例】
无论如何，医疗物资会在一周内到达。
At any rate, the medical supplies will reach you within a week.
救援物资已空投到地震灾区。
Supplies were parachuted into the earthquake zone.

rènyì
任意　⊜ 恣意　（丙）副
arbitrarily; wantonly
【常用搭配】
任意涨价 raise prices arbitrarily
任意行动 act wantonly
【用法示例】
从一副牌中任意选出一张。
Chose a card at random from the deck.
一旦确定了计划双方都不能任意更改。
Once we decide on the plan, neither of us can change it.
我们上课的时候，你们不能任意说笑。
You shouldn't just talk and laugh as you please when we have class.

suíyì
随意　（丁）形
① as one wishes ② willfully
【常用搭配】
请随意！ Help yourselves, please!
【用法示例】
这些动物可以在公园里随意走动。
The animals are allowed to wander at will with in the park.
我的选择相当随意。
My choice was quite arbitrary.
你可以随意使用这些参考书。
You can use these reference books as you wish.

láosāo
牢骚　（丙）名
discontent; complaint
【常用搭配】
发牢骚 whine complaining

【用法示例】

他老是发牢骚。

He's always grumbling.

他总是满腹牢骚。

He is always full of complaints.

我太忙了,没空听她那没完没了的牢骚。

I am too busy to listen to her endless grievances.

wúzhī
无知 （丁）形

ignorant

【常用搭配】

无知的人 an ignorant person

出于无知 out of ignorance

【用法示例】

他很无知,连自己的名字都不会写。

He's so ignorant that he cannot even write his own name.

无知的孩子们有时会嘲笑乞丐。

Ignorant children sometimes laugh at beggars.

他的无知令人吃惊。

His ignorance is surprising.

tānwū
贪污 （丁）动

corrupt

【常用搭配】

贪污的官员 a corrupt official

贪污罪 a crime of corruption

【用法示例】

他因贪污被警察抓了起来。

He was caught by the police because of his corruption.

贪污腐败妨碍社会的发展。

Corruption stands in the way of the development of society.

对他的贪污行为提出了指控。

Accusations of corruption have been made against him.

jìjìng   xuānnào
寂静   反 喧闹 （丁）形

quiet; silent

【常用搭配】

寂静的夜晚 still evening

寂静的山村 the quiet mountain village

【用法示例】

这间屋内一片寂静。

There was nothing but silence in the room.

雷鸣般的掌声打破了寂静。

The silence was shattered by thunderous applause.

她常常在寂静的夜晚思念父母。

She often missed her parents on quiet nights.

wǔlì
武力 （丁）名

military force; military power

【常用搭配】

武力镇压 armed suppression

诉诸武力 resort to force

【用法示例】

警察不得不使用武力驱散人群。

The police had to employ force to break up the crowd.

如果其他手段均告失败,我们将诉之武力。

If other means fail we shall resort to force.

他们用武力逼他就范。

They used force to persuade him.

 词义辨析

任意、随意

　　"任意"和"随意"都是副词,都可以表示任凭自己的意愿的意思,一般可以交换使用。"任意"强调没有外界拘束和限制;"随意"强调按照自己的意愿。另外"随意"还可以用作形容词,可以用作谓语和定语,"任意"没有这种用法。例如:①在开会的时候,你们不能任意/随意走动。②"我可以喝一杯吗?""请随意。"③他的穿着很随意。

　　Both 任意 and 随意 are adverbs, meaning "at will", and they are usually interchangeable. 任意 stresses "no restriction, no limitation from others", while 随意 stresses "according to one's own wishes". 随意 can be used as an adjective, and it can function as a predicate, or an attributive; while 任意 can not be used like that. For example: ① You shouldn't walk around as you please when we have a meeting. ② "Can I have a drink?" "Help yourself!" ③ He wore casual clothes.

 练习

练习一、根据拼音写汉字，根据汉字写拼音

jì（　　）　láo（　　）　（　　）wū　suí（　　）　（　　）zhì
（　　）寞　（　　）骚　贪（　　）　（　　）意　物（　　）

练习二、搭配连线

(1) 有害　　　　　　　　A. 镇压
(2) 战略　　　　　　　　B. 腐败
(3) 武力　　　　　　　　C. 牢固
(4) 贪污　　　　　　　　D. 物质
(5) 基础　　　　　　　　E. 物资

练习三、从今天学习的生词中选择合适的词填空

1. 如果你对工作不满意，就要想办法改变，发 _____ 是没有用的。
2. 父母在满足孩子 _____ 需求的同时，不要忽视了他们的精神需求，要多与他们沟通。
3. 每到 _____ 的夜晚，他就能隐约听到远处传来的钢琴声。
4. 谈判破裂，他们想诉诸 _____ 解决领土争端。
5. 您是今天光临的第一位客人，您可以 _____ 选择就餐的位子。
6. 他以前是一家大企业的财务主管，后来因为 _____ 公款而入狱。
7. 他平时穿着很 _____，只有在重要场合才穿西装、打领带。
8. 为了摆脱愚昧和 _____，我们要努力学习、积极探索。
9. 中国为发生灾难的国家提供了很多救灾 _____。
10. 宿舍里的人都出去玩了，她觉得有点 _____，便给家里打了个电话。

答案

练习一：
略

练习二：

(1) D	(2)E	(3)A	(4)B	(5)C

练习三：

1. 牢骚	2. 物质	3. 寂静	4. 武力	5. 任意
6. 贪污	7. 随意	8. 无知	9. 物资	10. 寂寞

星期四

jīxiè
机械　　　　　　　　　　（乙）名

① machine ② mechanical

常用搭配
机械制造 machine manufacturing
机械故障 mechanical breakdown
机械装置 mechanical installation

用法示例
杠杆和滑轮是简单机械。
Levers and pulleys are part of simple machines.
我在大学时主修机械工程专业。
I majored in Mechanical Engineering at college.
因为有机械缺陷，那种新型汽车只好撤出市场。
The new car had to be withdrawn from the market because of a mechanical defect.

jiāngyào
将要　　　　　　　　　　（乙）副

① will ② be going to

常用搭配
将要离开 will leave
将要实现 will come true
将要结婚 be going to marry

用法示例
明年我将要去留学。
I will go abroad next year.
房子将要在七月建设完工。
The construction of the house will be finished in July.
我们的城市将要有一个新的火车站。
There will be a new train station in our city.

héfǎ　　　　　　　　**wéifǎ**
合法　　反　**违法**　　　（丙）形

legal; lawful

常用搭配
合法地位 legal status
合法身份 legal identity
合法行为 a lawful action

用法示例
王子是王位的合法继承人。
The prince is the legal heir to the throne.
做那事是不合法的。
It is not lawful to do that.
那块地是他的合法财产。
The land is his lawful property.

cānmóu
参谋 （丙）动／名
① give advice ② staff officer ③ adviser

常用搭配
参谋长 chief of staff

用法示例
我想买辆跑车,你帮我参谋参谋好吗?
I want to buy a sports car. Can you give me some advice?
参谋人员在地图上把这个地区精确地标了出来。
The staff officers mapped out the area thoroughly.
在困难时他是个好参谋。
He is a wise counselor in times of need.

tànsuǒ
探索 ◉ 摸索 mōsuǒ （丙）动
① probe ② grope after

常用搭配
探索真理 grope for the truth
探索……的奥秘 probe the secrets of…
探索事物的本质 probe into the essence of things

用法示例
我们正在探索这种现象的原因。
We are exploring the reasons for the phenomena.
科学家致力于探索宇宙的奥秘。
Scientists work at probing the secrets of the universe.

mōsuǒ
摸索 （丁）动
① grope ② feel one's way

常用搭配
在黑暗中摸索 feel one's way in the dark
摸索着开锁 fumble at a lock

用法示例
我们摸索着走过黑暗的街道。
We groped our way through the dark streets.
他在房间里磕磕绊绊地摸索电灯的开关。
He blundered about the room, feeling for the light switch.
他们在摸索发展的规律。
They are exploring the laws of development.

jìnéng
技能 ◉ 技艺 jìyì （丙）名
skill

常用搭配
生产技能 skill in production
语言技能 language skills
工艺技能 industrial skills

用法示例
为钢琴调音需要专门技能。
It takes skill to tune a piano.
我们的英语课程非常重视会话技能。
Our English course places great emphasis on conversational skills.

资源管理是一项重要的经营技能。
Knowing how to properly manage resources is an important business skill.

jìxiàng
迹象 （丁）名
indication; sign

常用搭配
种种迹象表明 There are various indications that …
下雨的迹象 a sign of rain

用法示例
所有迹象似乎都表明将要发生地震。
There seems to be every indication that there will be an earthquake.
科学家们正在研究火星的照片,寻求生命的迹象。
Scientists are studying the photographs of Mars for signs of life.
一有危险迹象,潜艇就会潜入水中。
At the first sign of danger the submarine will submerge.

héhuǒ
合伙 ◉ 散伙 sànhuǒ （丁）动
form a partnership

常用搭配
合伙人 copartner   与……合伙 partner with…

用法示例
两人合伙买下了这家公司。
The two of them formed a partnership and bought the company.
他们合伙经营一家商店。
They run the business as a partnership.

xiànsuǒ
线索 （丁）名
clue

常用搭配
提供线索 give a clue   寻找线索 look for a clue

用法示例
经过彻底搜查未发现任何线索。
An intensive search failed to reveal any clues.
警方正进一步寻找线索。
The police are on the hunt for further clues.
警察发现了能帮助他们抓住强盗的线索。
The police found a clue which will help them catch the robber.

cānkǎo
参考 （丙）动
consult; refer

常用搭配
参考历史文献 consult historical documents
参考资料 reference materials
参考书 reference books

用法示例
你应该参考字典。
You should make a reference to a dictionary.

他在文章中引用大量参考资料。
He loaded his pages with references.
这本参考书对我有用吗？
Is this reference book of any use to me?

cānyù
参与 （丁）动
participate (in sth)
常用搭配
参与者 participator
参与意识 sense of participation
用法示例
由于他的参与，我们赢了比赛。
We won the game due to his participation.
所有的孩子都参与了学校的活动。
All the children took part in the school activity.

 词义辨析

探索、摸索

"探索"和"摸索"都是动词，都有试图了解未知事物的意思。"探索"强调明确的目的或科学的方法，它的对象往往是抽象的，如奥妙、真理、本质等重大而宏观的领域。"摸索"有试探着进行的意思，它的对象可以是具体的，也可以是抽象的，如方法、经验、规律等。例如：①科学家正在探索自然的奥秘。②盲人摸索着找电话。③他一直在摸索更好的管理方式。

Both 探索 and 摸索 are verbs, meaning "to try to study something unknown". 探索 means an exploratory action with a definite aim that happens in a scientific way, and its objects are something abstract and grand, such as 奥妙 (reason and secret), 真理 (truth), 本质 (nature of something); while 摸索 has the meaning of "feel one's way", and its objects are something concrete or abstract, such as 方法 (method), 经验 (experience), 规律 (regularity). For example: ① Scientists are working at probing the secrets of nature. ② The blind man groped for the telephone. ③ He has been searching for a better method of administration

 练习

练习一、根据拼音写汉字，根据汉字写拼音
tàn (　) jì (　) jì (　) cān (　) (　)xiè
(　)索 (　)象 (　)能 (　)考 机(　)

练习二、搭配连线
(1) 机械	A. 资料
(2) 探索	B. 技能
(3) 寻找	C. 真理
(4) 参考	D. 线索
(5) 专业	E. 装置

练习三、从今天学习的生词中选择合适的词填空
1. 他跟一个大学同学 _____ 开了一家经营电子商品的公司。
2. 最后还得由你自己来决定，我们提的这些意见仅供 _____。
3. 通过大量的语言实践，可以逐渐提高学生的沟通 _____。
4. 他是一名活跃分子，积极 _____ 各种课外活动。
5. 有 _____ 表明，这个杀人犯作案后曾经回过家。
6. 我的这个朋友是个好 _____，我买东西都要征求一下他的意见，看看他怎么说。
7. 我们希望通过合理而且 _____ 的方式解决他们之间的利益冲突。
8. 他和另外几名年轻的科学家一直致力于 _____ 宇宙的奥秘。
9. 这个学期 _____ 结束了，他已经买好机票，准备回国了。
10. 很多事情，没有人告诉我怎么做，都是自己 _____ 着走过来的。

 答案

练习一：
略
练习二：
(1) E	(2)C	(3)D	(4)A	(5)B

练习三：
1. 合伙	2. 参考	3. 技能	4. 参与	5. 迹象
6. 参谋	7. 合法	8. 探索	9. 将要	10. 摸索

星期五

zhídé
值得 （乙）动

be worthy; deserve

常用搭配

值得注意 deserve attention

值得一看。It's worth seeing.

用法示例

他值得我们表扬。

He is worthy of our praise.

这本书值得一读。

This book is worthy of being read.

这个问题不值得讨论。

It is not worthwhile discussing the problem.

fāshè
发射 （丙）动

shoot; launch

常用搭配

发射火箭 launch a rocket

发射鱼雷 launch a torpedo

用法示例

新兵瞄准靶子发射，但没射中。

The new soldier shot at the target, but missed it.

下周将发射一颗人造卫星。

An artificial satellite will be launched next week.

duìyuán
队员 （丙）名

team member

常用搭配

替补队员 substitute

上场队员 players in uniform

篮球队队员 member of a basketball team

用法示例

一个板球队由 11 名队员组成。

A cricket team is comprised of eleven players.

我是学校足球队的队员。

I am on the school football team.

chuàngxīn
创新 ⊚守旧 shǒujiù （丙）动/名

① blaze new trails ② innovation

常用搭配

创新能力 ability to innovate

创新思维 creative mind

创新精神 creative spirit

用法示例

我在一家非常富有创新精神的公司工作。

I worked in a very innovative company.

年轻人要勇于实践，大胆创新。

Young men should be bold in putting things into practice, and blazing new trails.

wùpǐn
物品 （丙）名

articles; goods

常用搭配

私人物品 private things　　违禁物品 contraband

免税物品 duty-free articles

用法示例

这个大超市里有各种物品。

There is a great variety of goods in this large supermarket.

她把贵重物品放在了保险箱里。

She kept her valuables in a safe.

línglì　　　　　cōnghuì
伶俐 ⊜聪慧 （丁）形

clever; witty

常用搭配

口齿伶俐 have a glib tongue

聪明伶俐 intelligent and clever

用法示例

她不厌其烦地谈起她聪明伶俐的女儿。

She never tires of talking about her clever daughter.

他是一个聪明伶俐的孩子。

He is an alert and bright boy.

wùtǐ
物体 （丙）名

object

常用搭配

运动的物体 a moving object

物体的名称 names of the objects

用法示例

这台显微镜将物体放大了 100 倍。

The microscope magnified the object 100 times.

物理学研究作用于物体上的力。

Physics deals with the forces that act on objects.

duìlì　　　　　hùbǔ
对立 ⊗互补 （丙）动

① oppose ② be antagonistic to

常用搭配

对立关系 antagonistic relations

对立的立场 antithetical stand

对立情绪 antagonism

用法示例

我们原来相互对立的观点开始趋于一致。

Our previously held, opposing views, are beginning to converge.

我能觉察出他们之间有对立情绪。
I could sense the antagonism between them.
唯心论和唯物论是对立的。
Idealism is the opposite to materialism.

chuàngbàn
创办　　　　　　　　　　　　　　（丁）动
launch; establish

常用搭配
创办刊物 start a publication
创办一所学校 establish a school
创办企业 found an enterprise

用法示例
他创办了一家很成功的公司。
He has carved out a successful business.
创办这个组织花了好几年的时间。
The establishment of the organization took several years.
这所大学创办于一八六零年。
The university was established in 1860.

géxīn
革新　　　　　　　　　　　　　　（丙）动/名
① reform ② renovation

常用搭配
制度革新 reformation of a system
技术革新 technical innovation

用法示例
这是革新时期。
It was a period of innovation.
传统的手工艺技术不断革新。
Traditional handicraft techniques are being steadily innovated.

géshi
格式　　　　　　　　　　　　　　（丁）名
form; format; specification

常用搭配
公文的格式 the form for an official document
格式化 formatting

用法示例
保险合同有固定的格式。
There is a standard form for an insurance contract.
该图表的格式很雅致。
The form of the figure is very tasteful.

chètuì
撤退　　　　　　　chèlí　　　　　（丁）动
　　　　　　　　　　◎撤离
retreat; withdraw

常用搭配
从那里撤退 retreat from there
迅速撤退 retreat quickly

用法示例
伤亡太大,我们不得不撤退。
We have to draw back due to the losses suffered by our force.

我们的部队撤退到了城里。
Our forces retreated to the city.
敌人被迫撤退了。
The enemy was forced to retreat.

 **词义辨析**

创新、革新
　　"创新"和"革新"都是名词,都可以表示创造新事物的过程或行为,也都是不及物动词,表示创造新事物,都不能带宾语,有时可以互换使用。"创新"强调创造性,多用作名词。而"革新"指通过变革用新的事物取代旧的事物,强调革除旧的事物,多用作动词。例如:①我们要培养大学生的创新精神。②传统的管理制度在不断革新。

　　Both 创新 and 革新 are nouns, meaning "the process or act of innovation", both of them are intransitive verbs meaning "to innovate", and they can not be followed by objects. Sometimes they are interchangeable. 创新 stresses creativity; most times it is used as a noun. 革新 stresses "to improve or reform by alteration, or abolishment of the old ways"; in most cases it is used as a verb. For example: ① We should develop the creativity of college students. ② Traditional systems of administration are being steadily renovated.

 **练习**

练习一、根据拼音写汉字,根据汉字写拼音
(　)shè　(　)lì　chè(　)　gé(　)　gé(　)
发(　)　伶(　)　(　)退　(　)新　(　)式

练习二、搭配连线
(1) 替补　　　　　　　　　A. 精神
(2) 创新　　　　　　　　　B. 火箭
(3) 聪明　　　　　　　　　C. 队员
(4) 私人　　　　　　　　　D. 伶俐
(5) 发射　　　　　　　　　E. 物品

练习三、从今天学习的生词中选择合适的词填空
1. 具有 _____ 精神的年轻人在企业里受到了重用。
2. 超市提示说,顾客的贵重 _____ 请随身携带,不要存包。
3. 尽管花这么多的时间和精力,但我认为我们这样做很 _____。
4. 这是所有名的私立学校, _____ 于 1902 年。
5. 中文书信的 _____ 和英文的不太一样,尤其是商业信函。
6. 传统的手工艺技术已经落伍了,生产方式需要 _____。
7. 这个小姑娘聪明 _____,特别讨人喜欢。
8. 驻扎在这里的军队已经 _____ 了,小镇的生活又恢复了平静。

9. 两国的领导人都认为这种 _____ 的局面不利于两国的稳定和发展,希望能尽快改善关系。

10. 教练带领着这些年轻的 _____ 参加了世界杯足球赛,并取得了优异的成绩。

答案

练习一:
略

练习二:
(1) C   (2)A   (3)D   (4)E   (5)B

练习三:
1. 创新   2. 物品   3. 值得   4. 创办   5. 格式
6. 革新   7. 伶俐   8. 撤退   9. 对立   10. 队员

第12月,第2周的练习

练习一. 根据词语给加点的字注音

1.( ) 2.( ) 3.( ) 4.( ) 5.( )
伶俐   牢骚   为难   好奇   恶心

练习二. 根据拼音填写词语

jì   jì   jì   dài   dài
1.( )静 2.( )象 3.( )能 4.( )款 5.( )遇

练习三. 辨析并选择合适的词填空

1. 经过( ),这种车的性能完全达到了国家要求的标准。(测验、测试)

2. 我们每个月都有一次英语( ),这个月我的成绩不理想。(测验、测试)

3. 为了提高成绩,这些运动员在参加比赛前一直在高海拔地区进行( )。(训练、操练)

4. 为了参加国庆阅兵式,这些士兵正在进行严格的队列( )。(训练、操练)

5. 他回答那个问题时显得很( ),好像并没有意识到问题的严重性。(任意、随意)

6. 在买彩票的时候,他( )选择了一个号码,居然中了一个二等奖。(任意、随意)

7. 他在黑暗中( ),终于摸到了墙上的开关,打开了灯。(探索、摸索)

8. 人类对外太空的( )一直没有停止。(探索、摸索)

9. 这种管理模式在多个方面都有所( ),值得我们仔细研究。(创新、革新)

10. 通过不断( )政府人事制度,政府的工作效率大大提高了。(创新、革新)

练习四. 选词填空

维修   委托   寂寞   参与   对立
维持   委屈   寂静   参考   队员

1. 这个消防队有名( )在执行任务时壮烈牺牲了。

2. 郊区农村的夜晚非常( ),夜间出行的人也很少。

3. 这个工厂现在根本不赚钱,只能勉强( )。

4. 在国外留学,每当感到( )的时候就给家里打电话。

5. 我知道你没有错,是他们错怪了你,让你受( )了。

6. 老师动员大家参加留学生运动会,说重在( ),得不得奖无所谓。

7. 妈妈( )一位来北京旅游的朋友给我捎来了一封信。

8. 我房间的水龙头坏了,一直在滴水,你知道该找谁( )吗?

9. 这两人之间的( )情绪非常严重,还是不要让他们在一起工作了。

10. 老师有很多( )书,这对老师备课很有帮助。

练习五. 写出下列词语的同义词

1. 撤退( )   2. 牢固( )
3. 卑鄙( )   4. 讽刺( )
5. 技能( )

练习六. 写出下列词语的反义词

1. 对立( )   2. 额外( )
3. 合法( )   4. 创新( )
5. 寂静( )

 **答案**

练习一.
1.líng   2.sāo   3.wéi   4.hào   5.ě

练习二.
1. 寂   2. 迹   3. 技   4. 贷   5. 待

练习三.
1. 测试   2. 测验   3. 训练   4. 操练   5. 随意
6. 任意 / 随意   7. 摸索   8. 探索   9. 创新
10. 革新

练习四.
1. 队员   2. 寂静   3. 维持   4. 寂寞   5. 委屈
6. 参与   7. 委托   8. 维修   9. 对立   10. 参考

练习五.
1. 撤离   2. 稳固   3. 卑劣   4. 挖苦   5. 技艺

练习六.
1. 互补   2. 分内   3. 违法   4. 守旧   5. 喧闹

12月 第 3 周的学习内容

星期一

yíwèn
疑问　　圓 疑惑　　（乙）名

query

常用搭配

疑问副词 interrogative adverb　　提出疑问 raise a query

用法示例

毫无疑问,他是有罪的。
There is no doubt that he is guilty.
在英语中有些疑问句需要用升调。
In English, some interrogative sentences have a rising inflection.
这是毫无疑问的。
There's no question about it.

búbì
不必　　圓 务必　　（乙）副

need not

常用搭配

不必担心 don't need to worry
不必解释 don't need to explain

用法示例

你不必告诉他这个消息,他已经知道了。
You needn't have told him the news; he knew it already.
不必走,还早着呢。
No need to go yet, it's still early.
你不必天天来。
You need not come everyday.

dāngdài
当代　　（丙）名

present age; contemporary era

常用搭配

当代文学 contemporary literature
当代社会 modern society

用法示例

他把他的一生都献给了当代艺术研究。
He had devoted his whole life to the study of contemporary art.
她算是当代最有才华的一位作曲家之一。
She ranks among the most gifted of the current generation of composers.

huānlè
欢乐　　圓 悲哀　　（丙）形

joyous; happy

常用搭配

欢乐的样子 a joyful look
欢乐时光 happy hour

用法示例

我们都沉浸在春节的欢乐气氛中。
We were all immersed in the gaiety of the Spring Festival.
童年时的相册经常让我想起儿时的欢乐。
My album of boyhood photographs often reminds me of past happinesses.
他们唱着、跳着庆祝这欢乐的时刻。
They were singing and dancing to celebrate this joyful occasion.

jǐngxiàng
景象　　（丙）名

view; scene

常用搭配

壮观的景象 spectacular view
繁荣的景象 a prosperous scene

用法示例

小羊在牧场上跳来跳去,这是一幅多么恬静而又生气勃勃的景象啊。
What a quiet but lively scene. Lambs gambolled in the pastures.
庆祝活动呈现一派壮观的景象。
The celebrations were a magnificent spectacle.
你一定会被那美丽的景象所感动的。
You will never fail to be moved by the beauty of this sight.

yíxīn
疑心　　（丙）动／名

① suspect ② suspicion

常用搭配

起疑心 become suspicious

用法示例

他无法消除自己的疑心,总觉得妻子不忠。
He can not rid himself of the suspicion that his wife is unfaithful.
他这人疑心太重,连自己的母亲也不相信。
He's so suspicious that he would distrust his own mother.

huáiyí
怀疑　　（丙）动

doubt; suspect

常用搭配

持怀疑态度 take a skeptical attitude

引起怀疑 arouse suspicion

用法示例

他怀疑这件事是否属实。

He has his doubts as to this being true.

警察怀疑银行职员与强盗有勾结。

The police suspected that the bank clerk was in league with the robbers.

谁也不怀疑她能胜任教师工作。

No one doubts her competence as a teacher.

huānhū
欢呼 (丙)动

acclaim; cheer for

常用搭配

欢呼声 shout of joy   欢呼雀跃 shout and jump for joy

用法示例

让我们为我们队欢呼三声,他们赢了。

Let's give three cheers for our team — they've won!

观众为自己支持的球队欢呼。

The crowd cheered their favorite team on.

喜讯传来,人们顿时欢呼起来。

People broke into cheers when they heard the good news.

wùbì
务必 (丁)副

① must ② be sure to

常用搭配

你务必得小心。You simply must be careful.

务必要信守诺言。Be sure to keep your promise.

用法示例

务必在六点之前把工作完成。

Be sure to get the work finished before six o'clock.

务必把这些东西放对地方。

Be sure to place them correctly.

务必写信告诉我所有的消息。

Be sure to write and give me all the news.

xūqiú
需求 (丁)名

requirement; demand

常用搭配

满足需求 meet demand

对贷款的需求 demand for advances

用法示例

尽管这些书价钱昂贵,对它们的需求量仍然很大。

Demand for these books is high, despite their high price.

如果你有什么需求,请告诉我。

If you need anything, ask me.

随着进口的增加,需求已经减少了。

Demand has been brought down by the increase in imports.

dāngchū
当初 ⑩ 起初 (丁)名

(qǐchū)

① originally ② at that time

常用搭配

早知今日,何必当初?

If I had known it would come to this, I would have acted differently.

用法示例

损害程度比当初预想的要严重得多。

The damage is much greater than was first anticipated.

当初你就不该这么做。

You should never have behaved the way that you did in the first place.

jiē èr lián sān
接二连三 (丁)

one after another

常用搭配

事件接二连三地发生。The events happened one after another.

用法示例

我很走运,在最后几场马赛中,接二连三地获胜。

Fortunately, I picked back to back winners in the last few races.

校长斥责那个学生不该接二连三地迟到。

The principal reprimand the student for his chronic lateness.

 词义辨析

疑心、疑问、怀疑

1. "怀疑"和"疑心"是动词,有不太相信的意思,对象是人或事。"疑心"和"怀疑"的意思是一样的,但"疑心"很少当作动词使用,作为动词也往往只带宾语从句;"怀疑"则应用得非常普遍,宾语可以是名词或从句。"怀疑"可以用于被动句,"疑心"不可以。例如:①他看上去很穷,可是我怀疑/疑心他很有钱。②我怀疑她的动机。③我的能力受到他们怀疑。

Both 怀疑 and 疑心 are verbs, meaning "have doubt in somebody or something". 疑心 has the same meaning as 怀疑, but 疑心 is rarely used as a verb, and when it is used as a verb, its object is usually a sentence. 怀疑 is used as a verb very widely, its objects can be sentences or nouns. 怀疑 can be used in the passive voice, but 疑心 can not. For example: ① He seems poor, but I suspect that he has quite a lot of money. ② I had suspicions about her motives. ③ They had suspicions about my ability.

2. "疑问"和"疑心"是名词。"疑问"表示有不明白或不确定的问题,"疑心"指心存疑虑。一般不能互换使用。"毫无疑问","毫不怀疑","对……起疑心"是固定搭配,不能与另外两个词相互替换。"怀疑"不是名词,"疑问"不是动词。例如:①请打消对此事的疑心。②老师认真讲解完以后,问我们有没有疑问。

Both 疑问 and 疑心 are nouns. 疑问 means "having

a question about something or feeling confused or uncertain about something"; 疑心 means "being doubtful of mind". The two can not be interchanged. In the following collocations—毫无疑问 (there is no doubt), 毫不怀疑 (make no doubt), 对……起疑心 (become suspicious of), the three words can not be interchanged. 怀疑 is not a noun, and 疑问 can't be used as a verb. For example: ① Please dismiss all doubts about it. ② After explaining it carefully, the teacher asked us if we had any questions.

练习

练习一、根据拼音写汉字，根据汉字写拼音
( )yí ( )hū wù ( ) ( )chū xū ( )
怀( ) 欢( ) ( )必 当( ) ( )求

练习二、搭配连线
(1) 满足　　　　　　　A. 时光
(2) 欢呼　　　　　　　B. 疑问
(3) 欢乐　　　　　　　C. 需求
(4) 引起　　　　　　　D. 雀跃
(5) 毫无　　　　　　　E. 怀疑

练习三、从今天学习的生词中选择合适的词填空
1. 他的话有些自相矛盾,这让我们对他的身份起了_____。
2. 他研究_____文学,和许多知名作家都有交往。
3. 那是一个_____的夜晚,每个人的情绪都很高,都为我们取得的胜利而自豪。
4. 他被_____泄露了技术机密,正在接受警方的调查。
5. 这篇文章描绘了农村发展的繁荣_____。
6. 张秘书,请你们经理_____给我回个电话,我有重要的事情和他商谈。
7. 人们对这种商品的_____量减少了,我们不得不降价处理这些积压的货物。
8. 这几天_____地发生了好几起抢劫案,这引起了当地居民的不安。
9. _____是他千方百计找我合作,现在也是他第一个提出解除合作关系的。
10. 对我们的产品您还有什么_____可以都提出来,我会一一为您解答。

答案

练习一:
略
练习二:
(1) C　　(2)D　　(3)A　　(4)E　　(5)B
练习三:
1. 疑心　　2. 当代　　3. 欢乐　　4. 怀疑　　5. 景象
6. 务必　　7. 需求　　8. 接二连三　9. 当初　　10. 疑问

星期二

děngyú
等于　　　　　　　　　　　　(乙)动
be equal to
常用搭配
设 x 等于 y。Let x be the equal of y.
用法示例
六十分等于一小时。
Sixty minutes is equal to an hour.
六减去二等于四。
Six minus two equals four.
一华里等于半公里。
One li is equal to half a kilometer.

dāngdì
当地　　　　回 **běndì** 本地　　(乙)名
locality
常用搭配
当地政府 local government
当地的风俗 a local custom
用法示例
他们把当地人迁移到别处定居。
They moved the local people and settled them in another place.
这位足球教练受到了当地报纸的批评。
The football coach was criticized by the local newspaper.

zhìliáo
治疗　　　　　　　　　　　　(丙)动
treat; cure; remedy
常用搭配
给病人及时治疗 to give timely treatment
精神治疗 psychotherapy
用法示例
她正在进行治疗。
She is under going treatment.
医生用针灸治疗他的病。
The doctor treated his illness with acupuncture.
他已经在医院治疗两个星期了。
He has been hospitalized for two weeks.

wàibù
外部　　　　反 **nèibù** 内部　　(丙)名
① external ② outside part
常用搭配
事物的外部联系 external relationship of things
外部世界 the external world

用法示例

车间的外部漆成了绿色。

The workshop was painted green on the outside.

房子的外部需要粉刷。

The outside of the house needs painting.

市场的外部条件不太好。

The external market conditions are not very good.

外界 wàijiè (丙) 名

① the outside world ② external

常用搭配

外界的压力 external pressures

用法示例

我们需要外界援助才能完成。

We'll need outside help before we can finish.

这个村子周围有湖泊和沼泽地,隔断了与外界的联系。

The village is isolated from the world by lakes and marshes.

敢于 gǎnyú (丙) 动

dare; venture

常用搭配

敢于尝试。Dare to try.

敢于斗争,善于斗争

dare to struggle, and know how to struggle

用法示例

他敢于说出他认为正确的东西。

He has the courage to speak out about what he thinks right.

他们不怕遭围攻,敢于冒这样的风险。

Unafraid of attack, they dared to run such risks.

这位体操选手敢于做惊险的高难度动作。

The gymnast dared a breathtakingly difficult move.

导游 dǎoyóu (丁) 名 / 动

① guide ② conduct a tour

常用搭配

从事导游的工作 work as a guide

用法示例

导游在旅游车的前部为游客进行现场解说。

The tour guide gave a running commentary from the front of the coach.

我们随着导游参观了城堡。

We went on a guided tour round the castle.

导游带领游客参观博物馆。

A guide conducted the visitors round the museum.

粗心 cūxīn (丙) 形

careless

常用搭配

粗心的作者 a careless writer

粗心大意 be negligent

用法示例

他是个粗心大意的医生。

He is a careless doctor.

你没锁门,太粗心了。

It was careless of you to leave the door unlocked.

由于粗心大意,他数学考试没及格。

He failed his math examination because of his careless work.

导演 dǎoyǎn (丁) 名 / 动

① director ② direct

常用搭配

电影导演 a film director　　戏剧导演 a stage director

用法示例

导演在为新片物色合适的拍摄场地。

The director is looking for a suitable location for his new film.

他一直在讨好导演,想在剧中扮演主角。

He has been courting the director, hoping to get the leading role in the play.

他正在导演一台新的歌剧。

He is directing a new opera.

当场 dāngchǎng 同 现场 xiànchǎng (丁) 名

on the spot; at the scene

常用搭配

当场测试 spot test

当场抓住 be caught red-handed

当场拒绝他的要求 turn down his request on the spot

用法示例

我们当场抓到了那个走私犯。

We caught the smuggler on the spot.

他被闪电击中,当场死亡。

He was struck by lightning, and killed on the spot.

他偷看我的论文时,我当场抓住了他。

I caught him peeping at my paper.

粗暴 cūbào 反 温和 wēnhé (丁) 形

rough; rude

常用搭配

粗暴的态度 a rude attitude

粗暴的行为 crude behavior

对某人粗暴无礼 be rude to sb.

用法示例

学生不听她的话时,常遭到她粗暴的申斥。

Her pupils often get the rough side of her tongue when they disobey her.

哪个政府也不能粗暴干涉别国内政。

No government can wantonly interfere in the internal affairs of other countries.

粗暴的士兵野蛮地抽打俘虏。

The brutal soldiers beat their prisoners ruthlessly.

yì fān fēng shùn
一帆风顺 （丁）

① plain sailing ② proceed smoothly without a hitch

用法示例

她的生活至今仍一帆风顺。

Up to now, her life has run smoothly.

一系列的幸运事使她的事业一帆风顺。

A series of fortuitous circumstances advanced her career.

到现在为止，这个项目进行得一帆风顺。

Up to now, the project has proceeded smoothly, and without a hitch.

 **词义辨析**

外部、外界

"外部"和"外界"都是名词，都表示超过某个范围或界限的地方，有时可以互换使用。"外部"强调表面，事物露在外面的那部分；"外界"强调某个集体或地区以外的社会。例如：①这种植物对外部／外界环境很敏感。②这种水果的外部是红的，内部是绿的。③他们要求外界的支援。

Both 外部 and 外界 are nouns, meaning "the space beyond a boundary or limit"; sometimes they are interchangeable. 外部 stresses outward an aspect or appearance, or the part that faces outside; while 外界 stresses the outside world of an organization or an area. For example: ① This kind of plant is very sensitive to external factors. ② The fruit was red outside, and green inside. ③ They requested outside assistance.

 **练习**

练习一、根据拼音写汉字，根据汉字写拼音

zhì（　）dǎo（　）（　）chǎng（　）bào gǎn（　）

（　）疗　（　）游　当（　）　粗（　）　（　）于

练习二、搭配连线

(1) 当地的　　　　　　A. 压力

(2) 外界的　　　　　　B. 态度

(3) 粗心的　　　　　　C. 导演

(4) 粗暴的　　　　　　D. 风俗

(5) 著名的　　　　　　E. 孩子

练习三、从今天学习的生词中选择合适的词填空

1. 经过一年的住院 _____，他的身体状况逐渐好转了。

2. 你太 _____ 了，把"甩"写成"用"了。

3. 他提的要求被老板 _____ 拒绝了，这使他感到很难堪。

4. 老师鼓励我们说要 _____ 提出不同的观点，这样才能写出有价值的论文。

5. 朋友要去旅行了，我打电话祝她旅途 _____。

6. 外出旅游的时候，除了欣赏风景，我还喜欢了解 _____ 的风俗习惯。

7. 由于大雪阻隔了交通，这个村庄无法与 _____ 联系。

8. 他教育孩子的方式很 _____，经常打孩子。

9. 自从拍了那部电影，这个 _____ 就名声大振，很多演员希望能与他合作。

10. 这座建筑的 _____ 使用了一层防水的材料，所以不用担心下雨。

 **答案**

练习一：

略

练习二：

(1) D　　(2)A　　(3)E　　(4)B　　(5)C

练习三：

1. 治疗　2. 粗心　3. 当场　4. 敢于　5. 一帆风顺

6. 当地　7. 外界　8. 粗暴　9. 导演　10. 外部

星期三

wǔqì
武器 （乙）名

weapon

常用搭配

核武器 nuclear weapons

常规武器 conventional weapons

用法示例

政府已经禁止使用化学武器。

The government has banned the use of chemical weapons.

这些武器是对世界和平的威胁。

These weapons are a menace to world peace.

渔夫用矛作为武器。

The fisher man used a spear as his weapon.

wǔshù
武术 gōngfu 功夫 （乙）名

martial art; Chinese Kungfu

常用搭配

武术比赛 martial arts competition

学习武术 learn Chinese Kungfu

用法示例

练武术可以强健体魄。

Practicing Chinese Kungfu strengthens the physique.

他爸爸是武术教练。

His father is a martial arts instructor.

chīkuī
吃亏 （丙）动

① suffer losses ② in an unfavourable situation

常用搭配

靠欺骗得利,准要吃亏。

Ill gotten gains will burn one's fingers.

用法示例

跟他做生意,你是要吃亏的。

You will be the one to lose if you do business with him.

他不会说法语,这使他很吃亏。

His inability to speak French puts him at a disadvantage.

他因粗心而吃了亏。

He suffered for his carelessness.

hánliàng
含量 （丙）名

content

常用搭配

净含量 net content

酒精含量 alcoholic content

用法示例

往炖煮的食物上加一匙麦麸,以增加其纤维含量。

Sprinkle a spoonful of bran onto the stew to increase its fiber content.

这种矿石中铁的含量是多少?

How much iron is in the ore?

wǔzhuāng
武装 （丙）名/动

① military ② armed (forces)

常用搭配

全副武装 armed to the teeth

武装斗争 armed struggle

武装侵略 armed aggression

用法示例

一群武装盗贼袭击了无依无靠的旅客。

Armed thieves descended on the helpless travelers.

战争期间,农民武装起来,对付敌人。

During the war, farmers armed themselves against the enemy.

政府为到访的元首派出了武装卫队。

The government provided an armed escort for the visiting head of State.

lùqǔ
录取 （丁）动

recruit; enroll

常用搭配

录取通知书 enrolment notification

录取新生 enroll new students

用法示例

不到两星期,我就收到了大学的录取通知书。

Within two weeks I received a notification of acceptance from the university.

我申请的学院已经录取我了。

The college I applied to has accepted me.

他们寄来了 202 表格,确认我已被录取。

They sent me the 202 form indicating my acceptance.

lùyòng
录用 pìnyòng 聘用 （丁）动

hire; employ

常用搭配

录用这位求职者 employ the job applicant

他被录用了。He was employed.

用法示例

这家公司从几百名应聘者中录用了 5 名。

The company took on five out of several hundred candidates.

我们不想录用没有经验的工人。

We don't want to hire an inexperienced worker.

chīkǔ
吃苦 xiǎngfú 享福 （丙）动

bear hardships

常用搭配
吃苦耐劳 bear hardships and with stand hard work
用法示例
他小时候吃了不少苦。
He suffered a lot in his childhood.
怕吃苦,就干不成大事。
Those who fear hardships will not accomplish anything great.
他工作很努力,能吃苦耐劳。
He is hard-working and unafraid of hardships.

shànliáng
善良 反 歹毒dǎidú (丁)形
kind-hearted
常用搭配
心地善良 be kind-hearted
善良的姑娘 a kind-hearted girl
用法示例
她是个善良和气的老太太。
She was a very kind and amiable old woman.
那位善良的老人给了他一些钱。
That kind old man offered him some money.

hányì
含义 (丁)名
meaning
常用搭配
深刻的含义 profound implications
这句话的含义 meaning of the sentence
用法示例
你能告诉我这首诗的含义吗?
Can you tell me the meaning of the poem?
我没能正确领会他讲话的含义。
I couldn't accurately grasp the gist of his remarks.
这个词的含义不明确。
The meaning of the word is not clear.

hányǒu
含有 (丁)动
contain
常用搭配
海水含有盐分。 Sea water contains salt.
啤酒含有酒精。 Beer contains alcohol.
用法示例
橙子含有维生素 C。
Oranges contain vitamin C.
软饮料中含有二氧化碳。
Soft drinks contain carbon dioxide.
该书含有诽谤性的内容。
The book contains scandalous text.

sì miàn bā fāng
四面八方 (丙)
from far and near

常用搭配
来自四面八方的游客 visitors from far and near
用法示例
四面八方立即伸出援助之手。
Offers of help are coming in thick and fast.
声音从四面八方传来。
The sounds are coming from all quarters.
来自四面八方的歌迷聚集到音乐会的举办地。
Pop fans are pouring into on the concert site from miles around.

 词义辨析

录取、录用
　　"录取"和"录用"都是动词,都有接受申请者的意思。"录取"指允许或被允许进入组织,尤其是学校,它的对象是学生。"录用"指任用,接收新职员,他的对象是工作人员。例如:①他已被这所大学录取。②老板同意录用这位求职者。
　　Both 录取 and 录用 are verbs, meaning "to receive applicant(s)". 录取 indicates to admit somebody, or let somebody be admitted into a group, especially a school, and its objects are students. While 录用 indicates to employ, or to take somebody onto the staff, and its objects are employees. For example: ① He had been matriculated in the university. ② The boss agreed to employ the job applicant.

 **练习**

练习一、根据拼音写汉字，根据汉字写拼音

lù（　　）　hán（　　）　shàn（　　）（　　）kuī（　　）qì
（　　）取　（　　）量　（　　）良　吃（　　）　武（　　）

练习二、搭配连线

(1) 武术　　　　　　　　A. 武器
(2) 化学　　　　　　　　B. 比赛
(3) 酒精　　　　　　　　C. 耐劳
(4) 吃苦　　　　　　　　D. 斗争
(5) 武装　　　　　　　　E. 含量

练习三、从今天学习的生词中选择合适的词填空

1. 农村没有电影院,听说要在这个村子里放映电影,附近村庄的人们从 _____ 涌来。
2. 这句话 _____ 深刻,一般人看不懂。
3. 他的分数非常高,几个大学同时 _____ 了他。
4. 这个人很精明,跟谁打交道他都不会 _____。
5. 麦克因为喜欢中国文化和 _____ 而来到了中国。
6. 我们要用知识来 _____ 自己的头脑。
7. 现在的年轻人跟父母那一辈比起来大都不能 _____。
8. 威士忌 _____ 酒精的成分很高。
9. 经理觉得这个应聘者很合适,所以当场就决定 _____ 他。
10. 1000 克啤酒的酒精 _____ 大概是 10 克。

答案

练习一：
略

练习二：
(1) B　　(2)A　　(3)E　　(4)C　　(5)D

练习三：
1. 四面八方　2. 含义　3. 录取　4. 吃亏　5. 武术
6. 武装　7. 吃苦　8. 含有　9. 录用　10. 含量

星期四 Thursday

cǎiqǔ
采取　　　　　　　　（乙）动
adopt (measures, policies,)

常用搭配
采取行动 take action
采取措施 take measures

用法示例
我们不得不采取预防措施。
We had to take preventive measures.
工会说他们将采取行动维护会员的工作权益。
The union said that they would take action to defend their members' jobs.
政府在独立的问题上采取了毫不妥协的态度。
The government adopted an uncompromising stance on the issue of independence.

cǎiyòng
采用　　　　　　　　（乙）动
adopt

常用搭配
采用新技术 adopt a new technique

用法示例
他们采用了我们的办法。
They adopted our methods.
这所学院采用新的外语教学法。
New methods for teaching foreign languages have been adopted by this institute.

dònglì
动力　　　　　　　　（丙）名
power/driving force

常用搭配
原动力 motivity
蒸汽动力 steam power

用法示例
火车的动力通常是蒸汽或电。
The power trains usually comes from steam or electricity.
帆船靠风的动力行驶。
A sailing ship is driven by wind power.
流水可以产生动力。
Running water produces power.

dòngjī　　　　　**qǐtú**
动机　　　同 企图　　（丙）名
motive; motivation

常用搭配
动机不纯 impure motives

谋杀的动机 motive for murder

用法示例

贪婪是他盗窃的唯一动机。

Greed was his only motive for stealing.

他做这件事的动机是好的。

He did it with good intentions.

你曲解了我的动机。

You have twisted my motives.

wǔtái
舞台 （丙）名

stage; arena

常用搭配

政治舞台 political arena   旋转舞台 revolving stage

舞台效果 stage effects

用法示例

舞台上有很多聚光灯。

There are many spotlights on the stage.

奴隶制度已经退出了历史舞台。

The system of slavery has left history's stage.

随着经济的迅速发展,中国在国际舞台上的地位变得愈来愈重要了。

With its rapid economic development, China's position on the international stage grows more and more prominent.

shānghài   sǔnshāng
伤害   ⑤ 损伤   （丙）动

harm; injure

常用搭配

受到伤害 be hurt

伤害某人的自尊心 injure a man's pride

用法示例

别怕,我们的狗不会伤害你。

Don't be scared! Our dog won't harm you.

她不想伤害孩子的感情。

She hesitated to hurt the child's feelings.

他伸出手去,保护他的孩子免受伤害。

He raised his arm to protect his child from harm.

cǎinà   jiēshòu
采纳   ⑤ 接受   （丁）动

accept; adopt

常用搭配

采纳意见 adopt an idea

采纳他的建议 accept his suggestions

用法示例

但愿我的建议能被采纳。

I hope that my proposal will be accepted.

委员会采纳了我们的意见,修改了计划。

The committee accepted our idea and altered the plan.

wǔdǎo
舞蹈 （丙）名

dance

常用搭配

舞蹈动作 dance movement   舞蹈家 dancer

舞蹈作品 works of dance

用法示例

以音乐和舞蹈庆祝他的胜利。

His victory was celebrated with music and dancing.

她做了一串连续的舞蹈动作。

She created a sequence of dance movements.

伦巴舞是拉丁美洲的舞蹈。

The rumba is a Latin American dance.

jiāwù
家务 （丁）名

housework; household duties

常用搭配

家务事 household affairs

做家务 do house work

用法示例

刘先生有时帮他的妻子做家务。

Mr. Liu sometimes helps his wife with the housework.

我们轮流做家务。

We take turns in doing the housework.

家务劳动使母亲整天忙忙碌碌。

Housework keeps mother on the go all day.

diāndǎo
颠倒 （丁）动

① reverse ② turn upside-down

常用搭配

颠倒主次 reverse the order of importance

颠倒是非 confound right with wrong

用法示例

那幅画挂颠倒了。

That picture is hung upside-down.

那小孩假装看书,但他把书都拿颠倒了。

The boy pretended to be reading, but he was holding the book upside down.

从左到右介绍来宾,千万别颠倒次序。

Introduce the guests from left to right. Be sure not to reverse the order.

diānfù   tuīfān
颠覆   ⑤ 推翻   （丁）动

subvert

常用搭配

颠覆政府 subversion of the government

武装颠覆 armed subversion

用法示例

反叛者想颠覆政府。

The conspirators want to overthrow the government.

他们这些颠覆性的思想是对我们年轻人的精神污染。

They are contaminating the minds of our young people with these subversive ideas.

luàn qī bā zāo
乱七八糟 （丁）

be in a muddle or a mess

常用搭配

把屋子弄得乱七八糟的 turn the room upside-down

用法示例

房间里乱七八糟的。
The room is in a dreadful state.
他屋里有一堆乱七八糟的衣服。
There is a messy heap of clothes in his room.
你的书和杂志乱七八糟的,去整理一下。
Your books and magazines are in a mess; go and put them in order.

 **词义辨析**

采取、采用、采纳

　　三个词都是动词,都有经过选择或考虑而接受并执行的意思。"采取"指根据情况而有选择地使用,它的宾语通常是措施、手段、态度、形式、方针、政策等。"采用"指认为合适而利用,它的宾语通常是工具、方法、技术、稿件等。"采纳"是指考虑并接受一项建议或提案,它的宾语通常是意见、建议、方案等。

　　They are verbs, meaning to accept something after making choice or consideration. 采取 indicates to make use of something based on certain conditions, and its objects are usually 措施 (measures), 手段 (means), 态度 (attitudes), 形式 (forms), 方针 (guide lines), 政策 (policies), and so on. 采用 indicates to make use of something suitable, and its objects are usually 工具 (tools), 方法 (methods), 技术 (technology), 稿件 (manuscripts), and so on. 采纳 indicates to consider and accept a suggestion or proposal, and its objects are usually 意见 (advice), 建议 (suggestions), 方案 (schemes), and so on.

 **练习**

练习一、根据拼音写汉字,根据汉字写拼音

( )dǎo　( )nà　shāng( )　( )wù　( )fù
舞( )　采( )　( )害　家( )　颠( )

练习二、搭配连线

(1) 颠覆　　　　　　　A. 措施
(2) 颠倒　　　　　　　B. 意见
(3) 受到　　　　　　　C. 政权
(4) 采纳　　　　　　　D. 是非
(5) 采取　　　　　　　E. 伤害

练习三、从今天学习的生词中选择合适的词填空

1. 她觉得每天在家里做 _____ 太没意思了,她希望找个工作。
2. 这个舞蹈演员一直在非常努力地练功,她希望能有机会在国际一流的 _____ 上表演。
3. 如果 _____ 这项新工艺,我们的生产效率会大大提高。
4. 母亲殷切的期望是他努力学习的 _____。
5. 政府将 _____ 有效措施降低日用品的价格。
6. 你把电池装反了,把它 _____ 过来,就可以了。
7. 妈妈上楼后发现,孩子们在玩游戏,把房间弄得 _____ 的。
8. 抢劫犯说他不想 _____ 谁,他只要钱。
9. 我们应该 _____ 合理的建议,不断提高我们的工作水平。
10. 这个穷小伙子和一个富家小姐结婚时,很多人会怀疑他 _____ 不纯。

答案

练习一:
略
练习二:
(1) C　　(2)D　　(3)E　　(4)B　　(5)A
练习三:
1. 家务　2. 舞台　3. 采用　4. 动力　5. 采取
6. 颠倒　7. 乱七八糟 8. 伤害　9. 采纳　10. 动机

星期五

qúnzhòng
群众 　民众　（乙）名
the masses
常用搭配
群众的利益 interests of the masses
群众运动 mass movement　群众组织 mass organization
用法示例
群众聚集在国王要经过的街道旁。
Crowds a massed along the road where the king would pass.
我们要团结群众。
We should unite the masses.
警察驱散了群众。
The police dispersed the crowd.

dǎbài
打败 　战胜　（丙）动
defeat; beat
常用搭配
被打败 be defeated　打败敌人 beat the enemy
打败对手 beat a rival
用法示例
我的祖国可能被打败，但决不会被征服。
My country may be defeated, but can never be conquered.
他们队以很高的比分打败了我们队。
Their team beat ours by a wide margin.
他们曾向世界上最强的球队挑战并将其打败。
They had challenged, and beaten, the best team in the world.

gōujié
勾结 　勾搭　（丙）动
collude with; collaborate with
常用搭配
与……相勾结 in collusion with…
暗中勾结 secretly collude
用法示例
他被怀疑与敌人相勾结。
He was suspected of collaborating with the enemy.
那两个罪犯彼此勾结在一起。
The two criminals were in cahoots with each other.
他装着不认识她，其实他们在暗中勾结。
He pretended not to know her, but in fact they were secretly in league together.

wǔrǔ
侮辱 　凌辱　（丙）动
insult

常用搭配
侮辱妇女 insult a woman　忍受侮辱 swallow an insult
莫大的侮辱 a gross insult
用法示例
他当众侮辱我。
He gave me an affront.
他们对俘虏百般侮辱。
They inflicted all kinds of indignities on their captives.
虽然他很懦弱，却无法忍受这样的侮辱。
Coward though he is, he can't bear to be slighted as such.

jiēlù
揭露 　　（丙）动
expose; unmask
常用搭配
揭露丑闻 reveal a scandal　揭露阴谋 expose one's plot
揭露真相 uncover the truth
用法示例
这名记者因为试图揭露一个阴谋而被杀害。
The reporter was killed because he tried to expose a plot.
他们揭露了这次战争的真实目的。
They exposed the true aims of the war.
我们要勇敢地揭露工作中的矛盾和问题。
We should boldly expose the contradictions and problems in our work.

jiēfā
揭发 　　（丁）动
reveal; disclose
常用搭配
揭发罪行 expose a crime
揭发检举 expose and denounce sb.
用法示例
一定要毫无保留地揭露贪官的罪行。
The crimes of the corrupt officials must be publicly disclosed.
这些问题被揭发后，有几个大臣辞职了。
As a result of these exposures, several ministers resigned from the government.
他的同事揭发了他的贪污行为。
His colleagues uncovered his embezzlement.

dǎoháng
导航 　　（丁）动
navigate
常用搭配
无线电导航 radio navigation　导航雷达 navigation radar
导航系统 navigation system
用法示例
他的职责是为出港船舶导航。
His duty is to captain the ships out.
机场引进了一些新的导航设备。
The airport introduced some advanced navigatioal equipment.

dǎoshī
导师 （丙）名
tutor

常用搭配

导师制 the tutorial system

研究生导师 teacher of graduate students

用法示例

我的导师是一位学识渊博的学者。

My tutor is an accomplished scholar.

她兼做导师工作和研究工作。

Her work was divided between tutoring and research.

研究生得阅读导师写的东西。

The graduate student should have read what his tutor had written.

gōutōng
沟通 （丁）动
① link up ② communicate

常用搭配

互相沟通 communicate with each other

沟通思想 promote mutual understanding

用法示例

我喜欢和我的家人沟通。

I like to communicate with my family.

父母亲常发觉很难跟他们的小孩沟通。

Parents often find it difficult to communicate with their children.

我们安装了传真机,与总部的沟通更快了。

Communicating with the head office has been quicker since we installed the fax.

dǎfa
打发 （丁）动
① dispatch sb to do sth ② send sb away

常用搭配

打发人请医生 send for a doctor   打发时间 kill time

用法示例

时间已晚,妈妈打发孩子们去睡觉。

As it was getting late, mother sent the children to bed.

他父亲把他打发到叔叔家去了。

His father sent him off to his uncle's.

她来串门只是为了打发时间。

She stopped by just to pass the time of day.

quèrèn
确认 （丁）动
verify; confirm

常用搭配

确认所属事实 confirm the statement

确认签字 verify one's signature

用法示例

旅馆给我们打电话确认所预定的房间。

The hotel confirmed our reservations by telephone.

请给我来封信,确认你在电话中传达的消息。

Please send a confirmation of your telephone message to me in writing.

我们正在等待确认那个消息。

We are waiting for confirmation of the news.

yì gān èr jìng
一干二净 （丁）
① thoroughly ② completely

常用搭配

忘得一干二净 forget completely

用法示例

我本该昨天回信的,但我把这件事忘得一干二净。

I should have answered the letter yesterday, but it slipped my mind.

这个男孩把饭菜吃得一干二净。

The boy gobbled up his dinner.

词义辨析

揭露、揭发

　　"揭露"和"揭发"都是动词,都表示使隐藏的事或秘密为人所知。"揭露"是中性词,它的对象可以是问题、本质或真相;"揭发"含有贬义,它的对象是错误或罪行。例如:①多年以后,有人揭露了真相。②他揭露/揭发他们的阴谋。

　　Both 揭露 and 揭发 are verbs, meaning to reveal, or to make known something concealed or secret. 揭露 has a neutral sense, and its objects can be a problem, or the nature or truth of something. 揭发 has a derogatory sense, and its objects are mistakes or crimes. For example: ① Many years later, the truth of the matter was revealed. ② He exposed their plot.

练习

练习一、根据拼音写汉字,根据汉字写拼音

(　　)rǔ　jiē(　　)(　　)háng　gōu(　　)qún(　　)

侮(　　)(　　)露　　导(　　)(　　)通　(　　)众

练习二、搭配连线

(1) 揭露　　　　　　A. 思想

(2) 暗中　　　　　　B. 侮辱

(3) 沟通　　　　　　C. 系统

(4) 导航　　　　　　D. 勾结

(5) 忍受　　　　　　E. 阴谋

练习三、从今天学习的生词中选择合适的词填空

1. 如果你认为记录的都是真实的,请签字 _____ 。

2. 有人给公安局写信 _____ 了他的贪污行为。

3. 轮船在海上航行时,可以用指南针 _____ 。

4. 今天妈妈很累,她早早就 _____ 孩子们回自己房间,然后她也去睡觉了。

5. 冰箱里什么吃的都没有了,被我的室友吃得 _____ 。

6. 丑闻被 _____ 后,好几名政府官员都被迫辞职了。

7. 父母与孩子缺少_____,导致他们不能相互理解。
8. 他们吵架的时候用了很多_____性的词语。
9. 这个警察居然与犯罪分子相互_____,他肯定会被开除。
10. 在攻读博士学位的时候,他的_____给了他很大的帮助。

答案

练习一:
略
练习二:
(1) E (2)D (3)A (4)C (5)B
练习三:
1. 确认 2. 揭发 3. 导航 4. 打发 5. 一干二净
6. 揭露 7. 沟通 8. 侮辱 9. 勾结 10. 导师

第12月,第3周的练习

练习一. 根据词语给加点的字注音
1.( ) 2.( ) 3.( ) 4.( ) 5.( )
颠覆 打败 治疗 导航 当初

练习二. 根据拼音填写词语
wǔ wǔ wǔ gōu gōu
1.( )术 2.( )辱 3.( )蹈 4.( )通 5.( )结

练习三. 辨析并选择合适的词填空
1. 这个人( )很重,他总是( )别人对他好是因为看上了他的钱。(疑心、怀疑、疑问)
2. 我还有一些( ),但是已经下课了,只好下次再向老师请教。(疑心、怀疑、疑问)
3. 有人把我们公司的机密泄露给了另一家公司,技术主管受到了大家的( )。(疑心、怀疑、疑问)
4. 房子的( )看上去很普通,但房子的内部装修却十分奢华。(外部、外界)
5. 国内的局势并不像( )宣传的那么严重。(外部、外界)
6. 他被国外一所大学( )了,即将去那儿读研究生。(录用、录取)
7. 他面试的时候表现得很好,很快就被公司正式( )了。(录用、录取)
8. 政府下令要尽快( )措施,把损失降到最低程度。(采取、采纳、采用)
9. 他说如果当初领导( )了他的意见,就可以避免发生类似的事故。(采取、采纳、采用)
10. 他曾多次向编辑部投稿,但从没被( )过。(采取、采纳、采用)
11. 他在这本书中( )并批判了这次战争的真实目的。(揭露、揭发)
12. 他的犯罪行为被群众( )检举了,他肯定会坐牢。(揭露、揭发)

练习四. 选词填空
欢乐 粗心 动力 当地 吃亏
欢呼 粗暴 动机 当场 吃苦
1. 听推销员介绍了减肥茶的神奇功效,琳达( )就买了五百块钱的。
2. 小王太( )了,上课忘了带书,回去取书时又忘了带钥匙。
3. 警察掌握了这个人犯罪的证据,却不能理解他犯罪的( ),所以怀疑他有精神病。
4. 你到了那个城市以后,可以向( )人打听,他们会告诉你市政府的具体位置。
5. 看到7号又进了一球,支持他的球迷激动得( )起来。
6. 为了让孩子能接受良好的教育,这对贫困的父母甘愿( )受累。
7. 崇高的理想是他努力奋斗的( )。
8. 这个作家的前半生是在痛苦和孤独中度过的,后半生才享受到了( )和幸福。
9. 在跟别人相处时,这个人总怕( ),所以一个朋友都没有。
10. 警察在执法时态度( ),有人用手机拍摄了整个过程,这个警察肯定会受到处罚。

练习五. 成语填空
1. 接二( )( ) 2. 一帆( )( ) 3. 四面( )( )
4. 一干( )( ) 5. 乱七( )( )

练习六. 写出下列词语的同义词
1. 录用( ) 2. 当初( )
3. 颠覆( ) 4. 当地( )
5. 打败( )

练习七. 写出下列词语的反义词
1. 务必( ) 2. 粗暴( )
3. 善良( ) 4. 外部( )
5. 吃苦( )

答案

练习一.
1.fù 2.bài 3.zhì 4.háng 5.chū
练习二.
1. 武 2. 侮 3. 舞 4. 沟 5. 勾
练习三.
1. 疑心,怀疑 2. 疑问 3. 怀疑 4. 外部
5. 外界 6. 录取 7. 录用 8. 采取 9. 采纳
10. 采用 11. 揭露 12. 揭发
练习四.
1. 当场 2. 粗心 3. 动机 4. 当地 5. 欢呼
6. 吃苦 7. 动力 8. 欢乐 9. 吃亏 10. 粗暴
练习五.
1. 连三 2. 风顺 3. 八方 4. 二净 5. 八糟
练习六.
1. 聘用 2. 起初 3. 推翻 4. 本地 5. 战胜
练习七.
1. 不必 2. 温和 3. 歹毒 4. 内部 5. 享福

12月 第4周的学习内容

星期一

yāoqǐng
邀请   **yuēqǐng**
⑩ 约请   （乙）动／名

① invite ② invitation

常用搭配

邀请朋友吃饭 invite friends to dinner
接受邀请 accept an invitation
应某人邀请 at the invitation of sb

用法示例

她邀请我们参加聚会。
She invited us to the party.
能被邀请参加晚宴我感到很荣幸。
I consider it a great honor to be invited to dinner.
感谢你的邀请。
I appreciate your invitation.

dàxiǎo
大小   （乙）名

size

常用搭配

大小不同 different in size

用法示例

国家不论大小,应该一律平等。
All countries, big or small, should be considered equals.
这些东西大小不同,实质一样。
They differ in size, but not in type.
这两本书大小一样。
The two books were the same size.

dìzhì
地质   （丙）名

geology

常用搭配

地质构造 geological structure
地质勘探 geological prospecting

用法示例

我在大学里学过地质学。
I've studied geology in my college.
李教授是著名的地质学家。
Professor Li is a very famous geologist.

yìngyāo
应邀   （丙）动

① on invitation ② at sb.'s invitation

常用搭配

应邀出席会议 attend a meeting by invitation
应邀访问中国 visit China on an invitation

用法示例

她应邀演奏了一曲。
She played a piece on request.
经理应邀在宴会上发言。
The manager was called on to speak at the banquet.
我应邀参加他们的婚礼。
I've been invited to their wedding.

yǎngfèn
养分   （丁）名

nutrient

常用搭配

吸收养分 absorb nutrients   土壤的养分 soil nutrients

用法示例

水中的养分能促进这种植物生长。
The nutrients in the water act as a stimulus to the growth of the plant.
这里的土壤缺乏养分。
The soil is lacking in nutrients.

yǎngliào
养料   （丙）名

nourishment

常用搭配

从……吸取养料 draw nourishment from…

用法示例

牛奶供给婴儿养料。
Milk nourishes a baby.
不同的食物提供不同的养料。
Different foods provide different nourishment.

jiè
届   （乙）量

① period ② session ③ measure word for graduates or meeting

常用搭配

88 届毕业生 graduates in 1988
第 3 届世界粮食会议 the third World Food Conference
第 29 届奥运会 Games of the XXIX Olympiad

用法示例

下届选举我可能选她。
I may vote for her in the next election.
我们是校友,我是 06 届毕业生,他是 07 届的。
We are schoolmates. I graduated in 2006, and he graduated in 2007.

第七届全国人民代表大会有着重要的意义。
The Seventh National People's Congress was of great significance.

dìxíng
地形　　　　　　　　　　　　（丙）名
terrain; topography

常用搭配
复杂的地形 varied topography
崎岖的地形 rugged topography

用法示例
司令员对地形作了仔细研究。
The commander made a detailed study of the terrain.
他了解这里的地形。
He knows the lay of the land here.

dǔsè　　　　　shūtōng
堵塞　　　　反 疏通　　　　（丁）动
① block ② clog

常用搭配
交通堵塞 traffic jam　　管道阻塞 a block in the pipes

用法示例
城里的交通天天堵塞。
Traffic jams in town happens everyday.
管子渐渐被堵塞了，水流不出去。
The pipes are clogging, and the water can't drain away.
管道被垃圾堵塞了，我请人清理了一下。
The pipe was clogged with rubbish so I had it cleared.

huǐmiè　　　　　xiāomiè
毁灭　　　　同 消灭　　　　（丁）动
perish; ruin

常用搭配
毁灭证据 destroy evidence
毁灭性打击 a crushing blow

用法示例
正在嫌疑人要毁灭证据的时候，警察阻止了他。
The police stopped the suspect as he was going to destroy evidence.
一切都毁灭了。
Everything was destroyed.
那次失败毁灭了我所有的希望。
That defeat meant the death of all my hopes.

huǐhuài　　　　　bǎohù
毁坏　　　　反 保护　　　　（丁）动
damage

常用搭配
毁坏公共财产 damage to public property
毁坏庄稼 damage the crops

用法示例
桥已毁坏，我们无法过河。
The bridge was destroyed, so we couldn't get across the river.

大雨毁坏了许多房子。
The heavy rain damaged many houses.
蝗虫群毁坏了所有的庄稼。
The locust swarm has destroyed all the crops.

wú kě nài hé
无可奈何　　　　　　　　　　　（丙）
① have no alternative ② feel hopeless

用法示例
她争执一番后，无可奈何地缴纳了罚金。
She had no alternative but to pay the fine.
老师对那个调皮的学生无可奈何。
The teacher thought the naughty boy was hopeless.
我想出去，可是没钱，只能无可奈何地呆在家里。
I wanted to go out, but I had no money. I had no option but to staying at home.

 词义辨析

毁灭、毁坏
　　"毁灭"和"毁坏"都是动词，都可以带宾语，宾语一般是具体的，但有时也可以是抽象的。"毁灭"比"毁坏"的程度更高。"毁灭"指彻底摧毁或消灭，使对象不存在或无法修复。"毁坏"指损坏、破坏，其对象仍然存在或可以修复。例如：①很多珍贵的油画在这次大火中遭到毁灭。②地震并不太严重，只有少数老建筑物受到了毁坏。

　　Both 毁灭 and 毁坏 are verbs, and their objects are usually something concrete, and sometimes something abstract. The consequence of 毁灭 is worse than 毁坏. 毁灭 indicates to ruin or destroy completely in order to make its objects vanish into nothing, or be beyond repair; while 毁坏 indicates to damage something which still exists or can be repaired. For example: ① Many priceless paintings were completely destroyed in that big fire. ② The earthquake was not very serious; just a few old buildings were damaged.

 **练习**

练习一、根据拼音写汉字，根据汉字写拼音
( )yāo yǎng( ) dǔ( ) huǐ( ) ( )zhì
应( ) ( )分 ( )塞 ( )灭 地( )

练习二、搭配连线
(1) 毁灭   A. 养分
(2) 吸收   B. 邀请
(3) 交通   C. 勘探
(4) 地质   D. 证据
(5) 接受   E. 堵塞

练习三、从今天学习的生词中选择合适的词填空
1. 她是上一 _____ 的毕业生，去年七月刚刚毕业。
2. 水果的一些 _____ 有助于身体健康发育。
3. 她 _____ 了很多人来参加她的婚礼。
4. 这次失败对他们来说是 _____ 性打击，他们再也没有发展的机会了。
5. 由于下水道都被 _____ 了，下雨时街道上水流成河。
6. 孩子又哭又闹，连她的妈妈都对她 _____ 。
7. 这个地方 _____ 复杂，游客很容易迷路。
8. 人们没有保护文物的意识，很多古建筑都被 _____ 了。
9. 星期天我 _____ 参加了一个朋友的生日晚会。
10. 这件衬衫 _____ 合适，就是颜色有点儿暗。

 **答案**

练习一：
略
练习二：
(1) D   (2)A   (3)E   (4)C   (5)B
练习三：
1. 届   2. 养分   3. 邀请   4. 毁灭   5. 堵塞
6. 无可奈何 7. 地形   8. 毁坏   9. 应邀   10. 大小

 星期二

wùjià
物价   （乙）名
(commodity) prices
常用搭配
物价指数 a price index
物价上涨 price rise
用法示例
有迹象表明物价将上涨。
There are some indications that the prices will go up.
物价仍有上涨趋势。
The trend of prices is still rising.
政府必须采取行动稳定物价。
The government must act to stabilize prices.

cāicè   chuǎicè
猜测   ⊙揣测   （丁）动
guess; conjecture
常用搭配
猜测……的结果 guess the result of…
用法示例
我们只能猜测她的动机。
We could only guess at her motives.
科学家猜测在金星上没有生命。
The scientists guess that Venus is without life forms.
谣言引起了很多猜测。
The rumor raised much conjecture.

diàndìng
奠定   （丙）动
establish; settle
常用搭配
奠定……的基础 lay the foundation of…
用法示例
他为细菌学科学奠定了基础。
He laid the foundation of the science of bacteriology.
学习和勤奋为他的成功奠定了基础。
He laid the foundations of his success through study and hard work.

yǎnjiǎng
演讲   （丁）动
give a speech
常用搭配
演讲比赛 speech contest
用法示例
他的演讲很受欢迎。
His speech was favorably received.

这位著名的经济学家给我们做了一次演讲。
The famous economist gave us a speech.
他用一则有趣的笑话结束了演讲。
He closed his speech with a funny joke.

yǎnshuō
演说 （丙）名／动
① speech ② give a speech

常用搭配

演说家 speaker
发表演说 make a speech

用法示例

他正在准备明天集会的演说。
He is preparing his speech for the meeting tomorrow.
他的演说不时被暴风雨般的掌声打断。
His speech was frequently interrupted by tumultuous applause.
她发表了热情的告别演说。
She had a fervent farewell speech.

bèiyòng
备用 （丁）动
spare

常用搭配

备用轮胎 a spare tire　　备用磁带 a spare tape

用法示例

每张床上都放有备用毛毯。
Spare blankets lay on each bed.
我的车胎扎破了，备用的也瘪了！
I've got a puncture, and my spare is flat too!
我的车里有一些备用工具。
There are some spare tools in my car.

dǐng
顶 （乙）名／量
① peak ② top ② measure word used for a hat

常用搭配

山顶 top of a mountain　　屋顶 roof
一顶帽子 a hat

用法示例

这只鸟的头顶上有一小簇红色的羽毛。
The bird has a tuft of red feathers on top of its head.
当我到达山顶的时候，我有一种巨大的成就感。
I felt a great sense of achievement when I reached the top of the mountain.
他有两顶高尔夫球帽。
He has 2 golfing hats.

yùcè
预测 （丁）动
forecast; predict

常用搭配

主观预测 subjective forecast
预测比赛的结果 forecast the result of a match

用法示例

委员会预测情况将继续好转。
The committee predicted that the improvement would continue.
很难预测出谁将获胜。
It is hard to predict who will win.
他预测了明年的经济形势。
He forecasted the economic outlook for next year.

zīzhù　　　　juānzhù
资助　　圆捐助 （丁）动
provide financial aid

常用搭配

资助大学生 aid a college student with money.

用法示例

她用教书挣的钱资助丈夫。
She supports her husband on the money she earns from teaching.
基金会资助他做这项事业。
The foundation aided him in his enterprise.
她很独立，拒绝一切金钱上的资助。
She is so independent that she refused all pecuniary aid.

huígù　　　　zhǎnwàng
回顾　　反展望 （丁）动
look back; review

常用搭配

回顾过去 review the past
历史回顾 a historical retrospect

用法示例

她回顾自己的经历觉得心满意足。
She can look back on her career with great satisfaction.
回顾过去就很容易明白我们的错误了。
In retrospect, it's easy to see where we went wrong.
回顾他的生命历程，我们发现他太伟大了。
Looking back on his life, from the cradle to the grave, we realised he was an amazing man.

chuàngyè　　　　shǒuyè
创业　　反守业 （丁）动
start one's own business

常用搭配

艰苦创业 start a business with difficulty

用法示例

他放弃了一份安定的工作而自己创业。
He left a safe job and set up his own business.
他决定独立创业。
He decided to go it alone and start his own business.
创业容易守业难。
It's easy to open a shop, but hard to keep it open.

wú lùn rú hé
无论如何 （丙）
whatever; anyway; anyhow

常用搭配

我无论如何也得去。I'll go in any case.

用法示例

屋子锁着,我无论如何也进不去。

The house was locked and I could not get in anyway.

无论如何我要去看他。

I shall go and see him anyway.

我们无论如何要完成计划。

We must complete the plan, whatever happens.

 词义辨析

猜测、预测

　　"猜测"和"预测"都是动词,都表示预先推测(某一结果或事件),有时候可以作主语或宾语。"猜测"强调没有足够的依据而臆断或想象;"预测"强调用科学方法提前估算,尤其指预测天气、天象、地震等。例如:①我们都不理解她的行为,只能猜测她的动机。②总统的讲话引起很多猜测。③科学家预测明天将出现日食。④他对经济发展的预测非常准确。

　　Both 猜测 and 预测 are verbs, meaning "to predict (a result or an event) in advance". 猜测 means "to guess", stressing to imagine or predict without sufficient information; while 预测 means "to forecast", stressing to estimate or calculate in advance by scientific means; it is especially used in predicting the weather, astronomical phenomena, earthquakes, etc. For example: ① We did not understand her behavior and we could only guess at her motives. ② The president's speech raised much conjecture. ③ The scientist predicted that there will be a solar eclipse tomorrow. ④ His prediction about economic developments is very precise.

 练习

练习一、根据拼音写汉字,根据汉字写拼音

diàn( ) cāi( ) ( ) gù chuàng( ) zī ( )

( )定 ( )测 回( ) ( )业 ( )助

练习二、搭配连线

(1) 独立 　　　　A. 轮胎

(2) 历史 　　　　B. 演说

(3) 备用 　　　　C. 回顾

(4) 发表 　　　　D. 比赛

(5) 演讲 　　　　E. 创业

练习三、从今天学习的生词中选择合适的词填空

1. 去长城玩时,为了防晒,我买了一 _____ 遮阳帽。

2. 由于 _____ 上涨过快,人们的消费能力下降了。

3. 出远门前,我总是拿点常用药 _____。

4. 她特别擅长数学和物理,这为她学习计算机 _____ 了坚实的专业基础。

5. 今天晚上我 _____ 也要把作业做完,因为明天老师要检查。

6. 大会首先 _____ 了去年的工作,总结了工作中的经验和不足。

7. 总统没有参加国庆招待会,这引起了人们对他的种种 _____。

8. 记者报道了这个大学生靠打工 _____ 贫困山区孩子的事迹。

9. 经济学家 _____ 明年经济发展的速度可能会放缓。

10. 现在越来越多的大学生毕业后不去找工作,而是选择自己 _____。

🔑 **答案**

练习一:

略

练习二:

(1) E 　　(2)C 　　(3)A 　　(4)B 　　(5)D

练习三:

1. 顶 　2. 物价 　3. 备用 　4. 奠定 　5. 无论如何

6. 回顾 　7. 猜测 　8. 资助 　9. 预测 　10. 创业

星期三

dù
度
（乙）名／量
① degree ② measure word for electricity and so on

【常用搭配】
三度烧伤 a third-degree burn
90 度的角 an angle of ninety degrees
一度电 1 kilowatt-hour

【用法示例】
水在摄氏零度结冰。
Water freezes at 0 degrees celcius.
今天气温比昨天高两度。
The temperature today is two degrees hotter than yesterday.

wēixié
威胁
（丙）动
① threaten ② menace

【常用搭配】
用死威胁他 death threat
受到……的威胁 be menaced by

【用法示例】
他们威胁说要对该国实行封锁。
They are threatening to impose a blockade on the country.
局势对世界和平构成了严重的威胁。
The situation poses a grave threat to world peace.
人民正受到战争的威胁。
The people are being menaced by the threat of war.

cánkù   **cánbào**
残酷   ⚁ 残暴   **（丙）形**
cruel; brutal

【常用搭配】
残酷的竞争 cutthroat competition
残酷的现实 the brutal facts

【用法示例】
命运有时是残酷的。
Destiny is sometimes cruel.
那个皇帝是个残酷的暴君。
That emperor was a cruel despot.
这的确是一场残酷的竞争，但我们最终胜利了。
It was a cutthroat competition, but we triumphed at last.

cánrěn   **réncí**
残忍   ⚁ 仁慈   **（丁）形**
① merciless ② bloody

【常用搭配】
残忍冷酷 cruel and cold hearted

残忍的士兵 cruel soldier

【用法示例】
他是个残忍的杀手。
He is a cruel assassin.
我们不应该对动物这么残忍。
We shouldn't be so cruel to animals.
他那样打孩子真是残忍。
It is cruel of him to beat his boy like that.

chénliè
陈列
（丙）动
display; exhibit

【常用搭配】
陈列室 exhibition room
陈列柜 showcase

【用法示例】
珠宝陈列在柜台里。
Jewelry is displayed on the sales counter.
博物馆里陈列着大量的珍贵文物。
A lot of valuable cultural relics are exhibited in the museum.
等她的时候，我浏览陈列窗来消磨时间。
While I was waiting for her, I killed time by looking in the display window.

huǎnmàn
缓慢
（丙）形
slow

【常用搭配】
行动缓慢 slow in action
缓慢进行 make slow progress

【用法示例】
卸货的过程很缓慢。
Unloading the cargo was a slow process.
船在汹涌的大海中缓慢前进。
The ship made slow progress across the rough sea.
鼓声平稳而缓慢。
The beat of the drum was steady and slow.

huǎnhé   **jiājù**
缓和   ⚁ 加剧   **（丙）动**
① ease (tension) ② moderate

【常用搭配】
缓和紧张的气氛 to ease the atmosphere
对……起缓和作用 ease something

【用法示例】
自从开始谈判以来，两国关系已得到缓和。
The relationship between the two countries has been more relaxed since the beginning of the talks.
外交部长对缓和那个地区的紧张局势做了很多工作。
The foreign minister did much to ease the tensions in the area.

wēiwàng
威望   shēngwàng 声望   （丁）名

prestige

常用搭配

崇高的威望 high prestige

有威望的科学家 a scientist of high prestige

用法示例

中国在国际上的威望越来越高了。

China enjoys a higher prestige in the world.

他在教育界有很高的威望。

He has high prestige in educational circles.

hàofèi
耗费   （丁）动

spend; consume

常用搭配

耗费人力物力

consume manpower and material resources

耗费时间、金钱 expend time and money

用法示例

他们在这一工程上耗费了很多资金。

They have spent a great deal of money on this project.

写这本书耗费了我大部分的时间和精力。

Writing the book consumed most of my time and energy.

案头工作耗费了委员会很多时间。

Paperwork took up much of the committee's time.

chénshù
陈述   （丁）动

to state

常用搭配

陈述自己的意见 state one's views

陈述理由 state one's reason

用法示例

几个证人的陈述并不一致。

The witnesses' statements just don't agree with each other.

他的律师陈述了他们对此事的看法。

His lawyer stated their views about the affair.

lì suǒ néng jí
力所能及   （乙）

in one's power

常用搭配

提供力所能及的帮助 offer all the help within one's power

用法示例

这完全是你力所能及的工作。

This is a task well within your ability.

人只能做力所能及的事。

A man can do no more than his best.

这不是他力所能及的。

It's beyond his power.

wú néng wéi lì
无能 为力   （丁）

cannot do anything about

常用搭配

我无能为力。There is nothing I can do.

用法示例

我们只好等等看，现在无能为力。

We shall just have to wait and see; there's nothing we can do at the moment.

我们无能为力，只好坐着等候宣布结果。

There was nothing more we could do, so we just had to wait until the result was announced.

这事我也无能为力。

That is beyond my power.

词义辨析

残酷、残忍

　　"残酷"和"残忍"都是形容词,都有凶狠、野蛮的意思,都含有贬义,有时可以互换使用。"残酷"可以形容人、人的行为或环境、形势等。"残忍"一般只用于人,"残忍"通常比"残酷"的语义更重。例如:①残忍的士兵凶狠地虐待俘虏。②他残忍地杀害了他的邻居。③我们得面对这个残酷的事实,我们失败了。

　　Both 残酷 and 残忍 are adjectives, meaning "extremely cruel and brutal", and both have a derogatory sense; sometimes they are interchangeable. 残酷 can be applied to modify a person, one's behavior, circumstances, or a situation, etc. While 残忍 is usually applied to modifying people. For example: ① The brutal soldiers beat their prisoners violently. ② He killed his neighbor brutally. ③ We have to face the harsh fact that we failed.

 练习

练习一、根据拼音写汉字，根据汉字写拼音

( )xié ( )kù huǎn( ) hào( ) chén( )
威( ) 残( ) ( )慢 ( )费 ( )述

练习二、搭配连线

(1) 崇高的　　　　　　A. 竞争
(2) 残忍的　　　　　　B. 威望
(3) 残酷的　　　　　　C. 过程
(4) 缓慢的　　　　　　D. 威胁
(5) 死亡的　　　　　　E. 士兵

练习三、从今天学习的生词中选择合适的词填空

1. 我想帮助她,却_____,因为我当时的生活压力也很大。
2. 历史博物馆里_____着很多文物。
3. 我没做什么了不起的事,只是给了他一点_____的帮助而已。
4. 这个九十岁的老先生在戏曲界享有很高的_____。
5. 由于太激动,她_____理由时有点混乱。
6. 今天只有十_____,冬天临近了,天气变凉了。
7. 这个行业的待遇很高,但是竞争非常_____,每年都有很多人被淘汰。
8. 人老了,行动难免_____,对此我们年轻人要理解并给予力所能及的帮助。
9. 这部著作_____了老人一生的心血。
10. 我说的话可能有点_____,但确实是事实。

 答案

练习一:
略
练习二:
(1) B　　(2)E　　(3)A　　(4)C　　(5)D
练习三:
1.无能为力 2.陈列　3.力所能及 4.威望　5.陈述
6.度　　7.残酷　8.缓慢　9.耗费　10.残忍

---

zhíxíng
执行　　　　　　　　　　　　(乙)动

carry out; execute

常用搭配
执行计划 carry out a plan
执行命令 execute a command
执行一项决定 implement a decision

用法示例
警察与法官执行法律。
Policemen and judges enforce the law.
他要执行他的计划。
He will carry out his plan.

lì
粒　　　　　　　　　　　　　(乙)量

grain (a measure word)

常用搭配
一粒沙子 a grain of sand.
一粒盐 a grain of salt

用法示例
在风天,我们能看到无数粒沙子。
We can see numerous grains of sand on a windy day.
他的领子上有一粒米。
There is a grain of rice on his collar.

jiǎngjiu
讲究　　　　　　　　　　(丙)动 / 形

① pay attention to ② be particular about

常用搭配
讲究卫生 pay attention to hygiene
讲究吃喝 be particular about what one eats

用法示例
我不怎么讲究衣着,我不在乎我穿什么。
I'm not particular about my clothes; I don't mind what I wear.
他吃东西很讲究。
He is very particular about his food.
新的经理非常讲究实际效果,他不在乎做事的方式。
The new manager put great emphasis on practical results; and doesn't care how they are achieved.

jiāodài
交代　　　　　　　　　　　　(丙)动

① hand over ② make clear ② confess

常用搭配
交代工作 hand over work to one's successor
交代罪行 confess one's crime

用法示例

按照交代你的话做。

Do as you're told.

嫌疑犯交代了罪行。

The suspect confessed to the crime.

jiānyù

监狱 （丙）名

prison

常用搭配

被关入监狱 be taken to prison

用法示例

那个好色之徒被关进监狱。

The lascivious person was put in prison.

那个骗子被关进监狱。

The deceiver was put in jail.

他在监狱中呆了 10 年。

He had been in prison for ten years.

huànxiǎng   mèngxiǎng

幻想   圓 梦想   （丙）名／动

① fantasy ② fancy

常用搭配

沉湎于幻想 indulge in fantasy

他的幻想破灭了。His illusion crumbled.

用法示例

我对他的能力不抱任何幻想。

I have no illusions about his ability.

他正沉浸于对未来的幻想之中。

He is indulging in reveries about his future.

龙是中国人幻想出来的动物。

Dragons are creatures of Chinese fantasy.

chǎojià   zhēngchǎo

吵架   圓 争吵   （丙）动

quarrel

常用搭配

跟某人吵架 quarrel with sb

为某事吵架 quarrel about sth

用法示例

他们经常为小事吵架。

They often quarrel with each other about trifles.

他和朋友吵架了。

He quarreled with his friend.

他们因为钱而吵架。

They had a quarrel about money.

zūnzhào   wéikàng

遵照   圓 违抗   （丁）动

be in accordance with; be in obedience to

常用搭配

遵照上级命令 act in obedience to orders from superious

遵照党的政策办事

act in accordance with the policies of the party

用法示例

遵照指示，警察在展览会期间维持秩序。

The police have been instructed to keep order at the fair.

他是遵照上级指示行动的。

He obediently followed the instructions of his superior.

zūnxún

遵循 （丁）动

follow; abide by

常用搭配

遵循党的路线 follow the party line

遵循和平共处的原则

follow the principle of peaceful coexistence

用法示例

在商标注册方面，不同的国家遵循不同的原则。

Different countries follow different rules for trademark registration.

我不管你个人是怎么想的，你必须遵循我们的教育方针。

I don't care what your personal views are; you must follow our educational policy.

在社会中生活，就要遵循社会行为准则。

You must adapt to the norms of the society you live in.

chǎonào

吵闹 （丁）动

make noise

常用搭配

大吵大闹 kick up a fuss

别再吵闹了！ Stop making such a fuss!

用法示例

邻居的孩子总是吵吵闹闹的。

The children of our neighbors always make noise.

邻居们请他们停止吵闹，可他们不听。

The neighbors asked them to stop making a noise, but they kept on at it.

吵闹声使他很烦躁。

The loud noise grated on him.

chóuhèn   ēndé

仇恨   圓 恩德   （丙）名／动

① hatred; enmity; hostility ② hate

常用搭配

满腔仇恨 be seething with hatred

仇恨敌人 have animosity towards an enemy

用法示例

不知怎么的，他仇恨富人。

Somehow or other, he has a resentment against the rich.

这种仇恨是由种族偏见引起的。

This hatred was generated by racial prejudice.

他们之间有仇恨。

There exists an animosity between them.

wú qíng wú yì
无情无义 (丁)
heartless and faithless

常用搭配

无情无义的家伙 a heartless guy

用法示例

她离开了生病的丈夫,并带走了他所有的钱,她是个无情无义的女人。

She left her sick husband and took all of his money. She is a heartless woman.

他是个无情无义的人。

He is a man without a soul.

没想到他这么无情无义。

It was beyond belief that he could be so heartless and faithless.

词义辨析

遵循、遵照

"遵循"和"遵照"都是动词,都表示依照指示、规矩或希望做,都是书面语,有时可以互换使用。"遵循"强调事物内在联系的一致性,它的宾语往往比较抽象或概括,如路线、方针、政策、原则、客观规律、理论等;"遵照"强调"严格的参照或依照",宾语相对具体或明确,如上级指示、法规、合同、遗嘱等。

Both 遵循 and 遵照 are verbs, meaning "to act in accordance to another's command, rule, or wish"; they are often used in written language and sometimes are interchangeable. 遵循 stresses internal agreement, and its objects are something abstract and generalized, such as 路线 (guiding line), 方针 (guiding principle), 政策 (policy), 原则 (principle), 客观规律 (objective rules), 理论 (theory),etc. 遵照 stresses "to conform or abide by strictly", and its objects are something concrete and definite, such as 指示 (instruction), 法规 (laws and regulations), 合同 (contract), 遗嘱 (testament), etc.

练习

练习一、根据拼音写汉字,根据汉字写拼音

huàn( ) zūn( ) chóu( )( )yù zhí( )
( )想 ( )循 ( )恨 监( )( )行

练习二、搭配连线

(1) 执行　　　　　A. 卫生
(2) 满腔　　　　　B. 罪行
(3) 遵照　　　　　C. 命令
(4) 交代　　　　　D. 指示
(5) 讲究　　　　　E. 仇恨

练习三、从今天学习的生词中选择合适的词填空

1. 他把饭吃得干干净净的,一_____米都没剩。
2. 那个国家的人民对侵略者充满了_____。
3. 经过审讯,犯罪分子_____了盗窃的全过程,以及同伙的情况。
4. 所有事情都是_____死者生前的嘱咐办的。
5. 别人在他关键时刻帮了他,他不但没有回报,还把对方出卖了,真是_____。
6. 教学楼内必须保持安静,所以禁止学生在进入教学楼以后大声_____。
7. 军官挑选了二十名精明能干的士兵,去_____一项紧急任务。
8. 他穿着一向很随意,从不_____品牌。
9. 他本来还_____着吵架后再跟她和好,结果一个月后得知她出国了。
10. 他在_____里度过了四十多年,被释放后已经是一位老人了。

答案

练习一:

略

练习二:

(1) C　　(2)E　　(3)D　　(4)B　　(5)A

练习三:

1. 粒　　2. 仇恨　　3. 交代　　4. 遵照　　5. 无情无义
6. 吵闹　　7. 执行　　8. 讲究　　9. 幻想　　10. 监狱

星期五

zhū
株 （乙）量
measure word for plants

常用搭配

一株杨树 a poplar   几株珍稀植物 some rare plants

用法示例

寒霜冻死了几株幼苗。
Frost has killed some seedlings.
门前有两株橡树。
There are two big oaks in front of the gate.

chóngxīn
重新 （乙）副
① re- ② again ② once more

常用搭配

重新考虑 reconsider
重新确认 reconfirm
重新开始 start anew

用法示例

我建议你重新做一遍。
I suggest you do it again.
你的作文错误太多，重新写。
Your composition contains too many mistakes; begin anew.
我们得重新做一次试验。
We have to do the experiment once more.

hǎibá
海拔 （丙）名
① elevation ② height above sea-level

常用搭配

海拔高度 altitude
海拔 4,000 米 4,000 meters above sea level

用法示例

这所房子在海拔 1,000 米处。
The house is at an elevation of 1,000 meters.
这座山的山顶海拔 3,000 米。
The top of this mountain is three kilometers above sea level.
在西藏海拔很高的地方呼吸很困难。
At the high altitudes in Tibet it is difficult to breathe.

zhōngchéng
忠诚 （丙）形
loyal

常用搭配

忠诚可靠 loyal and trustworthy
对……忠诚 be loyal to…

用法示例

他是一位忠诚的士兵。
He is a loyal soldier.
他宣誓他将永远忠诚于国王。
He swore that he would be loyal to the king forever.
他的忠诚无可置疑。
His loyalty is above suspicion.

zhōngshí   zhōngchéng
忠实　⑩ 忠诚 （丙）形
faithful; devoted

常用搭配

忠实的朋友 devoted friend   忠实的信徒 faithful disciple

用法示例

他总是忠实地履行自己的职责。
He always fulfils his duty faithfully.
我一直是他最忠实的朋友。
I have been his most devoted friend.
翻译作品要忠实于原文。
A translation should be faithful to the original.

jiàqī
假期 （丙）名
holiday; vacation

常用搭配

假期作业 holiday task   愉快的假期 a good holiday
四周的假期 four weeks' vacation

用法示例

你假期过得愉快吗？
Did you have a nice holiday?
我们今年假期要去意大利旅行。
We are touring Italy during our holidays this year.
你是在什么地方度过假期的？
Where did you pass your vacation?

děnghòu
等候 （丙）动
wait

常用搭配

等候时机 wait for one's chance
排队等候 wait in a queue
耐心等候 wait patiently

用法示例

他没有耐心,对他来说排队等候是活受罪。
He's so impatient that waiting in a queue is torture to him.
我们正在等候客人的到来。
We are waiting for the guests to arrive.
你等候多久了？
How long have you been waiting?

huǐhèn   huǐwù
悔恨　⑩ 悔悟 （丁）动
repent; remorse

常用搭配
表示悔恨 profess regret
用法示例
他对自己过激的行为深感悔恨。
He repented his rash behavior.
当他流着泪表达他的悔恨时,我们最终原谅了他。
We finally forgave him when he expressed his repentance with tears.
他打过孩子后感到悔恨不已。
He was filled with remorse after hitting the child.

hémù
和睦　⊜ 融洽　（丁）形
① harmonious ② concord
常用搭配
夫妻和睦 conjugal harmony
和睦的家庭 a harmonious family
与某人和睦相处 live in concord with sb.
用法示例
这些相互毗邻的国家几个世纪以来一直和睦相处。
These neighboring states have lived in harmony for centuries.
所有村民都和睦地生活。
All the villagers live together in peace.
我妈妈总能和邻居和睦相处。
My mother always gets on well with our neighbors.

héjiě
和解　（丁）动
reconcile; compromise
常用搭配
与某人和解 compromise with sb
已达成和解。An amicable settlement was reached.
用法示例
我们希望促成双方和解。
We hope that we can bring both sides together.
两国之间的政治和解已经取得了进展。
Progress has been made towards reaching a political compromise between the two nations.
我们不能根据这样的条件和解。
We can not compromise on such terms.

děngjí
等级　⊜ 级别　（丁）名
grade; class
常用搭配
等级观念 class system
薪金等级 pay grade
用法示例
牛奶是分等级出售的。
Different grads of milk are sold.
我们根据阅读能力将学生划分等级。
We grade the students according to their reading ability.

这些苹果已经按照大小划分了等级。
These apples have been graded according to size.

wú wēi bú zhì
无微不至
very thoughtful; very careful
常用搭配
无微不至地照顾 to thoughtfully care for
用法示例
由于这位母亲对儿子照顾得无微不至,他很快就康复了。
The mother took so such good care of her son that he soon recovered from his illness.
现在大多数国家的儿童受到无微不至的关怀。
Children have very good levels of care in most of countries now.
她对病人照顾得无微不至。
It was very thoughtful of her to look after the patients.

 词义辨析

忠诚、忠实、
　　"忠诚"和"忠实"都是形容词,都表示对人、事物或想法坚定或忠心。"忠诚"是褒义词,强调尽心尽力,它的对象往往是国家、事业、人民、领导、朋友等。"忠实"是中性词,一般用于形容人的品格是老实可靠的,有时还有真实的意思。如:①他对朋友一向很忠诚/忠实。②人民忠诚于他们的国家。③这本书忠实地反映了中国老百姓的生活。
　　Both 忠诚 and 忠实 are adjectives, indicating "adhering firmly and devotedly to a person, a cause, or an idea". 忠诚 has a commendatory sense, stressing being faithful to a country, cause, people, leader, friends, etc. 忠实 has a neutral sense, and is applied to describe one's quality which is honest and trustful; sometimes it means "being consistent with truth or reality". For example: ① He is always faithful to his friends. ② The people stayed loyal to their country. ③ The book is an authentic account of the common people's life in China.

 练习

练习一、根据拼音写汉字,根据汉字写拼音
( )bá ( )mù ( )jí ( )qī zhōng ( )
海( ) 和( ) 等( ) 假( ) ( )实
练习二、搭配连线
(1) 重新　　　　A. 等候
(2) 忠诚　　　　B. 和睦
(3) 海拔　　　　C. 可靠
(4) 排队　　　　D. 高度
(5) 家庭　　　　E. 开始

练习三、从今天学习的生词中选择合适的词填空

1. 由于这个地方 _____ 高,气候比较冷,空气也比较稀薄。

2. 发现自己写错了字,她 _____ 写了一遍,这次她写对了。

3. 狗是人类 _____ 的朋友,现在大城市里养狗的老年人越来越多了。

4. 生病期间,她 _____ 地照顾我,我特别感激她。

5. 吵架后,同屋想 _____ ,可他拒绝了。

6. 我想利用 _____ 去国外旅行,你去吗?

7. 她拿了一束花在机场 _____ 她丈夫归来。

8. 我们的宿舍特别好,我和两个同屋相处得也很 _____ 。

9. 这名老警察始终 _____ 于自己的职责,全心全意为人民服务。

10. 他酒醒之后对自己的酗酒行为 _____ 不已,发誓再也不喝酒了。

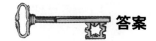**答案**

练习一:
略

练习二:
(1) E   (2)C   (3)D   (4)A   (5)B

练习三:

1. 海拔   2. 重新   3. 忠实   4. 无微不至   5. 和解

6. 假期   7. 等候   8. 和睦   9. 忠诚   10. 悔恨

第12月,第4周的练习

练习一.根据词语给加点的字注音

1.(　　)　2.(　　)　3.(　　)　4.(　　)　5.(　　)
　应邀　　重新　　和睦　　堵塞　　奠定

练习二.根据拼音填写词语

　　　　jià　　　　jià　　　　jià　　　　xíng　　　　xíng
1.物(　)　2.吵(　)　3.(　)期　4.地(　)　5.执(　)

练习三.辨析并选择合适的词填空

1.暴雨使这里的农田受到了不同程度的(　　)。(毁灭、毁坏)

2.那次战斗给敌人造成了(　　)性的打击,不久敌军就宣布投降了。(毁灭、毁坏)

3.听说要换个新老师,学生们非常兴奋,都在(　　)新来的老师长得怎么样。(猜测、预测)

4.专家(　　)未来几天会有暴风雪。(猜测、预测)

5.你怎么能当着她的面说出这么(　　)的话。(残酷、残忍)

6.邻居的猫进入了她家厨房,她居然把那只猫关进冰箱里冻死了,这个女人可真(　　)。(残酷、残忍)

7.无论做什么事都要(　　)自然规律,否则一定会受到大自然的惩罚。(遵照、遵循)

8.(　　)老人临终前的遗嘱,把财产平均分配给他的孩子们。(遵照、遵循)

9.翻译小说很难,既要(　　)于原作,又要让作品符合外国读者的阅读习惯。(忠诚、忠实)

10.他一生(　　)于祖国的教育事业,为国家培养了很多科技人才。(忠诚、忠实)

练习四.选词填空

邀请　缓和　和睦　悔恨　吵架
应邀　缓慢　和解　仇恨　吵闹

1.积极有效的民间交流逐渐化解了两国人民互相(　　)的心理。

2.他生长在一个十分(　　)的家庭,家庭成员都相处得很融洽。

3.我的好朋友(　　)我参加她的婚礼,并让我做她的伴娘。

4.这里经济发展的速度十分(　　),所以再次来到这里的时候,发现变化不大。

5.这位科学家参观了我们的实验室,还(　　)为学生做了一次精彩的讲座。

6.每次跟女朋友吵完架,都是他主动道歉才能(　　),否则他女朋友就不理他。

7.经理要求售货员要耐心与顾客沟通,绝不能跟顾客(　　)。

8.他动手打了妻子,妻子走后,他对自己的行为(　　)不已。

9.签订停火协议以后,两国边境的紧张局势得到了(　　)。

10.周末一大早,我被邻居孩子的(　　)声吵醒了。

练习五.量词填空

株　　粒　　度　　顶　　届

1.爸爸让我每次都把碗里的米饭吃干净,一(　　)也不能浪费。

2.他家门前的那(　　)枣树生长得特别茂盛。

3.今年夏天比较热,据说比往年的平均气温高3(　　)

4.我们是校友,我是2008年大学毕业的,他比我早一(　　),是2007年毕业的。

5.导游给旅游团的每个人发了一(　　)红色的帽子。

练习六.成语填空

1.无微(　)(　)　2.无论(　)(　)　3.无可(　)(　)
4.无情(　)(　)　5.无能(　)(　)

练习七.写出下列词语的同义词

1.威望(　　)　　　2.和睦(　　)
3.幻想(　　)　　　4.猜测(　　)
5.毁灭(　　)

练习八.写出下列词语的反义词

1.回顾(　　)　　　2.仇恨(　　)
3.堵塞(　　)　　　4.毁坏(　　)
5.残忍(　　)

 **答案**

练习一.
1.yìng　　2.chóng　　3.mù　　4.sè　　5.diàn
练习二.
1.价　　2.架　　3.假　　4.形　　5.行
练习三.
1.毁坏　　2.毁灭　　3.猜测　　4.预测　　5.残酷
6.残忍　　7.遵循　　8.遵照　　9.忠实　　10.忠诚
练习四.
1.仇恨　　2.和睦　　3.邀请　　4.缓慢　　5.应邀
6.和解　　7.吵架　　8.悔恨　　9.缓和　　10.吵闹
练习五.
1.粒　　2.株　　3.度　　4.届　　5.顶
练习六.
1.不至　　2.如何　　3.奈何　　4.无义　　5.为力
练习七.
1.声望　　2.融洽　　3.梦想　　4.推测　　5.消灭
练习八.
1.展望　　2.恩德　　3.疏通　　4.保护　　5.仁慈

附录
全书词义辨析包含词汇和页码

责任编辑：韩芙芸
封面设计：王　薇
印刷监制：佟汉冬

图书在版编目（CIP）数据

HSK 核心词汇天天学 . 下 / 刘东青编著 . —北京：华语教学出版社，2009
ISBN 978-7-80200-596-9

Ⅰ.H… 　Ⅱ. 刘… 　Ⅲ. 汉语 — 词汇 — 对外汉语教学 — 水平考试 — 自学参考资料
Ⅳ. H195.4

中国版本图书馆 CIP 数据核字（2009）第 089350 号

HSK 核心词汇天天学·下

刘东青　编著
*

© 华语教学出版社
华语教学出版社出版
（中国北京百万庄大街 24 号　邮政编码 100037）
电话：(86)10-68320585
传真：(86)10-68326333
网址：www.sinolingua.com.cn
电子信箱：hyjx@ sinolingua.com.cn
北京外文印刷厂印刷
2009 年（16 开）第一版
2009 年第一次印刷
（汉英）
ISBN　978-7-80200-596-9
定价：49.00 元